COLLECTIVE BEHAVIOR

COLLECTIVE BEHAVIOR

A REVIEW AND REINTERPRETATION OF THE LITERATURE

MICHAEL BROWN
AND AMY GOLDIN

GOODYEAR PUBLISHING COMPANY
PACIFIC PALISADES, CALIFORNIA

Library of Congress Catalog Card Number: 72-89588

Current Printing (last digit):
10 9 8 7 6 5 4 3 2 1

Y-1869-0

ISBN: 0-87620-186-9

Printed in the United States of America

CONTENTS

1796973

UNIT I   THE STUDY OF COLLECTIVE BEHAVIOR

The Concepts and Phenomena of Collective Behavior: A Critical View. *The Crowd: A Prototype of Collective Behavior / The Concept of an Issueless Riot / The Description and Definition of Riot / The Inadequacies of Contemporary Analyses*

Perspective and Theory: The Interrelationships. *Perspective-free Theory / The Roles of Perspective / The Criteria for Perspectival Critique / The Perspective of "Generalized Belief."* The Selection of Data: The Problem of Discovery. *A Political Analysis of the 1968 National Advisory Commission on Civil Disorders / The Paradoxes of Political Legitimacy / The Marginality of Advisory Commissions / Discovery as an Act of Attribution.* Researching Unauthorized Political Action

Perspectives in the Study of Disaster. *Disaster: The Emergency Social System.* What is Disaster? *Disaster as Impaired Social System / Disaster as Disruption / Disaster as Occasion / Disaster as Occurrence / The Public Process of Definition.* Collective Behavior on the Occasion of Disaster. *A Sociological Framework for Disaster Behavior*

UNIT **II**   MODERN THEORIES
OF COLLECTIVE BEHAVIOR

PREFACE

This book began as an extension of my political involvement in Students for a Democratic Society, the antiwar movement, the St. Patrick's Witness, and the New University Conference. It evolved through my courses in collective behavior and my work with the Center for Movement Research at Queens College of the City University of New York. But it was the collaboration with Amy Goldin that provided an opportunity for a critical and elaborate treatment of the subject matter.

The book itself is designed to contribute to a critical and speculative attitude toward both the literature on collective behavior and the language of its analysis. In this book, collective behavior is viewed primarily as a study in phenomenology and dialectics. It takes as a cardinal principle the proposition that theories of collective behavior are not, and need not be, independent of their subject matter. The work assumes the usefulness of Garfinkel's (1967) observations:

1. that the recognizedly rational accountability of practical actions is a member's practical accomplishment, and
2. that the success of that practical accomplishment consists in the work whereby a setting, in the same ways that it consists of a recognized and familiar organization of activities, masks from members' relevant notice members' practical ordering practices, and thereby leads the members to see a setting's features, which include a setting's accounts, "as determinate and independent objects" (p. 288).

As a result, a large part of the effort is devoted to establishing the perspectives from which particular theories (as accounts), including the "theoretic prospectus" (chap. 10) of the authors, are constructed and to establishing the bases of the perspectives of episodes of collective behavior themselves. The book draws heavily on the sociology of knowledge, political sociology, and recent phenomenological approaches to the analysis of situated social action.

Basically, we view collective behavior as rooted in strategic constructions of situations in process. These constructions are conceived to be more than ideational and cultural and as growing through a dialectical process in which the past, as well as the future, is continually discovered and remade. We maintain that collective behavior takes place in situations that are intrinsically and inevitably conflictful.

The book is best read as a whole, or at least in large chunks, because different sections contribute to an understanding of concepts that are deliberately open and intended to unfold as they are used. At this stage in the study of collective behavior, it is necessary to adopt a flexible attitude toward concepts but an extremely critical attitude toward the prevailing theories and their paradigms. This entails playing hunches, juggling with language and bibliographical material, and experimenting with concepts. The theoretic prospectus put forth here is more a prolegomenon than a theory. Its value lies in its capacity to stimulate thought rather than to establish a formally adequate inferential scheme or methodology for the description and analysis of determinate phenomena.

The organization of the unit on disaster, the selection and arrangement of topics, generally follows the conventions of other sociological reviews of disaster. However, there is no research currently available that is based on the model we present and that follows the lines of ethnographic methodology required by it. Consequently, we have arranged the material so that our approach to disaster can be illustrated through criticisms and reinterpretations of the prevailing literature rather than through attempts to analyze new data and list new findings. If the reader feels that we have painted social reality as unusually fragmented and unstable, he has understood our theoretic intent. What is apparent in disaster is that social reality is stable and replaceable at the same time. The constructive character of social action; the divisions among people and groups that emerge and dissolve; and the fact that individuals, groups, places and events have social meanings and identities that vary with the occasion and that may be topics of affirmation and confrontation were what we want to show. Our analysis of disaster provides the basis for the subsequent sections on theory.

In developing a theoretical program for the study of collective behavior we take advantage of some of the insights provided by Smelser (1963), Turner (1964), and Goffman (1961). In addition, we utilize some of the new developments in theory derived from the work of the ethnomethodologists and symbolic interactionists, and selections from the large body of empirical research that has appeared since the middle 1960s. Much of that material seems to demand a reevaluation of theory and method in the study of collective behavior.

We have selected the political activities on the American campus in the 1960s to illustrate some of the principles of the analysis of collective behavior. These activities were chosen for several reasons:

1. During the 1960s, student protest was often described as crowd behavior and, for purposes of analysis, was categorized with riots, urban disorders, and insurrection,

2. The activities took place in complex circumstances that invite an analysis of protest as situated social action,
3. Because the student political activities of the 1960s were so articulate, they allow examination of the relationship between episodes of collective behavior and their socio-political context,
4. Response to student protest was also articulate, and it generated a large literature and exposed an official practice that illuminates the relationships between theory and official policy and between official and unofficial definitions of social reality,
5. It is appropriate that a book on sociology direct its theoretical energies toward the matter that inspired it.

Our concern with collective behavior as situated action will involve us in a discussion of the university as an establishment with its own patterns of internal life and social action. The relationship between the contemporary American university and its context, American society, is also relevant. Both factors are crucial to the emergence of the patterns of interference that are at the root of collective behavior and that constitute the major topic with which we are concerned in the last section of the book. Second, the transformation of collective action into collective behavior will be discussed, with special attention to the role of perspectives in that transformation. The analysis that comprises the last unit of the book will allow us to probe the explanatory power of some of the concepts we have been developing. These concepts will therefore be juxtaposed to the categories that have already been applied to student protest as a phenomenon. This comparison focuses on the question of what data are to be considered relevant for explanation, and what implications are to be drawn from the presence of relevancy claims.

We are indebted to the intellectual stimulation provided by Frithjof Bergman, Harvey Wagner, Jerry Bernstein, Kenneth Feldman, Douglas Robbins, Lewis Meyers, Marie-Annick Huet, the staff of the Center for Movement Research (especially Louis Markowitz, Lawrence Sloman, and Louis Brill), the Ad Hoc Committee to End Political Repression (Queens College, 1969), and various members of the chapter of the New University Conference at Queens College of the City University of New York. In addition, we would like to thank Beth Lanum for helping to organize the material.

Michael E. Brown

INTRODUCTION

Like Hollywood, American sociology tended to look at the frontier more than at the muddled and sultry ambience of the cities, a frontier of technology and plans as well as of wide open space and heartfelt ideals. When sociologists turned to the city, they were rather like the gentlemen of genuinely well-intended and hopeful charity approaching a somewhat repulsive object. The city was rarely examined in terms of its existential heat; instead, it was examined in terms of its failure, dereliction, or prospect. The idealizations of the frontier met the dirt of the city—and won. However, the vision of exploration and cultivation was transformed into a vision of technological possibility. Hope, rather than perception, gave this vision to sociology, and sociologists gradually moved more and more into the airy realms of prophecy, giving their professional minds to the people who ruled rather than to the people who suffered rule, or the people who simply suffered. Even the late magnanimity of those sociologists who probed the wounds of a society apparently gone to seed was tempered by the philanthropist's respect for the good intentions, if not the good works, of the strong, the sure, and the powerful.

More and more sociologists began to treat the present state of Amercian life as a transitional moment, rarely as an indication of things to come. It was hardly surprising when many professionals reacted virulently to those who acted as if the present state provided lessons about a dangerous and, perhaps, sad future. The attack on the New Left during the 1960s was doubtless informed by a desperately reckless desire to wipe away the terrible vision of America – explicated by those who noted racism rather than discrimination, official repression rather than popular scapegoating, genocide rather than war, exploitation and oppression rather than poverty and disease, and conquest rather than international concern. It might be suspected that the attack was also directed at sociologists whose ideals were too well formed and whose courage spoke of too great a dedication to struggle against the institutions that stymied the humane potential of the American people. Such activist intellectuals stood for everything that sociological professionalism was against: the involvement of one's work with one's life and the involvement of one's life with the lives of others.

Even Robert Ezra Park, the eternal optimist of an earlier day, viewed modern urban life as, at worst, a minor pathology during the adolescence of a truly progressive society and therefore as less real than the future that the society had in store. With such an attitude, there was no room for tragedy in American life, much less in American sociology. Unlike European intellectuals who rarely deluded themselves with the idea of a frontier escape from the conflicts endemic to confined space, American sociologists rarely glanced back. They saw a calm that they called consensus. Where they found conflict they referred to problems. Where they saw power they thought of authority, service, and function in a modern revision of the "divine right of kings."

This nontragic attitude was retained in the work of Neil Smelser (1963), the major theorist of collective behavior, and to some extent in the work of others. The impatience Smelser attributed to the people who engage in unauthorized actions assumed a normally calmer, more deliberative state that could provide a more effective orientation for action in a responsive and continually equilibrating social system. In a sense, modern theories of collective behavior are happy theories about unhappy or troublesome events. The crowd is a foil to "society," as the mass was to "culture" in the nineteenth century (Williams, 1960). But, unlike the mass, the crowd of contemporary theory, while a bother, is not a grave danger. Turner (1964), for example, saw the crowd and episodes of collective behavior as mildly instructive rather than threatening:

> Collective behavior contributes toward *legitimating decision* in areas in which the culture is insufficiently specific.
> Collective behavior contributes to *solidarity* by countering the distance-provoking effects of formality in society.
> The third contribution of collective behavior is to the requirement for *action* in the face of counterbalanced values and complex regulatory systems. The acting crowd breaks the stalemate of inaction; the expressive crowd bursts the limits of qualified commitment.
> Finally, collective behavior contributes to the discovery of commitment in the absence of experienced alternatives (pp. 421-22).

And Smelser (1967) viewed collective behavior as a curiosity of man and society. He began his book by saying:

> In all civilizations men have thrown themselves into episodes of dramatic behavior, such as the craze, the riot, and the revolution. Often we react emotionally to these episodes. We stand, for instance, amused by the foibles of the craze, aghast at the cruelties of the riot, and inspired by the fervor of the revolution (p. 1).

The lack of irony in Smelser's use of the term "we" could only have been possible in the balmier days of sociology in which sociologists recorded the societal calm and, from a detached viewpoint, social problems. It is a long stretch from those times to Goffman's (1963) ironically compassionate, yet formally less secure, reference to "we normals" in his book titled *Stigma*.

What we are suggesting is that sociology had for so long been caught up in the heroics of executively planned change, the ambitions of the upwardly mobile, and the quiescence of an apparently consensual mass, that it approached unauthorized politics and collective behavior, like deviance, with gloved hands. This attitude was not out of respect for the topics and the phenomena but out of a need for self-protection and an almost touching concern for the delicate happiness that is the profession of social science.

The topic of collective behavior is anything but a curiosity; its threat is the threat of institutions, situations, and lives. The reader can become acquainted with the standard literature through the excellent anthology edited by Robert Evans (1969), the important theoretical review by Ralph Turner (1964), Neil Smelser's monograph (1962), and the recent review by Stanley Milgram (1969a). New directions have been suggested by Erving Goffman (1961), Jerome Skolnick (1969), Mitchell Goodman (1970), and Max Heirich (1971).

The sociology of collective behavior has drawn new life from several important developments. A number of sociologists have turned to the ethnography of situated social action and the dialectics of meaningful interaction. This interest reflects the availability of several alternative paradigms—in particular, ethnomethodology and symbolic interactionism—to the standard paradigm of the American school of functionalism. Sociologists also found that many of the classical and most attractive problems of the discipline were virtually eliminated from the orbit of established professional concern by recent developments in the political economy of research. The concentration and specialization of resources within the heavy research industry have produced an economy of poverty for many young sociologists. This economy of poverty has, however, generated a range of problems and methods that do not require the organization or the capital necessary for heavy research. The result is an underground of new and often highly intellectual sociologists who are interested in such matters as the relationship between intellectual and political work, the development of the political capacity of undergroups, the role of coercive power in social life, the conceptual and perspectival analysis of social theories, the social construction of reality, the relation of theory to practice, and the institutionalization of consciousness within close and immediately accessible collectivities.

Many of these sociologists have brought to their work a new vision that is informed by a perspective, by a practice, by values, and by traditions at odds with many of the established perspectives, practices, values, and traditions of their discipline. This contrast is largely because of the accelerated growth of the academic system since the end of World War II, which has brought new strains into the relationship between educational institutions and society. Among the issues that have been raised are the nature of sociology and the role of the sociologist. Is a positivist sociology possible? What is the role of values in sociology? What is the relationship between theory and practice? What are the implications of the traditional relationship between the "science" of society and official institutions? What have been the practical consequences of theory and research? Is the sociologist an intellectual, a professional, an activist, or a "man of science?" What is the moral relationship between the public occupation of the sociologist and his private and political activities? Is there a "history of sociology" and, therefore, an historic mission of sociologists? Or is there simply a multiplicity of available legitimating biographies of a loosely organized discipline? Do the practice and identity of the discipline depend more upon its relations with the rest of contemporary society than upon its position along the putative time line of the history of ideas (Berger and Luckmann, 1967)?

Many of the young men and women entering the discipline during the 1960s grew up with the outlaw romanticism of the beat generation. In addition, their newly critical sense of America was successively sharpened by Korea, the Cold War, the recognition of racism and widespread poverty, and the continuing official persecution of the Left. Many were students during the political and moral struggles of the 1960s and became committed to a socialist critique of society and of their own politics and political organizations (Oglesby and Shaull, 1967; Long, 1969; Marcuse, 1969; Teodori, 1969). This critique included a number of important proposistions relevant to the study of collective behavior:

1. That social change and official policy emanate from the interplay of interests, power, and struggle,
2. That what is ordinarily offered as "change" or "reform" is a projection of differences in power, position, and class,
3. That structural change can occur only by virtue of a reorganization and redefinition of these dimensions of societal order through a process of struggle,
4. That any effective politics and, consequently, any effective sociology must be practical and self-critical.

These propositions reflect a renewed interest in Marxist theory as well as a sharp division within sociology concerning the choice of the positional perspective from which models of society should be drawn.

These two developments—a new interest in situated social action and the reemergence of what C. Wright Mills (1961) called "the sociological imagination"—have opened the possibility for new models of collective behavior. In addition, they have revitalized the study of unauthorized political action by focusing on the content and organization of such action and its relationship to official institutions.

Such concerns have grown within a context of occupational change for academic sociologists. The emergence of the heavy research industry and a political economy of research, resulting from shifts in patronage, funding, and the sponsorship of research, have produced a much more bureaucratic orientation to the discipline than the more entrepreneurial orientation of the past. The sociologist is seen less as a source of problems and ideas and more as an agent for a principal whose practice is explicitly at issue. The organization of research has taken on the managerial ethos and the forms of rationalization that are identified with business and the traditional professions. Despite tremendous conflict within the field, sociology has come to be organized as a profession and, in terms of the heavy research industry, dependent upon official sponsorship and official or quasi-official investment. This organization and subsequent dependency, coupled with the fact that the discipline has always been identified with a liberal outlook, has led to legitimations of the practice of sociology in terms of the exigencies of official practice, system maintenance, and reform.

A sharp distinction can now be drawn between academic and professional sociology, between sociology as a profession and as a discipline. Increasingly, the public performances of sociologists are legitimated in terms of the professional roles of expert, consultant, and prophet, and in relation to official or quasi-official clients within the political economy of corporate capitalism. Thus, the new areas of research, or subdisciplines, have arisen in a context in which normal sociological problems are tied directly to the institutions of social control, for example, the study of disaster and the study of unauthorized political action. Nevertheless, these subdisciplines have provided a literature that has, to some extent, freed the theorist from the anecdotal and uncriticized descriptions of crowds and social movements that constituted the empirical basis of the classical theories of collective behavior.

Because this book originated out of a distinctively American experience, it should not be surprising that its ideas reflect the experiences of urban life, with all its vitality and oppression; a sense of the profound decay of American institutions and their words during a period of empire and repression; and a sense of tragedy that is new to the middle-class American spirit.

UNIT I

THE STUDY OF COLLECTIVE BEHAVIOR

CHAPTER ONE

COLLECTIVE BEHAVIOR: THE EMPIRICAL DOMAIN

The term collective behavior has been applied to phenomena that have traditionally escaped organizational analysis because they appear to be exceptions to the order and consistency usually ascribed to social systems. As recently as 1964, such phenomena included:

> social unrest, crowd behavior, riots, manias, crazes, fads, mass alarms, mass hysteria, public revolts, protest movements, rebellions, primitive religious behavior, reform movements, and revolutionary movements (Blumer, 1964 p. 167).

Collective behavior is primarily a label for a group of observations and theoretic notations. The term also appears as the title of books, the tables of contents of which list the items included in this group. There are essentially two principles by which items are selected for inclusion under the label of collective behavior: scholarly tradition and an apparent divergence from what is considered to be ordinary institutional behavior (Turner, 1964).

THE CONCEPTS AND PHENOMENA OF COLLECTIVE BEHAVIOR: A CRITICAL VIEW

The table of contents of what was the major text in the field for many years *Collective Behavior*, by Ralph H. Turner and Lewis M. Killian (1957), listed:

> Societal Conditions and Collective Behavior; Individual Reactions to Crisis; Social Contagion; Interaction in the Crowd; Crowd Process: Symbolization and Change; Crowd Conventionalization and Control; Mass Society and Mass Communication; The Diffuse Crowd; Nature of the Public and Public Opinion; Dynamics of the Public; Social Movements: Character and Processes; Value-Orientations of Social Movements; Control Movements and Power Orientations; Separatist Movements; Participation-Orientated Movements; Participation-Orientations; The Following and Leadership; End-Products of Social Movements; Collective Behavior; Social Behavior: Social Change; and Social Stability.

Included are theoretical concepts—such as "social contagion"—that lack formal status in most contemporary theories of social organization, and phenomena,—such as the crowd, the public, and the social movement—that appear to be exceptions to the range of organizations and activities ordinarily taken for granted as the empirical domain of sociology.

These concepts and phenomena are the unassimilated residue of a sociology devoted to the problems of social order and planned change. In such an approach, the characters of the various human social types have generally been understood as products of socialization and opportunity within the framework of the man-in-society paradigm. Such a sociology identifies the legitimate, the institutional, and the formal with the official. It views the natural history of social systems as tending toward a rational and inclusive ideal wherein power is equated with service, coordinated performance is equated with consensus, and contradiction is equated with strain.

A number of authors have gone beyond a simple catalogue of theoretic exceptions and have attempted to both reconstruct the field of study and develop a general model of collective behavior. Turner and Killian, for example, stated that "collective behavior refers to the characteristics of groups . . ." (1957, p. 12). This statement distinguishes the study of collective behavior from the study of cognitive and motivational bases of group participation, of individual reactions to stress, and of other strictly psychological phenomena. Turner and Killian further delimited the term: the field of collective behavior involves the study of groups that are "governed by emergent or spontaneous norms rather than formalized norms" (1957, p. 12). According to Turner and Killian, formalized norms are "established rules of procedure which have behind them the force of tradition" (1957 p. 12). Therefore, groups subsumed by the heading of collective behavior are not the enduring organizations that are the active elements of societal order.

Many of the phenomena included in the table of contents of the text lack the required characteristics of collective behavior—interaction and ad hoc or situated norms—as set forth by Turner and Killian themselves. The formal limits that Turner and Killian placed on the sociology of collective behavior should have excluded from their book phenomena such as the mass, the public, and the social movement.

Turner and Killian's definition of the mass as "a number of separate individuals each responding independently to the same stimulus in the same way" clearly excluded the mass from the study of collective behavior because mass, so defined, "is less than a collectivity since it lacks interaction tying the entire group together" (1957, p. 167). Mass is thus a statistical aggregate rather than a situated system of action. Similarly, Turner and Killian asserted that the public:

> is a dispersed group of people interested in and divided about an issue, engaged in discussion of the issue, with a view to registering a collective opinion which is expected to affect the course of action of some group or individual (1957, p. 219).

This appears to refer to the communicative behavior that accompanies institutional as well as noninstitutional operations rather than to the emergent and intensely situated phenomenon that Turner and Killian formally defined as collective behavior. Turner and Killian defined a social movement as "a collectivity acting with some continuity to promote a change or resist a change in the society or group of which it is a part" (1957, p. 308). Thus, the only thing that differentiates a movement from any other organization is its role as a struggle group and its unofficial standing within the polity.

The fact that Turner and Killian did include the phenomena of the mass, the public, and the social movement in their text may indicate an intention to leave traditionally unassimilable phenomena open for special consideration. Alternatively, Turner and Killian may have offered their theory not as a general model but as an insight, the value of which lies in its marginal application to social affairs.

THE CROWD: PROTOTYPE OF COLLECTIVE BEHAVIOR

Although Turner and Killian's theory of emergent norms—by its own terms—does not apply to the mass, the public, or the social movement, it does apply to the crowd. Turner (1964) made this point explicit when he declared that the crowd is the central and distinctive phenomenon of the sociology of collective behavior.

Following Turner's lead in taking the crowd as the prototype of collective behavior, the focal points for the study are: the concept of collective behavior and the impact of labeling social action as crowdlike or riotous; and the dynamics of the crowd when considered as nonroutine, situated social action. Consideration of the crowd as an example of situated social action assumes that it is fruitful to study the implications of the distinction ordinarily made between groups and organizations to which identity is attributed over time (transsituational social forms) and groups and organizations in which interactions appear to be temporary and contingent (situated social action). In addition, the implications of this distinction are assumed to be at the heart of what is ordinarily meant by collective behavior.

Our empirical domain, in its most general aspect, includes the catalogue of events traditionally subsumed by the label "crowd." However, it is proposed that the crowd, so conceived, can also be a point of departure for the study of social life in general. In this sense, the study of collective behavior is compatible with the work of sociologists for whom the identification of inclusive order is both a derivative of local conditions (settings) and an aspect of a dialectical process of analysis, rather than a primary sociological fact (Meadows, 1967, p. 77; Garfinkel, 1967, p. viii).

An examination of the sociology of collective behavior and the phenomena associated with the crowd requires preliminary discussion of three closely related fundamental issues. First, the empirical domain for the study of collective behavior becomes an issue in the context of a distinction that is frequently made between *acting* and *expressive* crowds. The basis for the distinction will be examined and its implications for the study of collective behavior explored. Second, the extratheoretic sources of theory and the influence of these sources on the development of theory require examination. The concept of *perspective* and its implications for understanding the development of theory and the character of theorizing about collective behavior is contingent upon understanding the extratheoretic sources of theory. This issue will be discussed in chap. 2. The third issue concerns the relation between description and theory and focuses on some aspects of the problem of discovery, as will be discussed in chap. 2. Because what is taken as fact depends in part upon the relation between the theorist and his topic—the theoretic and practical contexts of inquiry—discovery must be understood as an act that takes place within, and explicates, a particular social setting.

A Distinction between Action and Expression. Whether or not a discussion of collective behavior and the sociology of the crowd is fruitful depends first upon the empirical domain from which illustrations are drawn. Our illustrations are taken from the literature on student protest, urban unrest, and disaster. Consequently, we may be criticized for overemphasizing unauthorized political action and other instrumental forms of the crowd and disregarding those forms of the crowd that are consummatory, expressive, or otherwise noninstrumental. This possibility may be evaluated by examining several attempts to establish the noninstrumental forms of crowds as significant phenomena for the study of collective behavior.

Elias Canetti (1963) opened his book, *Crowds and Power*, with the statement:

There is nothing that man fears more than the touch of the unknown.

* * *

All the distance which men create round themselves are dictated by this fear.

* * *

It is only in a crowd that man can become free of this fear of being touched. That is the only situation in which the fear changes into its opposite. The crowd he needs is the dense crowd, in which body is pressed to body; a crowd, too, whose psychical constitution is also dense, or compact, so that he no longer notices who it is that presses against him. As soon as a man has surrendered himself to the crowd, he ceases to fear its touch. Ideally, all are equal there; no distinctions count, not even that of sex. The man pressed against him is the same as himself. He feels him as he feels himself . . . The more fiercely people press together, the more certain they feel that they do not fear each other. This reversal of the fear of being touched belongs to the nature of crowds. The feeling of relief is most striking where the density of the crowd is greatest.

* * *

Only together can men free themselves from their burdens of distance; and this, precisely, is what happens in a crowd. During the discharge distinctions are thrown off and all feel *equal*. In that density, where there is scarcely any space between, and body presses against body, each man is as near the other as he is to himself; and an immense feeling of relief ensues. It is for the sake of this blessed moment, when no one is greater or better than other, that people become a crowd.

* * *

The first point to emphasize is that the crowd never feels satiated. It remains hungry as long as there is one human being it has not reached (pp. 15-22).

The crowd is here described as transcendental and superorganic. Canetti envisions an expressive union in which the terror of the individual is exchanged for the beatitude of the component and self-conscious system devolves to spontaneous collective enthusiasm. For Canetti, the crowd is pure melted identity; its activity is expressive and consummatory. He classified crowds by their emotional content, or mood, and found in each crowd a mixture of vulnerability and lust that delivers it readily to the spirit of the millenial and the hands of the demagogue. Canetti's concept of the crowd is generic. Any action that may flow from the crowd is the result of external factors, of manipulation or accident.

More prosaically, Herbert Blumer (1951), in his distinction between the acting and the expressive crowd, recognized the role of enthusiasm in collective behavior. In this typology of crowds. Blumer suggested that some crowds are purposeful and instrumental and that other crowds are autistic and expressive. Such a distinction differs from the classical observation that there are both rational and nonrational features of crowds, particularly LeBon's claim that action and expression are aspects or components of collective behavior, rather than characteristics of types of crowds (LeBon, 1960).

Blumer (1951) described the typical crowd as:

Aggressive . . . represented by a revolutionary crowd or a lynching mob. The outstanding mark of this type of crowd is the presence of an aim or objective toward which the activity of the crowd is directed. It is this type of crowd which is the object of concern in practically all studies of the crowd. The remaining type is the *expressive* or "dancing" crowd, such as is so common in the origin of religious sects (pp. 178-79).

Turner and Killian (1957) later refined Blumer's distinction and placed it within an explicit theoretical framework. They asserted that:

The type of objective which the crowd has . . . determines whether it may be classified as active or expressive. The objective of the *active* crowd is such that the criterion of its attainment is some action upon an external object—some physical object, or some person or persons not part of the crowd. This action need not necessarily be a direct, physical assault. It may be indirect, as when a crowd drives a speaker from his platform with boos.

* * *

The measure of achievement of the objective of the *expressive* crowd is, in contrast, the production of some sort of subjective experience or some behavior in the crowd members themselves . . . Whatever the specific objective . . . the criterion of its accomplishment is subjective and internal (pp. 85-86).

If Turner and Killian's distinction is justifiable, Blumer was correct in his assertion that the study of collective behavior has concentrated almost exclusively on the acting crowd, and, by implication, that theory has been unduly restricted by this empirical bias.

The Basis for a Typology. The modern study of collective behavior has received its greatest stimulus from the occurrence of unauthorized political action. As a result, many theorists emphasize the beliefs of participants, the apparent goals of collectivities, and the mobilization of the crowd, with a concomitant deemphasis on the expressive and internally practical elements of crowd behavior. Nevertheless, most descriptions of crowds have included references to enthusiasm, rhythm, varying intensity of emotion, mutual stimulation, and other apparently expressive or autistic aspects of behavior. Despite a certain vagueness in the terms, the regularity of reference to feeling suggests at most that expression is as much a part of action as action is of expression. It does not require Blumer's explicit distinction—that crowds are either acting or expressive.

A distinction between action and expression does not expose a bias in the choice of objects of study as much as it suggests a bias in the choice of labels applied to those objects. Blumer has not justified his distinction between the acting and expressive crowds. He has, at best, merely reaffirmed the classical observation that the crowd has all the features of other systems of social action. Because that observation is rooted in a belief in the essential continuity of ordinary and extraordinary behavior—a belief based on an assumption that all behavior, both "normal" and "abnormal," has a rational base (Parsons, 1949)—it is of fundamental importance to any study of collective behavior that wishes to locate its topic within general sociological theory.

It can be argued that the expressive or active components of a crowd may be sufficiently exaggerated as to constitute certain crowds as expressive or as active, or that the distribution of episodes of collective behavior according to degrees of expressiveness-activity is bimodal such that the quantitative extremes are not simply the rare ends of a normal distribution. Both of these claims are at the core of Gary Marx's (1970) discussion of the issueless riot as an example of the expressive crowd. It is worthwhile to examine Marx's argument in some detail—because he has attempted to make his concepts operational and has tied them to the more general theory proposed by Neil Smelser (1962, 1970)—before deciding whether or not Blumer's distinction provides the basis for a typology of crowds and therefore one basis for criticizing the apparent narrowness of the empirical domain of the sociology of collective behavior.

THE CONCEPT OF AN ISSUELESS RIOT

Marx, like Blumer, attempted to redress the apparent imbalance in the contemporary emphasis on the protest riot, or the acting crowd. He began by dropping the distinction between expression and action. He replaced this distinction with a typology of riotous crowds in which he asserted that:

> The most important dimensions [are] To what degree is a generalized belief present? and, To what degree are riot actions themselves instrumental in collectively solving a group's problems? (Marx, 1970, p. 26).

This statement is the basis for his discussion of the issueless riot—a type of diffusely hostile outburst in which there is neither ideological nor strictly instrumental justification for the selection of the crowd's object, for its behavior, or for its organization. Issueless riots, Marx (1970) asserted, lack "a critique of the social order and the belief that violence will help bring about needed social change . . ." (p. 24). Both the issueless riot and the protest riot are included in Marx's general definition of a riot as "relatively spontaneous illegitimate group violence contrary to traditional group norms" (p. 24).

What is important here is that Marx has dispensed with Smelser's (1963) idea that an issue is necessary in order for collective behavior to occur. This fact leads to the novel proposition that strain in a social system as well as its usual concomitants—fear, anxiety, or a sense of deprivation—are also not necessary conditions of collective behavior. The notion of the issueless riot therefore means that people may be mobilized for collective behavior without any prior sensitization about targets or about the appropriateness of particular activities. Such a concept could mean that the term riot, as used by Marx, does not refer to a single, homogeneous phenomenon. Alternatively, Marx may be calling for a new general theory of collective behavior. He does not develop either possibility, however, and therefore leaves his position ambiguous at its core.

Whether or not the concepts put forth by Marx revitalize the idea of the expressive crowd, and thereby substantiate Blumer's criticism, depends upon the degree to which his definitions of the issueless riot lends itself to theoretical work and to empirical interpretation. The definition itself depends upon the two dimensions of his typology of riots—that is, the presence or absence of generalized beliefs (see also chap. 9) and the degree of instrumentality of the crowd's actions.

The Dimension of Generalized Belief. For Marx, generalized belief seems to be an overriding definition of the situation, an account of a condition, which transcends the local limitations on interaction and uniformity within a large gathering. Presumably, Marx accepts Neil Smelser's (1962) characterization of a generalized belief:

> a belief in the existence of extraordinary forces -threats, conspiracies, etc.—which are at work in the universe. They [generalized beliefs] also involve an assessment of the extraordinary consequences which will follow if the collective attempt to reconstitute social action is successful. The beliefs on which collective behavior is based (we shall call them *generalized beliefs*) are thus akin to magical beliefs (p. 8).

The generality of such beliefs lies in the fact that they define a condition of social life in abstract and inclusive, rather than in concrete and structural, terms (Smelser, 1963).

It should be noted that although Marx apparently accepted Smelser's notion of the generalized belief, he did not restrict himself to Smelser's formal definition. Marx's choice of examples of riots suggests a much broader concept. First, he appears to assume that any ideology or definition of a situation that bypasses the legal limits of action indicates the presence of a generalized belief. If this is the case, the only distinction between issueless riots and ordinary joint action is the illegality of the actions of the crowd and, perhaps, the fact that the actions include violence. Second, his examples suggest that when people cannot give explicit reasons for their behavior, they lack belief—their behavior is issueless.

The concept of spontaneity does not have a determinate meaning in Marx's analysis and, thus, does not appear to constitute a formal part of his definition. His use of the term " relative spontaneity" suggests an element of judgment that is inconsistent with the positivistic tenor of his discussion. In any case, the term is not intelligible as Marx has used it and will not be considered here, as a critical part of his definition. (See also Mead [1932] for a discussion of social time that sheds light on the concept of spontaneity; Goffman [1961] for a use of the term spontaneity in a theoretic context.)

Marx (1970) included in his examples of riotous behavior based on a generalized belief: the Luddites which were, according to Rude (1964) a relatively organized movement that responded to a decline in working conditions and income during a particularly depressed period in the history of Great Britain; bread riots, which seem to illustrate a highly specific and verifiable, rather than a generalized belief; prison riots, which may or may not be predicated on a generalized belief; pogroms, which may reflect a traditional and effective hostility that has official support, rather than reflecting an emergent generalized belief; and communal riots. Marx does not discuss the interpretation of collective behavior. Rather, he addresses himself to the allegedly objective qualities of independently observable episodes. But, the examples Marx has listed raise questions about the concept of generalized belief and its usefulness for comparing protest with issueless riots. How can it be decided whether or not a particular episode or activity is predicated on a generalized belief? Which of the many beliefs ordinarily mentioned by participants in collective behavior are the generalized beliefs that characterize the whole? Do statements of participants reveal the degree to which their activity—and the collective action of which their activity is or was part—was or was not predicated on a generalized belief or an issue? Does the fact that participants may express confusion when asked about their beliefs indicate a lack of belief? Where social analysts differ on the degree to which a particular belief is generalized, whose judgment should be accepted; and what criterion should be applied in order to determine what constitutes a generalized belief (Currie and Skolnick, 1970)? Can it be assumed that the beliefs of putative leaders represent the generalized beliefs of the crowd, or should the beliefs of all participants be surveyed? Does the absence of consensus within a gathering mean that there is no collective belief, ideology, or definition of the situation?

The Assessment of Instrumentality. With respect to instrumentality, Marx (1970) is again ambiguous. Initially, he seems to say that the instrumentality of the crowd resides in the fact that means are selected for the pursuit of goals, regardless of the effectiveness of the means (p. 11). The selectivity of riotous crowds with regard to means and targets does not guarantee the success of the means or even insure that they will have much of an impact on surrounding and competing collectivities. Subsequently, however, Marx emphasized those effects of riotous activity that are over and above the intended effects when he said that:

> If the riot is seen as instrumental, we may further ask if the violent action itself directly solves the problem . . . or if it is . . . a resource and a threat, which compels one's adversary to negotiate and offer concessions? (p. 26-27).

It is difficult to assess the intended effects of actions from outside the situation as it is defined by the participants. This perspective, however, is precisely that from which Marx hopes to evaluate the intended effects of riots. In addition, Marx does not indicate what should be investigated in order to gain information about intentions. Moreover, because all riots have some impact, it is never quite clear whether or not the particular impact—or any impact—was, in fact, intended by the rioters. Both of these judgments—of intention to have an effect and of intention to have created the specific effects that actually occurred by virtue of the riot—depend, in turn, on the judgment that the riot was mobilized on the basis of a generalized belief.

Marx's examples of collectively noninstrumental riots illustrate the difficulty in using the dimension of instrumentality to define the issueless riot. In his discussion of issueless riots, Marx (1970) said that they:

> develop out of two kinds of circumstances: a) in the face of a pronounced weakening of the agents of social control, and b) expressive outbursts which occasionally accompany victory celebrations or ritualized festivals (p. 30).

Included in his list of examples of collectively noninstrumental riots were: pogroms, communal riots, riots during police strikes, and riots following victory. It is, however, as easy to describe the first three examples as instrumental, according to any of Marx's criteria, as it is to describe them as noninstrumental, For example, it may at least be argued that even riots following victory are often rehearsals or demonstrations of newly found power or of a cultural or social rebirth and are, therefore, not issueless, although they may lack a specific target or intended effect. Marx's own report of the 1969 Montreal riot, for example, that took place during a police strike describes the action itself as well as listing several background factors: "the issue of French separatism, student and labor dissatisfactions, and economic rivalries . . ." (1970, p. 31). Marx included riots during police strikes in his list of types of issueless riots, yet listed these background factors for his example of an "issueless riot." From Marx's recitation of facts concerning the Montreal riot, it might rather be concluded the collective behavior was a protest predicated upon the sudden realization of power in relation to temporarily disarmed authorities. Furthermore, Marx asserted that the Montreal riot "seemed to have several elements of issueless rioting . . ." (p. 30-31). At this point, he seems to be suggesting that issuelessness may be an element even of protest riots, that a riot may both have and not have an issue at the same time. Thus, Marx contradicts his own assertions, and his illustrations and discussion of his proposed typology are inconsistent with the formal restrictions of the typology.

THE DESCRIPTION AND DEFINITION OF RIOT

It should be kept in mind that reports of riots frequently yield equivocal and, often, contradictory descriptions. Most of the examples of issueless riots discussed by Marx are drawn from journalistic descriptions and are therefore questionable as to accuracy and detail, which are precisely those qualities that are essential if insight concerning riots is to be gained from Marx's point of view. The National Advisory Commission on Civil Disorders (1968, p. 362-89) report on the portrayal of the 1967 urban riots in the mass media exposes some of the dangers of basing a sociological analysis of collective behavior on newspaper accounts. Without self-conscious criticism of the conventional procedures and categories of public accounts of riots and without a formal acknowledgement of the implication of such accounts in the settings they describe, an analysis runs the danger of being little more than an elaboration of the descriptive cliches of the journalism of riot.

Clearly, all instances of social action can be described according to both their rational and their nonrational aspects. Sociologists do not ordinarily typify organizations, groups, or societies by one term or the other. A typology of riots based on an artificial separation of rational and nonrational aspects neither clarifies the nature of riot nor helps in understanding the noninstrumental aspects of riotous behavior. It is a requirement of formal typologies that their differentia be independently observable. In the case of Marx (1970), for example, how can the instrumentality of riotous acts and the presence or absence of generalized belief, which are the two essential dimensions by which riots can be distinguished, be isolated and independently observed? Numerous difficulties are posed by the vagueness of Marx's definitions, the ambiguity of his riot examples and their interpretations, and his reliance on newspaper reports as primary sources of information on riots. Many of the problems of Marx's analysis derive from the vagueness of his definition of riot. Marx (1970) identifies a riot with the hostile outburst described by Smelser (1963) and distinguishes it from other forms of collective behavior. According to Marx, the two elements that distinguish the riot from other types of collective behavior are its illegitimacy and its violence, neither of which is easily defined.

Illegitimacy as a Criterion of Riot. Illegitimacy, for Marx, may mean either general unacceptability or illegality. If illegitimacy is synonymous with general unacceptability, riot is not distinguished from other forms of collective behavior since, in that case, illegitimacy would appear to be redundant with "contrary to traditional group norms," or at least so in the sociological usage ordinarily associated—for example, by Smelser—with the analysis of collective behavior (Marx, 1970, p. 24). Nor can illegality be considered a distinctive feature of riot. For example, victory celebrations are not clearly illegal even though some of the incidents that take place during the celebrations involve violations of the law.

Even if illegality were acceptable as a distinctive feature of riot, there is an operational difficulty. Because a special official determination—often made after the fact—is necessary for official (for example, police) actions to be deemed illegal, the label, in effect, applies only to the actions of individuals in nonofficial positions. For all practical purposes, the possibility of a riot by officials or their agents is excluded. Thus, the decision as to what constitutes a riot is a matter of official rather than social scientific determination. The use of illegitimacy as a criterion of riot commits Marx to a definition that excludes significant phenomena. In addition, such a definition is operationalized in terms of, and is subject to, the partisan judgment of one of the interested parties.

Violence as a Criterion of Riot. The criterion of violence remains as the distinctive characteristic of riot. Yet, it should be noted that not all events labeled riotous are examples of group violence. Furthermore, the fact that violence occurs on the occasion of a gathering does not necessarily indicate that it is the "group" that behaves violently, nor does it indicate that the gathering is a riot. It is often difficult, and sometimes impossible, to determine whether the violent actions of some participants in collective behavior are representative of the collective action or are even a part of it.

The term violence itself is equivocal (Skolnick, 1969). According to *Webster's New Twentieth Century Dictionary* (2d ed., 1962), violence is:

(1) physical force used so as to injure or damage; roughness in action. (2) a use of force so as to injure or damage; a rough, injurious act. (3) natural or physical energy or force in action; intensity; severity; as, the *violence* of the storm. (4) unjust use of force or power, as in deprivation of rights. (5) great force or strength of feeling, conduct, or language; passion; fury. (6) distortion of meaning, phrasing, etc.; as, to do *violence* to a test. (7) desecration; profanation.

Marx (1970) does not provide a formal definition of violence. He leaves the reader with the ordinary uses of the term and, thus, with too many kinds of violence for a useful definition of the term riot. His examples of riots indicate that he prefers the first three dictionary listings; but in each case, as with the other listings, judgments are required that are not objective in the sense of Marx's analytic program. Insofar as "violence" is a key element in his definition of riot, and therefore in his discussion of the issueless riot, Marx's concept of riot is either uncritically value laden and subjective or unable to be translated into observable effects. The way in which particular episodes, participants, or activities come to be regarded as violent is never delineated by Marx.

Concerning violence, the Skolnick Report (1969) to the National Commission on the Causes and Prevention of Violence commented:

First, *"violence" is an ambiguous term whose meaning is established through political processes.* The kinds of acts that become classified as "violent," and, equally important, those which do not become so classified, vary according to who provides the definition and who has superior resources for disseminating and enforcing his definitions. The most obvious example of this is the way, in a way, each side typically labels the other side the aggressor . . . (p. 4).

* * *

Second, *the concept of violence always refers to a disruption of some condition of order; but order, like violence, is politically defined.* . . . Less dramatic but equally destructive processes may occur well within the routine operation of "orderly" social life. Foreign military ventures come quickly to mind. Domestically, many more people are killed or injured annually through failure to build safe highways, automobiles, or appliances than through riots or demonstrations. . . . It would not be implausible to call these outcomes "institutional violence. . ." (p. 5).

It is difficult to see how the concepts of illegitimacy and violence can be used in a definition of riot that purports to offer theoretical and, presumably, practical implications as well as clear empirical reference. Without a definition of "riot," Marx is unable to define and establish the issueless riot as a phenomenon.

THE INADEQUACIES OF CONTEMPORARY ANALYSES

Despite Marx's and Blumer's failure to give conceptual and empirical status to the concept of an issueless riot, the idea persists. Why does the idea seem to have an intuitive appeal? First, many theorists have been influenced by the dramatic descriptions of apparently pointless and rhythmical activity found in the writings of some classical theorists and in the mass media of riotous times. Such descriptions have been used to construct classifications and theories without due regard for the empirical weaknesses and biases of the descriptions (Turner, 1964). Second, there is a tendency to exaggerate the tentative, experimental, and unformulated aspects of collective behavior and to avoid those aspects of "normal" or "institutional" behavior. This tendency is probably caused by the typification of collective and institutional behavior as polar opposites that define the limits of social action (Parsons, 1949; Williams, 1960, 1961; Turner 1964). The codification of these putative opposites as ideal types has encouraged sociologists to use as normal data, descriptions of those aspects of collective behavior that fit the ideal. Third, the claim that a riot is issueless is often supported by the observation that the rioters' justifications seem to be inventions after the fact. However, many protest riots also find their justifications during or after the fact. As collective actions develop, they may be heavily pluralistic; the participants may differ markedly in their intentions, ideologies, and activities, and in the extent to which these are articulated. In this respect, all riots, indeed most situated social actions, are issueless so far as that term refers to the absence of an initially consensual belief, plan, ideology, or definition of the situation. Although this general characteristic of collective, situated ventures lends intuitive weight to the notion of the issueless riot, it cannot provide a basis for distinguishing one riot from another; nor can it even provide a basis for distinguishing riot from other forms of situated action. In fact, "normal" or "institutional" action is often "issueless," in the sense of being without explicit goals, beliefs, etc.

The problems of Marx's theories are compounded by the fact that in accepting Smelser's (1963) theory of collective behavior, he was obliged to accept the value-added approach to explanation. In this approach, each determinant is a necessary condition of everything that follows (see chap. 9). According to this approach then, a failure to find strain and/or generalized belief in an episode of collective behavior invalidates Smelser's theory. Because each of Smelser's determinants is defined in terms of the other (a generalized belief is about a condition of strain; a precipitating incident confirms a generalized belief), it is not possible to rearrange or simplify his scheme without redefining the terms and reexamining their interrelationships, problems to which Marx did not address himself. Thus, the concept of mobilization, which Marx needed, is unintelligible without the notions of strain and generalized belief, because mobilization is defined in terms of goals, or beliefs, rather than in terms of, for example, interaction and control. Marx's attempt to establish the issueless riot as a phenomenon is, in effect, an assertion that Smelser has not provided a general theory of collective behavior. But he fails to meet the implicit obligation of this critique and of his own comparative approach: to reconsider the adequacy of Smelser's theory as an explanation of the protest riot and, thus, as a basis on which to develop the notion of the issueless riot.

It must be concluded that Marx has failed to demonstrate the value of the concept of the issueless riot. Whatever the value of the distinction between expression and action for describing episodes of collective behavior, it does not provide a typology of crowd, and it does not justify Blumer's original contention that the study of collective behavior overemphasizes the acting crowd. The closer the observer gets to the phenomena of collective behavior, the less the term expressive, as a label for a type of crowd, seems to be applicable. Marx has not shown the presence or absence of a generalized belief to be an essential variable of riot and, thus, has not revived the expressive crowd as a topic of major concern for collective behavior theory. Nor has he justified his own belief that recent studies of collective behavior have not given due regard to the issueless riot, because he has failed to show that the issueless riot exists or that, if it exists, it is anything but a rare bird of no apparent significance for society or sociology.

Marx's discussion can, however, be taken like that of Blumer: as a criticism of the failure of contemporary analyses of collective behavior to allow for enthusiasm, intensity, and variation in the actions of the crowd. In this case, Marx's dissatisfaction with the existing literature may lie with its overuse of a static decision model of collective behavior that emphasizes consensus, goals, beliefs, and leadership instead of, for example, interaction, excitement, and the practice and dialectics of meaningful activity. Because this model is most elegantly expressed by Smelser, Marx's dissatisfaction is most appropriately directed against the very theoretic framework within which he has conducted his inquiry.

CHAPTER TWO

COLLECTIVE BEHAVIOR: PROBLEMS IN THE FORMULATION OF THEORY

I am not inclined to believe that the language or the theories that scientists adopt are discontinuous with the language or theories of the nonscientific layman. The "language of science" is natural language; science is done, for example, in English and with the purpose *(inter alia)* of explaining phenomena that have proved refractory to casual or unsystematic investigation. It therefore seems implausible in the extreme to represent the concepts and theories that psychologists use in their accounts of behavior as unrelated to, or as mere homonyms of, the concepts and theories in terms of which the layman's understanding of behavior is articulated (Fodor, 1968, p. xxi).

* * *

In doing sociology, lay and professional, every reference to the "real world," even where the reference is to physical or biological events, is a reference to the organized activities of everyday life (Garfinkel 1967, p. viii).

The study of collective behavior has no technical language of its own. The words with which students of collective behavior regularly describe their phenomena are drawn from ordinary language. The meanings of words such as riot, violence, mob, crowd, hostility, protest, mass, leadership, belief, aggression depend upon the history of their ordinary public use. Each of these words carries the imagery of common sense interpretations of unfamiliar, dramatic, or untoward happenings (R. Williams, 1960, 1961).

That these are not technical terms is illustrated by the work of a number of social scientists. Ted Robert Gurr (1969) uses the terms "violence" and "strife" to refer to activities as diverse as civil rights demonstrations, urban disturbances, and terrorist activities (1969, p. 573ff). Gary Marx (1970) uses the term "riot" to describe selective attacks on property, police, and civilians, and enthusiastic outbursts at gatherings of the victorious. Neil Smelser (1963) uses the term "collective behavior" to cover situated action, such as the hostile outburst, and transsituated action, such as the value-oriented or norm-oriented movement. The Skolnick Report (1969) described the urban disturbances of 1967, student demonstrations, and antiwar activities as protest; and many investigations have used the terms "unrest," "disturbance," and "disorder," to refer to all unauthorized social or political action involving large numbers of people and/or activating agents of official control (National Advisory Commissions on Civil Disorders, 1968). In many cases, formal definitions are offered, but they are rarely used consistently and rarely cover the cases taken as examples. Even Smelser, whose work with that of Ralph Turner goes farthest in its technical claims, at one point asserts that some movements arise without the appearance of a generalized belief (Smelser, 1970). Yet, he continues to assimilate such movements to a model of collective behavior that includes panic and the hostile outburst, and which depends on generalized belief as a necessary condition of collective behavior as well as its criterial attribute.

The use of unexamined analogies and the appeal to a kind of common sense of collective behavior means that important methodological, theoretical, empirical, and practical issues are frequently resolved simply by the use of a word. More precisely, words such as riot, the meanings of which are limited by the settings of their use, are allowed to play the role of context-free, objectve terminology in situated accounts that are offered as general theories (Garfinkel, 1967, pp. 4-9).

The casual use of popular terminology is likely to give theory a particular slant that evades scrutiny by virtue of its utter normality. The perspective implicit in the use of such terminology is often revealed by official policies that are suggested by theorists and by the selection of theories by officials in order to justify their policies. James F. Short and Marvin E. Wolfgang (1970), referring to the work of the President's Commission on Law Enforcement and Administration of Justice (1965), the National Advisory Commission on Civil Disorders (1968), and the National Commission on the Causes and Prevention of Violence (1968) noted that:

> the Crime Commission virtually ignored the influence of the economically powerful in defining the nature of crime in our society, and in the making and implementing of laws for its control. The National Advisory Commission on Civil Disorders . . . labelled as a "riot cause" of ghetto riots "white racism," but failed to explore the implications for its continuance in the traditions and practices of the Congress of the United States, through seniority privileges and other means by which vested interests are protected. The Violence Commission called for a reordering of national priorities, but stopped short of analysis and full exploration of the implications for violence at home of the war in Indo-China, pleading instead for commitments to solve domestic problems "as soon as resources are available" (p. 3).

PERSPECTIVE AND THEORY: THE INTERRELATIONSHIPS

It is no longer possible to deny what is by now a cliche in the history and sociology of sociology: theory always reflects, expresses, and is limited by the perspective of its author. But perspective, like authorship, is a social fact that links the individual to the categories of which he is an instance and to the collectivities of which he is a part. Perspective does not operate simply as an intellectual limit to the construction of theory or as a source of personal bias. To speak of theory and practice as aspects of the same enterprise is to give perspective formal status within theory and to give theory moral and political significance within society. For now, as the concept is being used, perspective is the extratheoretic, extradiscipline analogue to paradigm (Kuhn, 1962). It defines the relationship between the author and his topic, between the theorist and his data, and between the scientist and the scientific community. The notion of perspective points to the fact that theories incorporate concepts, judgments, and imagery, the meanings of which depend upon the social characteristics of the theorists relative to the social attributes of their objects. People who publicly address themselves to the events of their lives or to the life of their society do so from a perspective that they, and their audiences, often take for granted.

Few issues in the sociology of collective behavior are more likely to arouse passionate controversy that that of the role of perspective in theory and observation. Sociologists are rarely given to detailed metatheoretic consider-ations and rarely given to the critique of perspective. The consequent naivete about the problem leaves the sociologist unprepared for an intellectual encounter over perspective. He often feels unjustly suspected of being unscientific, biased, or covertly ideological. Yet, if the general proposition that theory and perspective are complexly intertwined is accepted, the naive response is an obstacle to theorizing rather than a valid defense of objectivity (Mannheim, 1936; Lynd, 1939; Mills 1961; Sartre, 1963; Gouldner, 1965; Horowitz, 1965; Kuhn, 1962; Berger and Luckmann, 1967; Sjoberg, 1967).

Questions that arise are:

1. Is there a perspective-free theory?
2. What are the criteria for the critique of perspective and how do they relate to the criteria by which particular theoretical realizations of a perspective can be criticized?
3. Are extratheoretic concepts, propositions, and perspectives properly excluded from theoretic work and theory itself, or are they properly included as explicit elements of theory?
4. What is the relationship between theory, observation, and perspective?

PERSPECTIVE-FREE THEORY

The first question may tentatively be answered by saying that there is no perspective-free theory. A theory of perspectives can appear to be perspective-free, but it is an illusion of the fact that it is perspective-free relative to the data of the various theories that are its own data. Insofar as all theories are drawn from particular, socially organized points of view, they are subject, in their totality, to the limitations of those points of view. The role of perspective is especially problematic in theories that draw heavily on the ordinary use of terms and common sense notions of reality. For example, a person who views human behavior as essentially purposeful will assign an entirely different meaning to the term belief than someone who views behavior as essentially reactive.

A description of contemporary social change by W.E. Moore (1963) illustrates the ambiguity of accounts in which the author's perspective is left unstated. Moore specifies "the particular features of contemporary change . . . by a set of generalizations":

1. For any given society . . . change occurs frequently . . . .
2. Changes . . . occur in sequential chains rather than as "temporary" crises, . . . and the consequences tend to reverberate through entire regions or virtually the entire world.
3. Thus . . . contemporary change . . . has a dual basis.
4. The proportion of . . . change that is either planned or issues from the secondary consequences of deliberate innovations is much higher than in former times.
5. Accordingly, the range of material technology and social strategies is expanding rapidly and its net effect is additive or cumulative. . . .
6. The normal occurrence of change affects a wider range of individual experiences and functional aspects of societies in the modern world . . (p. 2).

The fourth generalization appears to be the key here. Whether this is a description of systematic change or a description of the consolidation of power by ruling elites depends upon whether power is identified with function or with position and interest. Moore's (1963) "tension-management" model of society identifies power with function in a way that does not answer crucial questions pertaining to coercion; the relative capacity of different interested parties to control the direction and scope of change; and the dialectical relationship between change and the nature and distribution of power in a system. The fact that such questions are unanswered is not simply a paradigmatic difference; it appears to be a difference in perspective as well.

The identification of power with function typically assumes that the exercise of power is legitimate and, consequently, representative. It should be noted, however, that a social system can be defined independently of the managed groups. Schools, universities, and, to some extent, empires are social systems whose operation does not depend upon a conception of its managed as members and that, consequently, define legitimacy independently of the values and beliefs of the managed groups. According to the terms of Moore's description, this assumption is not a matter of empirical determination that takes into consideration the various points of view nor does it attempt to explicate more than one point of view. The assumption that the exercise of power is legitimate and, therefore, representative can be seen as a justification for a political status quo. In the context of Moore's discussion, such an assumption is an expression of a perspective that is both managerial and elitist (Krausse, 1968; Cloward and Pliven, 1969). From this perspective, problems of power give way to considerations of function. From the perspective of those who are managed, however, discussions of societal guidance can easily be seen as descriptions of the intentions and capacities of those who hold power in the society.

Obviously, Moore has chosen his language, if not his propositions, carefully. His terms do not refer to change as a manifestation of the operations of power and interest but, rather, to change as a natural phenomenon that has a "normal," and presumably an "abnormal," course within which putatively legitimate planning plays a catalytic role.

THE ROLES OF PERSPECTIVE

Moore's discussion of social change illustrates two roles of perspective: as a parameter of theory and as a source of meaning for the terms of theoretic discourse. As a parameter, the ambiguity of Moore's perspective dictates a range of possible models of society but not the ways in which terms are to be understood, operationalized, and given conceptual status within theoretical propositions. As a source of meaning, the elitist and managerial perspective penetrates Moore's theory, giving meaning to terms such as "planned," "reverberate," "change," "proportion of change," "material technology," "social strategies," "individual experience," and "functional aspects of societies" (1963, p. 2). This perspective supports some analogies and submerges others, thus affecting the ways in which propositions will be combined to produce new propositions. For example, the extent to which a political response to planned change is anticipated, rather than social unrest or mass behavior, depends upon: (1) whether planned change itself is viewed as a political event or as the disinterested outcome of some process of the system; (2) whether the reverberation of effect is conceived as a continuous spread with similar consequences or as a discontinuous spread with differing consequences; (3) whether "deliberate innovations" are deemed representative or unrepresentative; and (4) whether or not unauthorized political actions are considered to be genuinely political.

The Attitude of Neutrality. Moore's use of overtly neutral terms not only masks his perspective but also illustrates the fact that the failure to explicate perspective is, in itself, functional to a particular sociological interest. By artificially taking theory outside of the socio-political (practical) setting in which it is devised, the failure to explicate perspective imputes to theory the transcendent qualities of pure reason. This failure seems to be part of the professional attitude of ethical neutrality assumed by many social scientists who wish their accounts to be read as accurate throughout history (Horowitz, 1965). It assumes a philosophy of social science that views the development of sociology in terms of contributions and additions to a body of knowledge, rather than in terms of presentations, criticisms, elaborations, practical suggestions, and replacements. Such a philosophy attempts to establish the discipline wholly outside of the events and processes that shape its tools and its very subject matter. This philosophy is inconsistent with what appears to be the most important recent developments in the sociology of knowledge and the philosophy of social science (Kuhn, 1962; Garfinkel, 1967).

THE CRITERIA FOR PERSPECTIVAL CRITIQUE

The criteria for criticizing perspective are generally moral or political. Criticism of perspective establishes constituencies for theory and the range of theories within which a particular theory can be evaluated, but it is not necessarily a basis for an internal critique of a specific theory or for a comparison of one theory with another. On the other hand, when a theory assumes its perspective by virtue of, for example, the explicit use of normative premises or ideal types, or by virtue of its use of common sense notions in illustrations and lateral applications of theory (the use of analogy to extend theory to new phenomena, as with, for example, the application of theories of laughter to the study of embarassment) both theoretic criticism and criticism of perspective may be part of the same project.

Morality and the Choice of Hypotheses. The perspective of a theory can be taken as an issue when hypotheses resemble normative propositions. When a theory, for example, involves a hypothesis that asserts a causal relationship between the weakness of official structure and the incidence of collective behavior, the perspective becomes an issue. In the choice of hypothesis, there is a selective mechanism at work that often goes beyond the ease of the test, the generality of the hypothesis, or the occurrence of the hypotheses within a schedule of inference. That mechanism is ordinarily extratheoretic and normative. Particularly where hypothesis testing is often impossible—as in theories of collective behavior—the selection of hypotheses indicates that the theory from which the hypotheses are derived is somehow incorporated in explicit or implicit moral or normative systems (Von Wright, 1963). This inference may be drawn when the terms of a theory presuppose a familiarity with particular realms of discourse or modes of thought and interpretation. For example, theories of social pathology and deviance usually assume a familiarity with certain types of moral thought. Moreover, all theories of crisis are obliged—as a matter of sheer understandability—to be up to date for some practice. Where a theory goes far enough beyond its data to constitute an idea among ideas, the same inference may again be drawn.

THE PERSPECTIVE OF "GENERALIZED BELIEF"

A recent controversy between Neil Smelser and two of his critics, Elliott Currie and Jerome H. Skolnick, illustrates both the confusion and the resistance that attend a critique of perspective. Currie and Skolnick (1970) argued that according to Smelser's (1963) theory of collective behavior, unauthorized socio-political action is the result of irrationality and immorality, or at least amorality. They pointed to his emphasis on the role of generalized beliefs in transforming frustrations into premises for action and his failure to adequately explore the rational and political bases for unauthorized actions. Currie and Skolnick further argued that this imputation stemmed from a nineteenth-century antidemocratic outlook transformed into the managerial or elitist perspective of twentieth-century sociology and applied to the study of deviance, marginal politics, and collective behavior. To this critique, Smelser replied that Currie and Skolnick misunderstood and exaggerated the role of generalized belief in his theory and, in any case, had introduced nonpositivistic criteria into what ought to be a positivistic criticism of a scientific theory. It is clear that Smelser considered the Currie-Skolnick argument an attack *ad hominem*; his reply is entitled "Two Critics in Search of a Bias: A Response to Currie and Skolnick" (1970). Each party to the dispute cited different passages of Smelser's book, *Theory of Collective Behavior* (1963), in support of his position.

It appears however, that Smelser's formal definition of the term generalized belief, and his theoretical discussion of its status as a "necessary condition" of collective behavior, does suggest that he takes collective behavior as "the action of the impatient." If impatience is a type of irrationality, mindless of procedure and the necessity to schedule performance, then Currie and Skolnick are essentially correct in their identification of Smelser's perspective.

A brief survey of Smelser's references to the nature of generalized belief and its role in collective behavior supports Currie and Skolnick. For example, in his closing remarks, Smelser (1963) stated that:

> We chose—in contrast to many others who analyze collective behavior—to make the defining characteristic *the kind of belief under which behavior is mobilized.* Collective behavior is action based on a generalized belief . . . (p. 383).

As to the rationality of such a belief, Smelser was explicit:

> These beliefs differ . . . from those which guide many other types of behavior. They involve a belief in the existence of extraordinary forces . . . The beliefs on which collective behavior is based . . . are thus akin to magical beliefs (p. 8).

And:

> Generalized beliefs restructure an ambiguous situation in a short-circuited way . . . Short-circuited involves the jump from extremely high levels of generality to specific, concrete situations (p. 82).

Smelser might have argued that a belief is generalized only relative to a particular system of reference and is thus impatient, magical, or irrational relativity to that system alone. What bypasses procedures or conditions of action for one system may be a conservative and orderly expression of another system. Marginality is a social phenomenon that reveals this most poignantly although the reality of rationality is revealed as well by other phenomena. For example, unauthorized demonstrations against government actions may be part of a relatively organized movement. From the perspective of government, these demonstrations bypass official procedures and are predicated upon generalized beliefs. From the perspective of the movement they may be fully rational. Similarly, collective martyrdom or heroism (for example, draft resistance and sabotage) often involve acts of agency—altruistic as opposed to egoistic "crimes"—for a community of interest (M. Brown, 1968). As such, they may be conservative, realistic, and orderly expressions of that system of action. Rather than take this conceptual option, Smelser described generalized beliefs in absolute rather than relative terms, giving legal membership a peculiar social psychological significance and leaving himself open to the Currie-Skolnick critique.

Moreover, generalized beliefs are essentially extravagantly reactive rather than constructive, as illustrated by Smelser's list of the "major types of generalized belief": hysteria, which envisions "an absolutely potent, generalized threat"; wish-fulfillment, "which reduces ambiguity by posting absolutely efficacious, generalized facilities"; hostility; norm-oriented beliefs, "which envision the reconstitution of a threatened normative structure"; and value-oriented beliefs, "which envision the reconstitution of a threatened value system" (p. 83).

Some of the statements from his book appear to be inconsistent with Smelser's later reply to the criticism offered by Currie and Skolnick. In that reply, he denied that he conceived of generalized beliefs as "distorted," that the beliefs guiding collective behavior differ from those guiding ordinary behavior, and that generalized beliefs are necessarily exaggerations. Whether or not it is an accurate portrayal of his earlier position, Smelser's (1970) response to the Currie and Skolnick critique seems to indicate a refinement of his concept of generalized belief, which is unfortunately not developed in the context of his theory:

> My basic theory of generalized beliefs is that they are purposive collective efforts to redefine and restructure the social environment, that crystallize when individuals and groups are subjected to certain stresses (strain) and certain types of constraints on their opportunities to resolve these stresses (conduciveness) (p. 49).

In this statement, a generalized belief seems no different from any action premise. It appears as a belief about what is possible under the circumstances. Collective behavior is thus an example of problem solving by ad hoc or temporary groups. What is lost here is the power of Smelser's original notion that a generalized belief is a leap of faith that bypasses the ordinary, and rational, bases of problem solving. In that leap, collective behavior resembles action on principle and includes a desituationalization of vision and concern. Thus, his original concept allows him—as his later analysis does not—to assimilate crowds and movements to the same model.

It is fairly clear that Smelser does not consider irrationality or impatience to be the essence of collective behavior, but the does consider it to be an attribute that is derived from more fundamental conditions. He speaks as if irrationality is an aspect of social action that inevitably arises out of anxiety, ambiguity, frustration, or strain. Despite the fact that this opinion represents a departure from the mass psychology of the late nineteenth and early twentieth centuries, it is understandable that many of Smelser's critics—who are attentive to his emphasis on uniformity, the generalized belief, and leadership—see his theory as a variant of that tradition. Moreover, it is understandable that critics find a managerial perspective in Smelser's concept of control, as in his more general political sociology, in particular its exclusive emphasis on elite-generated solutions to frustration, deprivation, and other symptoms of structural strain, and on crowd suppression. Both bypass the unauthorized efforts of those who lack official standing to influence the conditions of their lives.

Smelser's positivist statement avoids the major issue raised by the Currie and Skolnick criticism: not that Smelser is biased, but that he has not clarified the perspective within which he has framed his theory, and therefore has not clarified some of his key concepts. Since his theory, like all social theories, is intertwined with the perspective of a particular practice and the common sense of that practice, it is fully comprehensible only by those who take that practice and its common sense for granted or by those for whom that perspective, to some measure, has been explicated. While Currie and Skolnick also demand moral accountability, the gist of their critique is that Smelser has failed to state and examine, in an intellectual controversy that demands such a statement and examination, for *whom* his theory is practical and theoretical.

It must be concluded from this discussion that so long as a theory appeals to a particular community of interest for whom the issue of perspective has not been raised, it can be treated solely within the practice of that community. Presumably, it is in this spirit that Garfinkel (1967) has described the work of Talcott Parsons, for example, as "awesome for the penetrating depths and unfailing precision of its practical sociological reasoning on the constituent tasks of the problem of social order and its solutions" (p. ix). However, when there are counterclaims against that practice as a whole—and such counterclaims inevitably arise as part of crisis research—the perspective within which both theory and practical action are contrived must be made explicit and, perhaps, attacked or defended.

The perspective of the authors here emphasizes the managed groups for whom unauthorized action is often the only recourse for change that touches their lives. Such groups bear the brunt of official interpretations of collective behavior and of official strategies of control. The analysis shares the intellectual tradition, the perspective, and the hunches of radical left social thought. Its success depends upon whether it is, in Sartre's (1970) words, an "effective analysis of the situation"; whether it makes a difference, ultimately, in practice; whether it contributes to the continuing critique of contemporary society and the possibilities for progressive change; and whether it contributes to the analysis of the role of situated social action in movements for change. Because this work offers a counterclaim to the perspective of most modern theorists of collective behavior, the authors will attempt to clairfy their own perspective, the perspective of those theorists, and the grounds for a confrontation between the two.

THE SELECTION OF DATA: THE PROBLEM OF DISCOVERY

Second hand accounts of collective behavior are often unself-conscious and uncritical of their principles of selection and interpretation. In relying on them, the student of collective behavior faces a literature that is more than a collection of empirical reports and far less than theory. As a result, it is not clear what the data are for the study of collective behavior, much less what might be taken as relevant phenomena. Shibutani (1966), for example, argues persuasively that two phenomena typically associated with crowds may actually be artifacts of laboratory attempts to simulate collective behavior. He questions both the suggestibility of participants and the distortion of communications during collective behavior in his discussion of rumor as the alleged process of communication among crowd participants. Similarly, Turner (1964) suggests that the apparent homogeneity of crowds is an illusion. In both cases, the criticism is not directed at the classical theories of rumor and collective behavior but, rather, at the phenomena that those theories purported to explain. If the criticism is valid, then it discredits new theories that have accepted such phenomena as contagion, homogeneity, impatience, and mass mobilization—the classical phenomena of collective behavior—without examining whether or not these categories have been consistently and accurately applied and without reexamining their contemporary usefulness for the construction of theories of collective behavior. It is only by examining empirical reports as activities in their own right that the problems engendered by the necessity of relying on such reports can be dealt with.

Michael Lipsky and David J. Olson (1969) have exposed some important aspects of the problem of discovery that bear on the interpenetration of theory, method, and use in crisis research. Their discussion of "Riot Commission Politics" explored the relationship between an account of untoward action and the organizational and institutional life of its authors (Scott and Lyman, 1970, pp. 490-91). Their remarks concerning the relationship between the strains inherent in official advisory commissions and the descriptions and explanations that are the output of such commissions are expecially pertinent to a discipline that is dependent on officially sponsored, or at least, officially interested research.

Commenting on the work of the National Advisory Commission on Civil Disorders (the Kerner Commission), Lipsky and Olson (1969) asked:

> should we despair . . . that riot commission reports are irrelevant? Or should we agree with public officials that riot commissions provide an invaluable service for helping society understand complex events? Or should we think cynically that riot commissions are no more than the tools by which chief executives placate and arouse people? (p. 9).

They argued that these questions cannot be answered without "examining the place and function of riot commissions in the political life of the country" (p. 9). Such an examination would aid in answering questions concerning the value of officially sponsored research for the discovery and understanding of collective behavior. In their discussion, Lipsky and Olson focused on the personnel, the tasks, the organization, the strategies, and the functions of riot commissions.

A POLITICAL ANALYSIS OF THE 1968 NATIONAL ADVISORY COMMISSION ON CIVIL DISORDERS

The Kerner Commission (National Advisory Commission on Civil Disorders), like most riot commissions (Waskow, 1966), was dominated by essentially conservative men who were, according to Lipsky and Olson (1969), "either public officials or the heads of established American institutions" (p. 11). The commission attempted to deal with a number of complex problems in a very short time. It had to sift diverse and often contradictory material in order to develop a reasonably accurate picture of the civil disorders that took place in over 160 American cities during 1967. In doing so, the commission could not disassociate itself from the political implications—for both the commissioners and their official sponsors—of its report. The commission was also asked to determine the causes of the riots, to focus on those causes that could be reversed by governmental action, and to develop proposals for the prevention of future disorders. Clearly, the implicit purposes of this task were: to develop proposals for official policies that would bypass the energies of citizens engaged in unauthorized political action, thereby preserving official structure as a constant of reform; to justify the suppression of unauthorized political action as an intrusion on, and an obstacle to, reform; and to create a sense of urgency among officials and their publics based on the threat that, without immediate reforms involving short term and observable effects, widespread chaos would occur. In considering the output of the commission as a social system, Lipsky and Olson discussed the impact and influence of three organizational contingencies: (1) the scarcity of time and resources, (2) the problem of commission integration, and (3) the development of political legitimacy.

Initial Problems of the Commission. The commission had less than a year to complete its various tasks. The shortage of time and a scarcity of resources had several effects. First, the staff had to be hired quickly. Second, data were often overly sparse and unrepresentative. Third, data were compiled in the light of a hastily and relatively uncritically adopted working theory of riot causation, which asserted:

> that systematic deprivation and discrimination in the past, when added to reasonable expectations of positive change and when accompanied by continued indignities and community resentments, become focused by a single incident or series of incidents into behavior that takes the form of . . . hostile activities (Lipsky and Olson, 1969, pp. 11-12).

Although Lipsky and Olson acknowledged the serviceability of such a theory, they pointed out that it does not account for certain important types of civil disorders or for variations in the characteristics of disorders. Nevertheless, there was little opportunity for the systematic and comparative investigation that might have led to a definition of the phenomena and a significant theory of riot causation. As a result, the commission was left with the task of developing descriptions and accounts of the events in terms of relatively few characteristics and of illustrating a theory that was basically accepted by the commission before the research staff entered the field. It may be added that the focus on frustrations and incidents and the characterization of the behavior as "hostile activities" avoided both the possibility of a structural analysis of the causes of riots and the possibility of a political analysis of their role. Moreover, it left the commission with an impoverished inferential structure, too simple to generate hypotheses—and therefore creative policy—and questionable in its emphasis on motivation as well as its assumption of a direct relationship between particular states of motivation and particular collective activities.

The fourth problem was the exacerbation, due to the scarcity of time, of the conflict between the commissioners and their staff. The commissioners, as public people with constituencies and multifaceted connections with the official structors of society, wanted to construct a case so that their conclusions would appear to be well founded. The staff members, on the other hand, wanted to use professionally acceptable research procedures, despite the ambiguities that might be left unresolved in the final report. According to Lipsky and Olson (1969):

> Building a case and good research procedures are not necessarily incompatible. But a strain is placed upon mutual satisfaction of both these goals when time is short. Statistics without relevance are collected; time-consuming procedures are honored to make an impression of thoroughness; theories with potential validity are rejected since they cannot be adequately tested, and so on (p. 12).

There was mutual distrust between the commissioners and the staff. The commissioners suspected a liberal and reformist bias among their staff members, and many staff members felt that the commissioners would use the investigation to whitewash government officials. While the tension ebbed and flowed, it influenced the work of the commission. The fifth problem, urgency, enforced a separation of two staff functions: research and the preparation of the final report, with a consequent distortion of the findings in that report.

Much of the organizational work of the commission involved the insurance of some measure of integration among the commissioners themselves, most of whom were politicians at the same time that they served on the advisory commission, and between the commissioners and their staff. There were various mechanisms utilized, which accounted for at least a show of solidarity among the commissioners. Some of these mechanisms depended upon the public positions of the commissioners, which made them vulnerable to threats of publicity about internal disagreements. In their discussion, Lipsky and Olson described the way in which Mayor John Lindsay of New York forced the other commissioners to accept a relatively hard hitting and liberal summary of the commission's work by threatening to publish the summary as a minority report. However, Lipsky and Olson also asserted that the acceptance of the Lindsay summary ultimately depended upon a shared sense of urgency among commissioners, which resulted both from direct contact with the volatility and the needs of the ghetto and from the belief that American cities were highly vulnerable to civil strife. The commissioners finally agreed "that the riots were not results of conspiracies nor mass behavior dominated by criminal or quasi-criminal elements" (Lipsky and Olson, 1969, p. 14) but, rather, were due "to long-standing factors of discrimination, deprivation, and neglect" (Lipsky and Olson, 1969, p. 14).

Such conclusions were acceptable precisely because they were consistent both with the information accumulated about discrimination, deprivation, and neglect, and with the political limitations of the commission. These limitations precluded a structural critique and a political analysis of both the riots and the American social system in which they occurred. The commission's conclusions represented an uneasy reconciliation of a liberal moral sensibility and a conservative political philosophy: the report offered a policy of reform within the context of an ominous warning that a race war would occur if its recommendations were not adopted. There was every indication at the time that the demands of such a policy on official structures within the American economy and polity would not be met in the short time required by the warning. Consequently, the commission's report became an argument both for an increase in official control and for the suppression of the unauthorized and marginal political activity that could be expected under such circumstances. The commission's continual emphasis on avoiding chaos indicates that the prevention of unauthorized political action has precedence over the prevention of further misery for black people, which was a value parameter of both their data gathering and their analysis (Skolnick, 1969).

THE PARADOXES OF POLITICAL LEGITIMACY

The development of political legitimacy for an advisory commission, or the maximization of the impact of its report, has several consequences. The desire for unanimity—a united front that increases the credibility of the report—decreases the likelihood of minority reports of findings and conclusions. Moreover, the commission may engage in the building of a self-image that obscures defects in its research and limits the capacity of the critic to discover the best use of the report. For example, Lipsky and Olson claimed that in order to avoid the accusation of bias, commissioners often:

> give the impression that all political groups are given their day in court . . . The Kerner Commission . . . took the testimony of many of the black militants whose names appear on the witness list at a period when many chapters in the report already had been approved in relatively final form (p. 16).

Thus, "the internal political dynamics of riot commissions can be characterized as the gradual development of a *pressure group*" (pp. 16-17). As a pressure group, a commission developes strategies:

> to overcome their relatively powerless status. These strategies include: (1) maximizing the visibility and controlling the exposure of the reports; (2) competing for legitimacy; (3) affecting the political environment; and (4) assisting the implementation process (Lipsky and Olson, 1969, p. 17).

But these strategies may also be viewed as limitations on both the research activities of riot commissions and the usefulness of commission reports. Such strategies are sources of a pervasive bias that goes to the heart of the data from which advisory commissions draw conclusions as well as to the conclusions themselves. As such, they constitute powerful extratheoretic limits on theory and research that cannot be examined and criticized without direct access to the commission and its work.

THE MARGINALITY OF ADVISORY COMMISSIONS

In their discussion, Lipsky and Olson (1969) concluded:

> that formation of riot commissions gives rise to public expectations which cannot be fulfilled and that riot commissions are charged with incompatible goals which cannot meaningfully be reconciled.

* * *

Insofar as this is the case, riot commissions are most profitably viewed as participants in the ongoing political struggle of American race relations. They may make marginal contributions to that struggle by providing status and support for interpretations of riots which may affect the decisions of other political actors. They may also provide information about riots that will influence others, and may lend legitimacy to information which is already available. Riot commissions further may help structure the terms in which debate over issues relating to riots will be pursued. They are initiated by public officials as part of the executive function, but they are transformed by their constituents and, by virtue of the involvement of commissioners in commission business, they transform themselves into pressure group competitors in the political process (p. 10).

Such conclusions suggest that riot commission reports are not suitable as primary sources of information about collective behavior, although they can be treated as documents—and therefore data in their own right—that reveal the practical concerns of officials confronted with unauthorized political activity. This suggestion, however, is somewhat at odds with a recent statement by the general counsel of the National Advisory Commission on Violence, James S. Campbell (1970):

National advisory commissions have a distinctive factfinding role to play that is related to—in a sense lies midway between—the respective roles of both the news media and the social sciences (p. 171).

Campbell's portrayal of the role of national advisory commissions assumes a continuum of usefulness (for the citizen, the scientist, and the politician) ranging from journalism to social science. The choice of one end of the continuum as positive and the other as negative depends upon the role of the user and upon his purpose: whether it is to vote, to develop theory, to prepare social prognosis, or to make policy. As represented by commission reports, the midpoint is presumably useful regardless of the perspective from which the continuum of usefulness is drawn. To represent journalism and science, however, as the two ends of such a continuum is at odds with the usual conceptions of both enterprises. The differences are not simply in the degrees of objectivity; the relative complexity of inferential structure; or the more or less specialized sorts of description, analysis, abstraction, or presentation.

It is more pertinent, however, to talk about national advisory commissions in terms of their role in the structure of government. Their role is primarily ideological, rather than being directed at gathering news or at establishing facts and devising sociological accounts of those facts. Commissions gain their capacity to exercise political pressure—via the public—from the news media, and they gain some of their legitimacy and credibility from their sponsorship of social scientific research. This characterization is more consistent with the conventional sense of the differences—of function, of method, of organization, of the definition of information, and so on—among journalism, social science, and commission reports. It is, however, inconsistent with the typical characterization of riot commissions as fact-finding bodies capable—even though they sponsor research—of providing information for sociologists.

Contributions to Social Science. Campbell does hint at some other ways in which social science can profit from the work of national advisory commissions. He suggests that commission reports can serve both as crude, first approximations of a sophisticated treatment of collective behavior and as tests of the clarity of sociological concepts. According to Campbell (1970) "Commission reports usually precede more thorough scientific or historical studies by months or even years" (p. 171). Commenting on the limits of the sociology of collective behavior, which have been exposed by commission reports that have stretched those limits, he concluded that "social science can make them [commission reports] even more useful by improving the blunt and clumsy tools with which commissions have to do their job" (p. 176). This conclusion is apparent from the attempts of national advisory commissions to apply such tools within the empirical range for which they were, presumably, formulated. Campbell's conclusion, indeed, states a genuine contribution of national advisory commissions to social science. But it has only been a contribution to a particular sociological tradition and not to other traditions and paradigms in the study of collective behavior. Campbell (1970) illustrated the narrowness of this contribution; he outlined the sociological and historical analyses that he felt should follow the finding of the National Advisory Commission on Civil Disorders that:

> "the causes of recent racial disorders are imbedded in a massive tangle of issues and circumstances," but . . . the "most fundamental" strand in that tangle is "the racial attitude and behavior of white Americans toward black Americans" (p. 174, citing the National Advisory Commission on Civil Disorders, 1968, p. 203).

Tentatively assuming the Kerner Commission's statement that an attitude—white racism—is somehow an underlying cause of the ghetto explosions of 1967, Campbell projected the implications of this finding for social science:

> Thus, if we ask whether the riots may not have a deeper cause that underlies even white racism, we will not overlook the possibility of a further historical and sociological analysis of the sources of prejudice against Negroes in this country. We can meaningfully ask what caused, and what continues to sustain, these attitudes which we have denominated "white racism." We can consider, for example, what the institution of slavery and the failure of Reconstruction did to blacks and whites, and hence to their attitudes toward themselves and toward each other. We can further try to identify those features of contemporary life (e.g., high Negro crime rates and low media visibility of Negro accomplishments) which tend to reinforce the attitudinal legacy of centuries of white supremacy and Negro subordination (p. 175).

This focus on attitudes and attitude change is the most plausible line of attack only when the Kerner Commission's conclusion and the culturological paradigm invoked by that conclusion are accepted. It is not plausible within the framework of institutional or organizational analysis.

Despite the fact that riot commission reports are interesting primarily as public accounts of untoward behavior (addressed within the adversary situation of a pressure group) rather than as repositories of basic information, sociologists regularly cite the findings of national advisory commissions and similar agencies to substantiate theoretic arguments and to test hypotheses. More often than not, these citations accompany additional analyses of data that have been gathered by official agencies for other purposes (census reports, for example) or secondary analyses of descriptions provided by the news media. This fact, however, testifies less to the inherent usefulness of such material for the sociology of collective behavior than to the lack of alternative sources of information. For better or for worse, sociologists have been dependent upon such sources as the news media, the national advisory commissions, and police reports.

Given these circumstances, to what extent can theories of collective behavior and explanations of unauthorized political action avoid being either explications of official ideology or concrete solutions to problems defined within the parameters of official practice? The answer to this question depends upon a critique of the perspective of official practice as well as of the conventional sociology of collective behavior. Perhaps the best use of the reports of officially sponsored research and, in particular, the reports of national advisory commissions is as sources of illustration, rather than as sources of information or evidence. Such reports can provide a simple substitute for the fictional accounts that are often essential in order to demonstrate the plausibility of theoretical ideas. Fictional accounts are often fruitfully employed by theorists who adopt a phenomenological approach toward their subject matter. In this use, such accounts are the same as historical, clinical, or case materials referred to (and thereby devised) by theorists in order to substantiate theoretic propositions (Goffman, 1963b; Smelser, 1962; Sartre, 1964).[1] There is nothing wrong with this time-honored methodology so long as the method is acknowledged and so long as the accounts are presented as illustrations, rather than as evidence, with regard to the theory at issue.

DISCOVERY AS AN ACT OF ATTRIBUTION

What is important here is the acknowledgment of discovery as an act of attribution that has what McHugh (1968) referred to as "theoreticity"—that is, the quality of being imbedded in an intentional structure that goes far beyond the formally stated limits of theory and method. The skepticism concerning commission reports is largely the result of their own theoreticity, their imbeddedness in an intentional structure that has become an issue. Thus, much of the information available for the development of a theory of collective behavior is based on accounts stated within particular perspectives and paradigms. Data have been gathered under conditions that limit their representative quality, and conclusions have been drawn without an acknowledgment of

1. In this, we disagree with Berger and Luckmann who asserted that phenomenology is "a purely descriptive method" (1967, p. 20). We consider it rather a variant of the method of what might be called fictive construction, a method employed by Goffman but having its roots in the classical urban ethnographies. Without going into detail, we assume that the terms of the phenomenologist's rejection of positivism precludes the extreme empiricist claim of Berger and Luckmann, and that case material is inherently constructive, illustrative, and contingent upon the rules of descriptive irrelevance, etc., accepted by the social scientist.

the intentional structures that are pervasive, yet hidden, sources of bias. As a result, the literature is not clear as to what is evidence and what is theory. The scientific, or quasi-scientific, posture of national advisory commissions suggests that illustration is evidence; that a description of an event is a replica of an objective reality, rather than a construction in its own right; and that an interested investigation can uncover disinterested findings, conclusions, and implications for official policy.

Because much of the sociology of collective behavior reflects official perspectives, as well as the official ideologies that can be applied most easily to the solution of official problems (Janowitz, 1968; Graham and Gurr, 1969), it is essential that the parameters of theoretical activity be included in the study of collective behavior. Without considering these parameters, it is impossible to discover the phenomena of collective behavior and to develop alternative theories that can avoid the weaknesses of the prevailing theories.

Surprisingly, there is considerable agreement among sociologists as to what phenomena occur during episodes of collective behavior. Among those phenomena, Smelser (1964) included imitation, milling, and social contagion. His concept of generalized belief refers to a type of mobilizing idea regularly attributed to participants in collective behavior. All of these phenomena are, however, part of an empirical image of the crowd that has been criticized by a number of sociologists, such as Shibutani (1966), Skolnick (1969), Turner (1964), and Couch (1968), on the grounds that they are derived from accounts that are of questionable value for the study of collective behavior. As a result, it is not at all clear that sociology is in a position to develop theories to explain *known* phenomena. It appears, rather, that in the course of developing theory, phenomena will also be developed. But that is as it should be. The development of theory and the construction of fact go hand in hand: the act of discovery is the act of doing theory and the act of doing theory is the act of discovery.

RESEARCHING UNAUTHORIZED POLITICAL ACTION

The reports of national advisory commissions on urban disorder, violence, protest, and civil strife are the most extensive part of a vast literature distributed around two conflicting themes: riot and violence and "the politics of protest." Each theme projects an empirical domain and a paradigm. Although there is considerable overlap between empirical domains, the paradigms are mutually exclusive.

Literature concerning riot and violence projects an analysis in terms of a break in culture or social organization. Literature concerning the politics of protest projects an analysis in terms of struggle for power and the socialization of grievance. The different values and perspective of each of these two themes are articulated in the ways in which collective behavior is described; that is, as unauthorized or as noninstitutional. The constituent elements of society are analyzed differently and different suggestions for policy are formulated. General, and often exclusive, attitudes toward official, as compared with unofficial, sources of social change are expressed in any given sociological work.

The thematic category of a paper or book can, thus, be identified by the language it uses:

violence versus force
disorder versus conflict
failure of authority versus power struggle
belief versus ideology
expression versus information and organization
suggestibility versus the socialization of grievance
social control versus official repression
collective behavior versus unauthorized political action
hostility versus protest.

The language in which an episode of collective behavior is described is a clue as to whether that episode will be identified as antisocietal or as action that represents a position in opposition to other positions. Language is also a clue to the choice of strategies that are offered to officials—negotiation, containment, or repression—and to the advice given explicitly or implicitly to the participants in collective behavior.

The selection of one of the two major themes of the literature on protest also establishes a descriptive emphasis on either the strictly external aspects of collective behavior—stylization (Feuer, 1969)—or the structure of situated action in its organized and practical aspects, including the accounts of participants in the activities (Goffman, 1961, 1963; Garfinkel, 1967; Skolnick, 1969; Brown, 1970.) Correlatively, the former tends to invoke dispositional and the latter, situational explanations for the activities of crowds (Brown, 1970).

The literature on unauthorized political action has sensitized sociologists to the fact that theories of collective behavior have, for the most part, been devised as part of the formulation and solution of the practical problem of maintaining official settings, organizations, operations, and institutions. Therefore, the discussion of the topic of collective behavior here will include the following:

the relationship between theory and practice
the inevitability of confrontation in stratified socio-economic establishments
the ways in which activity develops as part of the practical construction of a situation
the relationship between organization and power
the problematic status of the concept of legitimacy
the capacity of allegedly technical terms, such as riot, violence, unrest, and protest to evoke particular settings and occasions
the extratheoretic sources of theory and research—for example, perspective, paradigm, value, and terminology
the complexity of episodes of collective behavior
the fact that collective behavior occurs on every social occasion
the role of information, tradition, organization, and perspective in the formation of active collectivities
the paradoxes of official control
weaknesses in the standard empirical literature on collective behavior
the inadequacy of a political sociology in which the unofficial and unauthorized is excluded by definition from the study of the polity.

CHAPTER THREE

COLLECTIVE BEHAVIOR
AND DISASTER

Disasters are known by their consequences. The drama of disaster lies in the body counts, the range of devastation, the incomprehensibility of the cause, and the mythic reconstructions of the event that feed the culture and the politics of the stricken community. The fiery destruction of Rome in 64 A.D. is typical: the death, the confusion, and the material destruction, as well as the blame placed on the Christians, tell as much about disaster as is necessary to stimulate interest. If history can be written as a chronicle of conquest and the dissolution of empires, it can also be written as a chronicle of catastrophe and recovery: for example, the great epidemics in Europe, Asia, and Africa; the great volcanic destructions of Pompeii and Herculaneum, the catastrophic urban fires of historical times (see Kurtz, 1969, pp. 388ff.).

The incomprehensibility of natural catastrophes is very nearly matched by the "technological disasters" of modern times: airplane wrecks, industrial explosions, automobile collisions, massive chemical poisonings, and wars that bring calamity to the millions of people who bear the brunt of the ideals and ambitions of the powerful. Willingly or unwillingly, men and women have seen their lives go up in the smoke and flames of machinery and intentions ultimately as incomprehensible to them as the earthquakes, volcanic eruptions, epidemics, and floods that they knew as acts of God.

Industrialization brings people together in the human density of the city and the factory, sets industry beside the home and the school, and creates immense and complex social establishments. As modern capitalistic society replaced the earlier forms of feudal domination and small community, industrial growth immeasurably increased the vulnerability of societies—though not necessarily populations—to catastrophe. At the same time, it became possible, and desirable, for officials to anticipate disaster and to enlist the aid of social scientists, psychologists, and human engineers, in limiting its effects.

Insofar as disaster control is part of the more general problem of societal order, the study of disaster has always dealt with the effects of disaster on societal operations. It has considered the political and the technical consequences of catastrophic occurrences as well as the cultural, the institutional, and the social dimensions. The sociological study of disaster has dealt with the apparently improvised definitional and tactical behavior of collectivities as much as with the apparently planned and disciplined actions of official agencies. In addition, it has dealt with interaction that is contained within the boundaries of conventional groupings—the family, the neighborhood, and the organization, for example—and with interaction that is strictly situated. Disaster research is a kind of halfway house for the more general study of collective behavior because it relates directly to the formulation of official definitions of crises, to the strategies on the part of the official order, and to the unauthorized conduct of large numbers of people.

The situated, organized, and occasional character of crowd action has become clear primarily through ethnographic research on disaster. This research has stressed the relationship between crowds and their material conditions, their prior organized activities, their intergroup relations, and their constructions of situations. Disaster is, by and large, felt to be a politically and morally neutral ground for the sociologist. As a result, research and theory have been relatively free of the types of controversy familiar to students of unauthorized political action. In the study of disaster, concepts have developed against a background of theoretical simplicity accompanied by a great deal of intensive field research (Baker and Chapman, 1962).

At first glance, collective behavior during disaster fits the standard conceptions of collective behavior as "interactional episodes which may be distinguished as relatively spontaneous and transitory" (Evans, 1969, p. 1) or as uninstitutionalized action (Smelser, 1963) occurring outside the norms of the inclusive society (Turner, 1964). However, as the literature here included in the discussion of disaster is reviewed, it will become apparent that the actuality of behavior during disaster does not fit the standard conceptions of collective behavior. It forces a reevaluation of what collective behavior, as a whole, is. As a result, the major theoretical problems concerning collective behavior must be reformulated.

PERSPECTIVES IN THE STUDY OF DISASTER

Investigators have approached the study of disaster from two converging points of view, psychological and sociological. Research on the behavior of people under stress shows that urgency and danger often shift, on the individual's hierarchy of loyalties, from inclusive and formal to local and traditional groups (Hill and Hansen, 1962). This shift involves both a particularization and a newly specific and extreme socialization of consciousness (Kilpatrick, 1957). In addition, psychological investigations have centered on the situationalizing effects of stress. As a result, the dispositional analysis of individual behavior has begun to yield to the interpretation of that behavior as situated and socially organized action (Mintz, 1951; Kilpatrick, 1957; Form and Nosow, 1958; Kelley, et al., 1965; Drabek and Boggs, 1968; Drabek, 1969; Drabek and Hass, 1969).

The findings of sociological research on disaster converge with the findings of psychology. Sociologists have described the processes of:

localization or demobilization (Sorokin, 1942; Hill and Hansen, 1962; Thompson and Hawkes, 1962)

the structure and politics of collective behavior on the occasion of disaster (Bucher, 1957; Schneider, 1957; Form and Nosow, 1958; Barton, 1969; Swanson, 1964)

the relationship between definitions of the situation and collective behavior (Fritz and Marks, 1954; Hudson, 1954; Spiegel, 1957; Danzig, et al., 1958; Mack and Baker, 1961; Janis, 1962)

the role of precipitating incidents in the conversion of social form (Mack and Baker, 1961; Janis, 1962)

the relationship between time and organization (Fritz and Mathewson, 1957; Beach and Lucas, 1960; Baker and Chapman, 1962)

several processes that have been incorporated in the major theories of collective behavior—rumor, the emergence of norms, and leadership.

The sociology of disaster has also suggested that collective behavior on the occasion of disaster can provide clues to the nature of enduring social orders through its exaggeration of conventional social structure and process (Sorokin, 1942; Ikle, 1958; Moore and Friedsam, 1959; Thompson and Hawkes, 1962; Lang and Lang, 1964; Drabek and Boggs, 1968).

Despite its short history, disaster research has produced a substantial literature based on a large number of empirical investigations (Wolfenstein, 1957; Form and Nosow, 1958; Disaster Research Group, 1961; Baker and Chapman, 1962; Grosser, et al., 1964; Barton, 1969). Between 1952 and 1959, the National Academy of Sciences sponsored laboratory experiments and an impressive list of field studies, which included investigations of twenty tornadoes, thirteen fires and explosions, twelve floods, twelve hurricanes and typhoons, eight earthquakes, eight accidents involving dangerous chemicals, five epidemics or threatened outbreaks of disease, four airplane crashes, three blizzards, two mine disasters, and six false disaster alerts (Baker and Chapman, 1962, p. 5). For example, Chapman (1962) reported that:

Under federal auspices, the United States Strategic Bombing Survey studied retrospectively the human consequences of the massive bombing of cities in Germany and Japan . . . . The British government sponsored research on the problems encountered in evacuating a large population from London during the wartime blitz . . . . Project East River, set up in this country under federal auspices, was in part concerned with applying concepts of the human sciences to problems of training and preparation for civil defense. The National Opinion Research Center at the University of Chicago, the Operations Research Office of Johns Hopkins University, and the University of Oklahoma undertook for government agencies a program of research on disaster behavior through field interviews of survivors of natural disaster (p. 4-5).

There have been studies of the effects of bombing on civilian populations (Ikle, 1958); of civil defense exercises (Livingston, Klaus, and Rohrer, 1954; Baker and Rohrer, 1960); and of responses to presidential assassination (Greenberg and Parker, 1965).

The early literature generated significant theoretical statements (Sjoberg, 1962; Barton, 1969) and helped to establish a number of disaster research centers. It also reflected the increased involvement of official agencies in disaster research following World War II and the willingness of government to sponsor research at such institutes as the Disaster Research Center of Ohio State University.

In this unit the modern theories of disaster will be summarized and the significance of the traditional inclusion of disasters in the context of collective behavior will be examined. For these purposes it is important to keep in mind the double perspective of disaster study: that of the official concern over the loss of control and that of the human response to the destruction of normal settings and occasions.

DISASTER: THE EMERGENCY SOCIAL SYSTEM

The story of disaster not only is a record of destruction or of individual behavior but is also an account of the development of new and emergency social order. Form and Nosow (1958) remarked:

> In disaster, rescue is facilitated, and indeed can only come to pass if a system of complementary performance of necessary functions arises. Thus, it is clear that rescue activity should be perceived as the functioning of relatively complex systems of social relationships and not solely as behavior directed toward the helping of victims (p. 24).

Much of the activity immediately following disaster may appear frenzied, and often unsuccessful, but it is purposive, socially oriented, and attentive to the needs and resources of the time and the place. The social units involved in the initial phase of a disaster are small and improvisational, as a person caring for another person's children, two people making a litter to carry an injured person, or people carrying messages between immobilized households. Despite the apparent individuality of behavior, disaster victims find themselves in what has been described as a loosely organized but, nevertheless, rational interim social system. The "system" includes definitions of the situation; functional differentiation; coordination among various groups and individuals; and continual mobilization of resources for collective tasks. In fact, the appearance of some sort of emergency social order is a regular phenomenon in situations of community disaster, almost as if the occurrence of disaster elicited a special sort of social behavior. Can this observation be made precise enough to provide the basis for a sociological definition of disaster?

WHAT IS DISASTER?

When the dictionary definition of the term disaster is compared with the definitions by sociologists and social psychologists, there is a striking difference.

> [Disaster is] misfortune, mishap, calamity; any unfortunate event, especially a sudden, serious misfortune (*Webster's New Twentieth Century Dictionary*, rev. ed., 1962, p. 519).

[Disaster is] the impinging upon a structured community, or one of its sections, or an external force capable of destroying human life or its resources for survival, on a scale wide enough to excite public alarm, to disrupt normal patterns of behavior, and to impair or overload any of the central services necessary to the conduct or normal affairs or to the prevention or alleviation of suffering and loss . . . it is *stress* on people . . . (Powell, 1954, p. 1).

Disasters are part of the larger category of *collective stress situations*. A collective stress occurs when *many members of a social system fail to receive expected conditions of life from the system* (Barton, 1969, p. 38).

Our reference to "disaster" is to sudden and disruptive events that overtax the community's resources and abilities to respond, so that outside aid is required (Thompson and Hawkes, 1962, p. 268).

Disaster is conceived for purposes of research as an event or set of events which may or may not actually occur, but which is perceived as sufficiently probable to justify the disruption of normal behavior that preparation for the event requires (Cisin and Clark, 1962, p. 36).

We define disaster as a severe, relatively sudden, and frequently unexplained disruption of normal structural arrangements within a social system or sub-system, resulting from a force, "natural" or "social," "internal" to a system or "external" to it, over which the system has no firm "control."

* * *

The term *disaster*, for us, refers to situations in which groups are affected, *accident* to situations in which individuals alone suffer loss (Sjoberg, 1962, p. 357).

The dictionary definition focuses on the outcome of disaster. In contrast, when social scientists speak of disaster, they focus on a state of a social system that may or may not be accompanied by physical or material loss for the system or its components or its members. Disaster is usually described as a state in which important resources are actually or apparently insufficient for maintaining the orderly participation of people in the roles and organizations which are ordinarily the active constituents of a social system. Sociologically, the roles and the organizations are important; the people are not. If the concern is with social systems, then the fact that human beings may be harmed, frustrated, or killed is sociologically significant only insofar as people represent systematically significant categories, aggregates, or collectivities

DISASTER AS IMPAIRED SOCIAL SYSTEM

The sociology of disaster focuses on the operations of social systems, and thus, on the impairment of those elements that can be said to be active parts of social systems, the attributes and activities of which are effective relative to the system. From this point of view, in Powell's (1954) definition of disaster, the concern with "stress on people" weakens his initial focus on "normal patterns of behavior" and "normal affairs." Similarly, Barton's (1969) definition of "stress" in terms of the distribution of feelings within an aggregate of people is less to the point than his use of the terms "collective" and "system."

The definitions offered by Thompson and Hawkes (1962) and Sjoberg (1962) are explicitly sociological. Neither definition assumes that social systems are made up of private individuals; both point to states of organization and interruptions of systems or lines of action. In addition, both definitions imply that the term "disaster" should be reserved for situations in which the resources or adaptive capacity of a social system are suddenly rendered insufficient—or apparently insufficient—to the tasks posed for the system by a particular event. Most important, both definitions somewhat vaguely suggest that a disaster is socially meaningful as well as consequential. That is, the depletion of resources alone does not explain subsequent social action; the social action depends upon the public identification of an occurrence as a disaster.

DISASTER AS DISRUPTION

Sjoberg's use of the terms natural, social, internal, external, and control in quotation marks indicates his awareness that these terms do not refer to objective qualities of a force but, rather, to interpretations of it. However, his perception remains undeveloped. Sjoberg's definition also indicates that it is sufficient that a force be disruptive in order for it to constitute a disaster; it does not matter whether the disruption is seen as natural, social, internal, or external. This assertion is inconsistent with the sociologist's ordinary use of the term. Sjoberg's attempt to state the conditions of disaster is weak because it includes too much; it eliminates the apparently critical sociological distinctions between a revolution, a riot, a strike, and an electoral campaign by a marginal political party, all of which are disruptions. Each of these episodes has a different natural history and different social consequences, but Sjoberg has not specified the bases for distinguishing among the actions that accompany the various occasions. Sjoberg should have taken advantage of the impulse that led to the inclusion in his definition of the key words in quotation marks to give greater weight to the fact that the words classify forces for the persons involved. Within a collectivity or organization, the classification of a "disruptive" force as natural and external inaugurates a different social occasion than does its classification as social and internal. Only the former is ordinarily considered to be a disaster; for example, the legal label "an act of God" removes any possible assumption of or attribution of human responsibility.

DISASTER AS OCCASION

A variety of authors have found it useful to proceed by analyzing the nature of a specific occasion. An example is Mary Douglas's (1970) analysis of pollution and danger. In order to arrive at the phenomenon of pollution, she writes:

> I start interpreting rules of uncleanness by placing them in the full context of the range of dangers possible in any given universe. Everything that can happen to a man in the way of disaster should be catalogued according to the active principles involved in the universe of his particular culture (p. 14).

In a similar manner, disaster can be viewed as a type of special occasion that is only one among the range of occasions of danger possible in modern society. With Goffman (1967):

> A sociology of occasions is here advocated. Social organization is the central theme, but what is organized is the co-mingling of persons and the temporary interactional enterprises that can arise therefrom. A normatively stabilized structure is at issue, a "social gathering," but this is a shifting entity, necessarily evanescent, created by arrivals and killed by departures (p. 2).

Goffman (1963a) has defined a social occasion as:

> A wider social affair, undertaking, or event, bounded in regard to place and time and typically facilitated by fixed equipment; a social occasion provides the structuring social context in which many situations and their gatherings are likely to form, dissolve, and reform, while a pattern of conduct tends to be recognized as the appropriate and (often) official or intended one . . . . Examples of social occasions are a social party, a workday in an office, a picnic, or a night at the opera (p. 18).

Goffman (1963a) has also pointed out that well-established occasions carry specific imperatives in that:

> Each class of such occasions possesses a distinctive ethos, a spirit, an emotional structure, that must be properly created, sustained, and laid to rest, the participant finding that he is obliged to become caught up in the occasion, whatever his personal feelings. These occasions, which are commonly programmed in advance, possess an agenda of activity, an allocation of management function, a specification of negative sanctions for improper conduct, and a preestablished unfolding of phases and a highpoint (p. 19).

On the other hand, ad hoc or organizationally unprepared occasions tend to reduce a person's participation to involvement with one's immediate surroundings, and "the individual may see a line of development in his own period of participation but not in the occasion as a whole" (Goffman, 1963a, p. 19). Goffman (1963a) also distinguishes between serious and unserious—that is, instrumental or expressive—occasions and between occasions that are regular (part of a series of occasions) and occasions that are irregular (one-shot affairs). He concludes that "the regulations of conduct characteristic in situations and their gatherings are largely traceable to the social occasion in which they occur" (p. 20)

In these terms then, a disaster is a relatively well-defined, publicly accountable, social occasion that is both serious and irregular. The authors prefer the terms "loose" and "bound" to "irregular" and "regular" because the former terms point specifically to socially structured properties of occasions—that is, their relationship to other occasions—while the latter terms call to mind expectations.

Disaster is a loose rather than a bound occasion in the sense that its occurrence is taken as out of the ordinary; it has no transitional links to other occasions. Disaster is the putative disruption of a systemic time line defined by systemic agenda and biography. Yet, not all occasions that could be termed loose (for example, insurrection) produce the localization, improvisation, and politics that are associated with disaster. For one thing, the suspension of normal structural arrangements in social establishments during disaster does not carry the onus of a violation of norms or duty. The state of emergency is not viewed as something that must itself be corrected.[1] By contrast, the temporary states of combat and turmoil associated with insurrection and rebellion are as much an issue as the grievances and values of the combatants.

There are times when new actions are not viewed or treated as socially deviant: when, for example, the prevailing normative framework is replaced by another frame of reference for action. In this case, an act may be unexpected, but it is not necessarily untoward. The act is deviant only in relation to the old normative framework and improbable only in a strictly statistical sense. The person who commandeers an automobile to rush someone to a first-aid station is not viewed as guilty of theft. Similarly, the person who breaks down the door of a house to rescue injured people trapped inside is not guilty of breaking and entering. In times of emergency, the gathering of people at places of information or material supply is not taken as wrong; it is not even a topic for discussion.

The occasion of disaster is, then, a fateful moment in which the boundaries of time and space are drawn close around individuals, their places, and their gatherings. It is a time in which, as Sartre (1964) says, the "intention of being" is transformed to an "intention of doing" (p. 74), and people are as fully external as possible, reading their situations aloud. During disaster, social action is dominated by a situational present rather than the inertia of past action or the dynamics of identity, plans, or tradition.

DISASTER AS OCCURRENCE

What characteristics must be attributed to an occurence—beyond the fact that "occurrence" itself is an attribution—such that it will be taken as a disaster? Specifically, what is disrupted during disaster? How does a loose occasion arise?

If disaster is recognized as an occasion, and therefore something that has special and established meanings of its own, then the fact that activity is distinctively organized on the occasion of disaster is acknowledged. It should be noted, then, that disaster is not uniquely signaled by widespread alarm, threat, or confusion. The definition of an occurrence as disaster relates to the social organization of communication, processes of mobilization, spheres of legitimate concern, interaction, and so on.

---

1. As we will see when we examine "recovery," the stage at which disaster ends, the return to acceptable normalcy is also experienced as unexceptional. But the dynamics of the initial and terminal states are quite different. Normalcy returns as transitional links are established between disaster activities (taken as a system) and "normal" activities. These links are usually social forms that exaggerate conventional authority and lines of traditional solidarity while justifying the exaggeration itself in terms of the requirements of the disaster. Thus, Barton comments: "It is probable that as the informal aspects of the therapeutic social system fade away and normal private interests replace generous personal emotions as dominant motivations, formal organizations may be a major factor in maintaining the continuity of participation in the restoration effort" (Barton, 1969, p. 297).

THE PUBLIC PROCESS OF DEFINITION

The concern with the politics of disaster flows from the primary observation that identifying a situation as a disaster tends to imply that the agency of disruption is external and not responsible. Thus, it tends to remove from normal locations of social responsibility and political control the human responses in the stiuation. The disaster interpretation creates a sanction for emergency measures. For example, when it was discovered that thousands of poor children in New York City were suffering from various degrees of lead poisoning, the situation was not typically taken as a disaster and the discovery was not followed by the emergency responses typical of disastrous occasions. On the other hand, the outbreak of thirty polio cases in one city in 1950 was viewed as a disastrous epidemic and was followed by the expected social reactions. The first case seemed to be a consequence of normal forces, a result of actions of responsible agents; the latter case appeared to be beyond responsible agency. Lead poisoning became a political issue, while the polio outbreak generated massive outside aid and new lines of organization.[2]

Whether an occurrence is natural or social, internal or external, disaster or the outcome of responsible action depends upon a public process of definition in which the occurrence is established as a type of thing—a social occasion. The task here is to develop a model of disaster that can deal with epidemics, famines, and droughts, as well as with more direct and immediate catastrophes such as tornadoes, floods, or fires. Whether thirty cases of plague is an epidemic is a matter of definition. Whether the starvation experienced by a million poor Americans in the midst of plenty is a disaster depends upon the interpretation of that fact within the social system that includes the victims. Moreover, even the meaning of a tornado or a flood is subject to public definition and its social consequences. No matter what the particular striking force and no matter what the outcome, the social impact of disaster can only be understood in terms of definitional processes that take place as matters of practice within the putatively affected society. For social action, the construction of an occurrence is as crucial as the physical limitations that the striking force places on activity. It may be concluded that the study of disaster is the study of social action in relation to a particular occurrence defined in a particular way.

The Components of the Public Definition. Four components of the ordinary public definition of an occurrence as a disaster can be identified:

---

2. It is interesting to note that as the lead-poisoning cases came to be understood as the unexpected and uncontrollable product of the "social system," or of such apparently impersonal states as poverty, housing crisis, or a shortage of resources to upgrade the lives of the urban poor, the lead-poisoning came to be described as disaster. Consequently, resources were mobilized to assist in the medical treatment of the victims, but the reduction of blame led to a gradual decline of political pressure on city officials, businessmen, and landlords to repair the dangerous buildings.

1. Those who see themselves as affected by the disaster view it as impinging on a specific, named, social system that they define as their own,
2. The specific social system referred to in disaster is taken to be differentiated, extended, and permanent,
3. The occurrence is taken as external in origin and therefore not voidable,
4. The occurrence is taken as sudden.

The first component asserts that naming something "disaster" presupposes the idea of organization and society—an idea comparatively recent in Western thought. Thus, "disaster area" is a nonterritorial concept; it relates to system damage and not to the destruction of goods and services. The identification of system damage with a destroyed area is always a matter of contingency. As a possible use of the term disaster, this component allows the inclusion of the situation of American Jews who identified the Nazi persecution of European Jews as their own disaster. It stresses the fact that the social system involved in the definition of disaster need only be a traditional social referent. Nevertheless, as sociologists use the term, a damaged system is a system in crisis in reference to severe threats to institutional functioning. The first component of the public definition of disaster reflects popular awareness of that element of disaster situations that can correspond to the Parsonian concept of strain or the Marxian concept of contradiction.

The second component of definition asserts that the reputedly affected system is something more than a family, a neighborhood, a network of friendly relations, or a casual encounter. It is an extended organization in which the social elements are groups rather than individuals, and it is an organization to which individuals can refer themselves in establishing a generalized social identity. An individual's capacity to take himself as a member of such a system is a matter of socialization (learning the rules by which membership can be demonstrated) rather than private motivation, personal advantage, or the attractions of specific interpersonal relationships. It is not enough that people see the occurrence as dangerous or disruptive to themselves, their families, or their friends; a disaster is first of all, a public affair. Thus, while the problems of disaster may be raised in reference to the capacity of "the system" to deliver services, they are normally formulated in terms of a threat to society. In that case, the failure of the system to mobilize resources is taken as a symptom rather than a cause of the crisis.

It may be objected that the material damage of disaster can be limited to a small geographical area or a small social area—it rarely extends throughout an entire social system. However, stating that disaster affects a system as a whole does not deny that only a particular segment of a system may be materially involved. It is generally understood that when a damaged sector is seen as a segment of a system, the system is affected as a whole.

The third component indicates that if an occurrence is taken as voidable—or avoidable in the most general sense—it is not called a disaster. As long as the acts of particular agents are identified as causes or conditions of avoidability, the occasion might be treated as one calling for combat, vengeance, or blame, but it is not a disaster. Only if agency is not indeterminate—where agents are sought or cannot be located—does avoidability become a question. The term "disaster" is reserved for situations in which accountability is problematic and agency is unintelligible.

This formulation is somewhat at odds with definitions such as Sjoberg's (1962). The naming of particular sorts of disasters (famine, blight, epidemic) evokes rather precise images of the nature or causes of disaster. Certainly, it is not that disasters are mysterious, but the fact that they arise within the order of nature rather than within the order of man that makes their import problematic. It is suggested here that the external "order of nature" refers simply to that which is not normally accounted for by reference to social or psychological factors, in particular, to those factors that establish agency, intention, and responsibility—in a word, action. In most western societies, the attribution of intention and responsibility is what establishes the difference between "social phenomena" such as revolutions and crime, and "natural phenomena" such as floods and insanity.

Finally, a disaster is seen as occurring suddenly. The term disaster suggests something that appears without warning and becomes full-blown in a short time. Yet many disasters, such as epidemics, famines, or floods develop over days, months, or years. What is sudden about such disasters? Why, and in what sense, is the time of their onset "short?"

It is suggested here that suddenness is the temporal coordinate of externality. Just as the normal conception of disaster implies that another order—the order of nature—has broken into the social order, it also implies that other processes have broken into the normal procedures of the social system. In relation to disasters, the term "sudden" does not refer to the absolute rapidity of an event (see Garfinkel's discussion of objectivity, 1967, chap. 1) The "suddenness' of disasters points to the realization that whole operations ordinarily—at least in retrospect—taken to be self-sustaining or uninterruptable have been interrupted. The term "sudden," then, refers to a certain type of interruption that annuls what is taken to be the overall project of a social system. In terms of everyday affairs, from the observer's point of view ordinary life has shifted its basis of accountability.

In terms of social phenomenology, disaster points to both a social system—something not normally available in everyday life—and dangers to that system; thus, the term "disaster" implies more and less than the disruption of everyday life. Disaster brings to public notice everyday life as a vulnerable condition and as a total social endeavor that must be actively sustained and protected. At the same time, behavior during disaster appears normal, even ordinary.

The perceived suddenness of disaster is an indication of the disrupted social context. It refers to the facts that dangers appear that were not formerly construed as disasters and that something—society—is vulnerable that was not previously noticed as a routine and practical matter. The construction of such dangers corresponds to the recognition that regular societal processes have failed to take all contingencies into account.[3]

The first two components establish the social boundaries within which disaster is an occasion. These boundaries locate a social universe. They establish the competent parties to a disaster—those entitled to participate—and the most general grounds of participation. The second two components establish the political dimensions of disaster behavior by establishing that there is a crisis of the social order and that the crisis stems from forces presumed to lie outside of that order. These two components account for the fact that the putatively affected social system is always referred to in orthodox terms and that restoration rather than change characterizes the accountable focus of disaster work. Together, these four components of the definition of an occurrence as disaster establish a reputational rather than a structural defect of a putative social system.

COLLECTIVE BEHAVIOR ON THE OCCASION OF DISASTER

Various investigations (e.g., Raker, et al., 1956) have corroborated the observation that most rescue, first aid, and immediate relief in the impact area is carried out by persons in the area or by people entering the area to help, often because they have friends or family there. Form and Nosow's (1958) account of a tornado, for example, reported that:

> By the time the emergency headquarters were established approximately three quarters of the dead and injured had been removed by civilian volunteers. Captain Murphy estimated that a thousand civilian volunteers were in the area by the time he arrived (p. 141).

A study of an Arkansas tornado (Marks and Fritz, 1954) showed that of those persons who provided rescue and relief in the impact area, residents, rather

---

3. In a more general sense, the problem of suddenness depends on what "time" is. More specifically, it depends on what social time is (cf. Levi-Strauss, 1967, p. 281ff). Social time has generally been conceived of in terms either of sequence or resource. As sequence, time is nothing more than the order of events taken as discreet epochs from the standpoint of an actor (in which case time is tied to routine) or an observer (in which case time is tied to history). As resource, time is defined in terms of the clock and the calendar, and presupposes competition. It is an objective measure of the capacity of an actor to perform a task without interference. Time conceived as sequence or passage begs the question of how epochs are defined and how they come to be arranged in a particular sequence. Time conceived as resource begs the question of objectivity by assuming a standard clock. Neither concept of time captures the idea of a social project which marks time and which makes the term "sudden" understandable and usable. "Sudden" refers to a certain type of interruption, one in which something is noticed that brings a history to light as an interruptable project that has in fact been interrupted. The suddenness of a disaster lies in the fact that an occurrence is taken in such a way that it appears to expose what are in retrospect seen as the underlying principles of action by which a social setting is usually taken for granted and its special features seen as "determinate and independent" rather than implicated in the setting itself (cf. Garfinkel, 1967, p. 288). In other words, an occurrence is sudden when it highlights a project that appears to be of the essence of a social system and is inconsistent with the logic of that project.

than outsiders, were a much higher percentage. This fact was true not only in the first half hour, when it would be expected, but also for the entire twelve-hour period following the impact. Commenting on this study, Barton (1962) noted that "only in giving medical aid by individuals is a higher proportion of the non-impact population active" (p. 228). Thus, participation in restitutive work immediately following a disaster is highly correlated with participation in the disaster itself and with proximity to it. Before official organizations are effectively mobilized, rescue and first-aid activities are accomplished through the improvised action of many small groups.

It would not necessarily be supposed that so many people would try to help each other during disaster. In modern urban societies, the fact that people live in the same area seldom gives rise to a network of emotional ties or mutual obligations. However, it would be an error to see this copresence of strangers as not being different from a collection of people who are alien to one another. It is true that cities are notoriously full of people who suffer terrible hardships silently and alone. Even where the presence of poverty, pain, and distress is recognized and acknowledged, misfortune functions more often as a signal for avoidance than for sympathy and support (e.g., Goffman, 1963b). Yet, provided that the striking force has not destroyed the types of resources that can serve many people and many purposes (Ikle, 1958), the suffering of disaster victims often finds simple, direct, and supportive response. Barton (1962) has asserted that mutual responsiveness in disaster situations stems from the emergency social system, which is characterized by highly altruistic norms. It is suggested here that an explanation can be found in the social dynamics of collective behavior on the occasion of disaster. It is not necessary to assume either a temporary or a constitutionally generous disposition in the individuals converging on the disaster scene or present within it. Nor is it necessary to assume, with Barton, the development of an articulated system in which performances are coordinated in the context of a special set of shared values.

A SOCIOLOGICAL FRAMEWORK FOR DISASTER BEHAVIOR

It is the socially organized behavior of people in disaster situations that poses the sociological problem of disaster study. The literature offers two types of explanation for the behavior of populations struck by disaster. The first type is a psychological explanation, which describes crisis behavior as the symptomatic result of an aggregation of individual states of stress. The second type, exemplified by Barton's (1962) "emergency social system," identifies disaster behavior as a functional adaptation of a social system to stress conditions. Close examination reveals that neither explanation addresses the sociological problem of disaster behavior; neither focuses on disaster behavior as practice. Individual psychological mechanisms and states cannot account for the operation of collectivities and organizations. Sociologists of disaster often interpret terms designed to refer to states of social systems and collectivities—system stress, collective stress, disruption of normal structural arrangements—as undifferentiated aggregates of individual states—stress, anxiety, low morale, uncertainty. This interpretation assumes unwarranted theoretical importance when the psychological mechanisms that explain the individual states are referred to in order to account for the operations of the social entities. In turn, the operations of the social entities (the emergency social system, for example) are asserted to explain the activities of the individuals whose aggregated psychological states defined the stressful state of the social system in the first place. This procedure can be saved from its otherwise fatal circularity by an independent description of the emergent social system and the systemic mechanisms that explain its operations. However, this is precisely what is usually missing from the literature: Barton's emergency social system asserts a socially functional adjustment to the same individual, psychological base, while that base, taken as an undifferentiated aggregate, serves to define both social function and the motivating conditions of the social system.

The basic problem involved in a consistent sociological framework for disaster behavior is the explanation of the social properties of collective behavior on the occasion of disaster. If Barton's concept of an emergency social system is adopted, it cannot be assumed that emergencies are objective facts and that the adaptation of a society to its emergencies arises automatically. Nor can it be assumed that modifications are adaptive and lead to a return to official normalcy. Among other problems, such a description of the situation cannot account for the resistance of the emergency system to reintegration, which is a regular phenomenon of late disaster politics.

The Role of Setting. It is in the concrete settings of the disaster situation that collective behavior takes on its socially meaningful and organized character. After a population is distributed among the socially organized settings available during a disaster, behavior must be understood in terms of the contingencies and imperatives of the acting collectivities. Participation in such ad hoc collectivities is characterized by an urgency, an inclusiveness, and a clarity of reference and accountability that prohibits the public examination of goals or limitations on commitment while it excludes a distant and alienating appraisal of role performance. Barton (1969) has cited evidence indicating that the social units that emerge during disaster are stable and relatively resistant to interference and personnel turnover. He also cited research on the tendency of individuals, given some initial measure of conflict among plausible social options,[4] to remain with the first group they join during postimpact periods (1969, p. 116). This observation is consistent with Goffman's (1963a) view that disaster, like all occasions, establishes:

---

4. Barton remarks on the sparseness of data on the incidence and outcome of a conflict in entrance considerations (not simply role conflict since that assumes entrance). According to Thompson and Hawkes (1962), when family is involved, "It appears that the conflict will be resolved in favor of the family and primary values—unless the individuals are, at the moment of perceived threat, already active in disaster-ready roles and in the physical presence of others in similar roles . . . . When members of disaster-ready organizations must be assembled after impact, however, they are more likely to decide role conflict in favor of family obligations" (p. 284).

a distinctive ethos, a spirit . . . that must be properly created, sustained, and laid to rest, the participant finding that he is obliged to become caught up in the occasion, whatever his personal feelings (p. 19).

The Polarization of Reference. On the occasion of disaster, social reference becomes polarized and the social identity of settings as public places becomes an issue. Disaster situations pose the imperatives of membership in the endangered social system as well as the imperatives of participation in the concrete, focused gatherings that occur within the setting. Because these are presented simultaneously, reference may involve obligations and activities that are mutually exclusive; disaster politicizes social settings by posing an either/or alternative. Arrangement and activity may be publicly accounted for or justified by exclusive reference to the claims of membership in extended cosmopolitan society. Alternatively, they may be accounted for by exclusive reference to the exigencies (as they are socially defined within a situated collectivity) of the immediate situation. The allocation of performance in reference to these competing sets of claims is a political process in which individuals and groups are placed in one context or another. It is this placement that constitutes the initial social problem for both individuals and groups on the occasion of disaster. The question is not "What should one do?" but "Where are we and who are we?"

Similar to other socially organized settings, disaster settings often provide ways in which activity is scheduled so as, temporarily and problematically, to avoid the conflict inherent in the polarization and intensification of reference.[5] But such conflict continually threatens to erupt because, in part, the act of social reference is collectively dramatized as settings acquire specific identities. In disaster, people become aware of the social body they claim as their own just as people become aware of their physical functioning in illness.

Politics and Disaster. Disaster settings are thus the loci of practice and organization in disaster situations. They are contingent, reflexive, and internally coherent sites of action. Their capacity to absorb their members is shown by their singular resistance to intrusions that threaten their identity and occasion, and the fact that they make momentous and exclusive claims on their members' environment and personnel, and the definitions of events.

Disasters occasion crises of identity, performance, and accountability, and they engender novel patterns of interorganizational interference. These considerations relate collective behavior on the occasion of disaster to a pattern that is also characteristic of more familiar socio-political phenomena. The similarity is

---

5. In Goffman's terms, the individual in disaster is forced to allocate spontaneity and role distance among mutually exclusive alternatives. An orientation to community (and therefore authority) yields a "spontaneous involvement" in official strategy and a stoical "role distance" regarding the activities of local *ad hoc* collectivities. An orientation to local *ad hoc* collectivities (and therefore association) yields a spontaneous involvement in the joint venture and a critical role distance from official actions. See also, Alexander and Knight's discussion: "What we need to understand are the processes by which identities are created and transformed so that it will become possible to specify how particular social identities influence actors' behaviors under varying situational conditions" (1971, p. 80).

instructive, particularly because it serves to remove collective behavior, as a phenomenon, from the perspective of official definition and practice. In doing so, it brings into theoretic prominence activity that has traditionally been treated as exotic, incidental, and unessential to the analysis of disaster behavior.

The literature on role conflict indicates some of the political features of individual entrance to and participation in collective behavior during disaster. Fritz and Mathewson (1957) have discussed "crisis role obligations" (p. 40) that arise when assumed but previously inactive structural ties (traditional ties) are revived on the occasion of disaster. Killian (1952) has described some of the consequences of the juxtaposition of such obligations with both the imperatives of local and ad hoc collectivities and the imperatives of official and transcendent institutional arrangements (p. 311). The polarization and intensification of social reference that links disaster studies to studies of political organization and conflict is the feature that makes the study of disaster interesting to the sociologist.

CHAPTER FOUR

RESEARCH PARADIGMS IN THE STUDY OF DISASTER

The study of disaster is a recent addition to the field of sociology. Of the more than 110 bibliographic items listed in Allen H. Barton's (1969) recent book, *Communities in Disaster*, only twenty were published prior to 1942. Only fourteen entries are directly related to the study of disaster: eight are empirical or quasi-empirical reports, articles, or books, and six are historical or general studies. An earlier review of the literature edited by Baker and Chapman (1962) listed twenty-four works published earlier than 1942, out of over 300 cited in their bibliography, of which only eight are directly pertinent to disaster.

Pitirim Sorokin's (1942) *Man and Society in Calamity* was an early effort to provide a paradigm for the study of disaster. His book illustrates the persistent emphasis of the early work in the field on the impact of particular disaster agents—flood, blight, and so on—and their effects on social organization and individual behavior. Sorokin considered war, revolution, famine, and pestilence as calamities. He explored the impact of each on mobility; on political, economic, and social organization; and on socio-cultural life. Several important hypotheses, framed in generalized terms, indicated important directions for research. Sorokin (1942) believed that calamity leads to "diversification and polarization . . . effects in different parts of the population" (p. 14). He argued that this principle could be applied both to individuals and to their organizations. It is the latter that is of primary concern here. The general proposition implies two opposing and politically consequential trends in a society struck by calamity. Calamity tends to disintegrate the larger society by weakening the ties among its constituent groups, and it reinforces the solidarity and hence the competitiveness, of the smaller groups, the internal cohesion of which becomes highly functional for the preservation of the members' lives as well as structurally necessary for the definition of those lives. Sorokin further noted that the effects of calamity are distributed throughout the society along already existing lines of social and class differentiation. Although he limited his attention to situations in which a striking force produces widespread devastation, Sorokin's book suggests a degree of organization in collective behavior and a degree of intergroup conflict during disaster that allows him to be treated as a forerunner of recent developments.

THE STUDY OF PANIC

In the interim between Sorokin and more contemporary developments such as Barton's, disaster research was generally overshadowed by the problem of panic. Indeed, investigations of the subject were undertaken on the assumption that the interruption of official control created the possibility of a general popular outbreak of uncontrolled behavior. Early literature on deviant behavior, for example, discussed panic in the same context as alcoholism, crime, and abortion. The idea was that such phenomena were aberrant effects for which causes should be found. The empirical material used was a highly dramatic literature (often journalistic memoirs) that described mass behavior in relation to plagues, earthquakes, fire, and so on. As late as the 1940s, radio and movie portrayals of behavior under stress emphasized the demonic character of crowds.

The extreme danger and urgency of disaster situations were believed to produce intense anxiety and a virulent contagion of emotion that eroded civility and revealed an intensely competitive individualism. Smelser (1963) defined panic as:

> a collective flight based on a hysterical belief. Having accepted a belief about some generalized threat, people flee from established patterns of social interaction in order to preserve life, property, or power from that threat (p. 131).

Smelser (1963) listed the characteristics of panic: "threat, anxiety, suggestion, contagion, flight" (p. 132). The individuation of a panicky mob lies in the fact that each member acts directly in reference to a goal; there is no division of labor or cooperation. Smelser considered panic likely when there is opportunity, particularly when there is opportunity to communicate in a situation in which scarce and essential resources are vanishing.

Panic is usually described as nonrational or irrational and as a form of collective behavior. Yet both the nonrationality and irrationality of panicky behavior on the occasion of disaster and its identification as collective behavior are thrown into question by recent investigations.

PANIC: A PARADIGM FOR COLLECTIVE BEHAVIOR

It is useful to note that the term panic may describe a number of different things. Wolfenstein (1957) has listed phenomena that fall into the category of panic: intense personal terror; fear-induced behavior that is useless or self-destructive; contagious alarm in a group; unnecessary group flight from a danger felt as imminent and overwhelming; a group situation in which each person is concerned for his own safety and other people are seen merely as rivals or obstacles to escape; and a group situation in which people hurt or destory others in the effort to save themselves. Wolfenstein (1957) added a valuable warning to this list:

Since definitions are sometimes confused with empirical statements, a definition of "panic" which includes all the items listed may be taken as implying the mutual involvement of these phenomena in actuality. For this reason it seems useful to point out the extent to which some of these phenomena may occur independently of others. Precipitate flight may be the most useful action in certain situations (as, for instance, from a fire which one is unequipped to combat) and may not exclude regard for others. Even where each individual is so preoccupied with his own threatened safety that he can think of no one else, there may be no mutual damage among those who are fleeing together. Thus the definition of "panic" as irrational and antisocial mass flight . . . should not lead us to infer that every instance of precipitate group flight . . . is useful . . . or involves mutual damage among the fugitives (p. 86).

Under what conditions do people panic? The common feature of situations in which people panic in a struggle for safety is usually thought to be entrapment. Smelser (1963) stated that:

Panic is not possible if the routes for escape are—or are conceived to be—completely open . . . . Nor can panic occur if routes are conceived to be completely blocked . . . . Reactions such as terror or infantile regression can occur in such settings, but not panic . . . . Limited (and possibly closing) access to exit characterizes certain "classic" panic situations (pp. 136-37).

Under conditions involving limited access to exits, other humans become physical obstacles or rivals (Wolfenstein, 1957). When the rather strict requirements for panic are defined, it can readily be seen that panic in a disaster situation is far less likely than it is generally thought to be. Fritz and Marks (1954) concluded that:

Panic, flight, and other highly uncontrolled forms of behavior appear to occur under quite restricted conditions present only in some disasters and only for some of the persons involved in such disasters. It is not the irrationality or uncontrolled nature of individual behavior that raises the *major* control problems in disasters; rather it is the lack of coordination among the large number of persons acting on the basis of different (and oftentimes conflicting) personal definitions of the situation (p. 41).

The fact that panic is improbable during disaster is consistent with the view, as set forth here, that disaster is a special occasion for social action. However, it says nothing about the mechanisms of social control intrinsic to panic. Fritz and Mathewson (1957) leave this question open by their reference to a "lack of coordination." Smelser (1963), on the other hand, lists such mechanisms threat, anxiety, suggestion, contagion, and flight. While these are responsive to the problem of explanation, they suggest autism, disorganization, and irrationality, which are critical issues for the arguments to follow. If such extreme forms of social response as panic are not irrational and asocial, then it is a reasonable hunch that less extreme forms of behavior under stress and on the occasion of disaster are also unlikely to follow the classical stereotypes.

SIMULATION STUDIES OF PANIC

Recent research has taken advantage of the technique of simulation in attempting to specify the determinants and form of panic (Zelditch, 1969).

Mintz (1951) published the results of an experiment designed to examine the roles of emotional and cognitive factors in panic. He set groups of people the task of extricating cones from a narrow-necked bottle in as short a time as possible. Each cone was attached to a string and only one could pass through the neck of the bottle at a time. The efficiency of the group was tested in two situations: when excitement was introduced by highly expressive behavior on the part of one or two accomplices slipped into the group, and when a system of ten-cent individual rewards and fines was set up. Mintz found that "traffic jams" at the neck of the bottle occurred more frequently in the second situation than in the first. He concluded that the possibility of individual failure leads to maladaptive group behavior "regardless of the presence or absence of face-to-face contacts between people and opportunities for mutual facilitation" (p. 157).

A similar, more recent study attempted to reexamine Mintz' contention that panic depends more upon the situation than emotional contagion. In a simulation experiment, Kelley and his associates (1965) studied the influence of several variables on the relative success of efforts to "escape," where subjects, threatened with shock, controlled their situation—presented by a bank of lights—by manipulating electronic switches. The results suggested that the greater the threat, the larger the group, and/or the less optimistic mutually oriented subjects are, the smaller will be the percentage of people who escape. These conclusions tentatively suggest that emotional contagion independent of organizational and rational factors cannot explain the regularities of panic behavior.

Both investigations raise questions about the accuracy of the classical stereotypes of emergency behavior and Smelser's (1963) characterization of panic. Both studies assume that panic can be simulated—that the collective behavior in which the investigators were interested is not interdependent with wider features of its natural setting. They also assume that the various simulations are analogous—that is, that the degree to which modes of response differ in their availability is not crucial to the action that follows a formal entrapment.

Despite its vagueness and ambiguity, modern literature on panic points to three provisional conclusions: (1) panic during disaster is unlikely; (2) if entrapment is sufficient to define the conditions of panic, simulation studies support the proposition that the occurrence of panic depends primarily upon information as to the degree of danger, the availability of resources for escape, and the likelihood that other people will or will not act in the interests of collective order; and (3) once underway, panic feeds on itself, and resists interference.

PANIC: AGGREGATE OR COLLECTIVITY

It is no longer clear that entrapment produces an individuation of performance and decision. Yet such individuation is one possible, if improbable, consequence of utterly extreme situations. It must now be asked whether panic—conceived of as the individuation of activity and at one time considered the most typical form of collective behavior—should be described as collective behavior at all. If the term "panic" refers to the individuation of activity under stress, then according to the definition of every major theorist, panic is not collective behavior. Individuals who share a focus or a condition may act similarly, without regard for each other and without conforming to an emergent norm. In this sense, panicky behavior is simply the individual behaviors of many people under stress in a small space. For each individual in such a situation, other people are not persons; rather, they are objects, much like furniture, to be dealt with during the emergency. The motion of such an aggregate of socially unrelated but mutually relevant individuals cannot be identified as collective behavior, but must be explained either by the psychology of individual stress and the individually projected ecology of the physical site, or by reference to the processes of observation and attribution—particularly the social relation of the observer to his phenomena—by virtue of which panic is said to exist.

If the term is used strictly behavioristically to refer to the motion of an aggregate—mass flight—then it does not permit the type of inquiry that could expose the internal dynamics of panic. This use would not allow a decision as to whether the observed motion is the product of social forces or simply a coincidence of individual behaviors. Whether, then, the term "panic" refers to the individuation of activity or to mass flight; it cannot be treated as collective behavior.

Nevertheless, it should not be concluded that there is no collective behavior associated with dangerous entrapment. Descriptions of panics indicate that as the situation becomes extremely restricted, so that each individual can see the actions of those around him but not the circumstances that would justify those actions, ad hoc social mechanisms begin to control individual behavior. Moreover, it is possible that collective behavior also occurs at the point at which a genuine collectivity—that is, a focused and reflexive gathering—is transformed into an aggregate of panicky individuals. The act that becomes a "flight model" can destroy the collective unity if, and only if, it is accompanied by certain other activities. A norm of social inattention must be established that depersonalizes other people so that individuals assume an exploitative role distance in reference to the collection and distribution of other individuals around them. After the instant has passed, and after the collectivity ceases to exist and the situation becomes defined as "every man for himself," collective behavior may yield to the extreme individuation that characterizes panic.

Unfortunately, this suggestion remains a hypothesis. The literature is too sparse to provide the kind of detailed description necessary for analysis. Investigators of panic have relied on the dramatic descriptions of others, noticing only the uniformities among individuals in panic, or have employed techniques of simulation without clearly delineating the phenomenon to be simulated. Nevertheless, even a cursory review of accounts of panic reveals more than might be expected and is suggestive for further research. One important implication is that panic is not a paradigm case of collective behavior. Another implication is that stress—even extreme stress—does not ordinarily produce irrational or even asocial response.

A PARADIGM FOR STRESS BEHAVIOR

These implications encounter resistance from another line of reasoning that is often cited in disaster literature: the tradition of cognition theory that is used to bolster the conclusions of the predominantly descriptive literature on panic. Even if behavior under stress appears to be rational and socially organized, some research on perception in "extreme situations" suggests that the apparent coherence of behavior is due to anxiety-induced suggestability. Kilpatrick (1957) offered six tentative generalizations from his research on perception and suggested that they "seem highly relevant to the problems of disaster":

1. There is an initial tendency to establish a dominant percept and assimilate all happenings to it. Usually, but not always, this dominant percept is a familiar one. . . .
2. Actions tend to be appropriate to the situation as perceived, even though they may seem illogical or inappropriate to others . . . .
3. Under stress there is a tendency to isolate oneself from immediate ongoing events, and hold on to a familiar stable perceptual organization. Concurrent with this perceptual restriction, there is a tendency to act in familiar ways that have proved reliable in the past, even though they are no longer appropriate to the immediate occasion . . . .
4. In the absence of reliable guides from past experience for perceiving or acting, suggestibility is high . . . .
5. Prolonged subjection to conflicting perceptual cues induces emotional depression, followed by elation when the conflict is resolved . . . .
6. The most effective way of accomplishing perceptual reorganization is through action by the perceiver . . . (pp. 20-22, original in italics).

THE EXPERIMENTAL SITUATION AS REAL

The usefulness of these observations depends upon the adequacy of the experimental situation as an analogue to the situation of disaster. In fact, these investigations are predicated upon a psychological model that makes neither the subjects' definition of the situation nor the social organization of the experiment explicit or theoretically problematic. Kilpatrick treated stress and behavior as objective facts linked as cause and effect. The definition of the situation by the subjects is understood as a factor that modifies the primary relationship between stress and behavior. Yet, the term "stress" summarily conceals what must be for the experimental subjects a variety of judgments, situations, and responses. Nowhere does the literature make the subject's situation explicit; rather it substitutes the experimenter's definition of "stress" for the subject's. Moreover, Kilpatrick neglected the fact that the experimental setting itself has a social organization with patterns of dominance, solidarity, and processes of communication, influence, and accountability.

Although Kilpatrick's methodology did not involve the social situation as a significant component of definitions of and responses to stress, he nevertheless believes that the results can help account for responses to disaster, a phenomenon in which the crucial role of the social situation is generally acknowledged. What can possibly account for Kilpatrick's suggestion that his work is relevant to disaster, and why have disaster researchers used this account of stress responses? The answer seems to be that Kilpatrick, like many disaster researchers, has been led to a false analogy between his laboratory situation (in which the social situation is taken as irrelevant) and disaster by the use of overly general and, therefore, systematically misleading terms, such as "stress" and "extreme"; and he has relied on incomplete or inaccurate descriptions of what happens during disaster.

In any case, a critical examination of Kilpatrick's language suggests that his subjects indeed, may have seen their situation as social and behaved accordingly. For instance, the use of the term "suggestibility" in the fourth observation predisposes the reader to view the behavior as an irrational suspension of self-control. However, the subjects' apparent unreasoning susceptibility to influence, as denoted by the term, as easily may be described as a willingness to engage in social action and to accept a local ad hoc socialization of performance and attention under conditions in which there appear to be no readily available alternatives. One cannot choose between these models without information that Kilpatrick does not provide.

Familiarity and Appropriateness. The term "familiarity," as used in Kilpatrick's third observation, is ambiguous. As a psychological concept, it suggests repeated experiences. However, complex action is rarely a replication of past action, and it can rarely be traced to the mechanisms by which a habit or hierarchy of habits—or even a "learned pattern"—are established. There is no question that individuals in unusual situations, such as the situations that Kilpatrick classifies as extreme, exhibit behavior that they appear to consider appropriate. But it does not follow that the selection of behavior in such situations is rooted in the automatism implied by "familiarity." In fact, the apparent ease with which people perform, or the familiarity of their acts, does not seem to vary with the "extremity" of their situation. Therefore, Kilpatrick has again pointed to the fact that people under pressure—that is, in situations in which situational peculiarities are brought to specific notice—seem to know what they are about, but he has not distinguished behavior under pressure from behavior in different situations.

The investigations summarized by Kilpatrick involve situations in which people perform complex acts on short notice, and in which their attention has been drawn to defects of their situation as a whole, despite the fact that an observer would not expect such a performance under these circumstances. In this way, the research highlights a general fact about human behavior, not a fact about behavior under special circumstances. Actions are complex ideas that occur despite the fact that they are never fully determined by situations (situations cannot be described in such a way that only particular acts may be expected to occur), and despite the fact that situations rarely, if ever, allow individuals to devise their acts from raw material. Thus, it is necessary to ask how the full-blown ideas or acts by which individuals identify their situations can arise in a span of time that is too short for them to be invented. In other words, how do acts and percepts become available to individuals in specific situations?

Ideas, Acts, and Percepts. Ideas that identify situations are part of what social phenomenologists call the "social stock of knowledge" (Berger and Luckmann, 1967), which is a wide context of socially produced meanings available to members of a society. The adoption of a "familiar" percept, or "perceptual organization," by experimental subjects indicates their entrance into a social situation—a practice—as opposed to privately learned associations. This observation affects understanding of Kilpatrick's second proposition. "Appropriateness" of action lies in its fitting into a structure of actions assumed by the individuals' identification of the situation. Because the individuals' act assumes that there is an inclusive structure of action, that act can only be understood as taking the perspective of a part (Goffman, 1963, p. 19). The failure of an observer to take this orientation into account yields the characterization of behavior given in Kilpatrick's second statement. That is, the act will appear to be isolated from ongoing events and inappropriate to the "immediate situation."

Perceptual Conflict and Reorganization. The behavior Kilpatrick describes in his fifth observation as induced by "prolonged subjection to conflicting perceptual cues" may be understood as social deprivation. The individual suffers the absence of socially meaningful and, therefore, "appropriate" behavioral options. Lacking any way of making his acts accountable, any action seems futile. Individuals in such circumstances are likely to behave as if their acts and their situations were, indeed, unintelligible to them and as if there were no hope that they would become intelligible (see Cook, et al, 1970).

Kilpatrick's sixth observation, which asserts the positive role of activity in "perceptual reorganization," suggests that work reflects the socially practical dimensions of the work setting. When individuals work, their behavior becomes accountably stable and intelligible—in other words, nonproblematic, spontaneous, and binding.

The methodology of this research makes it of dubious value for a sociology of disaster. The "stress" with which it is concerned is not clearly the "stress" of disaster. Moreover, even if it is assumed that the research is based on an adequate analogue of disaster, Kilpatrick's conclusions can support a different picture of collective behavior during disaster than he apparently intends. Despite the problems with the type of research that Kilpatrick has summarized, such research is assumed by a number of investigators to support models and typologies for the study of disaster. In particular, it is the background for the investigations of Lang and Lang.

LANG AND LANG: A TYPOLOGY OF DISASTER

Kurt Lang and Gladys Lang (1964) present a typology of disaster based on three dimensions. The first dimension refers to the distribution of effect. A disaster may be *discriminating* or *undiscriminating* in its effects. A discriminating disaster is one in which certain classes or groups are more vulnerable to danger than others. For example, if poor people live in flimsy houses and more wealthy people live in solid brick homes, an earthquake will affect the poor more than the rich and will, thus, be discriminating in its effects on the community as a whole. A bomb, on the other hand, will be undiscriminating in its immediate effects, although there may be discrimination relative to opportunity to recover losses during postimpact periods. The second dimension distinguishes between *anticipated* and *unanticipated* disasters, depending upon whether they were preceeded by a warning period. The third dimension distinguishes between *unprecedented* and *recurrent* disasters, depending upon whether similar disasters have struck the particular population before and have left traces on social organization.

THE CONCEPT OF MORALE

Lang and Lang (1964) have developed a social psychological concept, *morale*, to account for the relationship with which they are most concerned: the effect of impact on behavior. They define "morale" as "continued performance and coordination of roles in situations of stress" (p. 6). By making coordination of roles a defining property of morale, Lang and Lang are led to define any situation in which institutionally coordinated behavior does not take place as a demoralized situation and institutionalized response as evidence of high morale. Thus, shared behavior can be socially disintegrating, a situation that Lang and Lang (1964) described as occurring when "collective expressions of shared emotional disturbances [arise] that do not cope with the threat . . . such as . . . mass hysteria, propitiation rituals . . . scapegoating" (p. 6). This scheme assigns a peculiar meaning to the term morale because it is hard to view a society that reacts to the threat of pestilence, for example, with strictly formalized, round-the-clock, religious ceremonies as demoralized. Such societies may be misguided, perhaps, but hardly demoralized. Similarly, the Jews who behaved like model victims and marched into the gas ovens with every indication of accepting social discipline would be considered demoralized in the usual sense of the term. The same can be said for the working poor who fervently support the very laws that prevent them from changing their lives as well as the oppressed colonial populations who learn to accept the official legitimations of their condition (Freire, 1970).

These anomalous examples challenge the assumption of Lang and Lang that only institutionalized and strictly strategic behavior, and not collective behavior, will be functional during disaster. They asserted that: "collective responses that arise on an emotional basis . . . are likely, unless adequately channeled, to disrupt the group effort (1964, p. 167). This is a difficult statement to interpret. Their discussion suggests that "emotional" refers to low morale. But "low morale" refers to a social condition, namely, the failure of official or institutional control. So, by "emotional," in this statement, Lang and Lang seem to be adding to their definition of "morale" something that is not otherwise explicated.

Apparently, this added something pertains to unauthorized or noninstitutional activity and warrants the rejection of such activity by Lang and Lang as inadequate to the solution of the problems posed by disaster for an endangered populace. This interpretation clarifies the notion of the disruption of group effort and reveals the perspective from which Lang and Lang drew their descriptions and analysis. By "group effort" Lang and Lang seem to mean the action of the community as a whole. Action so conceived requires the coordination of disparate socially organized elements rather than the channeling of emotional individuals or individual emotions. The disruption, then, lies precisely in the unauthorized work of local groupings and not in the intrusion of emotion. It is the former unauthorized social action that Lang and Lang denigrate by their formulation, particularly by their identification of the survival of a populace with the unimpeded operation of official or institutional control. These are extreme implications to draw from the generalizations of Lang and Lang. Yet, the possibility of drawing such implications reveals serious theoretical problems that might otherwise remain obscure. To define "morale" sociologically while defining "demoralization" psychologically—"disaster involves the progressive weakening of affective ties and commitment to group goals and values" (pp. 66-67)—makes the process of gaining and losing morale inexplicable without an interpretation of the sort offered here. Similarly, to use the term "emotional" in such a way as to imply, without theoretical justification, the irrationality and unsuitability of unauthorized collective action makes it impossible to understand much of the behavior observed during disaster, including noninstitutional coordination and social conflict. Empirical data, in fact, suggest that during disaster, much of the actual rescue and immediate aid is conducted outside of official channels. As will be discussed in detail later, local solidarity and traditional ties usually increase during disaster, which can facilitate rescue; official agencies can be slow, easily immobilized, or discriminating in their operations. However, an increase in solidarity can also lead to socially organized activities other than rescue as well as to social conflict.

The idea of Lang and Lang that collective behavior is intrinsically maladaptive seems to depend, at least in part, upon certain myths about panic and the effects of stress. Their discussion is primarily directed at establishing the importance of local warning systems, and the threat of panic is always in the background. Their arguments point to two problems that the reader will find recurring throughout this book: (1) the interdependence of theoretical and practical considerations and (2) the theoretical difficulties that arise in making sociological generalizations on the basis of observations of individual behavior.

THE CAUSAL SCHEME OF THE
THREE-DIMENSIONAL TYPOLOGY

In terms of their causal scheme, in which morale mediates between impact and effect, the typology of disaster proposed by Lang and Lang allows them to say that undiscriminating, unanticipated, unprecedented disaster will probably pose the greatest threat to morale. As such, it will result in the greatest amount of social disorganization; but discriminating, anticipated, and precedented disaster, given adequate resources, will generally lead to well-organized and highly functional behavior. For Lang and Lang, it is obvious that unanticipated disasters, which allow no opportunities for preparation or rehearsal of possible disaster behavior, will cause the greatest intellectual confusion, at least on the part of those people who must look beyond their immediate locale for assistance, collaboration, and comfort. Undiscriminating disasters, in effect, enlarge the area incapable of rendering reassurances and aid. A social system struck by unanticipated, undiscriminating, and unprecedented disaster is unlikely to mobilize its components for emergency action. It is more dependent upon outside and, presumably, negotiated aid insofar as the preservation of the predisaster official order is concerned.

Most contemporary evidence is directly opposed to the portrait put forth by Lang and Lang of disorganized, chaotic, and atomized populations in situations of undiscriminating, unanticipated, and unprecedented disaster. It may be asked what theoretical assumptions have led Lang and Lang astray. The chaos they postulate would occur only if there were no basis for the local integration of the population; it would have to assume that people are social and orderly only in reference to the most abstract and inclusive system of which they are members. Moreover, Lang and Lang's concept of morale, drawn from an official rather than a popular perspective, fails to provide for the reorganization of social priorities (from the inclusive to the local) that occurs when inclusive systems fail, or to explain the fact that although many sources of order are impaired, people will work together (Shibutani, 1966). Their causal model does not allow for the most important features of disaster that have been observed—that is, altruism, cooperation, intergroup conflict, and so on (Baker and Chapman, 1962; Barton, 1969).

Lang and Lang assumed that disaster is an objective fact, the course of which can be adequately described by relatively straightforward causal models. They use a social psychological variable of dubious standing—morale—to account for a postulated relationship between different characteristics of the impact of disaster and the subsequent organization and survival of collectivities. This use of the term morale, however, limits the interesting applicability of their model to situations involving extreme and vivid danger to individuals and the utter destruction of resources and association. Can these situations even be called disasters in the sociological sense? They seem to describe either total dissolution of a social system or the aggregation of individual distress.

A PARADIGM FOR DEVELOPMENTAL STAGES

Turning from simple classificatory schemes and causal models, there is a different tradition that lends itself to a more sociological and social phenomenological view of disaster. This tradition evolved from the work of Powell and Rayner (1952) who proposed a descriptive scheme for disaster based on an analogy to problem-solving behavior and formulated in terms of developmental stages rather than types. They characterized each stage by its own integrative mechanisms, distinctive variables, and a set of unique tasks for each of the various sectors of the affected social system. Their scheme exposed a number of different processes by which an occurrence is defined and takes shape as an occasion for social action. In particular, this scheme specifies a variety of conditions in which collective behavior is likely to be found.

Powell and Rayner described seven stages of disaster, each involving different patterns of behavior: warning, threat, impact, inventory, rescue, remedy, and recovery. The preimpact stages involve the definition of the occurrence and predisaster organization; the impact stage establishes material limitations on collective behavior; the postimpact stages involve collective behavior linked to the socio-political processes by which an untoward occurrence is absorbed in a social system and its records. Powell and Rayner's analysis allows the conclusion that many of the phenomena associated with disaster can only be understood in terms of their meanings for affected collectivities.

WARNING

Warnings are given and received as social communications and indicate the stage of apprehension. In this stage resources are prepared for possible mobilization and dispositions to local and individual response appear. Research specifies three variables of warning that seem to modify the effectiveness of response to disaster: the content of warning messages; the context of communication, including medium, channel, recipient, and credibility of source; and the timing of the message, which refers to whether the warning message is presented only once or a number of times and to the length of time between a given presentation and the time of impact (Janis, 1962).

THREAT

Threat involves some sign of imminent danger. This phase is not simply an advanced stage of warning. Instead of a process of communication in which institutional channels play an important role, threat usually involves what Shibutani (1966) referred to as improvised processes of communication or rumor, as people receive and share news of the impending occurrence. As a result, the organization of social action at this stage of disaster is largely decentralized and interpersonal. The shaping of a sense of imminent danger is a much more variable and diffuse process than the process of warning.

IMPACT

Impact is ordinarily described as the period of maximum destruction. Chapman (1962) described the impact as the period "during which the disaster strikes, with concomitant death, injury, and destruction" (p. 7). Cisin and Clark (1962) asserted that "in one sense, this stage represents the maximum disruption of normal modes of behavior" (p. 32). This phase of disaster was the chief focus of early research; the typology described by Lang and Lang (1964) is based on it. Spatial descriptions of disasters usually represent impact as a series of concentric circles or zones at various distances from the point of maximum destruction. Within each zone there is a distinctive interpretation of the occurrence, a response, and an organizational base different from the interpretations, responses, and organizational bases of the other zones.

Despite its heuristic value, the term impact is ambiguous: a tornado sweeps across a region; an epidemic builds up slowly, with fluctuations in the incidence; drought develops over a long period of time; severe earthquakes may be followed by fires. Moreover, it is generally impossible to determine the period of maximum destruction except in retrospect. The ambiguity of the term lies in the failure to specify the perspective, including the values and principles of assessment, from which a period of impact is determined. Victims, biographers, representatives of the affected system, or officials may locate the period of impact differently. Based on the previous discussion of the definition of an occurrence as disaster, impact is the point at which an occurrence is seen as sudden. It is the point at which the suddenness of some incident is an accountable property of—a reason for—action. Impact is the condition of interruption by which members and system operators determine that their social system is at a turning point and, in a sense, is defiled. Impact, as defilement:

> is never an isolated event. It cannot occur except in view of a systematic ordering of ideas. Hence any piecemeal interpretation of the pollution rules of another culture is bound to fail. For the only way in which pollution ideas make sense is in reference to a total structure of thought whose keystone, boundaries, margins, and internal lines are held in relation by rituals of separation (Douglas, 1970, p. 54).

The Interrupted System as Indicating Normal Society. Like all such interruptions, the impact of disaster reveals the nature of the interrupted system. Impact ordinarily provides statistical indices of the distribution of damage that are consistent with the dimensions—class, race, age, initial investment, and so on—that define the relative positions of citizens in normal times. When Hurricane Carla hit Cameron parish, Louisiana, for example, 31 percent of the black population was killed, but less than 4 percent of the white population died. Reasons can be found. The black community was situated closest to the Gulf of Mexico, in greatest danger from high water. Lack of official interest, lack of cars available to evacuate the population, lower exposure to warnings, and a lower rate of response to such warnings as were received have all been cited as contributing factors (Bates, et al., 1963). The single factor most regularly contributing to the differential effect of disasters on black people, however, is probably housing. Poorly constructed houses are not only more easily damaged than substantial ones, but they offer the inhabitants less protection from the elements. Indeed, flimsy construction is itself, a source of danger. Homes of the poor are harder to insure. In Waco, Texas, 19 percent of the houses occupied by black people were destroyed by a tornado, compared to 7 percent of those occupied by white people. Thirty-four percent of the black families in the area struck by the tornado had to move, compared with 14 percent of the white families. According to Moore (1958), white families reported an average loss of $1,100 and black families reported an average loss of $494. Yet, 50 percent more blacks than whites were forced into debt as a result of the disaster. Moore remarked that:

> In view of the greater incidence of damage to Negro housing and household furnishings, their greater rate of injury, and the greater debt

they incurred, it is surprising that they received a smaller average amount of emergency aid than did whites (1958, p. 149).

These studies are consistent with the findings on the impact of bombing in World War II (Ikle, 1958). In all cases, the distribution of damage, receipt of aid, and capacity to recover followed the normal lines of discrimination.

Directions for Response. The impact of disaster also inaugurates directions for official and public response. During the period of impact, the disaster situation is acknowledged and defined. The boundaries of the affected system are established, as are material limitations on collective and institutional behavior, the statuses of individuals and groups in relation to the disaster, and the priorities of official agencies concerned with rescue and recovery. In addition, impact establishes the bases for the accountability of local settings and inclusive systems, and it establishes standards and procedural limits for the social work of inventory and rescue. Wallace (1956) has described some of the contingencies of rescue that followed a tornado in Worcester, Massachusetts in 1953:

> Organized aid in the form of police cruiser cars, fire equipment, and ambulances, reached the Home Farm, Great Brook Valley, and Curtis Apartments areas within five to ten minutes. This was owing in part to the fortunate accident that telephone communication with central Worcester had not been cut off by primary impact.

> * * *

> It is difficult to pick out the particular area which was last to be taken out of isolation by the arrival of aid, but probably portions of the Burncoat Street and St. Nicholas Development areas, and the Brattle Street area (difficult of access on account of narrow streets, hills, trees, and traffic jams) were last to be invaded by rescue forces. But even here the isolation period was not long . . . (p. 56-57).

It may be noted that the period of impact is not a period of "maximum disruption of normal modes of behavior" (Cisin and Clark, 1962). In fact, all the stages of disaster listed by Powell and Rayner (1952) involve action that is strikingly different from that found in other social situations. What is unique about each stage is the mode of social organization it implies rather than the degree to which behavior is or is not socially organized.

INVENTORY

Following the impact, with its numerous problems of definition and description, is the more clearly defined stage of inventory. Inventory is the period in which official and unofficial social units establish rules of action based on the boundaries, the social divisions, and the priorities established by the impact. Inventory is the mature stage of a political process. The jurisdictions claimed by social units and the relationships among them begin to appear as matters for negotiation. The rules of action and the situations to which they apply delineate a new order at the local and superordinate levels of a community. Reflections of the new order emerge from communication through a variety of channels, within a multiplicity of media, in a number of different settings, and on a number of different occasions. As during the period of threat, rumor is especially significant at this stage.

RESCUE

Rescue involves the care of survivors and the organization of work and solace among victims, rescuers, and witnesses. The phenomenon known as the "disaster syndrome" occurs during this stage. It is a prolongation of the stunned condition that is characteristic but momentary among victims (Wallace, 1956); Wolfenstein, 1957; Chapman, 1962, p. 17). Those manifesting the disaster syndrome do not quickly emerge from the stunned condition but continue to act dazed, withdrawn, immobile, and helpless and, in a sense, overly socialized to the disaster setting. Hospitalized disaster victims "have been observed to be exceptionally quiet and undemanding . . . . Frequently they ask hospital attendants to take care of others first." Accident victims, by comparison, "are apt to be demanding, complaining, excited and clamorous" (Wolfenstein, 1957, pp. 81-82). Wolfenstein attributes this difference in behavior to the difference between undergoing isolated damage and being one among many injured. Having been one victim among many, one who has been rescued, the disaster victim feels gratitude. The accident victim may be less grateful for help since he has been injured while surrounding others have not. Put in nonmotivational terms, the conception and presentation of oneself as "victim" depends on the occasion on which one does the part of victim and the special ways in which people know how to account for themselves in situations that differ in their wider social meaning. The way one tells about oneself (with words, gestures, and symptoms) is not the same for disaster as it is for accident.

Rescue and subsequent stages have been described by Barton (1962) as the "emergency social system" that arises when there is a sudden and "large unfavorable change in inputs" that "threatens and frustrates many members and disrupts the normal flow of activities in the system" (p. 222). Barton also claims that this emergent organization supports "distinctive social processes of adaptation" and "has the problem of organizing human behavior to produce needed outputs" (p. 222).

REMEDY

During the stage of remedy, efforts are made to deal with the effects of disaster beyond the immediate requirements of the victims. This stage involves attempts to reconstruct basic social and material conditions of life along predisaster lines. The success of these efforts depends to a great extent on the coordination of official and unofficial practice because, by this time, both types of organization will probably be working in the same area. This coordination usually involves a transfer of local power to officials and a consequent phasing out of unofficial and unauthorized activities. Officials may reduce subsequent tension by "cooling out" civilian commitment and reaffirming ideologies of hierarchy in place of situated ideologies of solidarity (Westley, 1956; Fritz and Mathewson, 1957). Even prior to the stage of remedy, official requests for civilian aid often serve to channel civilian activity along officially acceptable lines, lines that envision an ultimate return to official normalcy. In fact, throughout disaster, official communications to a populace serve to prepare for an ultimate realignment of the citizenry consistent with official definitions of normalcy as well as to provide information about the occurrence and its consequences. These are, as a matter of practice, inseparable operations.

RECOVERY

The period of recovery or adaptation normally involves a change in the ecology and social organization of an area, which may mean more than simply making the area inhabitable again. The reconstituted social order is likely to differ from the old one, at least in detail. It will probably incorporate anticipation of future disasters in warning and preparation systems as well as in the lore of the community. Thus, in the aftermath of a large fire or an earthquake, there are changes in building codes, in insurance rates, or in the distribution of the population. The priorities for officially instituted change reflect political, as well as other, considerations, which may explain why disaster rarely leads to significant changes in a social order, although official records of the disaster often refer to vast changes undertaken to protect the community from future danger. The various accounts of a disaster are often placed within the context of an official or publicly acceptable tale. This history takes its place among the various tales by which institutions are represented and dramatized within the community (Berger and Luckmann, 1967) and normally plays an important part in postdisaster politics. In this way, a disaster becomes part of the enduring culture of a place.

CHAPTER FIVE

THE POLITICAL ECONOMY OF DISASTER

As has been discussed, disaster can be defined as an occasion that generates its own community, discontinuous with the everyday life and many of the tasks, rules, and structures of nondisaster society. Yet the autonomy of the interim society of disaster is not complete. At the margins of disaster, where it meets the larger society, and especially in the preimpact and postimpact phases, the official procedures of institutional control continue to claim responsibility and authority. The interaction between regularly constituted official authority and civilian operations within the disaster area can reasonably be investigated as a political relationship. It includes the emphases on language and communication, exigencies of resource mobilization, divisions of interest, and the exclusiveness of collectivities and their claims, which are characteristic of politics. The following discussion will continue to review early disaster studies, but the primary concern will be with communication and its role in the politics of disaster.

COMMUNICATION AND THE POLITICS OF DISASTER

Disaster is defined through a succession of stages, each of which provides parameters for social action at subsequent stages. Each stage also involves a distinctive process of communication, a distinctive order for the components of this process, and different constituencies for messages (for example, officials, witnesses, marginals, victims, and the engaged).

THE PUBLIC

Shibutani (1966) has described the components of communication during crisis, in particular, publics and channels. While his analysis is a useful one, it fails to come to terms with the fundamental features of communication that underlie the dissemination and exchange of news. For Shibutani a public consists of "those who are in some way concerned with an event that has disturbed the routine of organized life . . . the term 'public'. . . will be used here in a . . . specialized sense of a 'following'" (p. 37-38). According to Shibutani, publics demand news and organize information from either an engaged or witness perspective as they define or accept the definition of an occurrence. Shibutani claims that the definition of the situation which is finally adopted by a public is the result of an evolutionary process in which the selection of ideas depends on the degree to which they account for the available facts and on the degree to which they are consistent with established ways of constructing reality. Publics emerge within transcendent or enduring social systems, the characteristics of which affect the organization of communication in regard to an untoward occurrence.

Shibutani's discussion of publics can be elaborated upon by referring to Gerald Suttles' (1968) description of *The Social Order of the Slum.* Insofar as he is correct in his contention that the slum resembles disaster society, Suttles' theory has a bearing on the prior conditions of the organization of publics during disaster. In particular, his description of slum society qualifies the term "following" in that it points out some of the organizational limits to the formation of publics interested in news about "their social system." For example, Suttles described some of the effects of neighborhood structure on the distribution of information:

> The segmental structure of the Addams area places certain rough metes and bounds on communication among residents. Items of information usually originate in a particular sex, age, territorial, and ethnic group and only gradually work their way across these boundaries (p. 73).

Of greater importance is the fact that highly differentiated subinstitutional and unofficial networks of contact are established within the conventional community organization. Contact is here governed by considerations of identity and past performance rather than the categoric considerations of role and norm (p. 92). These networks are presumably active within publics interested in untoward occurrences. Although these networks do not ordinarily deal with matters of official or general public interest, they are relatively stable channels of communication that are available on a number of occasions, even occasions that are not scheduled.

CHANNELS OF COMMUNICATION

The types of social control that characterize communication to and within publics, according to Shibutani (1966), are, organized as "channels" of communication. Such channels are "much more than mere points of contact; they consist of shared understandings concerning who may address whom, about what subject, under what circumstances, with what degree of confidence" (Shibutani, 1966, p. 21, italics in original). Shibutani described three types of channels: institutional, auxiliary, and improvised. It should be noted that Shibutani does not clearly distinguish channel from source. As a result, he does not adequately deal with the role of power in communication. This distinction, however, will be maintained in the discussion of crisis communication presented here. Shibutani hypothesizes that the fact that the demand for certain news may be greater than that available during a disaster forces people to search for essential information through other than strictly institutional channels, in particular, through improvised channels in which people on the scene collaborate in defining their situation (p. 164).

Institutional Channels. Shibutani asserted that:

> *Institutional channels* are well organized. Like other social institutions they are characterized by a stable set of rules, officers performing clearly defined roles, procedures so well established as to be followed by interchangeable personnel, and sustaining sanctions. There are fixed standards of acceptability, prescribed routes of transmission, verification procedures, and codes of reliable conduct (p. 21).

Institutional channels ordinarily transmit cosmopolitan news—that is, news that refers to the social system as a whole. Such channels are associated with official sources of information, the agents of which are often charismatic—by virtue of appearing on a screen, for example—and often accepted as reliable. Because the distinctive attribute of the particular communication operations Shibutani labeled institutional channels is that such operations are licensed or authorized, the term institutional will be used to refer to officially authorized systems of transmission.

Institutional channels are incorporated in the practice of everyday life. It is part of that practice that information about cosmopolitan affairs is taken to be essential to the ordinary life of citizens. Institutional channels also provide the opportunity to rehearse higher institutional ideals (Berger and Luckmann, 1967) and provide a touristic, nonengaged, access to distant events. Even during a crisis institutional channels confer routine credibility on communicators, whether or not a message is appropriate to a public demand for news. But—and this is a point with which Shibutani does not adequately deal—this credibility is of a different sort than is conferred on a party to a transaction, and it is not strictly comparable to the credibility of those people who operate within auxiliary channels of communication.

Institutional channels rarely provide premises for action, because the messages they present are not directly relevant to the situated practice of everyday life, except insofar as they provide a focus for special types of interaction at various times during the day (for example, watching television after dinner). Such channels appeal to individuals as social types and as members of indentifiably complex and extended arrangements. Institutional channels posit cosmopolitan society as a natural environment for their recipients. On the other hand, the participation of individuals in the affairs of their immediate settings must be accounted for in terms of those settings. Institutional channels are not strictly appropriate for this task.

News transmitted through institutional channels is both seductive and intimidating. It may give recipients a sense of intimacy with the practical affairs of the official society (Lang and Lang, 1968) which personalizes their concern with, and individuates and nullifies their engagement in, those affairs. At the same time, the structure of the news given by institutional channels tends to reject the social settings in which reception takes place and to draw attention exclusively to the identity of the individual recipient as a "member of society."

In this way, such news minimizes both the recipient's perception of power as a critical element in the organization of society and his involvement in the kinds of associations in which he can actively participate in political practice.

Auxiliary and Improvised Channels. For Shibutani (1966), auxiliary channels of communication constitute the formal or enduring organization of publics, and improvised channels are transient situated organizations of communication within temporary and focused gatherings. An auxiliary channel is a "grapevine" in which significant exchanges ordinarily occur through roles that, according to Shibutani:

> are not fixed in custom nor defined in law. These sources are evaluated largely in terms of the personal reputation of the participants for honesty, knowledge, sound judgment, and "connections" (1966, p. 23).

Shibutani considers auxiliary and improvised channels subsidiary to institutional channels, late choices for the procurement of news and, therefore plausible substitutes during emergency. "Auxiliary channels," says Shibutani, "are definitely supplementary; when 'grapevine' information conflicts with official news, the latter is generally accepted" (p. 22). However, it is necessary to qualify this description of auxiliary channels. The fact that conflict is ordinarily resolved in favor of official news does not imply that auxiliary or improvised channels operate merely as late supplements to institutional channels. Rather, communication in everyday life is conducted through a mix of channels consisting primarily of auxiliary and improvised channels, which process information that originates on a screen or from a radio or in the "outside world" itself. Here, auxiliary channels must be seen as institutional in everyday life and improvised channels as qualified emergents of special occasions.

A CRITIQUE OF SHIBUTANI'S THEORY OF CRISIS COMMUNICATION

Shibutani's theory—that an increase in the ratio of the demand to the supply of essential news results in a shift from institutional to noninstitutional channels of communication on the part of a news-needful and consensus-oriented public—hints at the existence of underlying social relations in the processes of information dissemination and exchange. However, it fails to come to grips with the most fundamental social relations involved in those processes. The theory underestimates the degree to which improvised communication during crises is continuous with everyday life, and it underestimates the degree of order and control—rationality—in both auxiliary and improvised channels. Consequently, the theory does not address the essentially problematic features of crisis communication that derive from the actual operations and organizational imperatives of official and unauthorized communication. Nor does it deal with the role of unauthorized channels in conflict during disaster. A large part of the problem is caused by the fact that key concepts—auxiliary, improvised, institutional, formal, control, informal, news, communication, channel, public, crisis—are not sufficiently explicated to establish the qualities of the phenomena they designate and the relations that underlie those phenomena.

Specifically, Shibutani uses the terms "social control," "communication," and "channel" in systematically misleading ways. For what he calls institutional channels, control is the organization of *transmission from* within a communications industry or an official structure. Such control is fundamentally different from the control of *communication within* a public. The same word—control— is used in such a way as to subsume different structures and processes under the same model without accounting for the differences. However, for noninstitutional channels, Shibutani describes control as embedded in informally organized interpersonal transactions that permit communication in the interactional and reciprocal sense implied by the term channel. Moreover, his treatment of news as a relatively undifferentiated category of information—something that can be gotten from a number of sources—leaves unexamined the relationship between news content and the setting in which news arises. The failure to discriminate processes and the failure to demonstrate his assumption that news is an item of exchange detachable from its origins allows Shibutani to conclude that various channels, or operations, are functionally equivalent ways in which "news" is exchanged through a process of "communication"; and they allow him to imply that channels are employed in serial order, depending on their capacity to meet an undifferentiated public demand for news. As a result of this imposition of serial form on the process of defining a critical situation, Shibutani underestimates the extent of conflict in disaster situations; since, by his hypothesis, channels do not occupy the same space or time, and since they do not represent different relations of interest or power, they are essentially noncompetitive.

A closer look reveals, however, that licensed transmitters have a special kind of corporate existence. They are organized as established industry or official agency. They relate to a populace objectively, as distributions of types, producing control rather than interaction. During crisis, they disseminate cosmopolitan news and official reassurance, thus establishing and coopting the most inclusive domain of an interested populace.

On the other hand, unauthorized channels provide different news, sociability, and the possibility of situated and collective action. In fact, auxiliary and improvised channels are not really coordinate: the former, like institutional channels, may involve the dissemination and exchange of news, but the latter are best understood as an aspect of the situated social action involved in the work of coping with the social and material problems of disaster. Thus, the various channels are suited to different tasks and their operations have different results. In addition, because the various channels are extensions of the noncritical settings of everyday life, they carry the weight of traditional uses and contexts as well as the special imperatives of use in the practical circumstances of crisis situations. In other words, they are persistent and insistent forms of action that are, to some extent, in vital competition with each other.

Shibutani's failure to see the force of politics in communication during disaster lies also in his emphasis on disaster as stress rather than occasion, and with his corresponding emphasis on excitement as the mechanism both by which news spreads through a relatively undifferentiated mass with different rates of speed, and by which channels break down. The rate of spread of news and the breakdown of channels might be better explained by the degree of organization of the collectivities that receive news and provide settings for interaction. Local organization enhances the continued operation of auxiliary and improvised channels to the detriment of institutional channels. By their nature, the latter cannot provide information sufficient to account for situated action, regardless of the degree of shared excitement among recipients. The breakdown of institutional channels, then, is an inevitable consequence of the operations of independent local acting collectivities and situated social action.

Shibutani's hypothesis that a process of natural selection accounts for a final consensus about the definition of the situation, without factual warrant, assumes a final consensus rather than, for example, a pattern of dominance or continued conflict. It also assumes that ideas compete in some fashion with ideas. Here again, the theory leaves obscure the underlying social relations of communication substituting an overall rationality of the public. Such an overall rationality is difficult to conceive of, largely because Shibutani's concept of the public does not easily lend itself to such a conception. The public seen as a following is too diffuse to be an arena for action or a social actor such that it can be characterized as having rationality. Since his assumptions of consensus and the process by which consensus is attained require that the public be a system of social action—something that, as he defines it, it cannot be—Shibutani's account of how situations are defined, how and under what circumstances various channels of communication are adopted, and how social order is accomplished during disaster lacks coherence.

In contrast to Shibutani's model, communication conceived of as a political process is characterized by power plays, coalitions, negotiations, and so on. Unauthorized or auxiliary channels, then, follow the organizational lines of normal unofficial public life within a community. They are neither supplemental nor informal, nor even public in the generalized unbounded sense of the term. This feature of auxiliary channels—their embeddedness within a community and their relative reliability, multiplicity, and exclusiveness—indicates that the public that is active during disaster is not a homogeneous collection of individuals, a following, as much as it is a collection of social orders organized and interrelated by far more than a shared interest in an untoward occurrence. Shared interest is necessary to the initial involvement in communication, but there is no entity such as a public that can be described as having that interest in the sense of social action that Shibutani clearly intends. There is, then, no process that can take place within a public or to which members of a public can subscribe, and a public cannot arrive at a decision or exhibit consensus, except in the purely statistical sense of the term.

The Effects of Crisis. Given these qualifications and revisions of Shibutani's view of communication, it can be concluded that a crisis exaggerates and brings into sudden juxtaposition simultaneous processes that are already part of a society, exacerbating conflicts inherent in the differences between official and unofficial structures, between collectivities and masses, and between situated and transcendent social actors. Moreover, from this point of view, it is incorrect to assert that the apparent "spontaneity, expedience, and improvisation" of improvised channels and rumor construction is caused by "the *lower degree of formalization* of many of its component communicative acts" (Shibutani, 1966, p. 23). Close observation of communication in focused gatherings does not clearly reveal the irregularity and lack of control implied by Shibutani's description. Moreover, his own qualifications of the concept of formalization reveals a discrepancy between his theoretic intent—to establish degrees of rationality among the types of channels—and the criteria by which he matches concrete processes to their theoretic type. His list of the formal attributes of institutional channels is qualified by terms like "stable," "clearly defined," "so well established," "sustaining," "fixed," and "coded." These qualifications are not strictly compatible with the concept of rationality. Rather, they indicate that when he classifies channels by degree of formalization, Shibutani is really classifying them by the degree to which they are established, powerful, linked to a multiplicity of institutions, routinely describable, and the like. Yet his assertion that the channels are ordered according to their capacity to service a need for news depends on interpreting the differences among them as differences in rationality. Thus, the relative low level of rationality of noninstitutional channels, in particular the unpredictability of improvised channels, is not given by theory or observation. It is, rather, a treatment or construction of events from within a practical perspective. Internal unpredictability is often, as was pointed out earlier, a construction from an official perspective. The peculiar features of improvised channels stem from a shift in control over the communication process from hierarchy to association and from controlling elites to indigenous organization and, in addition, from the fact that such channels reconstitute a public or a following as a setting for political activity and hard work.

THE SETTING OF COMMUNICATION

Fritz and Mathewson (1957) pointed out that:

> A disaster-struck population manifests overwhelming concern for human beings—family members, relatives, friends, neighbors, and other community residents—before it turns attention to property considerations (p. 31).

During disaster, location is a vital determinant of individual behavior. As people locate themselves within a setting consisting of mutually relevant actors, they breathe the imagery of the occurrence from the atmosphere of that setting and draw information about where to go, to whom to listen, and what associations are unsafe. Discussion presumably centers around the relationships among parties to a discussion and their shared relation to the occurrence: for example, "Did you see that?" "Did she get out all right?" "Let's find a policeman." As people are defined as witnesses, victims, marginals, and so on, they also supply each other with additional information, which is ultimately collated within collectivities engaged in extending the definition of the situation. However, the fact that individuals often linger in a crisis conversation beyond the point at which it supplies data about their circumstance or the occurrence itself indicates that such conversation provides more than information on the basis of which individuals can act.

The Polarization of Orientation. Fritz and Mathewson (1957) observed that:

> There are a number of disaster needs . . . in which disaster-struck populations have demonstrated a consistent preference for private and informal solutions over public and formal solutions, even when the latter objectively may be more adequate than the former (p. 41-42).

At the same time, individuals may become involved in a variety of channels of communication.[1] Officially initiated communications often contend with this politicization of the populace by attempting to inculcate a witness perspective—interested but properly disengaged—among the majority of communications recipients. Specifically, official communications may attempt to limit the sites in which individuals or groups can interact to those sites that are irrelevant to official jurisdictional claims or are easily contained. Concomitantly, officials may attempt to restrict communication to channels carrying official messages by releasing messages about communication such as "Please remain indoors and stay tuned to this station" or "Go immediately to your nearest shelter and wait until you are given further information."

The polarization of orientation during disaster initially leads to a heavy reliance on both situated interaction and institutional channels of communication. The result is a relative neglect of the network of credible sources that make up a community grapevine during ordinary times. In the United States, the extreme reliance on mass media during crisis may be due to the pervasiveness of the mass media and the cultural patterns they sustain.[2] By 1969, there were television sets in 98.5 percent of American homes and radios in 99.7 percent of American homes (Kurtz, 1970). Moreover, television, radio, and the newspapers have long been incorporated into the routines and places of everyday life, and they sustain a cultural pattern of attending to officials—a characteristic of citizenship during the present period of national mobilization.

Gerbner's (1969) discussion of the traditional relationship between newspapers and readers summarized the contemporary role of the mass media in American life:

> The principal sustaining service of the American newspaper is the creation and cultivation of a reading public of consumers concentrated in a market area which provides the base for the profitable operation of the chief

---

1. This is a different description of the same activities that were classically described as "milling" (Blumer, 1951).

2. Though most Americans have access to the mass media, the actual distribution of information depends on differences in life-style, differences in access to many media, the relative strength and traditional credibility of other channels within a given community, relative access to critical resources including a context in which a given message is intelligible, and the relative availability of settings in which information can be related to possible collective actions.

supporting clientele, the advertisers. These relationships and functions also shape the overall approach of the newspapers to other institutions and events, and affect the kind of attention it will pay to different publics. News and views are selected not only to be of broad general appeal but also to be of relevance and usefulness to the system of controls in which the press and its clients wield maximum influence (p. 217).

The political and economic base of the mass media in the United States establishes the media within the lives of citizens *qua* citizens, in terms of societal identity. Because disaster evokes precisely that identity, as well as specific location or place, it is not surprising that the intial referents of communication during a disaster are both extremely cosmopolitan and extremely local and that the most active channels are the institutional (licensed) and the improvised (interpersonal). In its evocation of official structures, disaster is an occasion for nostalgia, an occasion upon which social action is justified, as a whole enterprise, by reference to the past.

WARNINGS OF IMPENDING DISASTER

The intial stages of disaster can be characterized as the early phase of the process of defining an untoward occurrence and establishing its relation to social action. Thus, warnings not only state premises for individual action but also help to establish the meaning of the occurrence for collectivities and its significance as a framework for collective behavior. Because warnings are usually delivered by way of the mass media or through official spokesmen, they ordinarily transcend intimate face-to-face communication. By contributing to a widely shared definition of the anticipated occurrence as a disaster, warnings foreshadow a range of options for collective behavior and official action.

A verbal warning is a statement of a peculiar kind. There are several distinct processes associated with warning and each must be studied in its own right, in terms of its distinctive characteristics as socially organized activity. Moreover, the relationships among the various processes must be considered problematic. Warnings are assembled, credited or sanctioned, published, enacted, reenacted, reassembled, and so forth. The work of accomplishing each of those actions is different from the work of accomplishing any of the others. Warnings can provide news, as in the statement "a tornado is moving in a southwesterly direction from Dubuque, traveling at a speed of X miles per hour, and is expected to strike this area at approximately ten o'clock this evening." Warnings, however, are also acts, much like promises or vows. The content of warnings, or even the accuracy of the information conveyed, less important than their effect on the relationship between those who issue and those who hear the warning message. This relationship is usually characterized by disaster officials as the "degree of civilian preparedness." If a warning does not lead to a "state of increased preparedness," from the standpoint of those who issue it, it is a failure. Nevertheless, the nature of the relationship that warnings try to create is rather vague. H.B. Williams (1957) stated that:

The general function of communication in crisis is to provide the actor with information which will enable him to make choices to avoid, minimize or remedy the consequences of the crisis (p. 16).

THE DECISION TO ISSUE A WARNING

Williams' proposition avoids the political issue: Along what lines ought actions to be undertaken over and above their explicit reference to means and ends? The most important element of a warning is not its reference to specific sources of danger, but its reference to the system of action deemed relevant to disaster. Warnings help to prepare occasions and to establish the general limits of expected action. These limits reflect at least three decisions made by official warning parties based on answers to the following questions:

1. How will people act following the initial message?
2. To what extent is it possible to shape the warning to limit the degree of local independence that is likely as a consequence of the anticipation of a disaster?
3. How can political consequences that are dysfunctional to the maintenance of official control be minimized?

With regard to the first decision, H.B. Williams (1964) has described the behavior of officials in the Boston weather bureau prior to the 1953 tornado in Worcester, Massachusetts. These officials failed to issue early warnings about the likelihood of a tornado for a number of reasons, among which was a policy that "inhibited the issuance of unambiguous warnings." According to Williams:

> The forecasters were not to use the word "tornado." The system was blocked from the use of this word by fear that panic would result at least among those who were not close to cyclone cellars, if the people were warned of a tornado (1964, p. 88).

Williams pointed out that in this case:

> The system is acting in terms of the anticipated consequences of its own output, the anticipation in this case being based upon a stereotype about how human beings act when warned of impending danger (p. 89).

More precisely, officials in this case could not guarantee an officially preferred response and, therefore, issued no warning.

With regard to the second decision, warnings may establish stable sources of information so that the distribution of foci of attention within a populace centers on officials rather than on other figures. They may also suggest specific alignments among citizens that ease subsequent work of officials.

Finally, the third decision points to the political functions of warnings and their relationship to official structures. Williams commented that:

> If the decision maker decides against issuing a warning, and death and destruction occur, will he not be blamed? May he not even be blamed unreasonably? If he decides to issue a warning and the danger does not materialize, may he not be criticized by some people for "getting people upset?" (1964, p. 89).

Insofar as a warning states not only "the existence of danger," but "what can be done to prevent, avoid, or minimize the danger" (Williams, 1964, p. 80), it provides evidence of a capacity that will ultimately be put to the test. For example, the relationship between the stated capacity of official agencies and the actual disaster experience can provide the basis for later political conflict.

Desired Consequences. Early researchers tended to treat warnings as rational statements that often, mysteriously, failed to have the desired rational consequences. Although this tendency must be recognized as a weakness of analysis, a considerable amount of work has been done to investigate the different factors that determine the effectiveness of warning messages. Contemporary research on the effects of warnings has been dominated by interest in the priorities of those agencies which issue official warnings and has been directed primarily at the problem of minimizing social fragmentation and panic. Thus, warnings are aimed at reducing the individuation and localization of behavior by asserting cosmopolitan and official definitions of the event and of the actions appropriate to it. The study of warnings is in the tradition of communications research (Hovland, Janis, and Kelley, 1953; Janis and Feshbach, 1953, 1954; Janis, 1958; Hovland and Janis 1959; Janis, 1962; Larsen, 1964). Investigators have focused on two factors: the nature of the warning itself—its source, timing, and content—and the immediate social setting within which the warning is received.

WARNING MESSAGES AS SOCIAL CONTROL

The problem of control in disaster is normally formulated from the perspective of official agencies and, therefore, has to do with the relation of official action to the motions of aggregates and the unauthorized actions of unofficial collectivities. Research on the effects of warnings, however, has been primarily psychological, focusing on individual response to warning messages within the paradigms of the psychology of perception and thought. A critical examination of this literature highlights the importance of understanding disaster as a socio-political event rather than as a matter of individual problem-solving behavior.

Warnings engage recipients as social actors rather than as individuals. People often check out the warning message first, not only to assess its accuracy, which is often impossible, but to establish a social setting in which the warning can be interpreted and action undertaken. This feature of warnings has been overlooked by investigators working within the information-processing paradigm of communications research. These investigators see warnings as failing to achieve their purpose by erring in two directions. Warnings may fail to make the recipient aware of danger and thus be too weak to stimulate preparations. On the other hand, warnings may arouse so much fear that people reassure themselves by denying the danger or resigning themselves to a passive acceptance of whatever is going to happen, which is the more common reaction. In other words, from the point of view of the warning party, people can either underreact or overreact to warnings.

A study published by Powell (1953) described a variety of responses to warning. In 1951 in Atlanta, Georgia, 300 gallons of poisoned whiskey were distributed. The majority of the consumers were among the black population. Following public warnings, a number of people came to the clinics that had been set up to cope with the situation. Of those who came for medical help, 40 percent had actually been affected, 42 percent showed no symptoms, and the remaining 18 percent had hysterical symptoms but showed no medical trace of poisoning. Many people who heard the warnings did not report to the clinics; many people went to the clinics but did not subsequently follow the doctor's orders. Some people continued to drink whiskey in the face of the warnings, and other people rejected the warnings to the extent of looking for other reasons to explain the death of persons who succumbed to the poisoned whiskey (Janis, 1962, pp. 56-57). Based on this and other studies Janis (1962) concluded that the response to warning can be assigned to one of three categories: effective preparatory behavior, emotional sensitization, and underreaction (p. 55).

Preparatory Behavior. Janis hypothesized that warnings ordinarily give rise to some degree of "reflective fear" that, in turn, arouses two different but related needs: a need to be vigilant and a need to be reassured. Paradoxically, the need to be vigilant can become so overwhelming that it leads to dangerous behavior. For example, there are people who are so timid when they drive that they are an actual danger to other cars. The need for reassurance can also become overwhelming, leading people to comfort themselves with blanket reassurances that nothing very bad can happen to them or that God will protect them. On the other hand, there is also the possibility of rational behavior that can compromise between these needs and balance them, so that the individual plans and prepares for the danger ahead. In this case, vigilance becomes discriminating, and reassurance is gained from specifying plans. Whether or not the response to a warning is rational depends upon the warning itself as well as on the personality traits of the recipient.

Janis (1962) addressed himself to "the environmental conditions which foster high vigilance *versus* high reassurance needs when people are warned of impending dangers" (p. 66), and to the conditions under which these needs are transformed into rational responses to danger. According to Janis, the key is "the level of reflective fear induced by a warning stimulus" (p. 67). This level depends upon the ambiguity of the message and the degree and source of danger anticipated by it.

Clarity and Degree of Danger. Janis distinguished between two types of messages, ambiguous and unambiguous warnings. Both may posit different degrees of danger. According to Janis, when an unambiguous warning posits "remote, improbable, or relatively trivial" danger, people will tend to ignore the warning or adopt an attitude of blanket reassurance. On the other hand, an anticipated danger that is moderate will induce both reassurance and vigilance. An anticipated danger that is extreme will produce exaggerated vigilance and a consequent lack of discrimination "between safe and unsafe features of the environment" (p. 67).

If the message is ambiguous, it will foster vigilance where it arouses a moderate or high degree of fear and blanket reassurance where it arouses only a slight degree of fear. As Janis noted, the more general proposition is that ambiguous information tends to reinforce "whatever psychological set is dominant at the time of the exposure" (p. 69-70), but unambiguous information directly affects the level of fear. Thus, an unambiguous warning about a moderate danger will be more likely to provoke adaptive behavior than either an ambiguous warning or warnings that envision trivial or great dangers. Because the ambiguity of warnings can rarely be controlled, and because the officials issuing warnings generally assume their messages to be unambiguous, Janis would advise warning parties to concentrate on the degree of anticipated danger in order to maximize the likelihood of officially acceptable response. Table 5.1 summarizes the hypotheses put forth by Janis concerning the effects of ambiguity and the degree of danger anticipated by warnings.

Table 5.1 RESPONSES TO WARNINGS

Clarity of Message	Degree of Anticipated Danger		
	Extreme or High	Moderate	Trivial
Ambiguous	low adaptability; high vigilance	low adaptability high vigilance	low adaptability; blanket reassurance
Unambiguous	low adaptability; high vigilance	high adaptability; high discrimination	low adaptability; blanket reassurance

Based on information from Janis, 1962.

The degree to which an unambiguous warning arouses reflective fear depends upon two types of information: "the magnitude of oncoming danger" and "the magnitude of personal and community resources for coping with the danger" (Janis, 1962, p. 68). These two types of information determine the degree of threat implied by the warning and, consequently, determine whether the recipient should anticipate a low, moderate, or high degree of danger. The first type of information increases reflective fear; the second type of information reduces fear. Janis asserted that:

> The highest level of reflective fear, and hence the greatest likelihood of indiscriminate vigilance, will occur when there is a great deal of information of the first type and none of the second type. (p. 68).

Warning Themes. Janis listed four themes that lead to an increase in reflective fear if they appear in warnings that are delivered by a credible source following an initial disaster alert: (1) if the force strikes us, the danger will be greater than originally anticipated; (2) it is more likely that the force will strike us than had previously been expected; (3) we do not have as adequate resources to cope with the disaster as we had thought; (4) our resources cannot be mobilized as quickly as had been expected. These themes place the individual between his own fear and the resources available, both in himself and in his community, for coping with the source of his fear. Given the assumption that information suggesting inadequate resources tends to increase vigilance, Janis suggested four plausible hypotheses "which specify situational factors that change a person's self-appraisal and thereby influence his readiness to take action" (p. 75). When a disaster is anticipated:

1. A person will become more vigilant when he receives information to the effect that escape will be impossible when the danger materializes;
2. A person will become more vigilant when he receives information to the effect that escape will depend upon his own efforts rather than on the efforts of others;
3. A person will become more vigilant when he receives information to the effect that his own activity will be restricted at the time of impact, whether or not he believes that escape will depend upon his own efforts;
4. A person will become more vigilant when he receives information to the effect that "during a period of oncoming danger he will be out of contact with authority figures, members of his primary group, or other significant persons upon whom he is emotionally dependent" (p. 77, originals in italics).

Adaptation or Sensitization. Janis acknowledged that the relationship between information, fear, and the rationality of response must be qualified by the degree to which antecedent warnings and predisaster experiences induce an " 'emotional' adaptation" that decreases or a " 'sensitizing' effect" that increases vigilance when a new warning is issued. Whether adaptation or sensitization occurs seems to depend upon: the prior beliefs that people have about the dangers of particular types of disaster (Janis suggested that people often regard precipitant disasters as more dangerous than disasters with phased or gradual impact); whether or not there are additional cues that create a sense of urgency (Janis suggested that such cues characterize precipitant disasters); and the varying senses of imminence present in the schedule of messages (p. 81).

THE POLITICAL IMPLICATIONS OF WARNINGS

Janis' analysis of the effectiveness of disaster warnings assumes: (1) that the individual is an isolated decision-maker at the time that he receives and interprets the warning message; (2) that the individual's behavior is directly dependent upon disposition—fear—and; (3) that effective behavior depends upon the individual's formulation of explicit goals related to self-protection and the discovery of objectively specifiable means of protection or escape under the prevailing conditions. Thus, Janis described the normal response to warnings of high or moderate degrees of danger:

the arousal of reflective fear is expected to lead to reality-oriented compromise formations which satisfy both vigilence and reassurance needs in a discriminative way, with corresponding changes in attitudes and behavior. This sequence generally is adaptive in that the person is better prepared to cope with the danger situation if it subsequently materializes (1962, p. 65).

His hypotheses can only be tested in situations where his basic assumptions are met. They do not apply where individuals are not isolated and independently rational but are embedded in a social reality that provides interpretations, plausible alliances, and a design for action. However, such situations are precisely the ones of interest to the student of disaster and the ones to which Janis originally addressed his theory. The relevant question is not: Given individuation, when will a person become more vigilant? Rather, the question is: Given the ordinary facts of life—in particular, the fact that persons are primarily social actors and not simply "emotionally dependent" on other people—under what conditions will activity move in directions authorized by a warning party, and under what conditions will authorized acts occur that affect acting units and the coordination among them?

Social Forces Within the Setting. In this book, individual dispositions are assumed to be less important for action than the social forces at work in the setting. The importance of studying the psychology of individuals under stress is not denied here. However, that study should focus on changes in the social character of individuals as they enter new alignments, assume various roles, and adopt different attitudes toward their groups rather than on the relationship between danger signs and individual responses. These changes would in turn be predicted by reference to the variable quality of social life under various conditions common to disaster and predisaster situations. Specific states of motivation, apparently individual acts, and apparently individual attitudes would be treated as situated and, therefore, as social products, except in extreme and relatively rare cases. Because the mechanisms by which collectivities act involve more than the simple aggregation of individual tendencies, and because individual activity under stress tends to be at least as highly socialized as activity in nonstressful situations, an overemphasis on psychological factors leaves the fundamental problems of collective action (including individual participation in collective action) unresolved.

How did Janis arrive at a position that, at best, is able to explain only a rare case? To begin with, the initial research on warnings eliminated vital information by limiting attention to individual behavior coded as decisions. The process of deciding and the settings within which behavior occurred were simply ignored, even when information about them was available. Thus, there was no empirical basis upon which to consider the social determination of the various "responses." The adoption of a psychological model was economical to the data at hand, but it was insufficient given the social dimensions of warnings and response. Janis relied on a description of the "responses to danger" that was too specific and yet lacked important details. In addition, he employed a psychological explanation in terms of setting-free but cued dispositons, that is, dispositions cued by specific items of information, or content, rather than the social facts of delivery, interpretation, and use. This explanation led him to rely on "reflexive fear" as the motivational key to individual response rather than on social facts in relation to which vigilance is appropriate regardless of the degree to which individuals experience fear. From this point of view, Janis is obligated to assume similar levels of fear when he observes similar individual responses, which would not be necessary if he had examined the social settings of those responses. In any case, vigilance may be considered a social activity, rather than an individually motivated activity, that is available to individuals as a way of participating in groups on certain occasions.

Social System Designators as Political Cues. Janis saw two major components of warning messages that explain individual behavior and, thus, collective behavior: degree of danger and adequacy of resources for escape. However, there is an additional element that is almost always present in a warning: some social system designator, for example, "we," "us," "our," or "here." The four warning themes that Janis mentioned as likely to induce an increase in reflective fear included such social system designators. But Janis justifies neither his selection of one part of a message as relevant to the prediction of behavior nor his omission of other parts. In fact, it appears to be a social psychological canon that system designators normally dominate most other forms of public information, and there is reason to think that their significance in warning messages is exaggerated in crisis.

Among other functions, then, warnings suggest lines of participation as major premises of individual behavior. It follows that warnings and their effects cannot be analyzed without thoroughly examining the social settings in which they are received and acted upon. This analytic procedure assumes that it is not so much *what* a person is but *where* he is that determines his behavior. Thus, a message that states "our resources are inadequate" suggests that individuals realign themselves. The message designates a system and states that it is not available as a setting for individual participation and accountability. Under these circumstances, vigilance would be quite different from Janis' conception of it as the individual's search for specifically useful information. Instead, vigilance seems to consist of a search for alternate social forms rather than for information about states of material affairs (Festinger, et al., 1950). Because such a search occurs within and is of a social setting, it must be seen as collaborative rather than individual act. Janis' persistent reference to individuals as primary actors and as recipients of information obscures the social dimensions of action and the social dimensions of reception and interpretation. Where alternate social forms are unavailable, an increase in compulsiveness, apathy, or resignation on the part of individuals can be expected, rather than an increase in vigilance.

Janis' use of the terms resource and capacity is misleading. He separates resource from the social setting or system in which something has meaning as (can be said to be) resource. Thus, to mention official agencies within a warning message is to evoke a system rather than disembodied capacities. Again individuals are engaged along specific lines of participation rather than in individualistic and calculated acts of self-protection, including vigilance for danger-relevant information and blanket reassurance. Janis has described individual *capacities* to be affected by the environment and has transformed them conceptually into *determinants* or causes of behavior. Because stress opens an individual to a wider range of stimuli than before does not mean that he has a need for such stimuli; it only means that he can be affected by whatever is available (Williams, 1964 pp. 94-96; Parsons, 1958). In contrast to Janis, it can be claimed that warnings are meaningful only within a social setting, that responses to warnings are socially contrived through complex processes of collaboration, and that individuals respond to warnings by selecting location rather than by engaging in particular instrumental acts. Janis' failure to notice the system-designating content of warning messages also evades the political issues inherent in warning systems by neglecting the relationship between early stages in the definition of an occurrence as disaster and the ultimate socio-political shape of recovery.

In taking exception to Janis' analysis of warnings and their effects, the authors agree with Form and Loomis (1956) that:

> Perhaps the main reason for phrasing disaster research in individualistic terms is the commonly held premise that disasters completely destroy social systems, and they somehow strip the person of his social preferences and throw him back on his individual resources. Such reasoning automatically turns the research problem into one of studying the individual's morale, his adjustment, and personal reorganization. However, such a premise violates sociological theory and is inconsistent with what is observed of human behavior under disaster conditions (p. 185).

THE SOCIAL SETTING OF INTERPRETATION AND ACTION

Considered as part of a complex process of defining the danger situation, old data fall into new relationships. Apparent indecision and attempts to provide familiar explanations for unfamiliar phenomena can be seen as attempts at participation in collective problem solving or collective action. The restructuring of ideas about situations—the intended consequence of warnings—is too complex and unspecificable a task for individuals to accomplish by themselves. Moreover, there are many other forces at work that support activities inconsistent with the radical demands of warnings and that encourage individual skepticism. Yet, regardless of individually held attitudes toward a warning message, evidence indicates that individuals will participate in collective activities that may be, although they need not be, consistent with the conclusions and dicta of the warning message.

Researchers were worried because more than half of those people exposed to false civil defense alerts (Mack and Baker, 1961 p. 53) reacted as though they knew (although they could not have known) that there had been a mistake. These same researchers were doubtless encouraged by the results of Drabek and Boggs' (1968) investigation of the Denver flood of 1965. In the case of the Denver flood, over half of the warned population reacted to the warning with extreme skepticism; but on this occasion there was a flood. It destroyed property valued at $325,000,000, and 3,700 families evacuated their homes; but no lives were lost and no panic was reported. The general pattern of Drabek and Bogg's data suggests that under some circumstances, and despite skepticism, "appropriate" responses to warning can take place.

Warnings help to shape an occasion for social action. They tell the individual that circumstances will require him to participate in an episode of situated social action. But a warning is only one element of a social setting in which situations are defined, alignments formed, and projects undertaken. A setting in which individuals are distant from their roles or in which individuals experience themselves as isolated makes it less likely that they will receive warnings of impending disaster. Even when they do receive such warnings, isolated individuals are less likely to take them into account.

Social Isolation. Several studies have indicated that messages are less effective among social isolates or those who habitually receive "news" in temporary isolation, such as the aged and blue-collar workers (Moore and Friedsam, 1959; Friedsam, 1962; Spitzer and Denzin, 1965). The account of the Denver flood by Drabek and Boggs (1968) indicated that this is not simply because of a lack of education or a disability. They found that older families were no less willing to evacuate their homes after warning then younger families—if they had relatives in the area (p. 449). Because only three of the older families did not have relatives in the Denver area, Drabek and Boggs were unable to demonstrate that older families without relatives nearby were less willing to evacuate their homes. Nevertheless, they suggested that "it is not necessarily a psychological syndrome that characterized those elderly persons who were reluctant to leave, but rather a social characteristic, i.e., the absence of nearby kin" (p. 450).

Other research has indicated that when, by virtue of the conditions of communication or its content, a warning isolates individuals, it will not play a significant role in their subsequent behavior. Spitzer and Denzin (1965) found that people who learned about President Kennedy's death in a setting that provided access to interpersonal interaction as well as to mass media gained more information about the event than did people in settings where one of these components was missing (pp. 236-37).

The "Objective Reality". The effect of a warning depends, among other things, upon the degree to which individuals are absorbed in a setting that can include the warning as a meaningful component of a process of practically construing a situation. This formulation appears to be consistent with Mack and Baker's (1961) statement that, "The interpretation of a signal depends in part upon the observation of the behavior of others in the immediate environment" (p. 53; see also Scott, 1955, p. 20). But more than "observation" is required. Although Mack and Baker have recognized the relevance of the social setting to the interpretation of warnings, they have still located the interpretative process in the individual and the group is seen as merely supplementing the individual's information about his situation, which does not include the group. Thus, they assume that the theoretically problematic relationship is between the individual and a message—"person" and "environment"—which leads them to distinguish between the individual's interpretative activity and the "objective reality":

> People define a situation not only on the basis of the objective reality of the situation, but also on the basis of their own interpretation of signals which are intended to communicate that situation (1961, p. 53).

This formulation rather obscures the central problem, namely, the difficulty of knowing what the "objective reality" of the situation is. It is certainly quite different for the warning party, for the individual recipient, for the group recipient, and for anyone hearing the warning after the fact. The objective reality for the warned individual is his participation in a focused gathering, one topic of which is a signal from a particular transmitter (including imputations of source) mixed with signals from other transmitters, all within a social setting that is regular and in which there is already some definition of the situation. In these terms, it would be surprising if individuals acted predictably in the light of a single variable in the situation—that is, the specific information conveyed by a discrete message (Klapper, 1960; Lang and Lang, 1968).

In order to understand those situations in which individuals do heed warnings, other than psychological forces must be considered. At the very least, the relationships between the individual and his gathering and between the gathering and the warning party are essential in accounting for responses to w irning messages.[3] From this point of view, the collectivity, rather than the individual, is the agent of "observation" and "interpretation"; the individual must be understood as a participant.

THE EFFECTS OF SETTING ON RESPONSE TO WARNING

Drabeck and Boggs' (1968) investigation of the Denver flood of 1965 illustrates the complexity of social settings in which warnings are received as well as the ways in which such settings shape individual and group responses to warning messages. In the case of the Denver flood, presumably, the appropriate response to the flood warning was evacuation. The interpretation of the warning and the response were processed through a setting made up of family structure and particular relationships between the recipients of warnings and the various sources. In addition to families deciding to evacuate, Drabek and Boggs found that evacuation took place in three other ways: (1) as a compromise when family members disagreed about the danger; (2) by invitation when attempts to confirm the danger by consultation with friends and relatives resulted in invitations to come and stay (for 56 percent of those who evacuated, it was the invitation from a friend or relative that provoked the decision); and (3) by default, a category that included families that left their homes to go up to the nearby hill to see the river, only to find that the police had cordoned off the threatened area when they tried to return to their homes.

Social Relationships. The warning process was evidently successful. How was this success achieved? Because the area threatened by flood waters was so small, and the danger so acute and immediate, police cars with loudspeaker systems were sent into the endangered neighborhoods. These policemen represented the authority source as indicated in Table 5.2, which specifies the origins of evacuated warnings and the responses to them during the 1965 Denver flood.

---

3. In this regard, the literature on source credibility can be seen as referring to aspects of the relationship between the communicator and the social setting of the recipient rather than the reputation of the communicator, the putatively objective quality of his information, or the plausibility and coherence of his message.

Table 5.2 FAMILY REACTIONS TO WARNINGS

Family Reaction	Origin of Warning (Number of families and percentage)					
	Authority		Peer		Mass Media	
Immediate Evaluation	24	61 percent	33	30 percent	16	13 percent
Attempted Confirmation	12	31 percent	52	47 percent	63	51 percent
Discounted Warning	3	8 percent	25	23 percent	45	36 percent
Totals:	39	100 percent	110	100 percent	124	100 percent

Adapted from Drabek and Boggs, 1968, p. 342.

Attempts at Confirmation. The families who made some attempt to confirm warnings usually approached a different source from that which presented the first warning message. Over 50 percent of the confirmation efforts were directed toward mass media. The 47 percent who appealed to other people found confirmation less than 60 percent of the time, primarily because many of the people consulted had no information, had less information, or had information contrary to that given by the original source. Among other complicating variables is the fact that individual receivers will credit official information with different degrees of authority but will act according to the immediate conditions regardless of their initial skepticism or certainty. Drabek and Boggs reported cases of husbands who disagreed with their wives about the credence that should be given to warnings but who evacuated anyway "just to keep her quiet." The statistics in the mass media origin column (see Table 5.2) are interesting in relation to Katz and Lazarsfeld's (1955) early suggestion that a latent function of media is to stimulate a sequence of communication acts. Spitzer and Denzen (1965) considered mass media to be relatively inadequate in this regard, but Drabek and Boggs' statistics suggested otherwise. According to their data, it appears that people are highly suspicious of information received through the mass media but that those media do serve to stimulate other acts of communication.

Drabek and Boggs' research confirms the general tendency of people to seek confirmation of information during disaster. More importantly, it suggests that the social setting in which the warning is received is crucial for subsequent behavior and that a warning is only one element of such a setting. Their report makes it clear that the explicit content of warning messages is no more important than the implicit content and the situation in which a message is embedded. Ambiguity is no longer merely the formal property of an ill-defined message; it can also arise out of an incongruous relationship between the message and the setting.

The Pooling of Response. Apart from efforts at public or official verification, it is clear that a pooling of response takes place within the family. Over three-quarters of the families evacuated during the Denver flood moved as intact units, supporting Moore's (1958) earlier hypothesis that "families move as units and remain together, overriding dissent." According to Drabek and Boggs (1968), "recent empirical data suggest that kin ties, especially intergenerational ones, have more significance than was thought for the urban family" (p. 446). They added that "data further suggests that the significance of kin ties is not uniform across social classes."

Dotson (1951) found that about 40 percent of his working class sample had no intimate friends outside their own immediate families (p. 691). A number of researchers have found that roughly the same percentage—about 60 percent—of disaster evacuees take refuge with relatives and friends (for example, Young, 1954; Moore, 1958). This finding is interpreted here as indicating the importance of the logic of particular social settings in which warnings are received as well as the prepotent roles of conventional social groupings in shaping reactions to emergencies. Even though official warnings are highly credible, they are interpreted within the settings most relevant to the recipients. Quarantelli (1960) has suggested that as the scope of the affected community narrows, the more likely it is that the kin group will be a major source of help during a disaster.

The Drabek and Boggs study of the Denver disaster examines an usually full and intricate network of relationships and integrates a wide range of previously scattered data. As a result, it can be seen that warning, confirmation, and response are interwoven within a web of social relationships. The picture of the warning situation that now emerges is very remote from the simple, individual decision-making model that was used in earlier studies. In fact, contemporary research on families in disaster not only points to the role of the social setting in determining individual behavior during disaster but also locates the individual's response (e.g., to threat, warning, etc.) in reference to a specific social reality—as a mode of participation.

The Counterdisaster Syndrome. There remains the problem of the individual who finds no affiliation following a disaster. Research indicates that many people who fail to enter plausible acting units and who lack official and transcendent alternatives may develop what Wallace (1956) referred to as the "counterdisaster syndrome." The term refers to the compulsive hyperactivity and low efficiency characteristic of a lonely and individualistic orientation to stress (p. 143) and a dependent rather than a participative mode of involvement. It is characteristic of people who feel out of place, without a site in which to practice their humanity. Wallace reported that individuals showing symptoms of the counterdisaster syndrome frequently speak as if they had lost their social ground—not only their ties to other people but also to the very site within which those ties can be enacted. The counterdisaster syndrome most often appears in persons who are outside the impact area but who have strong attachments to victims in the area.

A "disaster syndrome," which is a prolongation of the stunned condition that is characteristic but usually temporary among victims has also been described (Wallace, 1956; Wolfenstein, 1957; Chapman 1962). Those manifesting the disaster syndrome do not quickly emerge from the stunned condition but continue to act dazed, withdrawn, immobile, and helpless.

The counterdisaster syndrome can be interpreted as an exaggeration and idealization of the rescuer "role," and the disaster syndrome can be seen as an exaggeration and idealization of the victim "role." Both "roles" are given within the social stock of knowledge, and are enacted in idealized fashion when they are removed from collective practice by the isolation or individuation of the actor. Their idealization in practice is, then, a result of the individual's failure to enter an active social unit during the postimpact period of disaster (Wallace, 1956, pp. 109-110). It is here concluded that the main effect of disaster warnings is to catalyze situated social action. The form and direction of that action depends on collective processes that are functionally autonomous of the conditions, including the warning message, under which those processes originated.

POLITICAL DIMENSIONS OF THE MACROSOCIAL EVENT

Consistent with the characterization here of disaster as an affair riven with political and economic contradictions, in which official operations are essentially political, and in which local operations are essentially incompatible with the unity and discipline required by official control, several descriptions of disaster as a macrosocial event suggest a more complex and diversified socio-political situation than the adaptive and temporary emergency system described by Barton (1969). H.B. Williams (1957) has stated that "the ready response of people to authoritative figures and the rise of emergent leaders have been repeatedly observed in disaster during the emergency period . . ." (pp. 16, 19). Turner (1957) has suggested that whatever structures emerge during disaster are strong ones: "the evidence seems to point clearly toward an increment of solidarity and an unusually strong norm of altruism" (p. 61; see also Fritz, 1961). Shibutani (1966) has noted the complex interactions that can be expected during disaster, although he ties these to a depletion of values rather than to the imperatives of strong structures. He has mentioned, in particular, that "political activities . . . can be found in any situation in which values are in short supply and where different parties find it necessary to compete for them", (p. 87).

Although all of these authors have recognized the political dimension of disaster, they have made no attempt to reconcile the larger picture with the implications of the microsocial developments of disaster collectivities, which they have also recognized in various versions. Rather than attributes of an extensive emergency social system, as implicitly assumed by Williams and Turner, authority and solidarity in disaster appear to be limited by boundaries that specify the disaster society and locate its distinctive collective components. Authority appears as one aspect of local structure, and solidarity refers to an increase in the structural isolation and autonomy of local settings. Both Turner and Williams assumed a greater degree of homogeneity within the society struck by disaster than is consistent with the process of collectivity formation that has been described. Turner (1964) himself criticized early theorists for this very "illusion of uniformity." In relation to Shibutani's statement, it would appear that competition for scarce values is not the predominant source of conflict or political differentiation but, rather, the social and practical imperatives of social organization itself. For example, in contrast with Shibutani's proposition which predicts that looting would be a prominent activity among those who share a disaster (those who suddenly lack essential resources), the looting frequently referred to in disaster accounts is apparently not carried out by people who are competent parties to the occasion of disaster.

LOOTING: PROPERTY REDEFINITION

Looting, like panic, is a phenomenon more frequently reported than directly experienced. However, the point of immediate significance is that exploitation of what can be called, for reference purposes, the disaster society, comes from those who have not been directly affected by the disaster and for whom the occurence has a different meaning. It is still a disaster, but it is not their disaster. White-collar looting on an impressive scale was reported in the aftermath of Hurricane Audrey. Bates and his associates (1963) reported that:

> At one point in the rehabilitation process the Federal Bureau of Investigation was called in to find out what had happened to such things as generators, water pumps, lumber and other relief supplies that had disappeared (p. 62).

Several points can be drawn from the data available on the topic of looting. First, it should be emphasized that Turner's (1957) statement concerning altruism can be used to refer to structural as well as attitudinal or cultural properties of disaster societies. Data on looting that identifies exploitative behavior as originating outside the disaster society may be considered to mark the limits of that society.

Second, Dynes and Quarantelli (1968) suggested that the appropriation of property inside the disaster society has a unique meaning: it is one technique by which people and things are fitted to the requirements of the occasion. They asserted that illegal appropriations of property in disaster situations should not necessarily be interpreted as looting:

> Here we come to the critical element of "property redefinition." Incidents of this sort are *not* looting [referring to situations in which individuals may break into stores and warehouses and appropriate cots, supplies, and other equipment that does not "belong" to them]. The notion of "property" involves a shared understanding about who can do what with the valued resources within a community. When a disaster strikes, property rights are temporarily redefined: There is general agreement among community members that the resources of individuals become *community property*. Individual property rights are suspended, so appropriation of private resources—which would normally be considered looting—is temporarily condoned (p. 11).

In this sense, the conversion of values during disaster is a civilian analogue to the exercise of the police power of the state.

Third, there is a widely acknowledged discrepancy between the frequency of looting reports and the verified evidence of looting. In White City, Arkansas, in the impact area of a tornado, only 9 percent of those questioned reported that they had lost property that they felt might have been looted, yet 58 percent reported that they had heard of others being looted (Fritz and Mathewson, 1957, p. 54), and only two major thefts could be verified by investigators on the scene (Dynes and Quarantelli, 1968, p. 10; Fritz and Mathewson, 1957, p. 54). This patterned discrepancy between rumor and fact has been repeatedly noted in accounts of wartime Britain, of peacetime disasters in the United States, and of the blackout that darkened New York City and much of the northeastern seaboard in 1967. Even the small percentage of reported looting may not indicate the degree to which ordinary standards of exploitation are suspended during disaster. Dynes and Quarantelli (1968) have asked:

> Since all evidence is that looting is rare or nonexistent in natural disaster, why do reports of looting in disaster situations occur over and over again? And why are these reports persistently believed, even when there is no clear evidence to back them up (p. 10)?

They answer the question by referring to:

> four conditions that usually prevail in the immediate post-impact period: misinterpretations of observed behavior; misunderstandings over property ownership; inflated reports of looting; and sensational coverage of disaster situations by the news media (p. 10).

The first three conditions could be considered examples of bad or unsophisticated judgment. It is, however, equally possible that the spate of accusation signals intramural defensiveness on the part of strictly situated and bounded collectivities within the disaster society. The content of such accusations is not important; what they signal is intercollective behavior—that is, collectivities accounting for or otherwise demonstrating their own practices while at the same time differentiating themselves from others (see Garfinkel, 1967, especially p. 3, 11, and 31-34).

EXPLOITATION AS AN INDICATION OF THE BOUNDARIES OF DISASTER

Bates and his colleagues (1963) described the widespread exploitation of the disaster by relief workers brought into the stricken area from outside:

> Entire bus loads of workers signed the work sheet each morning, and immediately reloaded the buses and returned to Lake Charles or other nearby towns. Yet each worker was given credit for 14 hours work and bills were submitted for rental on the buses they rode even though riders were charged as much as $2.00 each per day to ride some of them (p. 33).

Indeed, verified reports of exploitative activity seem to reinforce the claim that a quasi-political definition of boundaries marks the limits of the disaster society. The term quasi-political is used here because exploiters and victims are not differentiated by their respective social, economic, and political situations within the same society; rather, they identify different societies as their own.

Relief stealing (posing as disaster victims in order to get relief goods or services) is probably rare but is most frequently encountered during the emergency care phase of large scale disasters (Fritz and Mathewson, 1957, p. 56). It is often hard, however, to draw the line between exploitation and improvised operations. Form and Nosow (1958) gave an account of Salvation Army workers who protested the use of their canteen by nonvictims such as utility workers, national guardsmen, and police. Salvation Army officers defended the institutional generosity by saying that they were building good will and helping the victims indirectly (p. 180). The review here suggests that those people who are neither victims nor rescuers and who are bound to the stricken community only by professional responsibilities do not participate in disaster as competent parties to the occasion. Their activity depends upon settings for which the disaster society itself is an object.

CHAPTER SIX

POLITICS IN THE POSTDISASTER SOCIETY

By the end of the impact period, the occurrence of disaster is well defined, alliances have been formed, and priorities have been established within both the various collectivities and official structures. The intergroup relations implied by the formation of stable alliances and competing sets of priorities for disaster work make the postimpact stage intensely political. Bates and his colleagues (1963) asserted that in the wake of Hurricane Audrey "new conflicts arose . . . more severe in consequence for the social system than those that had existed before." Moore (1958) identified the beginning of the period of reorientation as the "brickbat stage" and considered adjustment to the ebbing of altruism to be crucial to the ultimate redefinition of goals that reduced resources (and presumably official priorities) require.

POSTDISASTER INTERACTION AND CONFLICT

Despite the fact that, during disaster, ties of family and site are likely to come into conflict with official authority and legal definitions of contract and property (Wallace, 1956, p. 92; Moore, 1958, pp. 42, 171), students of disaster have not squarely faced the politics of disaster. Disaster research has been geared primarily to the problems of official policy and action within a narrow definition of social control. The problems of officials during disaster are largely distributional. They do not easily include the consideration of particularistic interaction and conflict at the level of popular and local organization. The focus on distribution can be seen in the analysis of some of the more obvious phenomena associated with disaster.

CONVERGENCE BEHAVIOR

Fritz and Mathewson (1957) refer to convergent behavior as an important "source of difficult problems in disaster. Some of its effects, such as traffic congestion, have received much attention" (p. iii). But they pointed out that "all too often . . . it is discussed in terms too general to be helpful, as for example, when the people who move toward the disaster site are lumped uncritically into the category of 'sightseers' " (p. iii). The language dictates some of the problem. The term convergence refers to the refocused distribution of individual behaviors regardless of established patterns of association or the imperatives of interaction. Thus, the use of the term results in a predisposition to the fallacy of combining various recorded data without examining, as meaningful phenomena, the settings in which the data originated. One consequence of this fallacy is to underestimate the importance of collectivities because only a minority of the concerned population may become members. However, collectivities are actors and an unorganized mass is not. The final distribution of a populace depends on—and does not determine—interactions among collectivities that constitute centers of plausibility, attracting and repelling the human particles that comprise a statistical aggregate. After having committed this error, it is tempting to claim that a setting exists by attributing purposes and meanings to converging individuals without adequate or further examination of the particular social situations within which the individual behavior and its purposes and meanings are located and defined. For example, Fritz and Mathewson (1957) followed this procedure in their description of "five major types of informal or unofficial convergers: (1) the *returnees*, (2) the *anxious*, (3) the *helpers*, (4) the *curious*, and (5) the *exploiters*" (p. 29). But if crisis socializes people, the attribution of motives to individuals is of less importance to a theory of collective behavior on the occasion of disaster than the discovery of the boundaries and internal structures of associations within which individuals behave. Private motives do not provide the basis for the antagonisms and political interactions that have been described by Moore (1958) or by Bates and his associates (1963).

Similarly, and more generally, Goffman (1967) has concluded that:

> the proper study of interaction is not the individual and his psychology, but rather the syntactical relations among the acts of different persons mutually present to one another (p. 2).

Although it is true that "a tremendous amount of movement . . . occurs in the disaster area . . ." (Fritz and Mathewson, 1957, p. 64), this movement takes place within settings that are populated by officials and groups different in power, solidarity, and interest and that provide a background—often obscured by the clutter of personnel—within which complex social processes operate. Fritz and Mathewson get to the heart of the matter in a perceptive paragraph that they nevertheless fail to assimilate in their general discussion:

> In effect, what occurs in disasters is a reduction of size in the *unit* of effective communication and action. Individuals, families, and other small groups usually do act adaptively in taking protective and ameliorative action in the post-impact period, but the separate and independent actions of each of these small units often overlap or conflict with one another, creating a total picture of confusion to an outside observer. What the observer is witnessing is disorganization on a societal or community level, but not necessarily disorganization on the small group or individual level (1957, p. 65).

Similarly, Danzig and his associates (1958) hypothesized that people who receive a threat report "while they are part of an intimate group are more likely to behave in a group-oriented manner than are those who are not part of an intimate group" (p. 61). By locating individual behavior in collectivities, Danzig and his associates have qualified the individualistic emphasis of the conclusion of Fritz and Marks (1954) that:

> It is not the irrationality or uncontrolled nature of individual behavior that raises the major control problems in disasters; rather, it is the lack of coordination among the large number of persons acting on the basis of different personal definitions of the situation (p. 41).

Following this conclusion, Fritz and Mathewson (1957) recommended the decentralization of information as one tactic for reducing convergence. Their use of the term convergence at this point is misleading, however. The problem is one of official overload rather than of mass behavior. Moreover, their suggestion evades the central problem: how to coordinate the inherent conflicts among groups, officials, and unaffiliated individuals. More is required than the dissemination of "information" or the control of "rumor."

THE POSTCRISIS SOCIAL ORDER

As has been noted, Suttles' (1968) description of the social order of the slum is suggestive for the understanding of crisis and situated politics. For example, at one point he wrote that "the local people . . . view their way of life as a practical exigency" (p. 234) rather than as a career within a traditional order that is largely taken for granted. The slum is a relatively accessible site for social research, and its organization changes slowly enough to permit reliable observation. As a result, Suttles was able to expose some of the complexities of social organization in crisis that can rarely be discovered under the exigencies of disaster research. His conclusions offer hints as to what the sociologist might search for in future investigations of the politics of disaster.

Intergroup Antagonism. Suttles noted that the antagonisms of emerging groups seem to follow the lines of what he termed a "segmentary system" (p. 30). Social order within such a system is limited by crisis priorities and opportunities for exchange, and reflects the inevitable contradictions of site, traditionally solidaristic relationships, standard networks of communication and control, and official structures. Suttles stated that:

> First, each group is a socio-spatial unit. Second, inclusion in these groupings is mutually exclusive. Third, opposition is between "equivalent" units. Fourth, the order by which groups combine preserves the equivalence of oppositional units. While segmentary systems are usually restricted to corporate groups, however, the ones here include groups that are no more than corporate units of responsibility. Addams area residents are a group only in the sense that they are jointly held liable for each other's behavior (1968, p. 31).

Suttles' description resembles the anarchic model of disaster that has been presented here. In this regard, the most significant feature of the description is that it depicts an intensely political situation in which a populace is sharply divided along exclusive and regularly competitive lines that are continually subject to review. As in the slum, the postdisaster social order includes collectivities that are identified as mutually competent actors exercising specific and explicit claims over territory, tasks, personnel, or definitions of their situation.

The Public Person. As in the slum, in disaster society, members are continually engaged in explicating the socio-political and moral grounds of their acts. Individuals become social facts as they take on the attributes of public figures. The transcendental ego is no longer an accountable property of individual action. Individuals no longer "own" their behavior, nor is their behavior understood as individually pragmatic, personally expressive, or self-identifying (M. Brown, 1969a). Conflict between individuals stems from differences in practice and the fact that individuals are agents for collectivities of interest. This practical insistence that behavior should be read as public, with no egocentric implications, was reported by Bates and his colleagues (1963). They noticed an interesting phenomenon that initially appeared as a methodological problem during their study of Hurricane Audrey:

> It is interesting to note that respondents to the . . . interview could not or would not name leaders in the parish. Furthermore, they would not cite persons who particularly deserved praise because of the roles they performed in rehabilitation. There were only five or six exceptions to this rule in the 61 interviews conducted . . . (p. 60).

Interpersonal Contact. Form and Nosow (1958) reported that the population in four different tornado-struck communities "relied primarily on direct perception and word-of-mouth sources rather than on official disaster agencies" (p. 18). It cannot be denied that mass behavior takes place, but it can be asserted that much of what passes for mass behavior is well organized, differentiated, and complex. In addition, the behavior of collectivities is of greater significance than the motions of masses during disaster.

Popular reliance on interpersonal contact during disaster does not reflect a simple convergence of private persons in order to gain access to reputable sources of information or to attempt to check the accuracy of official reports. It signals a more complex process in which association is affirmed within relatively organized settings for social action and in which the establishment throughout a populace of any particular definition of an untoward occurrence depends upon the operation of socio-political processes. The description of the socio-politics of disaster here, however, is not compatible with Shibutani's (1966) hypothesis that public consensus during crisis tends to move toward those ideas that have utility and that are consistent with the a priori premises or "basic cultural axioms" of the public (chap. 6). The utility and plausibility of these common basic assumptions are matters of interpretation and, therefore, also subject to the socio-political processes involved in disaster. Initially, the definition of utility and plausibility may restrict the range of possible definitions of an occurrence along officially orthodox lines. However, the subsequent socio-political processes are likely to lead in new directions. Although the tendency of rumor content to move "in the direction of greater harmony with shared assumptions" (Shibutani, 1966, p. 179) may be a factor in the emergence of a collective definition of the situation, organization and power are even more important determinants.

ORGANIZATION AND POWER

A collective definition of the situation does not reflect a process of communication within a large following so much as it reflects a political process in which definitions are negotiated among collectivities differing in power and cohesiveness (Bucher, 1957; Goffman, 1963a, b). Because the balance of power and relative cohesiveness are more likely to favor official than unofficial structures during disaster, late disaster and postdisaster politics are characterized by the reappearance of official culture despite the anarchic structure of earlier periods. Official strategy of control during these stages often includes the decentralization of authorized centers of information and the opening of lines of communication between various areas of the stricken community, which reduce the likelihood that strong, independent, local collectivities will be sustained.

The discussion of communication in disaster has revealed two sources of postimpact political conflict. One type of conflict arises from the interplay among collectivities that have equal status relative to disaster work, and the second type of conflict results from the confrontations between those collectivities and official organizations.

Intercollectivity Politics. Collectivities consolidate within a mass of unaffiliated, often marginal, individuals and congeries of collectivities. All of these collectivities make claims and engage in activities that test their integrity and their practical directions. Part of their self-testing includes attempts to avoid confrontation with competitors, especially official agencies, and part of it involves proselytizing among unaffiliated individuals, for whom active collectivities are centers of plausibility. Competition thus involves collectivities in the expansion of practice, and in particular, in the elaboration of their definitions of the situation and in the cooptation of the energies and members of less cohesive assemblies.

Regardless of their adaquacy as rescue units, the survival of collectivities in the postimpact period depends upon the development of a rhetoric and special self-justificatory claims, accounts constructed along the lines of the ideologies of "action bureaucracies" (Krausse, 1968). Survival of collectivities also depends upon the emergence of specialized roles that deal directly with the socio-political aspects of proselytizing, negotiating, and ensuring the continued internal accountability of collective action. Collectivities that maintain their standing during this stage are in a position to influence the processes of postdisaster politics and the development of a final and official account of the occurrence.

The Reemergence of Official Control. The postimpact stage of disaster involves the reemergence of an officially orthodox political center amidst the interplay of power and what Barton (1969) refers to as "vested interests" (p. 225). This stage begins when local collectivities have largely exhausted their resources, have been absorbed by official structures, or have been replaced by alternate or inclusive forms. It usually includes aspects of the so-called emergency social system integrated with the official agencies of predisaster society. Political conflict now centers around the consolidation of official control in the face of residual pockets of resistance. Officials face the problems of neutralizing the surviving unofficial collectivities and mobilizing the populace around official structures and officially authorized activities. For citizens, the problems are to resume normal life, to avoid further suffering, and to receive a just compensation for damage. For surviving unofficial collectivities, the problems are to remain in existence by playing a role, perhaps as pressure groups, in the establishment of official priorities during recovery and to participate as acting bodies in postdisaster politics (Thompson and Hawkes, 1962). Because, at this stage, two different types of constituencies for official action have emerged—groups and individual citizens reconstituted as a public for official action—the successful consolidation of official control may involve playing one off against the other. For example, focusing on the public interest bypasses and weakens special interest collectivities, because it deprives them of the possibility of expanding their base, whereas forming coalitions with powerful special interest collectivities, or even coopting them, may require the deliberate maintenance of an ineffectual and uninformed mass.

The Increase of Official Domination. During the late periods of the postimpact stage, official and authorized channels of communication and official sources of information dominate the culture of the emergency social system. As centers of command, official channels and sources assume priority over the still active interpersonal channels (Thompson and Hawkes, 1962) and shift their focus to authorized topics and official operations so far as is possible. This shift is part of the depoliticization of the populace that characterizes the reemergence, often in exaggerated form, of a conventional political center during late rescue and recovery. The reemergence of authorized channels of communication and official sources of information illustrates the fact that when disaster occurs in a stable and nonrevolutionary situation, it is usually exempt from the dialectical development of a new society following a revolutionary collapse. Insofar as a social structure is hierarchical, stable, and dominated by a relative few, and given the neutralization of the vast majority of the people—especially those in lower positions in the economic and productive order—an untoward occurrence will ultimately substantiate that structure, no matter what the experience of people might be during the occurrence and during its immediate aftermath. Revolution does not occur because of a sudden break in the official order but because events sharpen the divisions that have already been defined for an already politicized populace. Disaster does not provide the opportunity for revolution or even vast social change.

Barton (1969) described the buildup of coordinating or command centers in terms of functional rather than political processes. He suggested that a coordinating center builds up "where there is communication equipment, or a socially central location for interpersonal contact that is known and accessible to the organizations and individuals interested in the disaster" (p. 172). Yet, he hinted at the role of power in this process when he noted that such centers are to some extent self-elaborating and self-perpetuating: "Once a concentration of information builds up, it attracts more communications from those with requests or offers; information 'snowballs' in proportion to the amount already present . . ." (1962, p. 253; 1969, p. 172). As coordinating centers mature, they are increasingly dominated by officials. According to Barton (1969), this domination occurs because officials are usually in a better position than others to use and control facilities and public places (p. 173), but it is also because of the nature of the political struggles that occur at this stage. The relative access of officials to key facilities is illustrated by a comparative study of four tornadoes done by Rosow (1955) and cited by Barton (1969):

> In the town of Harwood there was not much of a local police organzation, but there was an energetic Civil Defense leader who had maps, blood-type lists, and a centrally located office at the town hall. This office became a center of local communications, especially for word-of-mouth, on-foot transmission. The Civil Defense director consulted with the mayor, laid out search and rescue sectors, and dispatched volunteers to these sectors as they arrived at the town hall. A central listing of casualties and damages was virtually complete twelve hours after impact and provided information for all those seeking residents of the impact area (p. 173).

This study also illustrates the proposition that official control is rarely fully relinquished during disaster. The speed and extent to which the populace is depoliticized and official control reestablished depends upon prior official priorities and the state of official preparedness. It also depends upon the major attributes of the striking force and its physical consequences: the scope of the impact, the speed of onset, and the duration of the impact (Barton, 1969). Another important factor is the prior state of the society, in particular the extent to which there was a strong and consolidated political and economic center and relative distance (in terms of the degree of organization and access) between that center in its executive operations and the governed. The prior concentration and stabilization of power affects official priorities and the capacity of officials to reassert themselves during disaster. It is not directly related to the degree to which the reassertion of official control reduces damage within any particular sector of the populace or within the social system as a whole.

Relative Effectiveness of Official Actions. Sjoberg (1962) has pointed out that:

> formal organizational activity and control (especially by the government) increases in the post-disaster period, relative to the pre-disaster situation . . . Indeed, it is only in the modern industrialized and urbanized context that a vast roster of agencies can arise . . . to effectively assist the victims of disaster. Thus in England during World War II it was after various highly organized agencies had come into existence that cities and their inhabitants were really able to adjust to the bombings . . . . Extensive and efficient police, firefighting, ambulance, and rescue corps were all essential to reduce the impact of the recurrent disasters . . . . As a matter of fact, a careful

examination of the research studies on disaster reveals that many of these are geared to probing for more effective means to allow the formal organizations to operate through (and control) the informal ones, and in the end to hasten the reestablishment of normality (pp. 371-72).

Even if official action is seen by the constituency of individual citizens as having minimized damage and suffering, such action can still arouse resistance and backlash on the part of that constituency. Fundamentally, official relief agencies, particularly the Red Cross, whose resources are the greatest, are in an awkward position. Because it is widely known that such organizations have large funds at their disposal, bureaucratic caution and red tape may be resented as a blatantly ungenerous and inhuman response to distress. Differences in attitude and social style loom large in the catalogue of complaints against officials and "outsiders," especially the Red Cross.

The conceptual basis for postdisaster politics now emerges from the juxtaposition of official claims of effectiveness during disaster and of accounts by nonofficial sources. Conflicting claims for credit provide the basis for later blame, justification, excuse, and authority because each account now assumes a definition of the occurrence as an occasion for official action and claims credit for effective support. In this way the question of official responsibility is raised, placing the burden of justification on those in official positions.

THE RETURN TO NORMALCY: LATER POLITICAL DEVELOPMENTS

The special place of disaster in the autobiography of a society is indicated by the persistent importance of an established version of the episode in subsequent public developments. For example, Fritz (1961) cited a "restudy of a midwestern river town conducted more than 15 years after a severe flood in 1937 [that] showed that disaster was still a salient fact in the life of the community" (p. 692). Such persistence is, in part, doubtless supported by the continual reference of official and officially authorized activities to the established version of the disaster. Wallace (1956) noted that following the 1953 tornado in Worcester, Massachusetts, a number of studies were undertaken, often on the initiative of official agencies. He speculated that:

> These post-mortem studies of the effectiveness of counter-measure organizations—Civil Defense, Red Cross, churches, and hospitals in particular—must have resulted in a great many specific alterations and "tightening up" in social organization which are not reflected so much in any physical construction as in disaster plans, inter-agency agreements, and definitions of authority and responsibility . . . (p. 106).

THE ATTRIBUTION OF BLAME

Disaster studies that assume public opinion to be the primary directive mechanism of socio-political change put a great deal of emphasis on a "natural" tendency to interpret disasters punitively. These studies consider disaster and postdisaster politics to be largely made up of popular scapegoating and the attribution of blame. However, Bucher (1957) suggested that although blame often appears in post hoc interviews of individuals, it is not a common feature of disasters. Bucher stated that "this behavior appeared in interviews made in only two out of eight disasters, and there among a minority" (p. 467). However, Bucher's research does not indicate that the postdisaster period is free of politics. Instead, it forces a shift in the analysis of postdisaster politics from the vagaries and vicissitudes of public opinion to the complex interplay of groups, officials, and other system operators. For example, among various studies undertaken by the National Opinion Research Center, those studies relating to a series of three plane crashes in Elizabeth, New Jersey reported considerable attribution of blame. Bucher noted that the disaster situation, in the case of the three plane crashes, had to be viewed as a corrigible one before the blaming occured (p. 471). Indeed, as noted at the beginning of the discussion of disaster, unavoidability is a definitive attribute of disaster. In the case of the plane crashes, the immediate agents of harm—that is, the pilots—had to be distinguished from a wider causal picture of the disaster as somehow natural and beyond agency. Therefore, neither anger nor the assessment of responsibility is to be confused with a generally punitive interpretation of disaster. According to Bucher, in postdisaster politics, blame is ordinarily rationally and carefully assigned, and is normally linked to the desire to prevent future disasters.

The occurrence of blaming assumes a return to some measure of official normalcy. In this sense, and in terms of the discussion of the social and political aspects of disaster, blaming must be seen as part of a well-developed socio-political process rather than as a backlash of diffusely organized public opinion. As a late activity in disaster, fault finding reflects the redefinition of disaster as an occasion for popular support of official action. It rarely preserves any initial definition of the occurrence but concentrates on specific activities and events that took place within the framework of the disaster.

The Issue of Avoidability. When the definition of disaster is itself an issue, the usual claim is that, because of the outcome of the occurrence, the whole train of events must be recast as the result of conspiracy or a dereliction of duty. One party, for example, asserts that "given that a disaster occurred, no one can be blamed either for the occurrence or for the results of activities undertaken during extreme stress." The other party counters with the statement that "had reasonable controls been adequately enforced, the opportunity for disaster would not have arisen." Here, avoidability is the issue, and it arises as part of the political struggle among system operators as they attempt to establish the need for control and to influence the course of political events. Such struggles usually focus on responsibility, credit, and blame, precisely because the only possible political outcome envisaged is in terms of retaining or replacing specific operators rather than in terms of revising the social order itself. This outcome is not due to, as one investigator suggested, a cult of personality that underlies the fabric of American society. Rather, it is due to the fact that publicized politics in America establishes a culture of voting that revolves around personages instead of, for example, a context of conflict, around alternative conceptions of society established as cultures of work and transformed into political practice within interest-based parties. For example, postdisaster politics involves at least two distinct but related processes, public pressure and conflict among public operators. Public pressure standardizes politics by establishing boundaries within which conflict takes place among public operators. Such pressure reflects partisan considerations and the publication of claims. Following a disaster, publics often regroup around former or newly prominent operators simply by way of affirming the shared identities and practices appropriate to a putative return to normalcy. Marginal operators such as administrators of official agencies, or major operators who are not clearly identifiable with particular publics, are often subjected to a critique that refers to accounts of disaster experience that are widely taken as representative—in that sense, as public property. Abney and Hill (1966) report that public officials who volunteered to serve on relief boards have claimed that controversies growing out of their relief roles resulted in a loss of votes.

The reassertion of official control requires the transformation of the disaster society into publics differentiated along traditional lines: classes, territorial bounds, and traditioned political groupings. Publics are seldom found to emerge whose members are linked solely by similar disaster experiences. Form and Nosow support this hypothesis by their suggestion that resentment toward Red Cross workers often varies with class. They report that resentment may be more frequently expressed by lower middle class recipients of aid, who have become thwarted status aspirants as a result of the disaster, than by the very poor, for whom disaster raises no questions pertinent to status (Form and Nosow, 1958, p. 208). Support is also provided by reported differences in postdisaster attitudes between black and white citizens. Moore (1958) reported that despite the greater relative deprivation suffered by black people during disaster, they did not consistently criticize the Red Cross more than did white people. Blacks were, however, consistently more willing to criticize the performance of governmental agencies (p. 151). On questions relating to governmental agencies, Moore found that about half of the black people questioned declined to comment, compared to one-fifth of the white people. Moore also found that 78 percent of the blacks, as opposed to 60 percent of the whites, responded favorably to the Red Cross; 80 percent of the whites, as opposed to 64 percent of the blacks, responded favorably to city government; and 71 percent of the whites, as opposed to 47 percent of the blacks, responded favorably to the federal government. Such figures may reflect black consciousness of institutional racism and of the relationship between race and the inequalities in the distribution of damage and relief in a disaster (see Barton, 1962, p. 246).

Similarly, the formidable formal intricacies of applying for disaster relief puts a premium on familiarity with bureaucratic and political organization. The capacity to make effective claims for public resources depends upon established social differences, such as class, race, or geographical location. In such situations, conventional political antagonisms are exacerbated or allowed to continue unquestioned.

POSTDISASTER POLITICAL PRESSURE

Both public pressure and conflict among public or official operators may leave traces in legislation and executive practice. However, unless damage has been so catastrophic that the subsequent social order is treated as new rather than as a return to normal, it is difficult to assess the political repercussions of a disaster. For example, in Abney and Hill's (1966) study of the New Orleans mayoral elections that followed a hurricane and extensive flooding in 1965, ninety-two voters in the flooded area and ninety-nine voters in the unflooded areas were interviewed in order to determine differences in political attitudes attendant upon the disaster experience. In the unflooded areas, 28 percent of the ninety-nine voters rated the city's protection poor and, Abney and Hill added, "many of them used more explicit language to express their hostility." The same people also complained about the city's warning procedures, but hostility was so deflected from officials that even some of the flood victims praised the mayor and his work. Forty-seven percent of those in the flooded area and 36 percent of those in the unflooded areas said that they believed that the hurricane would affect the outcome of the mayoral election. But, when asked which organizations should be criticized for their actions in connection with the disaster, 63 percent of the voters in the flooded area and 66 percent of the voters in the unflooded areas replied that no one should be criticized.

The findings reported by Abney and Hill may highlight the difficulty of assigning blame after a disaster; it is not clear why it is not equally difficult to assign credit. It may be relevant to note that the setting within which interviewing and questionnaire answering takes place encourages a responsiveness that is invariably remote from the action setting referred to by the interviews and questionnaires (Cook et al., 1970). In this case, the political significance of such utterances is unclear. Although people can express attitudes when asked and may, in fact, have strong feelings about the topic in question, their political activity, including active participation in the public assignment of credit and blame, is held in abeyance unless and until they are engaged in a genuine political setting, such as that usually provided by publicized controversy among political operators. Because such controversy usually takes place along traditional political lines and ordinarily includes a multiplicity of topics besides disaster, expressions of popular resentment related to disaster, in themselves, are not likely to produce much in the way of politically relevant behavior or social change.

THE RETURN TO PREDISASTER PATTERNS

Perhaps the generalization that emerges most persistently from a review of the literature is that postdisaster politics like the distribution of information before and after the impact of disaster, takes a course that is consistent with predisaster patterns. Clifford's (1956) comparison of behavior during a flood of the Rio Grande that threatened neighboring American (Eagle pass, Texas) and Mexican (Piedras Negras) towns illustrates the continuity of disaster behavior with traditional patterns of social action, and thus the occasional character of collective behavior during disaster. In the family-centered Mexican community, the family was the focal point of behavior during and after the flood. In contrast, the Americans relied heavily on nonfamilial associations and official agencies for instructions and relief. However, this conclusion may be criticized on the grounds that reliance on family was reasonable rather than just habitual in the Mexican community, because official structures were weak and ineffectual. The damage was much greater in Piedras Negras than in Eagle Pass: 150 deaths to none, and 1,300 homes destroyed to only 55.

A source of potential conflict in the rehabilitation phase following a disaster occurs at the point where disaster operations provide explicit reminders of the normal patterns of discrimination, exploitation, and oppression in predisaster society. However, opposition to these undercurrents rarely emerges as an aspect of postdisaster politics. In fact, previous status differences appear to be reaffirmed as easily as if the possibility of rectifying them had never been raised, and old ideologies are reiterated to provide moral and political sanction for the reappearance of the differences. It is interesting that the occurrence of disaster does not ordinarily produce a critical attitude toward discrimination, exploitation, and oppression, just as it does not produce a reorganization of relations among the various strata of a community. Following the equalizing effects of disaster, there is little shame attached to a resumption of old distinctions of class, race, sex, and material advantage. Rather, prior ideologies replace the situated socialistic ideologies of the disaster period. Disaster victims are forced to play out their status fate as if loss was a part of their natural condition and as if the overwhelmingly unjust circumstances of predisaster discrimination and all its implications has not been exposed. It is the old society that is rehabilitated, a process aided by provisional rules, special social affairs, and a rhetoric that allow members of the society to rehearse the justifications of the conventional order, even before it reappears. Fervent expressions of religious piety, patriotism, or community loyalty frequently follow disaster. For example, at some point, disaster victims are expected to drop "inappropriate dependencies" and to apply for relief, but they are expected to receive whatever they get in a spirit of gratitude and appreciation (Wallace, 1956, p. 124). Moreover, they are expected to uncritically resume old statuses without "using" the disaster experience and its equalizing aspects to question the basis of old social, economic, and political distinctions. Such are the ground rules for postdisaster politics. They reduce the strains attendant upon the sudden visibility of the unappetizing facts of life hidden beneath the political surface of traditionally hierarchic society.

UNIT I: SUMMARY

Collective behavior, as a subject, is vaguely defined, and it is difficult to know where to draw the limits of inquiry. The boundaries of the subject often seem to have been chosen quite arbitrarily, under the pressure of historical and political conditions. The study of collective behavior was introduced by the topic of disaster under the assumption that the phenomena recorded by disaster researchers would be relatively clear and that the conceptions of collective behavior during disaster would be politically and morally neutral. However, like the study of collective behavior itself, disaster research has shown considerable elasticity of subject matter and a similar responsiveness to official concerns and elite perspectives.

Disaster was initially viewed as a manifestation of the violence of nature, just as crowds were first studied as manifestations of the violence of man. As a topic for research during the 1950s and 1960s, disaster was investigated under the auspices of a government more centralized and militarized than at any other time in American history and deeply concerned with the prospect of thermonuclear war. The desire to preserve the official order under all conditions engendered an interest in sudden, system-wide danger and in methods of warning and protecting key sections of the population. Because the requirements of civil defense were highly relevant to the investigation of disasters, early disaster studies often included information gathered in the wake of bombing attacks. The results of studies of Hiroshima and the bombed cities of Europe were applied to the general problems of panic, convergence, rumor, and the maintenance of official organization and control.

An examination of various attempts to construct a sociology of disaster leads to the conclusion that neither a causal nor a functional analysis is sufficient to explain the behavior regularly associated with disaster. Functional analysis, of the sort represented by Barton's (1969) model of the emergency social system, assumes an overall solidarity within the affected territory that is not justified by empirical research. It also assumes disinterest, flexibility, and precision of official response to the practical exigencies of official projects such as warning, rescue, and rehabilitation. However, close observation of official behavior during disasters suggests that such assumptions are misleading. Ultimately, functional analysis has failed to distinguish official structures from institutions and from formal organization. Consequently, it has neither differentiated official actions from the operations of the social system itself nor clarified the crucial relationship between official and unofficial activities in disaster situations.

Causal analysis has been applied almost exclusively to the unauthorized activities—that is, behavior that has been defined as problematic to the official order of disaster work—of unofficial groups. Thus, Janis (1962) speaks of the information provided by a "warning" rather than of the use of published material as an instrument of social and political control. His assumption that collective behavior during disaster can be controlled through the manipulation of the content of official messages delivered to the public appears to reflect official hopes more than the facts of social life. The failure to specify the perspective from which phenomena are defined and problems are posed for research has placed causal analysis within the framework of official practice.

Causal analysis has not been a successful method within general sociology. Because of the relative ease of fitting material gathered from individuals in isolation to its models, it is associated with the psychological reductionism characteristic of the work of Janis (1962) and, to some extent, Lang and Lang

(1964). As a result, it has not provided useful propositions for a sociology of disaster. Furthermore, the major factors that have been isolated for causal analysis—fear, anxiety, emergency, stress, adaptation, warning, organization, information, ambiguity, degree of threat, occurrence, and action—have not been defined independently of the settings in which these variables are alleged to be causes and effects.

Here, the study of collective behavior during disaster began by moving in a different theoretic direction. The ordinary use of the term "disaster" was examined, and it was concluded that disaster must be understood as a type of definition of a situation. This suggestion became compelling because most of the available models for disaster research were either too specific in their focus on types of behavior (looting, panic, convergence, flight, warning) alleged to occur during disaster or too general to be useful in distinguishing disaster behavior from behavior in other situations. The overspecificity of models such as that of Lang and Lang (1964) excluded from theoretic consideration many of the features of disaster that have been described in literature. The overgenerality of models, such as Sjoberg's (1962), seemed to lead to questionable hypotheses— for example, that disaster, similar to war and revolution, supports basic changes in the social order.

It was necessary, then, to develop an approach that could distinguish disaster from other affairs involving collective behavior. Such an approach would have to take advantage of the observation that disaster has been studied from a particular socio-political perspective that has not, itself, been investigated but that appears to resemble the perspective of official practice. In addition, an acceptable approach to the study of disaster would have to examine the variety of social activities that occur during disaster, particularly the interactions between official structure and unofficial assemblies and the interactions that take place between the various unofficial assemblies.

Four components of the definition of disaster were identified:

1. An occurrence must be taken as impinging upon a particular, identifiable, social system that is acknowledged by those who define the occurrence as their own,
2. The reputedly affected social system is known as a complex, extended, and permanent organization,
3. The occurrence is taken as having been unavoidable,
4. The occurrence is taken as sudden.

Together, these components establish a special social occasion, a wider affair, in terms of which specific structures and behaviors are socially organized and meaningful. As an element of the "social stock of knowledge" (Berger and Luckmann, 1967), the occasion of disaster entails specific forms of interaction, statuses, facilities, roles, stages, agenda, modes of account, and so on.

An analysis of disaster as an occasion establishes a basis for examining the meaningful organization of behavior during disaster, particularly the relationship between specific and novel activities and the wider affair that makes those activities intelligible to a large number of people and groups, most of whom are not in direct contact with one another. Basing a discussion on the nature of an occasion requires that a rather detailed discussion of the social process of definition be undertaken. The usual treatments of communication, publics, and rumor were inadequate to explain how disaster settings generate the sharing of responses and the formation of social units. There are also inadequacies in the use of a decision model in which information, circumstances, practical considerations, and the like are defined independently of the decision maker and his setting. The rationality of action does not depend upon the ability of the actor to fulfill some objectively defined set of goals but upon the sense that can be made of the action with reference to a particular occasion.

Insofar as disaster is a genuine social occasion, the definition of which is part of the social stock of knowledge, it is a socially "normal" event; people know how "to be" a disaster victim just as they know how "to be" sick, grief-stricken, a criminal, or a victim of an accident. Status as a "victim" does not stem from the quality of the individual's experience of harm, loss, or injury but from his participation in a society in which people recognize such experiences. Nevertheless, the problems posed to participants by disaster do not lend themselves to routine solutions.

Disaster entails a polarization of social reference that raises questions about the social identity of disaster settings and the proper location of individuals on the occasion of disaster. The organization of the action settings is an "ongoing accomplishment," an aspect rather than a parameter of activity. The social activities that occur during disaster identify their participants and their collective definitions of the situation at the same time that they accomplish practical tasks. Thus, the definition of reality is a political necessity as well as part of the practice of collectivities engaged in disaster work.

Disaster society can be viewed as a congeries of collective units rather than as a mass (Lang and Lang, 1964) or as a social system (Barton, 1969). The picture is one in which intensively organized collectivities dot a pluralized environment. In this setting, the precise definition of any given situation is a highly charged political issue. Inevitably, patterns of interference emerge among the various collectivities. Consequently, their interactions appear as socio-political processes involving negotiation, defense, proselytizing, power plays, and other political phenomena.

There are three basic conflicts that dominate the politics of disaster: intercollectivity interference; interference between official structures and non-official assembles; and traditional socially structured differences that persist within the disaster society. In addition, there are political activities that arise as interference ripens into conflict. In particular, official claims to legitimate hegemony over disaster society are usually bolstered by specific acts of control. It was also noted that local collectivities tend to deal with the problems of interference by proselytizing among unofficial assemblies and that such collectivities may resist official attempts to absorb and control them.

MODERN THEORIES OF COLLECTIVE BEHAVIOR

CHAPTER SEVEN

COLLECTIVE BEHAVIOR: THE FIELD AND ITS TRADITIONS

Theoretical efforts to understand collective behavior preceded serious research. The most recent attempts to develop a theory of collective behavior lean heavily on disaster studies such as presented in Unit I, but the paradigms of the major theoretical views were well established before World War II. These paradigms dominated description and explanation and helped to substantiate public and official responses to collective behavior. Indeed, the paradigms themselves were often part of those responses.

The empirical study of collective behavior undertook the examination of a catalogue of exceptions to the social activities expected by social theorists. It was primarily a catalogue of whatever was unofficial and unauthorized in social life. This catalogue included activities such as riot and rebellion, often thought by those who described them to be morally repugnant. But the catalogue also included such casual manifestations of collective involvement as fads and aspects of culture and politics that could not be assimilated by consensus theory (e.g., fashion, style, social movements).

The relatively simple theoretical ideas that arose as crisis accounts (response to collective behavior) became elaborate as they found points of articulation with general sociological theories. When theorists attempted to accomodate the findings provided by research on disaster to their paradigms, they focused on episodes that had been thought common in the past, but that are now known to be rare and relatively unimportant among the various activities that occur on the occasion of disaster—for example, panic. It was not until the "decade of protest," the 1960s, that new areas of research were opened and the proper theoretical explanation of collective behavior again became an issue. However, the legacy of the earlier period consists of beliefs about collective behavior that still pervade the field. These beliefs are still taken for granted whenever a social event is described as deviant (beyond the operation of the usual social controls) and is composed of the activities of a large number of people in relative proximity to one another.

THE FIELD AND ITS SUBJECT MATTER

Between 1882 and 1951, there were 4,725 reported lynchings in the United States, which is an average of one lynching every five and one-half days over a span of sixty-nine years. Of the victims, 3,432 were black (R. Brown, 1954, p. 848). In 1919, in addition to the riots that swept the country (Waskow, 1966), there were sixteen pogroms—violent attacks on black communities by gangs of white people. Although the period between 1919 and the 1960s was hardly calm, 1967 saw the cities of America explode in sudden complaint, an overwhelming but ultimately doomed surge toward liberation: a vast moment sandwiched between epochs of racism, oppression, and despair.

THE 1967 URBAN DISORDERS

Between January and September of 1967, 164 civil disturbances were recorded in which residents of urban black ghettoes attacked white-owned businesses and harrassed law enforcement officials. Whether these occurrences were tension-induced riots facilitated by a mixture of weather, incident, and personality, or protests against what Stokely Carmichael and Charles Hamilton (1967) called "oppressive colonialism" depends upon the perspective (Turner, 1969). Many of the participants who were interviewed following the events explained their participation in terms of protest, citing a host of grievances ranging from police brutality to unemployment, bad housing, and enforced poverty. As protest, the 1967 urban disorders might have been understood as an escalation of negotiable demands by a black community that had long been too patient and too willing to follow the course of institutions. However, the first, and ultimately the most significant official response came from the police and the National Guard and was a mixture of attack and containment followed by political repression. In the two cities of Detroit, Michigan and Newark, New Jersey, 68 deaths and 1,049 injuries were reported. The vast majority of those killed and injured were the victims of retaliatory action that involved the often overzealous employment of firearms, tear gas, and other weapons for civilian control. Moreover, official policy was dominated by an interpretation of those events as violent mass behavior. The capability of quasi-military domestic forces was improved, but little was done to heal the conditions of life that so oppressed black people and the poor or to recognize the legitimacy of their demands for power.

Interpretive Options. The choice of this interpretative option—seeing the events of 1967 as violent mass behavior—depended partly upon factors endemic to American politics (Marcuse, 1968), partly upon the orthodoxy of officially stimulated public opinion, and partly upon the way in which the events were presented by the mass media. Aggression, particularly on the part of under-groups, seems undemocratic, presumptuous, and self-indulgently defiant of authority in the liberal capitalist state. Moreover, attacks on property and large scale roaming are not credible as acts of communication or negotiation in the ordinary course of events. There is no American interpretative tradition by which these actions can be classified as political activities (Silver, 1969). The mass media tended to treat the events as the work of a small minority, which suggested an explosion of the impatient rather than the end product of a gathering storm. For these reasons and others, it is not surprising that public interpretations of the 1967 events tended to focus on irrational mass violence in which the many were led by the few. Like many public interpretations of public events, this version was encouraged by officials of both state and federal governments (see also Myers, 1948).

Implications of "Protest." An interpretation of collective behavior as protest acknowledges the possible righteousness of the action and makes an issue of official performance. Similarly, an interpretation of such behavior as political action envisions the possibility of a change in the structure or distribution of power in society. For these reasons, officials tend to adopt the interpretation that does not threaten their position. Events such as those of 1967 are thus considered simple violations of the law or "collective deviance." Of the many research reports submitted to the government following the "decade of protest," the conclusions of the Kerner Commission Report (National Advisory Commission Civil Disorders, 1968), the Skolnick Report (1969), and the Walker Report (1968) were largely ignored. The Kerner Commission Report spoke of the grievances of black people and the role of police in civil strife; the Skolnick Report suggested that a political interpretation was essential if America was to avoid becoming a police state; the Walker report recorded a "police riot" by Chicago law enforcement officials during the 1968 Democratic National Convention. Not one of these reports was accepted as an authorized version of the events it had been commissioned to describe.

Whether riot or protest, the 1967 episodes came thirteen years after the Brown decision on school desegregation. Seven years after the desegregation decision the civil rights movement began to use the sit-in—a tactic developed in the course of worker struggles—to attack the discrimination and racism that had oppressed black people since the days of the Reconstruction. During 1960 and 1961, 50,000 Americans took part in a variety of nonviolent civil rights protests; 3,600 of whom spent time in jail (Zinn, 1965; Newfield, 1967, p. 38).

THE PROTEST AGAINST THE VIETNAM WAR

By 1966, the sit-in had become a conventional method of demonstrating dissent, and by 1968, thousands of college students had participated in protests. They protested the United States invasion of Vietnam, university support of the military through defense research, ROTC programs, political repression, and recruitment by defense industries on campus. These protests took many forms: buildings were occupied on countless American campuses, variants of the sit-down strike and the civil rights sit-in; and rallies and marches took place as national politics grew vivid in contrast to the conventionality of local politics. Hundreds of thousands of people of all ages marched through the streets of New York, Washington, D.C., San Francisco, and other large cities in protest against the Vietnam war. As American involvement in Vietnam continued and escalated, protest grew; previously diverse issues gave way to a radical and structural critique of the social system; complaint was replaced by organization; and the spectre of political repression began to haunt America.

THE 1968 DEMOCRATIC NATIONAL CONVENTION

The coercive capacity and repressive potential of government was dramatically revealed during the 1968 Democratic National Convention in Chicago, when thousands demonstrated against the war. The demonstration took place after the city government had denied requests for parade permits and the use of various city parks and after the mayor had banned demonstrations, promising harsh treatment of any demonstrators during the time of the convention. Television viewers were given a ringside view as Chicago police indiscriminately assaulted civilians with fists and clubs. A number of delegates at the convention protested what one United States senator called the "gestapo tactics" of the Chicago police. The mayor charged the demonstrators with inciting the police by insults and argued that the use of official violence was restrained in the face of the provocation. The Walker Report (1968) to the National Commission on the Causes and Prevention of Violence (1969) disagreed.

HISTORICAL EXAMPLES OF COLLECTIVE BEHAVIOR IN THE UNITED STATES

Ghetto riots, student protest, and mass demonstrations are the classical phenomena of collective behavior. Yet, the events of the 1960s were hardly without precedent in the United States. The Skolnick Report (1969) criticized the "myth of peaceful progress" that described American history as a mixture of the melting pot and peaceful change (pp. 8-9). The report referred to regularly experienced "episodes of mass violence directly related to the achievement of social, political, and economic objectives" (p. 10). It listed, as examples, the nineteenth-century Indian revolts "aimed at securing their land and liberty against invasion by white settlers supported by colonial, state, and federal governments . . . . The suppression of Indian revolts was the chief occupation of the U.S. Army for more than a century after its creation" (pp. 10-11). Among many other events, the list also included:

the Whiskey and Fries rebellions in Pennsylvania
the wars of the Regulators
the war of the New Hampshire Grants
Shays' Rebellion
civil disobedience during the Stamp Act controversy
the American Revolution
civil disobedience during the Nullification controversy of 1828-1830
the Civil War
the terrorism following the surrender at Appomattox
lynchings
the "Native American" onslaughts against the Irish in Philadelphia in 1844
    and similar riots in Baltimore, Boston and other cities
collective assaults on Jews, Italians, Chinese, Japanese, and other immi-
    grant groups
the New York draft riots of 1863
the warfare between workers and capitalists that began in the 1870s
the Haymarket Square bombing and retaliation in 1886
the series of strikes by railroad men, steel workers, and others that resulted
    in the use of federal troops by the government
the riots of 1919
The Detroit riot of 1943.

THE RANGE OF ISSUES

There have been militant protests by members of all socioeconomic classes about issues ranging from compulsory military service to desegregated schooling, from taxation without representation to a refusal by the city of New York to aid landlords by removing rent controls, and from the expression of unpopular views on governmental policy to the expression of hostility toward dissenters. These protests have often resulted in pitched battles between police or government troops and civilians, and occasionally among the various civilian groups themselves.

But political violence is not the only dramatic form of collective behavior to appear regularly in America. The youth riots during school vacations at Fort Lauderdale, the campus panty raids that took place during the 1950s, and the various fads that captured large segments of the American public as advertising reached new pinnacles of sophistication and the commodities of leisure began to dominate the imagery of the American scene are all examples of collective behavior. Also included in the subject matter of the field are the peaceful political protests that took place during the 1960s in response to national policies on war, civil rights, and dissent.

COLLECTIVE BEHAVIOR IN EUROPE

Crowds, militant political action, and official force are not peculiarly American phenomena. Europe also has a long history of unauthorized political and social action. As in America, such activities have usually been issue-oriented and have occurred after official channels for the regulation of conflict have failed. A significant example, in which the myth still overshadows the facts, is that of the Luddites in nineteenth-century England. The Luddites were tightly coordinated bands of workers who destroyed the new machinery of mass production in the textile industries. The Luddite movement appeared in the wake of a severe economic depression that reached a climax in 1811 following the Napoleonic wars, when the impact of the collapse of trade between Britain and America was most sharply felt in the hosiery, cotton, and woolen industries. The social implications of the Industrial Revolution were still imperfectly understood, and the humanitarian efforts to relieve poverty through legislation such as the Poor Laws coexisted with the absolute belief in an employer's right to cut labor costs and maximize profits in any way he chose. Under these circumstances, and prior to the development of unions, the laboring class was virtually identified with "the poor." Because the chief hope of the poor ultimately and officially depends upon the generosity of the rich, the virtue most heavily enjoined upon the workers was patience.

In Europe, technological unemployment appeared very early, and "impatient" workers had occasionally destroyed the machinery that weakened their position as far back as 1710 in France. In England, the Luddites, named after the mythical Ned Ludd, deliberately employed the old tactic of machinery destruction in order to force concessions on the part of manufacturers after negotiations and peaceful protest had failed. Newspapers and officials of the day described the Luddites as "ignorant rabble" and "criminal mobs" who wanted to prevent "progress." However, the Luddites enjoyed widespread popular support and were well organized and selective both in their targets and in the means used against them (Rude, 1964).

More recently, 120 years after the "year of revolution" in Europe, the spring of 1968 saw revolt in France. The revolt was led by hundreds of thousands of students and a larger number of workers. Schools and factories were taken over and the streets became battlegrounds for civilians and police. In the same year, Mexican student demonstrators, protesting the alleged violations of traditional university autonomy by government police, were harshly repressed. In one case, a police attack on dispersing demonstrators left forty-seven civilians dead and hundreds injured and arrested. Similar events occurred in most of the major countries of the western hemisphere and in many of those in the East, notably Japan and India.

COLLECTIVE BEHAVIOR: CONVENTIONAL AND UNCONVENTIONAL

Such events comprise the drama of collective behavior, a drama that has singled out these events, and others like them, in history and produced a field of specialized study, the theories of which presumably apply to less noticeable events as well. Collective behavior is ubiquitous and, considering the events listed above, it appears to be unconventional. But how unconventional a phenomenon is it? It may be said that the formation and the subsequent acts of a crowd are unconventional by definition, because a crowd is a temporary social unit engaging in behavior that is always unauthorized and often illegal. On the other hand, even conventional social life is not free of crowdlike behavior. Some of the most time-honored institutions are characterized by such behavior: the development of bandwagon sentiments at political conventions; the behavior of large audiences at athletic contests, at rallies, or at parades led by a national hero; the gossip that often accompanies the discovery of discrediting information about well-known figures; the public adulation of movie stars; and so on.

One explanation for collective behavior that has been suggested is that people have an innate preference for acting in concert, on the model of children playing follow-the-leader or of animals living in herds or flocks. In contrast, the fact that choice is always limited should be noted. Every situation seems to pose its own set of contingencies and available alternatives, which implies that human beings may be individually selective. But when choice is limited, people who happen to make the same selections will appear conformative even though they are not. Moreover, where the array of behavioral alternatives is taken to be of low quality, any choice can seem to imply a debased standard of judgment, which, from the actor's standpoint, may not be the case at all. Another factor to be considered is that activities that appear to an outsider to be conformative in the motivational sense are often acts of participation.

COLLECTIVE BEHAVIOR: THE CROWD

All the phenomena discussed above have been labeled collective behavior. These phenomena have also been classified as social movements, publics, mass behavior, and crowds. The concept most useful for present purposes is th, the crowd because the literature on collective behavior has emphasized crowds and crowdlike actions. Publics, the mass, and social movements can be more fruitfully discussed in other contexts (see chap. 1). "Public opinion," for example, describes the response of a collection of individuals to an issue; it is a shared state of knowledge, belief, or preference, but it does not involve interaction among the assembled members. The socio-political significance of the public depends upon its function as constituency and on the capacity of each member to act on the basis of his opinion—for example, to vote or to write a letter. But the public has no corporate capacity; it is not, in Parson's terms, a system of social action. "Mass" is used in referring to a large focused gathering that is considered independently of all organizational ties. The term is also used to describe the condition of a collection of individuals in which organizational ties are broken. In this sense, "mass" refers to phenomena that are best described in other ways—for example, social unrest. The mass is part of the development of many episodes of collective behavior, but is not a distinctive form in itself. Social movements can be discussed as conflict organizations that resemble other transsituational systems of social action.

The term "crowd" is generally used to refer to a social unit whose action is distinctively recognizable as collective behavior. The precise nature of the crowd is difficult to specify. The term "crowd" is marginal to theory and common sense. It invariably applies to "an event" known "to have occurred," where that knowledge is taken for granted and is the product of a process not usually thought to be problematic. As discussed in chapter 1, most theorists argue that collective behavior (the crowd) is uninstitutionalized action (Smelser, 1963) occurring outside the norms of the larger society (Turner, 1964) or that collective behavior includes "those patterns of social action that are spontaneous and unstructured inasmuch as they are not organized and are not reducible to social structure" (Lang and Lang, 1961, pp. 3-4). Thus, the term collective behavior is ordinarily applied to behavior that is unexpected, unconventional, and/or unauthorized; that takes place within a given collectivity, which is any collection of people in some relation to each other; and that is initially uncontrolled. The term usually refers to precipitant social events that constitute a large-scale reorganization of a collectivity over a period of time too short for conventional routines or norms to take effect. In brief, collective behavior is considered by most sociologists to be action that is unofficial, unconventional, precipitant, and short lived or episodic, and that occurs throughout the collectivity. Taken together, this set of traits is not characteristic of movements, of publics, or of masses.

TRADITIONS IN THE STUDY OF COLLECTIVE BEHAVIOR

Modern theories of collective behavior are the conceptual residues that were selected from among various paradigmatic options as sociology grew. Not all the views cited by Roger Brown (1954) in his monumental survey contributed to the traditions that became the culture of the field.

THE LEGACY OF THE NINETEENTH CENTURY

The elitist perspective of Taine and Burke overcame Michelet's emphasis on the quality of popular protest. The former was a perspective that blended well with what the period defined as social problems and with the social disorganization critique of the crowd and of popular protest that was common prior to World War II. Moreover, the description of the crowd as lacking substantial goals within a culture of disorder provided a category of pathology that highlighted a rational and functionalist model of social organization. For the proponents of this model, collective behavior represented action under conditions in which goals were not operational because they were part of collective beliefs that were contradictory to fact, because the goals were beyond the capacity of the collectivity, or because appropriate means were not available.

The views of Taine, Burke, and eventually LeBon (1960) were the nineteenth-century legacy to the twentieth-century sociology of collective behavior. The persistence of these views was a result of the peculiar relationship between theory and official practice during periods of conflict and change in society. Moreover, that persistence reveals a class bias in social science that is represented by an often implicit preference for elite structures and authorized and genteel forms of dissent, and an often explicit denigration of the judgment and behavior of the "lower orders" of society. It also reveals something about the relationship of theory to its patrons and sponsors.

During periods of societal crisis, mainstream theories directed at crisis itself tend to shade explicitly into ideology and, more than at any other time, reveal the practice context of their inquiry. Crisis mobilizes official structures, thereby activating the obligations of sponsored personnel, particularly intellectuals. During crisis, the growth of a theoretical tradition as a process of selection and simplification demonstrates the loyalties, identifications, and professional options of theorists, as well as the prior distribution of paradigms within social science. The growth of a theoretical tradition also demonstrates the capacity of official structures to identify the traditions in apparently neutral fields as belonging to a system of official values, interests, and perspectives.

Collective behavior is usually studied as an aspect of social and political change. Interest in crowds and allied phenomena has always been greatest when society is most tumultuous. In nineteenth-century Europe, theories of collective behavior developed in the context of the intense social conflict and unrest that accompanied industrialization, urbanization, and the growth of large bureaucracies. Faced with sharpened discontinuities in social life, many previously liberal scholars looked upon the currents of their time with horror. They saw the reform movements within the working classes, the Paris Commune, and the French Revolution as eroding their most cherished values. They saw collective behavior as a symptom of a mass society emerging from the ashes of a disintegrating social order (Bramson, 1961; Rude, 1964). Out of their horror they developed a vivid picture of collective behavior as wanton irrational mobbism, and as an expression of society's "dangerous classes" (Silver, 1967). According to Rude (1964):

the French historian Taine, . . . though a liberal in 1848, had, . . . been soured by his experience of the Paris Commune. To him the revolutionaries of 1789 and the captors of the Bastille were the lowest social scum: "dregs of society," "bandits," "savages," and "ragamuffins"; the insurgents of October were "street-prowlers," "thieves," "beggars," and "prostitutes"; and those of August 1792, who drove Louis XVI from the Tuileries palace, were blood-thirsty adventurers, "foreigners," "bullies," and "agents of the debauchery" (p. 8).

The crowd seemed to be an outburst of people whose ties to each other—ties essential for the preservation of social order—had been broken. Burke, in England, and Taine, in France, saw the decay of the family, the erosion of authority, and the persistence of the individuating egalitarian ideals of the Revolution as society's loss of control over its members, in particular, members of the working class. They supposed that a populace detached from traditional culture and the social structures by means of which culture is transmitted inherently unstable, anxious, and susceptible to demagoguery.

Leon Bramson (1961) has argued that this view of the crowd is based on the assumption that human nature is selfish and impulsive unless kept in close check by institutionalized authority. Many proponents of this view were politically conservative and protective of the existing forms of society, which had been projected from positions of privilege. Consequently, they were hostile to forces pressing for radical social change, and they were likely to view any shift in the prerogatives of wealth, power, and privilege as far too radical or extreme. This ideological base is explicit in LeBon and even in the writings of Taine, the liberal historian; the ideology is characteristic of many of their American counterparts in the twentieth century, although a somewhat different tradition developed in the United States.

THE GROWTH OF SOCIOLOGY IN THE UNITED STATES

Despite a heavy European influence, sociology in the United States developed a unique perspective that was characterized by an interdisciplinary tradition, a positivistic program, and a liberal political philosophy. These components insured that American sociology would focus on social problems and offer solutions that were reformist and progressive. It is within this framework that American sociologists turned their attention to collective behavior.

Similar to Europe in the nineteenth century, the United States entered the twentieth century on the waves of social upheaval. In America, the formal study of collective behavior grew out of the interracial clashes of 1919 in Washington, D.C., Chicago, and other sections of the country. The commission appointed by the governor of Illinois to investigate the Chicago riots was influenced by University of Chicago sociologist Robert Ezra Park. The report of the Chicago Commission on Race Relations (1922), similar to the Kerner Commission Report (1968) on the 1967 urban disorders and characteristic of Park's viewpoint, focused on the grievances and frustrations of the black community.

Neither the clashes themselves nor the political and structural origins of powerlessness and deprivation were emphasized.

Park had explained collective behavior as part of the process of societal change—an initial stage that exposed the necessity for reform. He was concerned with the conditions that give rise to episodes of collective behavior and the ways in which collective behavior fits into the life of the society. In 1921, Park and his colleague E. W. Burgess published an important textbook, *Introduction to the Science of Sociology*, which included a discussion of the forms of interaction that take place in two types of collective behavior: that of the crowd and that of the public. In this way, and with descriptive techniques he developed, Park began the task of analyzing the crowd and opened the way for the more thorough theoretical treatment of the problem that developed some thirty-five years later.

Although Park accepted the general characterization of the crowd that developed in France and Italy, he differed from the Europeans in refusing to dissociate the crowd from its context and its long-range consequences. His discussion of the forms of interaction typical of collective behavior, specifically his distinction between the crowd and the public, suggested that there are social processes and a social order within the crowd. Thus, he introduced the sociology of groups and organizations into the study of collective behavior, which pointed out the fact that collective behavior is a normal part of any social system. As Freud did in the field of psychology, Park questioned the sharp distinction that had been drawn between the "abnormal" and the "normal" in social life. Most important, and perhaps partly because of the political neutralization of the working class in America, collective behavior was no longer seen as a threat to the established order. In this regard, Bramson (1961) noted that: "The rise of the masses as signifying the end of civilization is replaced by an evolutionary conception of institutions, in which crowd behavior represents the initial stages" (p. 64). Despite this fruitful beginning, however, collective behavior has not yet been fully integrated into academic sociology. Until the middle 1960s it remained at the fringes of the field.

THE THEORETICAL ISOLATION OF COLLECTIVE BEHAVIOR

There are several reasons why collective behavior has remained on the periphery of American sociology. Much of the initial work was done by psychologists and social psychologists (e.g., Ross, 1908; Freud, 1922; Allport, 1924) and when sociologists began to investigate the problem, they tended to take the psychological emphasis for granted and viewed the character of the crowd as a magnification of the personal qualities of its members. This definition of collective behavior limited the search for strictly sociological determinants.

An even greater stumbling block to a sociological treatment of the crowd was the original empirical data referred to by those classical theorists of the crowd who wrote in what Bramson (1961) called the "mass society" tradition. For example, LeBon (1960) attempted to explain behavior that he had described as bizarre, uncontrolled, and large-scale mobbism at its most violent pitch. On the one hand, these traits are the manifestation of the crowd that most urgently demands explanation. On the other hand, LeBon's characterization identified the crowd with the abnormal, the extraordinary, and the pathological. As an image of collective behavior, this characterization of the crowd oversimplified and falsified the facts by identifying only one extreme of a much broader continuum of crowd behavior. In any case, the domain of "salient fact" defined by this characterization has served as the empirical basis for American investigations of collective behavior. In the past, social theories in the United States focused on rational, adaptive institutions and social processes as ultimately serving the purposes of organizational expansion and social integration. Such theories were not equipped to deal with behavior that was extraordinary, unauthorized, apparently disorganized, or urgent. Although psychology initially studied the pathological and abnormal and subsequently extended its range to include the normal, sociology developed in the opposite direction, and it could not easily assimilate exceptional behavior in the paradigms of social order it had developed.

A third reason for the failure of American sociology to deal adequately with collective behavior involves the social organization and practice of sociology itself. Two related trends have helped place the study of collective behavior outside of the academic discipline. First, college and university departments of sociology have tended to accept and enlarge on the dictum that sociology should remain politically neutral (Horowitz, 1965). The research community, however, is a sponsored elite. Faced with the question of what is and what is not controversial, the community tends to resolve the matter consistent with the viewpoint of their sponsors—not simply as a matter of choice, but as a matter of practice. Thus, until very recently, both privately and publicly financed research has dealt primarily with the problems of managers and administrators rather than with the problems of people who lack power and either wish to get it or prefer that those who have it exercise it in a different way.

These trends have made it difficult to deal effectively with the intrinsically controversial problems of collective behavior. Either as politically conformative behavior (e.g., the political bandwagon) or as politically rebellious or revolutionary behavior (e.g., the mobs of the French Revolution), the action of the crowd embodies a kind of spontaneous socialization that seems to demonstrate the limits of rationalized institutional power. Mills (1961) said that:

> In order to judge the problems and methods of various schools of social science, we must make up our minds about a great many political values as well as intellectual issues, for we cannot very well state any problem until we know *whose* problem it is (p. 76).

Insofar as this dictum has not become a norm in sociology, the failure to raise questions of value and politics has limited the study of collective behavior.

Another reason for the marginal status of collective behavior in academic sociology stems from the search for theoretic hegemony over the reputed facts of social life. Many sociologists prematurely combine data in what appears to be a search for scale. They assert the existence of systems when observation yields only bounded aggregates or relationships that do not require the assumptions of system theory. The effort to "discover" the most inclusive system conceivable for any aggregate of actors sharpens interest in clearly structured aspects of society or in the attribution of structure itself. Compared with the complexity of enduring systems of action, collective behavior is traditionally taken as a temporary, local, and relatively simple phenomenon; its explanation has seemed obvious and theoretically uninteresting. For this reason, theorists have tended to assume that collective behavior is readily understood without additional work. For example, Smelser (1963) has accepted, without reservation, a host of descriptions of collective behavior, presumably because the phenomena seemed to offer none of the empirical challenge or ambiguity of conventional organizational research.

Finally, collective behavior poses problems for traditional theories of social change (Ryan, 1965). These theories emphasize the way small changes and innovations gradually feed into the long-range structural adjustments that facilitate the growth of society. Incidents that seem to interrupt that steady and moderate development and that seem to represent claims beyond the capacity of the official order are interpreted, according to these theories, as pathologies of order. The fact that such incidents and claims are seen as occurring outside the ordinary processes of social development means that they are unlikely to be studied in the context of theories that focus on those processes.

CHAPTER EIGHT

MODERN THEORIES OF COLLECTIVE BEHAVIOR

Following the publication of the textbook by Park and Burgess (1921), sixteen years elapsed before the next major contribution to the study of collective behavior occurred. It was a lengthy essay written in 1937 by Herbert Blumer that summarized the field and suggested directions for further study. First, Blumer listed the major forms of collective behavior: the crowd, the mass, the public, and the social movement. Second, similar to Park but in greater detail, he discussed some social psychological mechanisms that could account for interaction in episodes of collective behavior, particularly the contagion and spiraling of emotion that develop through mutual stimulation when people mill in close interaction. Instead of explaining collective behavior as the convergence of criminals, unsocialized individuals, and other undesirable types, Blumer followed Park in explaining the actions and intensity of crowds as the spreading of mood by the mechanism of contagion. His discussion of contagion is refined by his use of Allport's (1924) notions of circular reaction and social facilitation (Zajonc, 1965).

Following Blumer's essay, Richard T. LaPiere's *Collective Behavior* (1938) appeared. It was a fascinating study but was more a general text in social psychology than an investigation of what has come to be called collective behavior. One interesting suggestion that runs through LaPiere's book, and that has not been adequately acknowledged in later works, is his thesis that collective behavior is not merely a normal part of social systems but is a regular aspect of all forms of social organization. This hint was later taken up in the theories of Ralph Turner and Erving Goffman, as will be discussed.

Two influential theories of collective behavior have appeared in contemporary sociology. Neil Smelser's theory appeared in 1962. The other theory was initially presented in a text (see chap. 1) by Turner and Killian (1957) and was further developed by Turner (1964) in an important review article. Both theories asserted a formal relationship between hypotheses about collective behavior and more general theories of social action. But the most promising literature has come out of social phenomenology, in particular, the work of Goffman (1961), and the ethnomethodologists (McHugh, 1968). From these points of view, the study of collective behavior is one aspect of two more general problems: that of the nature of situated social action and that of the practical—in the sense of praxis—grounds of action.

This chapter presents the two theories of collective behavior that dominated the field at the beginning of the 1960s, those of Neil Smelser and Ralph Turner. Only Smelser's can be said to be a genuine theory of collective behavior, whereas Turner's theory is a set of lossely linked hypotheses. Yet Turner's work offers a promise of further theoretical development while, paradoxically, Smelser's work has been important primarily because of its implications for official policy and its usefulness in illustrating Parson's model of social action.

In addition to the theories of Turner and Smelser, the chapter presents a framework for the study of collective behavior that is derived from a consideration of the work of Erving Goffman. The purpose of this chapter is to lay the foundation for a theoretic prospectus (chap. 10) that draws from recent research and theory in sociology. In order to lay this foundation, each theorist's work has been presented in some detail. Moreover, an attempt has been made to resolve ambiguities in order to explore the implications and play the hunches of each theory. In this and the following chapter, the theories have been subjected to critique and an attempt has been made to provide a basis for the study of collective behavior that is consistent with some of the recent traditions of sociological analysis.

SMELSER'S DEVELOPMENTAL THEORY

Neil Smelser defined collective behavior as "mobilization on the basis of a belief which redefines social action" (1963, p. 8). Because his definition and explanation of collective behavior depend heavily upon the work of Talcott Parsons, some aspects of Parson's theory of action should be reviewed.

THE INFLUENCE OF PARSON'S THEORY

According to Parsons, the continued existence of a society depends upon the development of institutional mechanisms capable of solving four essential problems:

1. *Pattern maintenance:* There must be general agreement about basic values—that is, a consensus of opinion about the kind of society toward which the system is aimed. These collective values limit the range of societal goals and forms of organization.

2. *Integration:* Behavior must be organized normatively so that essential tasks are performed and the activities of the society and its parts are reasonably well coordinated by a variety of mechanisms of social control.

3. *Goal Attainment:* Specific goals must be set, means must be selected, and resources must be mobilized through the operation of a polity in which is vested the legitimate power to perform these tasks.

4. *Adaptation:* There must be adequate supply and distribution of resources for the attainment of societal goals.

These extremely general requirements account for the coordination of the activities and purposes of the constituent units (roles and organizations) of a society. Each constituent role and organization can be described in terms of the ways in which it contributes to the maintenance of internal order, both moral and social, or in terms of the ways in which it contributes to the operations by which a society meets environmental demands in the pursuit of its goals. The institutionalization of the mechanisms and procedures that correspond to the four basic problems of a social system constitute the conditions of social action for that system.

Societal order is never perfect. As a result, many of a society's activities are directed at internal adjustment. Parsons refers to serious incompatibilities among the four institutional mechanisms that define social action as *structural strain* and distinguish it from the local problems and intergroup conflict that inevitably take place within any large society. Strain is a state of the social organization as a whole rather than a local condition of particular individuals or small groups; it is disequilibrium caused by internal failure or external pressure. Strain appears, for example, when role commitment is inadequate or when there is a shortage of supplies for the performance of essential tasks of the system. A system in strain is likely to experience episodes of collective behavior as it moves toward a restructuring of the overall conditions of social action. Strain generates a continuum of responses from the rational to the irrational, all of which are moves toward alleviation of the strain; collective behavior represents the irrational end of the continuum.

Parsons (1960) illustrated his thesis about the relationship between structural strain and collective behavior with a discussion of the era of McCarthyism in America during the 1950s. Parsons considered the growth of McCarthyism to have been a general and widespread response to particular social tensions generated by the Cold War. America's attitude toward Russia involved an intense but nonmilitary struggle that produced an expansion and centralization of the power of the federal government which conflicted with the traditional American values of individualism. Americans found themselves in a situation in which they were forced to revise their ideas of what could safely be considered private and what citizens owed their country. The renunciation of an earlier state of assured domestic security was accompanied by feelings of tension and resentment. According to Parsons (1960), this crisis of commitment fostered:

> a set of beliefs that certain specific, symbolic, agencies are responsible for the present state of distress; they have "arbitrarily" upset a satisfactory state of affairs. If only they could be eliminated the trouble would disappear and a satisfactory state restored (p. 236).

McCarthyism took the form of seeking out agencies or responsible elements that could be charged with encouraging disloyalty at a time when loyalty was an issue. Communists, liberals, and intellectuals who were consciously critical of many aspects of American society were identified as disloyal. Their critical stance toward American institutions made them easy candidates for the type of scapegoat required by the crisis of commitment. As a form of collective behavior, McCarthyism expressed this crisis by its demand for specific action along counterinstitutional or noninstitutional lines.

SMELSER'S VALUE-ADDED APPROACH

Parsons (1960) essay, "Social Strains in America," is a typical application of his theory. His discussion of strain is the starting point for Smelser:

> Writers on collective behavior assume almost universally that people enter episodes of such behavior because something is wrong in their social environment. People panic, for instance, because they face some extreme danger. They take up fads or crazes because they are bored with their surroundings. They riot because they have experienced a sharp deprivation such as an inflationary price rise. They join reform and revolutionary movements because they suffer from the injustices of existing social arrangements. Such assumptions isolate an important set of determinants in the genesis of collective behavior. In this study we group such determinants under the heading of "structural strain" (1963, p. 47).

Smelser (1963) extended and elaborated Parsons' concept of response to social strain so that it could provide a general explanation for all types of collective behavior. Smelser did not specify how one decides that a particular social event is or is not collective behavior. He simply took everything previously labeled "collective behavior" as collective behavior. He described an episode of collective behavior as the exceptional and direct action of a collectivity. It is exceptional because the participants act outside the conventional norms and institutions of society. It is direct because it involves an immediate attack on something that is identified as the source of stress, without regard for the validity of that identification or the rational limits of action. Smelser viewed collective behavior as the outcome of a popular desire to do something about a situation that is initially felt to be both vague and oppressive. He identified the underlying condition as structural strain, and his theory focused on the generalized beliefs that arise in order to facilitate the collective understanding of the condition that leads to direct action in response to the strain. These "generalized beliefs" about the nature of strain, its sources, and its possible outcomes serve as the basis for the purposive, problem-solving action of the crowd. For this reason, these beliefs are the core of Smelser's definition of "collective behavior" as "mobilization on the basis of a belief which redefines social action" (1963, p. 8).

As with all instances of problem solving, collective behavior is a process. Moreover, it is not a process that gradually unfolds from a single case, but a complex development, requiring that specific conditions be fulfilled at each of several stages in order for the next stage to occur. Smelser's value-added approach identified the stages of an episode of collective behavior as follows:

1. the emergence of structural strain
2. the growth of a shared generalized belief

3. the confirmation of this belief by a precipitating incident
4. the mobilization of the collectivity
5. collective action and social control.

The following example will make this sequence clear:

In the year 1761 the citizens of London were alarmed by two shocks of an earthquake and the prophecy of a third, which was to destroy them altogether. The first shock was felt on the 8th of February . . . ; the second happened on the 8th of March . . . . It soon became the subject of general remark . . . ; and a crack-brained fellow, named Bell, a soldier in the Life Guards, was so impressed with the idea that there would be a third in another month, that he lost his senses altogether, and ran about the streets predicting the destruction of London on the 5th of April. Most people thought that the *first* would have been a more appropriate day; but there were not wanting thousands who confidently believed the prediction, and took measures to transport themselves and families from the scene of the impending calamity. As the awful day approached, the excitement became intense, and great numbers of credulous people resorted to all the villages within a circuit of twenty miles . . . . Such as could not afford to pay for lodgings . . . remained in London until two or three days before the time, and then encamped in the surrounding fields . . . . As happened during a similar panic in the time of Henry VIII, the fear became contagious, and hundreds who had laughed at the prediction a week before, packed up their goods, when they saw others doing so, and hastened away. The river was thought to be a place of great security, and all the merchant-vessels in the port were filled with people . . . . The greater part of the fugitives returned on the following day, convinced that the prophet was a false one; but many judged it more prudent to allow a week to elapse before they trusted their dear limbs in London (MacKay, 1932, pp. 259-60).

The Emergence of Structural Strain. In this case, ordinary social routines and institutions failed to protect people and failed to provide them with adequate information and a clear statement of the occasion. As the only available source of interpretations of the situation, rumor became an important process of communication among Londoners during the 1761 earthquakes. Rumor determined the generalized beliefs that offered the clarity necessary for the mobilization for flight. It should be noted that Smelser included an initial stage that he labeled structural conduciveness. Because it seems to refer to the fact that all forms of behavior (including unofficial activities that are ordinarily identified as deviance and collective behavior) are limited by the implicit rules and standards of the systems in which they occur, it does not appear to be a stage in the same sense as the others. Therefore, structural conduciveness has not been included in the discussion of Smelser's theory.

Smelser's definition of collective behavior depends upon the concept of social action that he shares with Parsons. Social action is the system-wide coordination of values, norms, performances, and facilities for the attainment of a goal in the environment or for the affirmation and regulation of some internal state of the social system. Thus, social action includes both integration and direction. The "redefinition of social action" that characterizes extreme responses to structural strain is a change in the relationships among the components—values, norms, performances, and facilities—of social action. Such a redefinition raises questions about the standards and scheduling of performance, the proper allocation of commitment, the legitimacy of power, and the rationale for action.

The concept of social action and its redefinition can be illustrated by noting the changes that often occur in American families as the children enter the transitional period of adolescence. Some students of socialization have held that adolescence disturbs the social order of the family. The adolescent, anticipating adult status, feels that he deserves adult privileges. He resents the standards of performance, the rights, the obligations, and the status that are appropriate to childhood. When the family traditions do not allow for an easy transition to adulthood, a struggle for power may take place in which respect for parental authority is staked against personal integrity. This crisis illustrates structural strain within the social system of the family. As they are brought into question, the various roles that comprise this social system are defined and articulated. Within the family, new forms of control and principles of authority may emerge to replace the mystifying and authoritarian setting of childhood. To win consent, parental decisions may have to be justified by the rationale of the decision maker rather than asserted as the word of authority. The adolescent may participate in decisions that were formerly exclusively parental. In this case, the conditions of family action get redefined in terms of normative, rather than coercive, control. As a result of this crisis, the social system is reorganized and directed toward new goals. The breaks in the social order of the family that accompany this transition can be explained in the same terms as collective behavior.

McCarthyism, the reaction to the London earthquakes, and family conflict during adolescence are symptoms of structural strain. In the first example, strain appeared as a crisis of commitment in the society; it seemed to the McCarthyites that lack of agreement about specific political values posed a threat to national security. The structural strain of the second crisis stemmed from a failure of information and facilities. Threatened with the possible destruction of London, people no longer considered or recognized the norms governing ordinary social behavior to be suitable to the solution of the problems posed by the disaster; those norms did not serve to coordinate escape. The third example, adolescent-parent conflict, is construed as a more general crisis that can bring into question all aspects of the family as a social system. In adolescence, parental approval no longer may be sufficient reward to win commitment to family undertakings. Family values, roles, authority, and the distribution of resources may all be brought into question as a natural consequence of changes in the relationships between individual family members and society.

Although Smelser has not made himself entirely clear, and seems to argue that strain can be measured absolutely in terms of degree of departure from equilibrium, his definition of "structural strain" suggests that degree of strain is always relative to a prior condition of strain. Similar to total mechanical efficiency, complete social integration is an unrealizable ideal, and some structural strain is always present in a social system. Thus strain as a determinant of collective behavior occurs when there is a sudden change in the relationships among the components of the system of action. If this is Smelser's meaning, he cannot argue, as he occasionally appears to, that a precipitating incident is merely a sudden noticeable change in the degree of integration toward an increase of strain. Such a redundancy would make the concept of strain trivial in the study of collective behavior. If strain is always present in a society, but only sudden noticeable changes in strain are determinative, calling these changes precipitating incidents would deprive Smelser of the possibility of using strain itself as a determinant. Consequently, his concept of precipitating incident will be distinguished from his notion of strain. The overall coordination of work in a social system may conceal and override underlying, omnipresent structural strain. But developments inside and outside the social system are continually redistributing the rewards and legitimations of such an order. Any sudden change can thus make that order dysfunctional in a particular sector and, consequently, start a chain reaction that spreads throughout the society. This account of structural strain explains why oppressive slave societies are not continuously in open revolt. It is also consistent with the hypothesis that political activism of the poor and of oppressed groups does not grow out of steady deprivation but, rather, depends upon sudden shifts in their relative socioeconomic positions (R. Williams, 1957), or in the amount of power they appear to be able to exercise.

The Growth of Generalized Belief. According to Smelser, structural strain is the most general condition of collective behavior. However, although it is necessary, it is not sufficient to produce an episode of collective behavior. Without strain, collective behavior will not occur; given structural strain, collective behavior may take place if other factors are also present. Generalized beliefs must arise to explain the source of strain and its consequences. These beliefs explain events and situations in very general terms that describe society as at a turning point. They indicate the nature of the problem, the possible responsible agents, the inability of institutional operations to meet the needs of the system, and the consequences of collective inaction. Generalized beliefs are the result of the initial attempts to reduce the uncertainty caused by structural strain. Worried people consult each other and try to discover what has happened to distress them, why it has happened, and what is going to happen as a consequence. Rumor is the improvised communication process that allows people to make interpretations of a condition or an event unaccounted for by standard communications channels (Smelser, 1963, p. 81; Shibutani, 1966). By means of rumor, social systems produce collectivities with shared generalized beliefs.

Killian (1956b) studied the development of generalized beliefs during a fireworks factory explosion in Texas. A spark at a fireworks factory near the center of Houston detonated twenty tons of explosives. Major damage was inflicted over a quarter-mile radius and debris rose in the air in a mushroom-shaped cloud. Killian interviewed people who had been at various distances from the explosion. Only 10 percent of the respondents knew immediately that the explosion had been caused by fireworks. Other respondents supposed it to be an explosion of an unspecified nature, a bomb, or an atomic blast. Most people relied on information provided by other people and did not seek official confirmation for the interpretations offered. Sixty-seven percent of those interviewed based their interpretations on information received over the telephone or through interpersonal contact; 14.4 percent guessed what happened, knew from the outset, or went to the scene of the explosion; 18.7 percent relied on the mass media for information. Thus, in the initial stages of the disaster, rumor played an important role in establishing generalized beliefs about the nature of the event.

Popular beliefs are a common store of interpretations that reflect social attitudes. Generalized beliefs arise when popular beliefs are attached to specific situations by a large part of the public involved in that situation. Smelser claimed that generalized beliefs usually assume the existence of extraordinary forces, such as threats or conspiracies, and suggest that these forces are responsible for the problems that suddenly appear acute. During McCarthyism, for example, these forces were identified as critics of American institutions and Communists and their "fellow travelers." In the case of the Texas firework explosion, various forces were posited as causes of the explosion; and the allegations varied from the failure of city officials to enforce safety regulations to the Cold War policy of the United States government or the imperialistic aims of foreign powers. Both of these examples illustrate the apparently nonrational, but not implausible, character of generalized beliefs.

Smelser (1963) identified two common types of generalized belief: hysterical beliefs and wish-fulfillment beliefs. The first is based on the idea that hostile forces are responsible for society's problems. A typical example is the nineteenth-century belief that the "yellow peril" would sweep down from Asia and destroy the West. Such beliefs were enshrined in the Fu Manchu stories, which revolved around the British protagonist's attempts to foil a vast conspiracy to rule the world led by Fu Manchu, an inscrutable Chinese of incredible intelligence and charisma. These and related beliefs played an important role in shaping American immigration policy, particularly the determination of quotas for non-European nations, during the first half of the twentieth century.

A contemporary example of a hysterical belief is the fear that marijuana saps the moral fiber of youth and is a major cause of crime and social alienation. Despite a lack of positive evidence, the popular literature and the laws are based on the belief that marijuana is a dangerous substance, the use of which results in the erosion of personality and the destruction of society (Brown, 1969a). Similar to the earlier belief in the "yellow peril" and the later belief in a "communist menace," the "scientific," hysterical drug myths have a "but for . . . ." quality—but for the existence of drugs and the strange states of consciousness they induce, life would be orderly and decent and society would return to a state of happy equilibrium.

Wish-fulfillment beliefs suggest that there is an adequate and immediate source of relief from immediately perceived tensions. A belief in an all-powerful hero is an ancient and recurring form of wish-fulfillment. Other wish-fulfillment beliefs are the belief that a particular political candidate is the only man who can save the country, that crime would vanish if punishments were severe enough, that racism would disappear if education were more effective, and that war would stop if men would only love their brothers.

It should be noted that Quarantelli and Hundley (1965) have reported a case of collective behavior in which precrowd participants apparently did not perceive an undefined danger with boundless consequences or a specific responsible agent. In other words, there was no generalized belief intervening between strain and collective behavior. If their observation is valid, it would disconfirm Smelser's theory as a whole because (1) collective behavior is defined as behavior mobilized on the basis of such a belief, (2) each stage is defined in terms of the other stages, and (3) belief is the mechanism that translates strain (which is not a potential for action) into action conceived as problem-solving behavior.

The Role of the Precipitating Incident. Generalized beliefs are important in the development of collective behavior because they provide certainty during a period of uncertainty, because they are shared, and because they provide specific premises for action. The particular clarity that a generalized belief introduces narrows the range of plausible options for collective behavior. Although structural strain and generalized beliefs provide the basic and most general conditions under which collective behavior occurs, a precipitating event is also necessary to spark an actual episode. The specific precipitating event gives "the generalized beliefs concrete, immediate substance" (Smelser, 1963, p. 17). It either magnifies and sharpens existing tensions or removes inhibiting uncertainty about the implications of a particular generalized belief. When individuals under conditions of intense strain share a generalized belief, otherwise innocuous events may assume the character of a precipitating incident. For example, Smelser (1963) stated that:

> Under conditions of racial tension it is nearly always a dramatic event which precipitates the outburst of violence a clash between two persons of different race, a Negro family moving into a White neighborhood, or a Negro being promoted to a traditionally white job. These events may confirm or justify the fears or hatreds in a generalized belief; they may . . . exaggerate a condition of strain . . . (pp. 16-17).

A recent study (Lieberson and Silverman, 1965) of seventy-six interracial clashes that occurred between 1913 and 1963 illustrates Smelser's description of precipitating incidents. Table 8.1 presents the immediate precipitants of the seventy-six clashes. The information was gathered largely from journalistic sources and, therefore, may illustrate only the theoretic assumptions and expectations of journalists. In the search for origins typical of the western social psychological tradition, observers may attribute precipitance to an event as a routine way of describing the event.

According to the authors of this study, the data indicate that a large proportion of the precipitating incidents of the seventy-six race riots involved interracial violations of important societal norms. According to Lieberson and Silverman (1965):

Noteworthy are the large number of events in which bodily injury is the precipitant as well as the smaller number of cases precipitated by violations of the interracial segregation taboos (p. 891).

Table 8.1 IMMEDIATE PRECIPITANTS OF RACE RIOTS, 1913-1963

Precipitant	Number of Riots
Rape, murder, attack, or hold-up of white women by black men	10
Killings, arrest, interference, assault, or search of black men by white policemen	15
Other interracial murder or shooting	11
Interracial fight, no mention of lethal weapons	16
Civil liberties, public facilities, segregation, political events, and housing	14
Black strikebreakers, upgrading of blacks, or other job based conflicts	5
Burning of an American flag by blacks	1
No information available	4
Total number	76

Adapted from Lieberson and Silverman, 1965, p. 889.

Mobilization of the Collectivity. Given structural strain, the formation of generalized beliefs that interpret the tensions arising from the strain, and the confirmation of those beliefs by a precipitating incident, Smelser (1963) asserted that:

> the only necessary condition that remains is to bring the affected group into action. This point marks the onset of panic, the outbreak of hostility, or the beginning of agitation for reform or revolution. In this process of mobilization the behavior of leaders is extremely important (p. 17).

During an episode of panic, flight tends to take place only after someone yells or begins to run. Smelser called this act of leadership a *"flight model"* (1963, p. 153). The flight model serves an executive function in that it mobilizes the rest of the group. However, active leadership is not always necessary to mobilize people for collective behavior. The spiraling of emotion that occurs in a tense situation may force action of its own accord. Thus, Smelser noted that panic has been called a "fear which feeds upon itself" (p. 154).

Collective Action and Official Control. Smelser's analysis of the stages of development of an episode of collective behavior has important implications for official attempts to control collective behavior (see also chap. 7). According to Smelser (1963):

> Stated in the simplest way, the study of social control is the study of those counter determinants which prevent, interrupt, deflect, or inhibit the accumulation of the determinants just reviewed (p. 17).

Smelser's emphasis on stages of development within the crowd suggests that deliberate countermeasures may be taken at every stage in a corresponding development of official control. He noted that the rationality of control depends upon the stage at which control is instituted. For example, strain can be minimized. Social reforms prevent the occurrence of collective behavior by ameliorating the strains that can result in such episodes. Other official controls can be mobilized after an episode of collective behavior has begun to materialize. The police, the press, officially recognized community leaders, or religious authorities can intervene in threatening situations to affect the speed, intensity, and direction of the developing episode (Besag, 1967; National Advisory Commission on Civil Disorders, 1968). Although Smelser explicitly recognized that social control operates at every stage of social action, he treated it systematically only as the final added value in the series of determinants of collective behavior. It is interesting that he did not consider control, especially officially sponsored control, as an independent emergent of strain in itself. This failure forced him to assert what amounts to a backlash theory of control, which bypassed the politics that occur when engaged parties encounter one another—that is, the transactional character of collective behavior.

Aside from the possibility that the research by Quarantelli and Hundley may be taken as refutation of Smelser's theory, and aside from the criticisms of the concept of generalized belief presented in chapter one, several problems of the theory should be noted at this point. Whether or not Smelser's theory is a "value-added" theory depends on whether or not the various determinants are of the same logical order, differing only in their generality of application. The relation of strain to generalized belief is too tenuous to constitue an ordered set of determinants: the former is a condition of a social system while the latter is a trait of a segment of the system. Control and conduciveness operate throughout the process and therefore are neither prior to or subsequent to any of the other determinants. In other words, they do not add value to the explanation. Instead, they qualify operations at every stage. The insistence on the order of determinants provided by the theory leads Smelser, in applying the theory, to accomodate strain to the more local causes, in particular, generalized belief. Thus, in specific accounts, strain appears as a local condition of frustration, or the like, rather than a condition of the system as a whole. This, then, begs the question of the relationship between such local conditions and structural strain.

Moreover, Smelser's concept of strain seems to preclude the processes of reform that he posits as suitable for the initial stage of collective behavior. Strain is a system trait, therefore, correctable only by a systemic operation. But systemic operations are themselves noninstitutional and are therefore likely to generate strain if they are undertaken. At best, Smelser's theory leaves room for reform only as a technique for undermining generalized beliefs and therefore as part of the coercive repetoire of authorities engaged in controlling collective behavior. But this means that there is no mechanism by which collective behavior can be fully controlled, in so far as the theory of action is concerned. If this is so, authorities are advised by proponents of the theory to focus on coercive forms of control and policies of containment.

Finally, many of the problems with Smelser's theory of collective behavior stem from the difficulty of operationalizing his concepts or interpreting them in such a way that the theory can be tested. Part of this is due to the fact that many of the concepts have only quasi-technical status, and are marginal to common sense usage. But that usage is not treated critically. As a result, the theory incorporates the ambiguities and vagaries of the common sense of deviance and riot. In addition, part of the problem lies in the fact that key variables refer to mental states—anxiety, belief—that are difficult to fix by known research techniques.

The upshot of these criticisms is that, despite its obvious heuristic value, Smelser's theory makes moral, intellectual, and political commitments that are the unexamined but inevitable consequences of the use of the theory. This is one reason why Smelser has been criticized so often for what appears to be biases in his work. Regardless of whether the critics are accurate, neither their claim of bias nor Smelser's claim of innocence (Smelser, 1970) can be evaluated without a tightening up of the theory and a clarification of the meaning of its language. The following application of Smelser's theory to an incident of collective behavior illustrates its heuristic value.

APPLYING SMELSER'S THEORY TO AN INCIDENT OF COLLECTIVE BEHAVIOR

The Los Angeles riot of August 1965 erupted against a background of strain. The black community in the Watts area had a history of unemployment and biased police behavior: "malpractice and ... 'brutality' " (Oberschall, 1968, p. 330). In the preceding year, the state had voted to reject fair housing legislation and city officials had long failed to provide the community with adequate hospital and transportation facilities. Understandably, community members regarded law and official authority as oppressive and intrusive. The police were seen as a hostile occupation force for an essentially colonial rule. The inconsistency between the historical values of justice and equal opportunity and the practices of officials and the policies of government, was the other side of an institutionalized inequitable distribution of resources—goods, services, and control. Attempts to remedy the situation had failed: federally financed poverty programs had neither improved the situation nor convinced residents that conditions were changing fast enough to make any difference to them.

Watts tends to be isolated from the rest of Los Angeles by the racial homogeneity of its population, by the lack of transportation facilities, and by poverty. Interaction and communication among Watts residents about their shared condition had led to the development of generalized beliefs about racism in the city administration and police hostility. At the same time, the police believed that the black community was dangerously volatile. Both for the police and the community, these beliefs had specific implications:

> A belief on the part of a Negro about to be arrested that the arrest is going to involve the use of force has the consequence of an attempt to avoid or resist arrest, thus increasing the probability that force will in fact have to be used to implement the arrest; whereas a belief on the part of police that an arrest is going to be resisted might produce a behavior in which

force is in fact used. Thus the ground is prepared for the fulfillment of the prophecy (Oberschall, 1968, p. 331).

Under these conditions, it is easy to see how an arrest could precipitate an episode of collective behavior.

On the night of August 11, 1965, a crowd of Watts residents gathered to witness an arrest. The police were slow to remove the prisoner from the scene, and bystanders openly doubted whether the arrest was lawful. Rumors spread that the police were acting brutally. Specifically, it was said that a policeman had kicked a pregnant woman. In the light of the beliefs prevailing at that time, this alleged violation of a basic norm of human conduct seemed to demonstrate the brutal and racist proclivities of the police and served to precipitate the riot. The riot itself was characterized by looting, the destruction of property, gathering and roaming, and occasional aggression toward the police. However, "the evidence, meager as it is, supports the view that there was a systematic relationship between the specific targets of aggression and the sources of the rioters' grievances" (Oberschall, 1968, p. 337). There was a tendency to avoid destroying the property of black residents and black businessmen. In addition, Oberschall (1968) said that "looting as well as other riot activity were essentially group activities during which participants and onlookers experienced a sense of solidarity, pride, and exhilaration" (p. 338).

The episode "became defined in global, dichtomous, we-they terms, where we and they stood for the two races and the long history of conflict associated with them" (Oberschall, 1968, p. 338). According to Oberschall (1968), earlier theories of collective behavior which stressed the peculiar characteristics of participants, do not apply to the Watts episode. The rioters were neither criminals (only 11 percent of those arrested during the riot had a prison record); nor irresponsible youngsters (58 percent of those arrested were older than twenty-five years); nor recent migrants to Los Angeles (75 percent had lived in Los Angeles County for at least five years); nor the uneducated (those persons who were convicted had the same median number of years of education as the general population of South Los Angeles, although they tended to be from lower socioeconomic strata).

Oberschall concluded that:

> The riot cannot be attributed to the lawless and rootless minority which inhabits the ghetto, though, no doubt, these were active in it as well. The riot is best seen as a large scale collective action, with a wide, representative base in the lower-class Negro communities, which, however-much it gained the sympathy of the more economically well-off Negroes, remained a violent lower-class outburst throughout. If there were numerous jobless among the participants and many youths from families with problems, it is precisely because such cases abound in the neighborhoods in which the riot occurred (1968, p. 329).

Thus, the Watts riot can be seen as occurring because of the formation of generalized beliefs in a situation characterized by a strain and cannot be attributed to the copresence of "special" types of people.

TURNER'S THEORY OF EMERGENT NORMS

Ralph Turner (1964) objects to the empirical image of the phenomena that Smelser's theory purports to explain and to Smelser's reliance on a variant of convergence theory to account for the allegedly peculiar characteristics of collective behavior. Turner writes in the tradition of Robert Ezra Park. The basic problem to which he addresses himself is: How and under what conditions does interaction among people lead to collective behavior? More specifically, what accounts for the integration of the crowd, its shared level of excitement, its apparent uniformity of behavior, and its acceptance of a common goal?

Smelser's theory was initially formulated to explain social movements—a type of collective behavior that exhibits complex organization and that develops over a relatively long period of time. The problem-solving model of social movements was then extended to the crowd. Turner, on the other hand, formulated his theory of collective behavior by initially addressing himself to the short-term phenomenon of the crowd itself. The difference in approach is reflected in their basic explanatory concepts. Smelser (1962) argued that episodes of collective behavior occur as a result of the development of generalized beliefs. Turner (1964), on the other hand, argued that episodes of collective behavior are characterized by the emergence of norms. The difference is partly one of emphasis; Smelser focused on the culture of the crowd and Turner focused on interaction. Nevertheless, their formulations offer different pictures of the crowd and competing hypotheses of crowd formation. Specifically, Turner reduces the theoretical problem of collective behavior to the problem of explaining conformity within the crowd.

CONFORMITY WITHIN THE CROWD

In the process of developing an explanation for conformity within the crowd, Turner examined the two major alternative theories that are used to explain fads, panics, riots, and rebellions. He asserted that:

> *Contagion* theories explain collective behavior on the basis of some process whereby moods, attitudes, and behavior are communicated rapidly and accepted uncritically. *Convergence* theories explain collective behavior on the basis of the simultaneous presence of people who share the same predispositions and preoccupations (1964, p. 384).

Although convergence theory traces collective behavior to the predispositions of the participants rather than to interaction among them, both types of theory agree on some basic characteristics of the crowd. Both types of theory assume that the crowd is homogeneous, that crowd behavior is irrational, and that the crowd exerts a peculiarly compelling force on its members as well as on marginal participants. In their focus on the terrible outcomes of crowd behavior (e.g., lynchings and riots) both theories attempt to account for the apparent failure of ordinary social and moral restraints operate when people congregate in large gatherings.

Convergence Theories. At its simplest, the convergence thesis suggests that the people most likely to be found in crowds are antisocial or unsocialized individuals, whose aggregated presence makes for a kind of spontaneous holiday from restraint. In its more complex form, the convergence thesis maintains that crowds are composed of people with similar dispositions, that such dispositions are magnified in a kind of culture of the crowd, and that there is a simple and direct relationship between these dispositions and the direction, intensity, and organization of collective action. The major objection to convergence theory is that the thesis assumes a simple and unwarranted similarity between a phenomenon and its determinants. The fact that an episode of collective behavior results in damage to lives or property does not necessarily imply that the damage was caused by people who are generally indifferent to the lives and property of others or even that the people had destructive intentions. Moreover, the hypothesis that crowds are made up of criminal, irrational, or otherwise deviant elements (people outside the mainstream of society) is not supported by evidence. There have been reports of lynchings in which participants of the lynch mob were highly respected members of the community (R.W. Brown, 1954); commodity riots by workers (Rude, 1964); civil disturbances, such as in Toledo, Ohio, in 1967, in which the majority of the people arrested were employed (National Advisory Commission on Civil Disorders, 1968); protests by academically respectable individuals and children of well-educated parents (Sampson, 1967a, b); and police assults in which the participants were the very people who, supposedly, are professionally opposed to criminal behavior (Walker, 1968).

Contagion Theories. Contagion theory was suggested by the apparent intensity of emotion generated by the crowd. Contagion theories argue that individuals feel anonymous in crowds and that, under such circumstances, moods are easily transferred, self-control is relinquished to the crowd, and individuals are consequentially emboldened to adopt behavior that they would repudiate in other settings. Contagion theory emphasizes the excitement of the crowd and sees this mood as an active force that infects everyone it touches and spirals upward in scope and intensity.

Contagion theory has been criticized on several grounds. First, contagion theories, similar to theories of convergence, are geared to token paradigms: they identify collective behavior with very rare and extreme episodes. Because initially sociologists had little opportunity to observe such unusual occurrences for themselves, they based their explanations on data from interviews of horrified and frightened observers. Calmer investigators who moved closer to the scenes of collective behavior noted that when revivals, riots, demonstrations, and similar events are closely studied, the contagion that supposedly distributes excitement throughout a gathering and that infects uncommitted bystanders seems to be lacking.

Second, contagion theory makes the questionable assumption that socialization merely overlays a permanently primitive human nature that can express itself with undiminished force when "the lid is off." In addition to its incompatibility with contemporary psychological theory, this assumption implies that crowds lack internal control and external competence. But do crowds behave irrationally and unsocially? Many examples of collective behavior suggest otherwise. During the civil disturbances in 1967, crowd behavior was often very deliberate. Black rioters usually selected white-owned business establishments and other symbols of white domination as targets. Looters were observed honoring traffic regulations and the ordinary courtesies of social life; and looted goods were often distributed unselfishly, as private property was converted to community property (Dynes and Quarantelli, 1968; Oberschall, 1968).

Third, contagion theory requires mechanisms to account for the transfer of emotion, and, if they exist, there is little empirical evidence that such mechanisms can carry the explanatory weight required by the theory. The term contagion is simply a label. The observation of contagion has been neither rationalized nor explained. Turner (1964) also pointed out that although excitement in general may be contagious, it is doubtful whether specific emotions are transmitted.

Fourth, similar to convergence theories, contagion theories seriously oversimplify the phenomenon of the crowd. Both theories move directly from psychological assumptions to a description of collective behavior that justifies those assumptions. They pay little attention to the fact that a crowd is a social manifestation that is subject to the forces that shape social behavior. Contagion theories are particularly weak in their failure to consider the crowd as a social structure when they interpret collective behavior as fundamentally privatized and asocial. Because they attribute an unrealistically static and undifferentiated composition to the crowd, both types of theory assume the uniformity that they supposedly set out to explain. The fact that a crowd seems to move in a single direction and that its members jointly fulfill a common goal drops from sight as a problem; its unity of action becomes a mere corollary of an underlying structural uniformity. Thus, the assumption of the uniformity of collective behavior is a premise of early theories, but a problem for later ones.

How does an assumption of uniformity arise? Lang and Lang (1953) examined the effect of different perspectives on descriptions of General Douglas MacArthur's parade into Chicago. This occasion, MacArthur Day, followed the general's removel from command by President Truman in 1952. Lang and lang placed some observers in the crowds that lined the streets and other observers at television sets. Those observers who watched the parade on television concluded that, on the whole, the crowd of spectators was uniformly enthusiastic. However, those on the scene reported that cheering was only one of many responses evoked by the occasion and that "the crowd" consisted of many different behaviors and collectivities. According to Turner and Killian (1957), who quoted from the 1953 study by Lang and Lang:

> The cheering of the crowd seemed not to die down at all, and even as the telecast was concluded, it only seemed to have reached its crest.

* * *

The cheering crowd, the "seething mass of humanity," was fictionally endowed by the commentators with the same capacity for a direct and personal relationship to MacArthur as the one which television momentarily established for the TV viewer through its close-up shots (pp. 180-181).

In contrast, Turner and Killian (1957) quoted Lang and Lang on the fact that one observer at the parade reported:

> Everybody strained but few could get a really good glimpse of him [MacArthur]. A few seconds after he had passed most people merely turned around to shrug and to address their neighbors with such phrases: "That's all," "That was it," "Gee, he looks just as he does in the movies," "What'll we do now?" Mostly teenagers and others with no specific plans flocked into the streets after MacArthur, but very soon got tired of following as there was no place to go and nothing to do. Some cars were caught in the crowd, a matter which, to the crowd, seemed amusing (pp. 179-180).

This description implies that the impression of a uniform public response is partly the result of the medium through which the response is perceived and partly the result of the way in which the event is presented and the way in which it is interpreted. Even in direct experience, an idea of the crowd's quality and intensity of response would vary depending on where its "emotional temperature" was taken. A spectator in a moving car or in the front row of the crowd would receive different impressions than would an observer at the margin of the crowd. The distance from which an observer views a crowd determines the degree to which the aggregate or its details dominates his image of the crowd. Moreover, inevitably, an observer's point of view is a matter of practical perspective as well as of physical location. What the observer perceives reflects the degree and direction of his involvement or indifference.

The contribution of theories of contagion lies in their insistence on the intensely compelling and social character of collective behavior. Convergence theories are valuable for their stress on the differential sensitization of participants to the development of the crowd situation. Both theories emphasize the discontinuity of collective behavior with ordinary social life. However, their insistence on the uniformity of feeling and behavior within the crowd and their identification of the dynamics of crowd behavior with the outcome leaves the question of crowd development unanswered. Moreover, their tendency to attribute destructive outcomes to all forms of collective behavior suggests an image of the crowd as antipathetic to social order and progressive social change, a corresponding sense of history that stresses what Skolnick called a "myth of peaceful change" (Skolnick, 1969), and a notion of politics that excludes unauthorized action from the normal operations of the polity.

TURNER'S FORMULATION

Turner's (1964) theory of emergent norms is an attempt to perserve the insights of the contagion and convergence theses and to avoid their weaknesses. Turner agreed that the crowd is sharply distinguished from ordinary institutional behavior. However, instead of assuming that collective behavior is intrinsically asocial, Turner assumed that individuals in crowds are participants in social structures activated by face-to-face interaction. In their textbook, Turner and Killian (1957) distinguished collective behavior from ordinary institutional behavior in three ways.

Characteristics of Collective Behavior. First, ordinary institutional behavior is intelligible in terms of the norms and goals of the surrounding society; collective behavior is not. Collective behavior is *functionally isolated*. For example, industrial work groups are usually classified by the products or outputs they contribute to a larger organization; however, the actions of a protesting crowd of workers are not defined in terms of production and the participants are workers by label rather than by role.

Second, in its initial stages a crowd has no tradition. It *lacks prior normative integration*—that is, the behavior of a crowd follows norms that emerge spontaneously out of interaction. These norms are spontaneous in that they depend upon the way in which a particular situation develops rather than upon norms and practices shared by participants before entering the collective situation. Thus, episodes of collective behavior are both unconventional and normative: they are unconventional as far as the larger society is concerned, but they are internally normative for the participants.

Third, episodes of collective behavior can be distinguished from one another and *classified in terms of a dominant norm*, whereas institutional behavior is ordinarily defined by the value it fulfills for the social organization.

Two Types of Dominant Norm. Turner (1964) classified crowds by two types of dominant norm. The individualistic norm, exemplified by the panic, provides "collective support for the pursuit of individual survival or gain" (p. 413) through interpersonal competition, for example. The solidaristic norm, however, involves interaction that is often cooperative and supportive. Examples of crowds displaying a solidaristic norm include the lynch mob and the political bandwagon that sometimes develops among delegates to a party convention. Although both the lynch mob and the bandwagon are solidaristic, Turner agreed with other writers in calling the lynch mob an acting crowd and the bandwagon an expressive crowd (see chap. 1 for a discussion of acting and expressive crowds). Turner asserted that:

> The emergent norm which governs the behavior of the acting crowd incorporates the response of the [outside] . . . object as a crucial condition in defining appropriate behavior. In contrast, the feedback to which members of an expressive crowd attend is the response of the fellow crowd members and their own . . . experience (1964, p. 417).

The solidarity expressed by the lynch mob is outwardly directed. Its members accept a new definition of legitimate behavior toward those designated as outsiders. On the other hand, the attention of members of a crowd on a political bandwagon is directed away from outsiders and toward the expression of enthusiasm. An expressive crowd sanctions behavior that would elsewhere be considered indulgent or childishly excessive (Turner, 1964).

Circumstances Leading to the Formation of Crowds. Turner's theory proposed that episodes of collective behavior appear when conventional norms fail or weaken in an ambiguous situation that provides an opportunity for individuals to interact. A situation leading to the establishment of a new norm and a new definition of the situation to which the norm is applied can arise only when conventional norms or their sanctions are neutralized. The neutralization of conventional norms is illustrated by the mock trials that often accompany lynchings. The trappings of justice which pay superficial homage to the requirements of due process serve to remove the potentially inhibiting effects of those requirements on the lynching. The emergent norm develops as part of a new interaction and it determines the direction and intensity of crowd behavior.

Prior Interaction. A pilot study by Bindler and his associates (1970) illustrated the relationship between the emergence of a norm and the prior interaction among potential participants in collective behavior. Bindler and his colleagues hypothesized that the speed with which a norm builds up and its ultimate strength depend upon whether there was an opportunity for open interaction at the point at which the setting became ambiguous. In their study, groups of three members each were asked to view a picture in which figure and ground were ambiguous and to announce when they observed a shift in the dominant image. One set of groups had worked together on a picture puzzle (prior interaction) before being placed in the experimental setting. The members of the other groups worked on the same puzzle individually (no prior interaction). Group responses to the ambiguous picture were then recorded at thirty-second intervals. Bindler and his associates concluded that a norm of responsiveness built up faster and with greater persistence in those groups in which there had been prior interaction than in those groups that had no prior interaction. According to their report:

> Three of the four PI (Prior Interaction) groups showed a low initial response that built up to a high response . . . . Five of the seven NPI (No Prior Interaction) groups showed very low initial responses and maintained a stable response rate throughout the six minutes . . . . Our data seem to indicate that for subjects who have previously interacted the group pressure is felt more strongly and high response rates build up more rapidly, as compared [with] the NPI groups (Bindler, et al., 1970. p. 35).

These results are consistent with the general implications of Turner's theory of collective behavior and his view of interaction as facilitating the emergence of norms.

SOCIAL CONTROL

Turner's theory of collective behavior does not imply that the crowd is independent of its environment. He describes the organization of the environment in relation to collective behavior as social control and lists three mechanisms that influence the operation of an emergent norm: conventional norms, mediating publics, and conventionalizing operations.

Conventional Norms as Social Control. Because situations are never entirely novel and individuals are never entirely disassociated from their ordinary social contacts, emergent norms are not independent of conventional norms. Emergent norms, Turner (1964) asserted, are often "exceptional applications of conventional norms . . . . institutional stratification, cleavages, and communication channels continually reemerge in collective behavior" (p. 418, see also Dynes and Quarantelli, 1968).

The way in which conventional norms act to control social behavior was illustrated in the zoot-suit riots of 1943. According to Turner and Surace (1956) the hostility of many white citizens of Los Angeles toward Mexicans could only have led to open violence if conventional norms prohibiting attacks on minority groups were neutralized. The presence of a new symbol of social deviance, the zoot-suiter, provided a focus for white racism. The zoot-suiter label actually identified a style rather than an ethnic group. The neutral and basically aesthetic label supported hostile crowd behavior by submerging the racism involved. It depersonalized the people to whom it actually referred and redefined them so that it was not necessary to treat them according to ordinary moral considerations. Thus, the way was paved for the overt expression of what had been a veiled antagonism toward Mexican-Americans.

The zoot-suiter image first appeared in local California newspapers about three years before the actual riots. Although the newspapers rarely made the association explicit, the label tended to appear in stories about Mexican-Americans. The zoot-suiter was someone who wore his hair long and greased and who dressed in long suit-coats; his trousers were tight at the waist, pegged at the cuff, and full at the knee. The zoot-suiter was accused of a whole roster of familiar social crimes and moral sins, such as draft-dodging, gang attacks, deliquency, and sexual misbehavior. Mob attacks on zoot-suiters were occasionally met with retaliation, which was in turn used to justify the original attacks. Turner and Killian (1957) quoted from the report of Turner and Surace (1956) that:

> Groups of sailors were frequently reported to be assisted or accompanied by civilian mobs who "egged" them on as they roamed through downtown streets in search of victims. "Zooters" discovered on city streets were assaulted and forced to disrobe amidst the jibes and molestations of the crowd. Streetcars and buses were stopped and searched. "Zooters" found therein were carried off into the streets and subjected to beatings . . . (p. 125).

What Turner called "continuous two-way interaction between collective behavior and the larger society" often includes patterns of retaliatory assault. In the California situation, the essential preliminary of collective behavior was the neutralization of the conventional normative order in reference to the Mexican-Americans. Before the crowds could mobilize for action and the participants could feel that their behavior was appropriate, Mexicans had to become zoot-suiters, because zoot-suiters could be treated in a way that Mexicans could not. The same process appeared in the 1960s with reference to the Black Muslims, the Black Panther Party, and hippies (Brown, 1969a).

Symbolic neutralization of conventional norms may also have been at work in Chicago during the 1968 Democratic National Convention. This episode was labeled a police riot in the Walker Report (1968) to the National Commission on the Causes and Prevention of Violence. According to the Walker Report, demonstrators who came to Chicago before the convention to express opposition to the war in Vietnam and dissent on other issues had been characterized in the media and by officials as "'hippy-Yippie,' entirely 'New Left,' entirely anarchist, or entirely youthful political dissenters . . ."(p. 4). The Walker Report noted that this characterization "is both wrong and dangerous. The stereotyping that did occur helps to explain the emotional reaction of both police and public during and after the violence that occurred" (p. 4).

Mediating Publics as Social Control. In addition to limits on crowd behavior imposed by conventional norms, the crowd is controlled by the way in which it is publically identified. In the United States, public identification often begins in the mass media, and incidents of collective behavior are usually news. Heavy coverage and conflicting reports leave the initial situation confusing (National Advisory Commission on Civil Disorders, 1968, p. 368). As news is repeated, discussed, and summarized, standard interpretations of events emerge. Turner called a group of people who share a particular interpretation of events a mediating public. This special type of public consists of those people who feel that they have a stake in how an episode is understood or defined. It constitutes "the principal mechanism through which society is affected by any instance of collective behavior" (Turner, 1964, pp. 418-19).

An interpretation of an episode of collective behavior ordinarily answers three questions (1) What is it about? (2) Where does justice lie? (3) How will it end? The third question implies two further questions: Will there be more trouble? If a cause is being advanced, can it succeed in changing things? The way in which these questions are answered determines whether or not others are likely to join the crowd, whether officials respond with reform or suppression, and what measures will be taken by the government in the future. For example, when William T. Gossett, the ninety-second president of the American Bar Association, commented on the forms of protest that characterized the 1960s, he offered an interpretation of episodes of collective behavior that answered each of the three questions:

> It is well known that mobs do not generate human progress; they retard it. It is known that mobs do not establish rights; they trample them. It is known that mobs do not inspire the advancement of civilization; they impede it. . . . Mobbism is, then, the antithesis of civilization -the dire step that moves backward precipitously and fiercely; undoing in a few wild hours the forward movement of generations. Obviously, mob violence and destruction cannot be tolerated by any nation that counts itself civilized (1968, p. 3).

Gossett presented the viewpoint of a mediating public that sees civil disturbances as irrational protest, heedless of the rights of others. This public believes that justice is on the side of those opposing the participants, and it feels that the law must operate forcefully and immediately if greater dangers are to be averted. Carmichael and Hamilton (1967), commenting on the same events to which Gossett addressed himself stated that:

> The eruption in Birmingham, Alabama, in the spring of 1963 showed how quickly anger can develop into violence. Black people were angry about the killing of Emmett Till and Charles Mack Parker; the failure of federal,

state, and city governments to deal honestly with the problems of ghetto life. Now they read in the newspapers, saw on television and watched from the street corners themselves the police dogs and the fire hoses and the policemen beating their friends and relatives. They watched as young high-school students and women were beaten, as Martin Luther King and his co-workers were marched off to jail. The spark was ignited when a black owned motel in Birmingham and the home of Dr. King's brother were bombed. This incident brought hundreds of angry black people into the streets throwing rocks and bottles and sniping at policemen . . . James Baldwin stated it clearly in 1963: "When a race riot occurs . . . it will not spread merely to Birmingham . . . . The trouble will spread to every metropolitan center in the nation which has a significant Negro population."

* * *

This country, with its pervasive institutional racism, has itself created socially undesirable conditions; it merely perpetuates those conditions when it lays the blame on people who, through whatever means at their disposal, seek to strike out at the conditions (p. 154-55, 161).

Carmichael and Hamilton represent another mediating public that answers the three basic questions quite differently. The civil disturbances are not attributed to mobbism but are interpreted as decent people struggling against indecent conditions for social, economic, and political justice. Justice does not lie with those people who condemn the disturbances but with those people who are fighting against oppression; the outcome depends upon the willingness of those in power to respond by revamping basic features of social, economic, and political structure.

The Role of Mass Media in the Formulation of Interpretations. Because mediating publics are both represented and guided by the news media, the role of the mass media in formulating interpretations must be examined. Commenting on the media's coverage of the Watts disturbances of 1967, the National Advisory Commission on Civil Disorders (1968) stated that:

We have found a significant imbalance between what actually happened in our cities and what the newspaper, radio, and television coverage of the riots told us happened . . . . We found that the disorders, as serious as they were, were less destructive, less widespread, and less a black-white confrontation than most people believed.

* * *

We are deeply concerned that millions of Americans, who must rely on the mass media . . . formed incorrect impressions and judgments about what went on in American cities last summer (p. 363).

Although the commission specifically denied that the contradictions between reports and actual events was solely a consequence of sensationalism, they did make the following observations:

First, . . There were instances of gross flaws in presenting news of the 1967 riots. Some newspapers printed "scare" headlines unsupported by the mild stories that followed. All media reported rumors that had no basis in fact. Some newsmen staged "riot" events for the cameras . . . . Second, the press obtained much factual information about the scale of the disorders . . . from local officials, who often were inexperienced in dealing with civil disorders and not always able to sort out fact from rumor in the confusion. At the height of the Detroit riot, some news reports of property damage put the figure in excess of $500 million. Subsequent investigation shows it to be $40 to $45 million . . . . Third, the coverage of the disorders—particularly on television—tended to define the events as black-white confrontations. In fact almost all of the deaths, injuries and property damage occurred in all-Negro neighborhoods, and thus the disorders were not "race-riots" as that term is generally understood.

* * *

Television coverage tended to give the impression that the riots were confrontations between Negros and whites rather than responses by Negroes to underlying slum problems . . . . The ratio of white male adults to Negro male adults shown on television is high (1:2) considering that the riots took place in predominantly Negro neighborhoods.

* * *

Newspapers tended to characterize and portray last summer's riots in national terms rather than as local phenomena and problems, especially when rioting was taking place in the newspaper's own city . . . . During the actual disorders, the newspapers in each city studied tended to print many stories dealing with disorders . . . in other cities. About 40 percent of the riot or racial stories in each local newspaper during the period of rioting in that city came from the wire service (p. 364-71).

The commission's conclusions concerning the role of the mass media stated that:

Closely linked to these problems is the phenomenon of cumulative effect . . . . What the public saw and read last summer thus produced emotional reactions and left vivid impressions not wholly attributable to the material itself (pp. 364-65).

The commission, however, refused to conclude that the media were a *cause* of the riots when they asserted that:

In some cities people who watched television reports and read newspaper accounts of riots in other cities later rioted themselves. But the causal chain weakens when we recall that in other cities, people in very much the same circumstances watched the same programs and read the same newspaper stories but did not riot themselves (pp. 366-67).

The commission's analysis of the content and tone of the media coverage shows how a specific interpretation of the events emerges. Both television and the newspapers were "cautious and restrained" and both emphasized "control of the riot." Of the television scenes of the riots, 53.8 percent emphasized control and "activities in the aftermath of the riot." Among newspaper articles, 15.5 percent focused on containment or control and 16.5 percent on proposals for legislation, plans to control ongoing riots, and plans to prevent riots in the future. By emphasizing the activities of law enforcement agencies, television newscasts tended to underplay the grievances and tensions that were generally conceded to be at the root of the riots (see Schiller, 1971).

The complexity of the development of mediating publics may be illlustrated by the fact the the commission report, itself, provided the basis for the formation of another public, namely those people prepared to accept the commssion's view of the reported events (Silver, 1969). The report also answered the three questions that provided the basis for interpretation. It asserted that the disturbances were caused by "Negroes acting against local symbols of white American society, authority, and property in Negro neighbor-hoods—rather than against white persons." The Negroes "appeared to be seeking . . . fuller participation in the social order and the material benefits enjoyed by the majority of American citizens. Rather than rejecting the American system, they were anxious to obtain a place for themselves in it." Implicitly, but unmistakably, the report claimed that justice lies in social and economic reform. It recommended "new initiatives and experiments that can change the system of failure and frustration that now dominates the ghetto and weakens our society." The report also described the probable outcome of the situation: "Our nation is moving toward two societies, one black, one white—separate and unequal."

Since 1919, special official reports have served to establish a tradition of interpretations of urban riots and other forms of collective behavior. Officially sponsored interpretations play a role in the social control of episodes, largely because of their unique effect on their mediating public—that is, the segment of the populace that supports the official interpretation. On the one hand, by raising the episode to the level of a problem and engaging the resources of the community in problem-solving activities, official investigations and interpreta-tions may justify a reduction of concern for the issues raised by the episode. Reports shift concern from politics to the more abstract and orthodox problems of research and interpretation, and the period of reflection they require is likely to be a period of inaction. Waskow (1966) indicated that when a commission appointed by the governor of Illinois investigated the 1919 Chicago riots, the political concern of whites with the issues raised by the black community was reduced as the focus of the white power structure shifted from reform to study and analysis. This reduction of concern occurred despite the fact that the commission's report listed many of the grievances of the black community.

On the other hand, the official reports and the commissions that prepare reports can also transform a potentially controversial and challenging political event into a managerial problem. This encourages public reliance on officials and official strategies, including violence, for the resolution of what come to be viewed as uncontroversial social problems. An official investigation suggests that what had been out of control is now under control, again part of the official order of society. The problem is disposed of by being placed "under consideration" and "in good hands." The control function of research commissions does not go unnoticed, however. The participants in collective behavior, and those people in sympathy with them, often regard official reports with the cynicism appropriate to substitutes for ameliorative or remedial action.

Both the coverage of the 1967 riots and the Kerner Commission's report on that coverage reviewed the acknowledged sources of strain in society and identified a range of issues to which individuals and interest groups could commit themselves. Because news media and official reports tend to broaden participation in the process of definition and interpretation, they draw larger sections of the society into mediating publics. By defining the issues and the approved responses to them, news media and official reports set some of the conditions for conflict.

Conventionalization as Control.

Processes of conventionalization are at work from the start, in every instance of collective behavior, because of the continual reassertion of the institutional order (Turner, 1964, p. 420).

From an official point of view, the main thrust of an episode of collective behavior is its violation of the prevailing socio-political order. The violation of order threatens the relative positions of officials and their constituencies. As an alternative to the crisis-generating pose of confrontation, emergent norms may be conventionalized and collective behavior, thereby, drawn into the traditional institutional framework of society. Conventionalization tends to be an official strategy—it is sometimes called cooptation. When the initiative for conventionalization comes from officials, it serves to protect specific office holders and to control the ways in which political issues are publicly defined. Yet the initiative for integrating emergent and established norms can arise within a movement or an episode of collective behavior itself.

The development of collective bargaining in the United States illustrates the conventionalization of emergent norms and collective behavior. Initially, the strike was collective behavior. Repetition within increasingly organized settings routinized it so that it became an identifiable form of social action. Its incorporation into organized conflict gave it at least a modicum of legitimacy. Instead of being interpreted as a general challenge to property rights and established order, the strike came to be identified as a move within a process of negotiation that required the demonstration by all parties of the limits of their power. Repetition stabilized the definition and interpretation of such episodes and established the power of the active collectivities. After strikes were given the status of a tactic for organizations legitimately engaged in conflict, it was only a matter of time before such actions became legal and were codified as an institutional part of "industrial relations." In this case, institutionalization followed the formation of a base of power mobilized in a tradition of action and interpretation.

This technique of conventionalizing emergent norms ultimately rests on the development of power—supportive publics, organization, and control over opposition resources—among the dissidents. Potential participants in collective behavior occasionally court such a development by attempting to enter the institutional framework without dealing with the facts of power and, consequently, without attempting to establish a position of negotiation. This attempt to enter the institutional framework usually occurs when issues seem to turn on legitimacy rather than when power and organization are weak. This type of approach can become a tradition of a movement whether or not it succeeds in gaining official acceptance of the goals of the participants and whether or not the organization develops the capacity to wield power. The approach can be illustrated by the civil rights movement, which worked largely within the courts and legislatures during the late 1950s and early 1960s, with some community organizing of voter registration. The legalistic approach to integration has been a persistent theme of organizations such as the National Association for the Advancement of Colored People (NAACP), despite the inefficiency or ineffectiveness of judicial and legislative action. Regardless of the minimal effects, the legalistic approach allows the movement to persist by virtue of official and public tolerance or even active support. At the same time, the approach justifies the official rejection of more radical demands and militant organizations (B. Moore, 1969b) and, consequently, diminishes the likelihood of the indigenous development of a base of power within the mass of black and poor people.

The attempt by a dissident group to conventionalize its own protest tends to establish limits to that protest and to obviate its capacity to escalate pressure in the event that official beneficence fails and the group finds it necessary to enter a period of active negotiation. This situation is due to the fact that initial moves toward conventionalization ordinarily discredit unconventional approaches and justify their suppression. Conventionalization presupposes absolute limits to action by projecting a future in terms of the values and norms of the present. It usually states the dissident case in terms that justify official control over the course of reform.

Whether it occurs on the initiative of officials or of dissidents, conventionalization always involves the modification of an official stance regarding an episode of collective behavior. New statements are made and old statements are changed or eliminated from the public arena. Thus, in 1968, during their campaigns, several presidential aspirants recited slogans from the civil rights movement: "We shall not be moved" or "We shall overcome"; in 1971, President Nixon was reported to have declared "Power to the people." When the attempt to conventionalize emergent norms and definitions of the situation is initiated by officials, the situation is defined as a demand for reform within the existing power structure. Conventionalization revises official rhetoric and, to the extent to which publics are engaged by the new rhetoric, affects the chance of any office holder to remain in authority. The paradox of conventionalization is illustrated by the course of the American invasion of Indo-China. President Nixon justified his escalation of the war, the invasions of Cambodia and Laos in 1970 and 1971, and the federal government's repression of the Left by reference to the explicit goal of the antiwar movement: "Peace now." It is precisely this paradox that leads radical organizations to resist conventionalization, even at the expense of remaining unacceptable to large numbers of people, and to insist that issues be clarified and understood in terms of their radical meaning.

AN EVALUATION OF EMERGENT NORM THEORY

Turner's theory assumes that conformity arises under the impact of an emergent norm, which means that participants in collective behavior experience social pressure against nonconformity and do not necessarily act out of the same feelings or beliefs. Turner argued that social pressure is usually strongest among people who identify with one another or who acknowledge shared experiences (Bindler, et al., 1970). This view suggests that the crowd's control over its members is greatest when the participants define themselves as having something in common—a hypothesis that Turner interprets as a challenge to earlier ideas about the catalytic force of anonymity. Actually, the hypothesis only distinguishes collective behavior, as defined by Turner, from the uncoordinated and individuated outbursts described by the early theorists of mass behavior. According to Turner, the more mutual recognition (and he seems to mean practical recognition) there is among people, the more likely it is that they will form a crowd that will act collectively under stress or on an unanticipated occasion.

This hypothesis can be translated into a prediction: As those people living in a specific area and feeling oppressed or dissatisfied become politically organized, they will be less likely to engage in uncoordinated, individuated, and "riotous" activity and more likely to engage in collective behavior, given the conditions for such behavior. Under these circumstances, official control would either recognize the existence of collectivities and shift from suppression to negotiation, or it would escalate into political and social repression (Skolnick, 1969). In other words, after an area or a gathering or collection of people has been mobilized for action, residents or members can no longer be treated by officials as individuals with regard to that action. Individuals have become members or agents of collectivities that have goals that must be dealt with through collectively authorized representatives. When this consequence of mobilization is not recognized, the refusal or inability—because organization clarifies conflict at the same time that it affords an alternative to confrontation—of officials to engage in political negotiation and their continued reliance on a strategy of political suppression increases the likelihood of episodes of collective behavior. Indeed, this very pattern describes the official action and political protest during the 1960s.

Turner's theory of emergent norms may thus be used to construct an account of the ways in which collective behavior extends into politics and institutional change. Turner does not articulate the full sequence but focuses on the emergence of the crowd. Nevertheless, a complete developmental pattern is implicit in his argument: the failure of prior norms followed by interaction gives rise to an emergent norm in conjunction with a definition of the situation as one in which that norm can fruitfully operate. An emergent norm is thus defined as a sanctioned regularity that characterizes interaction in situations in which already existing norms are inoperative. To the extent to which the emergent norm is organizationally elaborated or the institutional norms remain inoperative, the crowd can persist and grow into a more complex movement engaged in protracted struggle.

Emergent norm theory has several advantages over earlier theories. First, the concept of norm permits conventional social theory to be applied to an unconventional phenomenon. Second, it permits an empirical description of the crowd that is more refined than that offered by the theories of contagion and convergence. Emergent norm theory should not be viewed as explaining "why an unnatural unanimity develops, but as explaining the imposition of a pattern of differential expression which is perceived as unanimity by crowd members and observers" (Turner, 1964, p. 390). According to the emergent norm theory, the complete uniformity of the crowd is an illusion that is a result of positional and perspectival limits to observation.

Emergent norm theory can also account for commonly observed limits to the development of the crowd. An important problem in collective behavior stems from the fact that crowds do not always move to the final limits of possible action. Turner draws on Rude's (1959) example of the crowd that stormed the Bastille in 1789 but did not harm the highly available director of the prison. According to contagion theory, typically, a spiral of mutual reinforcement would lead to extreme behavior under extreme circumstances. This unrestricted escalation, however, is not what is usually observed. Collective behavior is often restrained as well as directed by its dominant norm. The crowds that will tear at the clothes of a hero or movie star will not strip him naked or deliberately harm him, because such an act will meet with disapproval and resistance, which would only dampen the spirit of the crowd. Emergent norm theory can explain the phenomenon of the restrained and orderly crowd as well as that of the unruly crowd, which significantly increases the range of intelligibility of crowd behavior. In this way, emergent norm theory constitutes an implicit reproach to contagion theory, which attributes to every crowd the same unlimited spiraling momentum; and to convergence theory, which sees every crowd as limited only by the dispositions of its members. Turner added that:

> Normative theory further gives rise to the hypothesis that many forms of crowd behavior are rendered possible as much by the conviction that behavior will not exceed certain upper limits as by the interstimulation of like-minded partcipants (1964, p. 391).

Emergent norm theory offers a hint of social structure that provides for differential response within the crowd, at least during early stages of crowd development. It also takes into account the apparent uniformity of the crowd as well as differences among crowds in the direction of action and the intensity of mood. Finally, the theory views the crowd as subject to three major forces: normative uncertainty, interaction, and social control. Thus, it offers insight into the complex interactions among crowd participants, officials, and surrounding publics.

GOFFMAN'S INTERACTIONIST THEORY

Erving Goffman has not formulated a theory of collective behavior. He has not explicity dealt with specific episodes of collective behavior, nor has he discussed the crowd. However, Goffman's analysis of ordinary face-to-face interaction has important inplications for a theory of the crowd that can be developed within the interactionist tradition in social psychology. The following discussion extrapolates an interactionist theory of collective behavior from the general body of Goffman's writings (e.g., 1961, 1963a, 1963b, 1967).

THE INTERACTIONIST TRADITION

The interactionist tradition, principally stated by the pragmatist-philosopher George Herbert Mead (1932, 1938), offers an important paradigm—compatible in many respects with social phenomenology—within contemporary American sociology. Mead examined the conduct of participants in social relations in order to find out how individual acts depended upon the collective actions of which they were part. It is a truism to say that all behavior is caused or that behavior takes place in a context; Mead set out to analyze the ways in which individual acts and social situations are dialectically interdependent. He tried to specify the relationship of individual and collective action to shared meanings, perspectives, and definitions of the situation.

For example, as a person carries on a conversation with his neighbor, gestures and statements give rise to an overall conversational pattern that, in turn, influences the meaning of its constituent gestures and statements. Each remark is a part of the flow of talk and would have a different meaning or carry a different weight in a different setting. When the person asks a question, he initiates an action that is completed or sustained by his neighbor's answer, and that is understood only as it unfolds. Each person contributes to the behavior of the other, and each individual act depends upon a mobile and reflexive setting to which both people contribute.

Thus, for Mead, acts are both temporary and collaborative; they are temporary because they are part of an ongoing and changing situation, and they are collaborative because the situation is sustained and defined by the interaction of the participants. From this point of view, it is not possible to separate the study of behavior and the study of situation. Rather, all behavior is seen as socially situated action and all situations are seen as projections of an act.

Mead's fundamental unit of analysis is the social situation, and his major questions are: How is a particular act intelligible to those who are "members to" (Garfinkel, 1967) its setting? How does a situation come to be defined as a setting for action? How does a situation change? For Mead, individual conduct is primarily understandable as an extension of a particular social situation to which participants are mutually responsive. The Luddite who protested working conditions in 1811 by destroying his master's machinery in Nottingham, England, was a participant in a social situation. His act was shaped by a social reality that consisted of a large protest movement, by the smaller band of protesters with whom he was allied, and by social gatherings in which the bases for particular activities were established. Similarly, many of the violations of the selective service laws of the United States during the late 1960s were political crime. As such, they were acts of participation—or, more accurately, acts of agency, the principal of which is a community of interest (Brown, 1968)—as much as they were expressions of individual moral positions. The meaning of these violations depend upon moral standards and alternatives that had devel-

oped and were shared within the antiwar movement. The actual decision to resist
the draft is always made in a local context of involvement in which the political,
social, and moral meaning of the act is part of a tangible and ongoing social reality.

As the above examples suggest, the collaborative nature of social situations
does not exclude opposition. A conversation can be extended and sustained by
disagreement. The extent to which disagreement or conflict can be accommodated varies within a social situation. Probably the chief considerations are whether
the participants consider a continuation of the interaction to be desirable—that is,
as likely to have good results—and whether there is an available alternative to the
interaction. Obviously, participants do not always see the total situation in
exactly the same way, although there must be considerable agreement about the
meaning or implications of specific acts. Because every social situation is ongoing
and developmental, its overall meaning and direction are continually open to
redefinition. Moreover, in order for any social situation to be sustained, the
separate interpretations of the interaction must be partially resolved or, at the
least, participants must not notice them as incompatible. Therefore, participation usually includes some elements of probing or testing to establish both
implications of the other person's behavior and the way one's own contributions
are understood. These reflexive moves provide at least a semblance of compatibility among the ways participants view each other and in the ways they define the
situation as a whole. A sense that something of a particular type is going on
enables each participant to move confidently with the ongoing situation, which
implies that interaction is both topical and self-regulating. Specifically, participants share a situation to some extent but spend a certain amount of interaction
on resolving differences among themselves. Such differences are often revealed
through the efforts of the participants to establish the meanings of acts and
situation.

SOCIAL INTERACTION IN TERMS
OF DRAMA AND THE STAGE

The vision of social interaction as intrinsically problematic and dynamic
led Goffman to formulate his own theory in terms of drama, using the language
and categories of the stage to discuss ordinary social behavior. Using this model,
he talked about the presentation of self and the performance of roles. He noted
the way participants usually work together as teams, and his model allowed him
to take into account the peculiar instability and complexity of situated social
action, whereby participants can play both against and with each other at the
same time that they shape and are shaped by their game or drama.

Goffman's theory does not imply that social interaction is always a matter
of pretending or that interaction is nothing more than the rehearsal of set
attitudes. Rather, he wanted to emphasize the aspect of drama that takes into
account the relevance of conventions, routines, and roles (implicit and explicit)
in determining human behavior. Whatever an individual does in society, he is in a
particular "scene" which involves a setting, a cast of characters, and a changing
scenario. The idea of role performance captures the smoothness and regularity of
most social situations as well as the awkwardness that occurs as individuals slip

in and out of their roles. The idea also suggests the meaningfulness of specific actions; Goffman argued that actions, like the actions of players, are gestures that are meaningful and absorbing, primarily as relevant parts of an interactive setting or process. Above all, performance is relevant and timely behavior. In this way, much of ordinary behavior is imbedded in a program—it fits into something larger that is also something social. Of course, in most ordinary situations the overall design is only loosely laid down. Social life has an improvisational character.

Social situations, or scenes, vary in the range of options they allow the participants. During a disaster, for example, rescue work is so detailed and urgent that roles and their performance requirements are only called into question under unusual circumstances—for example, when resources are unavailable or conflict arises among groups. Ordinarily, the activities of rescue are performed as a matter of course, for individuals are absorbed in their roles and time is filled with activity and concern.

On the other hand, participation can be less urgent and individuals less spontaneously involved in their activity. For example, in a conversation with strangers or with children, an adult is often at an emotional or intellectual distance from the roles that define the conversation. In this case, the adult knows his performance as an element of a pattern external to his "self." Sometimes this distance is marked by the awkwardness and self-consciousness that accompanies roles that are infrequently played or normally played in idealized fashion. This distance may also arise when a person becomes aware that he is entering a particular interaction that makes him subject to appraisal on moral, aesthetic, political, or biographical grounds. Under these circumstances, the individual is apt to plan his behavior and criticize his own performance and the performance of others, as he considers the situation as a whole. Often, a person will adopt strategies of interaction that allow him to perform his roles without fear of giving himself away.

Role distance is often a prelude to withdrawal or the assumption of power because of the loss of information or simplification that accompanies a shift in attention from detail to design. Considering the situation as a whole also raises the possibility of transforming or abandoning it; role distance evokes radical alternatives. Few social situations can sustain the question, "What's the point?" When an individual notices the negative aspects of role distance, he is likely to describe the situation as one of "inauthenticity," "alienation from one's acts," "failure to suspend disbelief," or, from a group perspective, "low morale." When its positive aspects are emphasized, role distance is often called "reflection," or, perhaps, the more ambivalent "self-consciousness."

This discussion of urgent and distant modes of involvement suggests that as a scene comes to resemble a disaster, or as time is filled with urgent detailed requirements and mutual dependence, participants are involved in their local setting to the exclusion of the wider situation: they are inattentive to alternative and marginal concerns. In such an overwhelmingly immediate situation, individual behavior becomes an intimate aspect of interaction. Face-to-face interaction in novel or uncertain situations shows some of these absorbing qualities; it involves participants more thoroughly than do interactions that are routine or remote.

Goffman called episodes of focused face-to-face interaction (interaction about a topic) *encounters.* His discussion of encounters has important implications for issues fundamental to the study of collective behavior. First, what is the basic unit for the analysis of collective behavior? Is it the crowd, the gathering, the episode itself, or interaction? Is collective behavior a particular sequence of steps, none of which is extraordinary in itself, as Smelser suggested? Or is collective behavior a peculiar form of social grouping—the generic crowd that Turner viewed as arising from the closure of normal channels of social activity? Second, how can the high degree of involvement that characterizes participation in episodes of collective behavior be explained? What leads individuals to perform actions that seem unrelated to their personal or social history? How do we account for actions that seem to bypass the self-criticism and reflection that are usually attributed to social behavior? This question, introduced by earlier contagion theorists and largely ignored by Turner and Smelser, must be dealt with. Third, how do episodes of collective behavior begin and under what conditions do they develop? In particular, can a precipitating incident regularly be found? What limits the direction or duration of collective behavior? And, under what conditions does collective behavior change or end?

AN ANALYSIS OF COLLECTIVE BEHAVIOR

The implications of Goffman's work for the analysis of collective behavior emerge from a criticism of Turner's solution to the problem of the composition of the crowd. Turner criticized theories of contagion and convergence for assuming that the crowd is a spontaneously formed collection of volatile like-minded people. According to Turner, the sociologist must ask whether the shared feelings and ideas attributed to the crowd by the classical theories of collective behavior really exist. Consequently, he began with the observation of concrete interactions at various points within a large gathering as the basic data for the analysis of crowds. His procedures, however, did not provide a basis for extending to crowds the conclusions he had reached about the emergence of norms from small group interaction. Turner's assumption that the way in which norms emerge remains constant through changes in the size of groups must be recognized as an unjustified leap from the known to the unknown. In the absence of somewhat stable face-to-face contact among all the members of a crowd, how can the apparent generalized conformity to a dominant norm be accounted for? How do the norms that emerge among locally interacting individuals come to characterize the whole crowd? Turner's suggestion that rumor accounts for the way in which the homogeneity of the crowd develops out of local units merely displaced the problem to the communication situation.

Turner was justified in criticizing the old theories of collective behavior for their failure to ground the concept of the crowd in observation, but the adequacy of his own discussion is thrown into question by the absence of mechanisms that explain how a variety of local interactions come to be integrated under a dominant emergent norm. His own theory requires an explanation of the way in which a large number of individuals come to participate in the same action. The difficulty of finding such mechanisms might have led Turner to ask whether the classical image of the crowd as a homogenous group was justified. His only gesture toward the solution of the problem, however, lies in his suggestion that when people are densely packed together they can communicate with each other about the event or issues that brought them together, so that norms can develop and spread rapidly. Even in situations of moderate social density, the norms that emerge in small scale interaction can spread as various groups come in contact with one another. This hypothesis, however, suggests that communication takes place between groups as it does between individuals—a highly dubious assumption. In any case, Turner noted that a shared focus of attention, a common concern, or a leader can help generate the shared norm.

It should also be remembered that, for Turner, the development of the crowd, apart from interaction based on physical closeness, is itself an expression of social control. His investigation of interaction led him to conclusions about differentiation within the crowd. Lacking an explanation for integration, Turner was unable to account for the precise ways in which social control—that is, the dominant norm—itself diffuses throughout the crowd. Turner is also unable to account for the transmission of such external social controls as new information, police action, and so forth.

In denying the accuracy of the classical picture of the crowd, Turner asserted that the alleged uniformity of mood and action was an illusion. But, because the term crowd has always been used to designate a homogenous mass of people, his denial amounts to saying that there is no such thing as a crowd. Although Turner undertook to explain patterns of conformity in episodes of collective behavior rather than to justify the classical picture of the crowd, the denial caused him difficulty when he wanted to distinguish between crowds and institutionalized behavior and when he tried to classify crowds by their dominant norms. In his discussion of these problems, Turner appeared to accept the very assumption that he had elsewhere rejected; namely, that there are relatively homogenous collectivities that satisfy the classical description of the crowd.

Goffman escaped Turner's difficulty by beginning with different analytic concepts. Without assuming anything about the crowd, Goffman proceeded as if the structure and dynamics of collective behavior were yet to be discovered. He made clear the distinctions between interaction, the occasion on which interaction occurs, and the interpretation of events. Obviously the first requirement for the development of an episode of collective behavior is a gathering of people. Goffman distinguished between a gathering and the occasion for any social action. All gatherings contain the potential for interaction. According to Goffman, the occasion is the specific framework of meaning within which interaction occurs. An occasion limits the range of acceptable activities and establishes an agenda and a schedule for interaction. Behavior is initially intelligible by virtue of its reference to an occasion, the violation of which raises the issue of propriety or decorum. For example, an occasion might be a spectacle that brings people together or an issue that provides a topical basis for interaction (see Unit I). The occasion may be anticipated, as with football games or political rallies, or unanticipated, as with automobile accidents, or disasters.

Features of Interaction. Two features of interaction on the unanticipated occasion of a large gathering are of special importance to the study of collective behavior. First, the interaction is face-to-face; second, the interaction is highly fluid. The availability and easy circulation of participants makes for rapid circulation of information. Clearly, the degree to which information is centrally released and widely distributed is inversely related to the circulation of personnel. As the central focus or issue is clarified, people will not have to move around to find out what has happened. However, they will not simply stand still and passively receive information about the initial focus of attention. On the contrary, as they begin to communicate with each other, the gathering breaks into islands of interaction.

Face-to-face Interaction. In relation to the problem of collective behavior, two characteristics of face-to-face interaction are crucial: the "richness of information flow" and the "facilitation of feedback" (Goffman, 1963, p. 17). Because face-to-face interaction is largely improvised, the participants are especially vulnerable to one another. They divulge more than they intend to and are constantly forced to correct impressions formed on fragmentary clues. Each communication provides information about the focal issue of interaction and also about the state of the communicator himself. The communicator usually cannot help but give an impression of his psychological state, and listeners constantly shift their attention, coordinating impressions based on slight indications given by facial expressions, intonations, gestures, and posture. In addition, each person is both sender and receiver. Each person can find immediate and tangible evidence of how his own behavior is taken. He can see that he is being experienced in some way, and he will guide at least some of his conduct according to the definitions and responses that appear to be made by his audience. Goffman observed that when people use their senses, as in face-to-face interaction, they are "made naked by their use. We are clearly seen as the agents of our acts" (Goffman, 1961). This special richness and mutuality of local, face-to-face interaction, coupled with its urgency as improvised communication, creates an attention to detail, an intensification of mutual dependence, and an absorption in the interactive moment. This concentration and localization of activity is one aspect of the compelling quality of face-to-face and body-to-body encounters.

Focused and Unfocused Interaction. A gathering can provide more than an occasion for interaction; it may also provide sufficient focus for a sustained interaction, specifically, a topic. A large number of people gathered in a park on a Sunday afternoon can share the same area without having any common focus of attention. On the other hand, an automobile accident may be an occasion for individuals to gather at the scene. As more spectators arrive, the simple fact of gathering itself is an occasion for others to join. Such focused convergence is not, itself, a form of collective behavior, because the action does not originate within a collectivity. When an individual sees an accident or an assembly of people who seem to be involved in something, he is not affected by the norms or definitions of the gathering he observes but by curiosity and/or the prospect of participation. His interest grows out of the special qualities of the object of attention rather than out of interaction with others. After arriving on the scene, a spectator may become a participant by talking to people in order to comment on the situation or by asking what has happened. In other words, the gathering and the accident provide successive frames of reference for focused interaction.

Goffman's distinction between focused and unfocused interaction depends upon the presence or absence of an initial focus for interaction. The distinction allows for the possibility that a focus of attention can develop within any gathering.

That an occasion exists means that people on the scene have some idea of what to do and what not to do and some basis for anticipating the behavior of their fellows. It accounts for the incorporation of conventional norms into most encounters and is true for both anticipated and unanticipated occasions. A concern that arises within a setting can spread in ways that cannot fully be anticipated and can focus and organize interaction from act to act as gestures are exchanged.

The Appearance of Regularities in Encounters. As an encounter continues, regularities appear that reduce the variability of behavior characteristic of improvisation. These regularities organize and define the encounter for the participants and help to keep tension at a tolerable level. If an encounter is to be maintained and elaborated upon in further, shared activities, it must be protected from disruption. Interruptions can come from two directions: from inappropriate behavior on the part of the participants or from the intrusion of matters external to the encounter. Such intrusions may be minor disturbances, interruptions, or bona fide disruptions, depending upon the way in which they are handled by participants. Encounters are protected by two types of regularity that participants interpret as normative. Goffman (1961) refers to these regularities as *rules of irrelevance* and *transformation rules*.

The rules of irrelevance are rarely explicit within an encounter, but they establish what "shall be attended and disattended, and through this . . . what shall be accepted as the definition of the situation" (Goffman, 1961, p. 19). These rules steady the focus of the encounter, distinguish the encounter from its alternatives, and identify it as a specific type of scene.

Goffman's rules of transformation are mechanisms by means of which aspects of reality that are not relevant to the focused gathering, but that nevertheless impinge upon it, can be accommodated without disrupting the occasion and the organization of the encounter. Transformation rules which govern the way in which externally based concerns are modified to enter the context of the encounter are often subtle and fluid. Adeptness at handling transformation rules is usually called tact; tactfulness calls for close attention to the requirements of the immediate social situation.

Both the rules of irrelevance and the rules of transformation help to define the encounter, giving it a boundary that insulates it from the rest of the world. They sustain "a locally realized world of roles and events [that] cuts the participants off from many externally based matters . . ." (Goffman, 1961, p. 31). As encounters guide and reinforce the spontaneous involvement of the participants, they acquire a momentum that allows them to persist beyond changes in personnel and, to some extent beyond the life of any particular topic or occasion (p. 238). This inertia of encounters is partially caused by their tendency to provide an exclusive domain, within which individual acts are intelligible.

But encounters also provide pleasure in the form of fun. In describing gaming encounters, Goffman (1961) noted that although people can win as players, it is only as involved participants that they can get fun out of winning (pp. 36-37). "Fun" requires a specific limitation of tension; it describes the ease experienced when involvement in a situation is total and not subject to question—when a person is a participant and not just a player, when a person is "in" or "of" the game and not simply making the moves. This ease of play is possible by virtue of the collective enforcement of the rules of transformation and the rules of irrelevance, which protect the basis of participation.

Goffman's Rules and Turner's Norms. Goffman's description of the rules by which encounters are defined and protected should be compared to Turner's discussion of the norms that emerge within unscheduled encounters. Both Goffman and Turner are looking at the same social process, but they are looking at the process differently and with a different degree of attention to detail. Turner's norms specify a preferred form and direction of behavior; his focus is on conformity rather than on the emergence of social structure. Goffman's rules are directed at the preservation of an encounter rather than at the control of individual acts. In this way he can account for the improvised quality and the variety of individual behavior within a stable determinate setting, which contrasts with Turner's assumption of uniformity—a lack of behavioral variety— at the level of the small encounter. For Turner, the function of norms is to direct and consolidate the activities of the members of an encounter. For Goffman, the rules segregate an encounter and bind its participants to an unstated, but shared and exclusive social reality. Goffman stressed the capacity of an encounter to absorb its participants and, thus, limit the range of behavior and qualify the way in which particular concerns can be handled intelligibly. Regardless of the content of the norms (which for Goffman is highly contingent, both theorists agree that some common recognition of a shared reality will develop among the participants in any encounter; and according to Goffman, a common recognition of the prospect of sharing a reality will also develop.

COLLECTIVITIES: CROWD COMPOSITION AND EXPANSION

It must now be asked whether Goffman's analysis can provide an answer to the questions that Turner left unsettled: How do large numbers of individuals come to participate in episodes of collective behavior? Is there such a thing as a large crowd? Or should the same phenomenon be described as an accumulation of commonly focused social clusters or encounters in which the apparent commonality of focus is a problem for investigation?

Both Turner and Goffman suggested that although collective behavior may seem to involve a large number of doing the same thing or conforming to some particular norm, it is more accurate to say that episodes of collective behavior involve a number of relatively isolated groupings or collectivities. Here, it is relevant to consider the binding and localizing qualities of face-to-face interaction on an unanticipated occasion. These qualities imply that an episode of collective behavior consists of floating "islands" of interdependent people. It is not a mass of otherwise unrelated individuals suddenly rendered similar to each other.

Goffman's theory also suggested an explanation for the fact that, in some episodes of collective behavior, all the "islands" float in the same direction. Insofar as the groupings share a single focus, they may develop similar definitions of the situation and, consequently, act similarly in relation to the focal object. But, at any moment, their actions may diverge as each grouping or encounter exerts its own local normative force on its members. Moreover, strictly external events may be handled differently in different encounters. The activities of each participant refer more to the activities of his immediate fellows than to external matters. The important point is that participants are not bound into an episode of collective behavior directly as individuals, but indirectly through their involvement in temporary groupings or encounters whose interrelationships are empirically and theoretically problematic.

The apparent easiness of exchange of members and the movement of transients among neighboring encounters introduces another dynamic factor: the tendency for encounters in complex or indeterminant scenes to proselytize. The proselytive character of collectivities within a gathering depends upon whether or not a disputable issue appears to be shared with other collectivities. The activity is apparently governed by considerable role specification. Not all members carry messages between engaged collectivities. Proselytizing is a variant of the operation of the rules of transformation. The presence of alternative definitions of the situation is a potentially disturbing conflict that threatens the integrity and exclusiveness of encounters for their members. Proselytization occurs when such conflicts are introduced into an encounter as a collective mission which requires specific acts to reduce the differences with those who might otherwise threaten the encounter and its definition of the situation. The extent to which a local collectivity succeeds in its mission determines the extent to which it shares a definition of the situation, and perhaps a focus and a direction for action, with other local collectivities. The extent to which mutual proselytizing leads only to a dramatization of irreconcilable differences is the extent to which an episode of collective behavior will appear atomized and chaotic. For the individual, participation in the mission of his collectivity is the only way in which he can remain in that collectivity in the face of the obvious differences of interpretation. Moreover, his collectivity and its version of the situation will continue to exist only if he and his fellows remain and help proselytize among other collectivities. Under these conditions, internal pressures develop toward preserving the security of the encounter as a frame of reference for dealing with the inevitable conflicts of an environment inhabited by a multiplicity of such potentially intrusive collectivities.

The collective mission by which encounters try to manage the potential intrusiveness of this pluralism is occasionally incompatible with their initial focus. For example, civilian rescue work during a disaster may be interrupted by official demands for cooperation, which may draw the civilians and the officials into a jurisdictional dispute that threatens the rescue work itself. Often, however, the jurisdictional dispute gives rise to a new definition of the situation that may include both rescue and cooperation as elements.

From these considerations, it appears that most episodes of collective behavior tend to be either highly integrated in the relationships among their constituent collectivities or highly disintegrated, so that the relationships among the constituent collectivities are, at most, competitive. Such episodes resemble neither a static mass nor a fluid and milling gathering of constantly shifting interactions. Moreover, and of key importance according to this picture of the crowd, episodes of collective behavior are not precipitated as a whole.

PRECIPITATING INCIDENTS AND SOCIAL CONTROL

Smelser made precipitating incidents a part of the causal scheme of collective behavior in order to account for the conversion of the volatile collectivity into a mobilizable crowd. For Smelser, the precipitating incident is a catalyst that precipitates a gathering as a whole. The question of how the ramifications of precipitating incidents are carried throughout the crowd either is solved by definition or requires the assumption that the crowd is a simple social structure composed of a mass of homogeneous and mutually accessible individuals—the assumption that Turner has shown to be defective.

Smelser's theory also stated that precipitating incidents are events that confirm a generalized belief, a proposition that is consistent with Lieberson and Silverman's (1965) conclusion that such incidents may draw their force from the violation of intensely held taboos. However, Smelser explained precipitating incidents primarily by reference to cognitive mechanisms rather than to motivational mechanisms, as were cited by Lieberson and Silverman.

According to Goffman's point of view, the force of a precipitating incident does not stem from the fact that it suddenly transforms moral and tolerable individuals into immoral and intolerable ones nor from the fact that it confirms the validity of a shared belief. The primary importance of the precipitating incident lies in its effect on the structure of encounters. A precipitating incident does not merely shift the focus of attention in an encounter; it transforms the total meaning of the situation.

Changes in the Structural Properties of Encounters. The sudden and radical transformation of one social or individual pattern of behavior to another is found in religious conversion, in revolution, and in collective behavior. In relation to collective behavior it is necessary to know what sorts of events can precipitate a sharp reorganization of the social structure of a collectivity and what their relationship is to the structure they disrupt. There are four variable properties of encounters that are structurally crucial: the occasion, the definition of the situation and its protection by the rules of irrelevance and transformation, the presence of vital alternatives, and personnel.

Goffman suggested that the better organized an encounter is, the more capable it is of taking outside events into account. That is, the more fully established and integrated the details and forms of interaction within an encounter, and the more spontaneously involved its members are, the less likely it is that the encounter will change in the face of external events.

The organizational strength—or goodness of organization—of the encounter depends upon the extent to which members' activities are accountable in terms of their immediate setting rather than the overall project that includes that setting. From an observer's perspective, that limited accountability depends on the completeness with which a definition of the situation covers its topic, its internal consistency, the clarity and consistency of its reference to its occasion, and the extent to which performance requirements limit the capacity of actors to become distant from their roles. When the structure of a well-established encounter is broken, it fails unequivocally.

An incident that is merely embarrassing, no matter how acute or how many participants are enmeshed in it, seldom serves to throw the encounter itself into question. It may shift the focus of the encounter or hasten its disintegration, but it does not create a totally new occasion for interaction. In order for an incident to precipitate a radical change of the occasion, the incident must transcend the capacity of the rules of transformation to limit and conventionalize potentially intrusive occurrences, and it must pose an alternative interpretation of the total situation that is both plausible and incompatible with the interpretation that had already been established. A precipitating incident demonstrates the availability of alternatives and, thereby, discredits the exclusiveness of domain asserted by an encounter.

Both Turner (1964) and Goffman (1961) explained the collapse of a defined situation as a consequence of a precipitating incident. For Turner, however, the result is a situation without definition; for Goffman, the original definition collapses under the influence of a competing definition of the situation. This difference highlights an important point: Goffman's concept of precipitating incident involves the forcible presentation of an alternative organization of reality. Thus, the term incident is a bit misleading for Goffman insofar as it suggests something free-floating and structurally isolated. Goffman's precipitating incidents are not isolated events; they carry implications of an alternative reality, and they are subversive in that they are capable of undermining and converting the ongoing reality of an encounter by forcing a confrontation between competing definitions of the situation and between competing policies.

The findings of Lieberson and Silverman (1965) may be interpreted in Goffman's terms: violation by blacks of a rule against agression toward whites poses incompatible definitions of the relationship between blacks and whites. One definition says that they both are equal, and one says that they are not. Aggression by a black man during the first two-thirds of the twentieth century violated the social reality in which blacks are subordinate to whites. An apparently aggressive black man indicates that submission is a temporary and reversible accommodation to an unequal power situation. Such aggression, therefore, suggests an alternative reality in which whites and blacks are equal. Thus, race riots conducted by whites against blacks are not simply retaliations for the violation of a specific norm or taboo, as Lieberson and Silverman suggested; rather, such race riots attempt to reestablish the very reality that is substantiated by the violated norm. Similarly, when police enter the scene of a political street demonstration, almost any expression of physical coercion on their part can redefine the situation for the demonstrators. Instead of a gathering in which enthusiasm for a cause is publicly displayed at a place protected by law enforcement agents, the situation changes to one in which the demonstrators must defend themselves against the repressive forces of the political establishment (Walker, 1968).

Thus, precipitation is the result of two alternative and competing definitions being brought into sharp contrast by an incident that could be part of either. The juxtaposition threatens the integrity and the exclusiveness of the definition of the situation and, therefore, the spontaneous involvement of participants in it (see Koestler's treatment of laughter, 1964).

Ramifications of Precipitating Incidents. The "flooding-out" of emotion (Goffman, 1961) subsequent to a precipitating incident may be defined as behavior unchanneled by both local, ordinary normative constraints and the constraints of the new situation. Such behavior is conventionally meta-situational. It often eases conversion by clearing the air and purifying or decontaminating the disruption. Flooding-out may involve what appears to be disorganized behavior, for example, laughter or coldly distant tightening up. In either case, it is a consequence of precipitating incidents and usually contributes to their ultimate effect. Moreover, a flood of emotion or a tightening up can, itself, function as a precipitating incident. A sudden burst of tears, an eruption of threats and foul language, or a lapse into an inappropriately solemn mood, can threaten the participants' assumptions about each other as well as their capacity and willingness to continue interaction on the same basis as before. As the behavior of participants transcends its setting, their behavior affects the definition of the situation for those who witness it. In this way, the ramifications of precipitating incidents move through, and beyond, an encounter. As a given encounter changes tone and becomes an issue for the immediately affected participants, it affects the scene for those on the periphery.

The Role of Rumor. From this perspective, rumor can be seen as an exceptional and improvised process by which the rules of transformation are brought to bear on potentially disruptive matters. Collectivities can neutralize their potential for disruption by interpreting new events in terms of old ideas, which helps to explain the familiar content of many rumors. Rumors are not simplifications and distortions of reality as much as they are local translations of unpalatable or ambiguous events into interpretations that validate the locally conventional social forms and meanings of an encounter. As an improvised process of communication, rumor initially functions to reinforce rules of transformation within an encounter and later among collectivities. Rumor, as an organized and differentiated process of communication among proselytive groupings, may neutralize the differences among the various corporate units in an episode of collective behavior. Ultimately, rumor, conceived of in this way, tends to eliminate all but one of the competing constructions of the situation that are available for any given encounter so far as those constructions refer to interactions among collectivities.

THE PRECIPITATED ENCOUNTER

Sociologically, a destructured or precipitated encounter will move either toward a restructuring or toward dissolution. Which development takes place depends, in part, upon the social implications of the precipitating incident—its content—and, in part, upon whether features of the situation force the individuals in it to interact or whether the situation is one from which they can readily depart. In most episodes of collective behavior, dissolution takes place. Because of the urgency of the situation and the discreditation of the old encounter by the introduction of plausible alternatives, participants in a destructured or precipitated encounter will tend to move toward new centers of action. If such centers are inaccessible, the original encounter may be reorganized in such a way that what was a precipitating event is reinterpreted as unintrusive in the light of a revision of the rules of irrevelance and transformation. Such a transcendent revison may depend upon leadership or upon a special and highly qualified (almost therapeutic) interaction about "what is to be done." In this case, the resultant structure may be simpler than the old because of its continual dependence upon the mechanisms by which restructuring was accomplished. Most likely, because it includes reference to a former state of affairs, the new structure will also have to tolerate a more agitated and internally conflictful—in the relationship between acts of detail and acts of design—type of interaction. If no new focus for interaction arises, encounters will use up their topics and slowly disintegrate as exhausted structures. Because encounters tend to have a certain inertia, the loss of an issue means that dissolution is likely to be uncomfortable. This discomfort may be sustained in the form of postdissolution resentment or relief. An etiquette of leave-taking has developed to ease people out of such exhausted encounters.

If a dominant focus of attention remains in disintegrating encounters within a large gathering, mass behavior may occur. Such behavior may occur along the lines of Smelser's model of an aggregate mobilized by a leader in some shared generalized belief. Whether or not mass behavior ops in this way depends upon several factors: whether or not the object of attention remains visible and dominant, whether or not the members of the gathering can remain on the scene, and whether or not the special requirements for leadership are met under such conditions.

On the other hand, the persistence of encounters will produce an episode of collective behavior throughout the gathering only if proselytive activities produce coalition among the various unrelated or competing assemblies. In some cases, an overwhelming occurrence that affects a large number of these groupings can produce coalition. Such an occurrence would require an additional process by which social alliances may be accomplished. It is clear that this type of collective behavior is more organized, internally more fragile, and yet more resistant to external controls than the mass behavior described by Smelser.

SOCIAL CONTROL

One of Goffman's chief contributions to the study of the social control of collective behavior—so far as control is coordinate with the actions of collectivities rather than transcendent to them—may lie in his ability to account for the ambiguous role often played by police actions. Because encounters are Goffman's units of organization, control must be studied as it applies directly to those units and their relationships to one another. From Goffman's point of view, a precipitating incident is something that controls the form and duration of encounters. It can transform a standing crowd into an acting crowd, or an acting crowd into a collection of noninteracting and vulnerable individuals. The presence of uniformed police suggests a situational definition to those people present. Thus, when some degree of organization has been established among the people already on the scene, the sudden appearance of police, or a rapid increase in the number of police on the scene can serve as a precipitating incident.

Police action, in particular, the undiscriminating use of force, often precipitates street violence, because it presents local units (whether initially involved in the officially proscribed action or not) with a new occasion for interaction and a new focus of attention. For example, assembled bystanders under police attack may redefine the situation as one in which they are imminent victims and, thus, potential allies of those people who are the immediate target of the police. For the police, bystanders may appear to assume the posture of the offenders and therefore may be interpreted as potential enemies. The presence of the police thus creates a situation that, on both sides, can be redefined as one of wider and imminent danger. The new definition can stimulate new interaction, especially flight or combat.

From the point of view of control, an ordinary civil disturbance—unauthorized action—in which police appear as a coordinate collectivity—a competent party—is an exchange of precipitants. Mutual violence probably occurs when the police definition of the situation interferes with that of engaged civilians. As a consequence, participants in the unauthorized collective behavior feel that they are under attack and must flee or use self-defense, and police may feel that the participants have dangerous intentions and must be forcibly restrained from carrying them out.

UNIT II: SUMMARY

The rediscovery of participants and their situations is one of Goffman's most important contributions to the study of collective behavior. His theory implies that it is not possible to distinguish between institutional and noninstitutional actions and that all social action is predicated on and determines the existence of the untoward. The extension of Goffman's model of face-to-face interaction to collective behavior has provided tentative explanations for the phenomena addressed by Turner and Smelser. The compelling character of the crowd for its participants stems from the special conditions of accountability and mutuality enforced by the contingencies of face-to-face interaction, the exclusiveness of encounters, and the nature of particular occasions. Conduct within the crowd is more complex and varied than Turner suggested in his discussion of conformity to an emergent norm. The shift from conformity to participation represents a critical conceptual move in regard to understanding the order of the crowd. Goffman's theory makes quite clear the inadequacy of the man-in-society paradigm for the study of collective behavior. Man is social and his acts intelligible primarily by virtue of his participation in close collectivities and their occasions. Involvement and individual action are precipitates of the local and often transient incidents of collective life. Only when we accept this does the apparently abnormal behavior of people in crowds become comprehensible. The following two chapters extend Goffman's ideas and incorporate some features of social phenomenology in a theoretic prospectus for the study of collective behavior.

UNIT III

NEW DIRECTIONS
IN THEORY

CHAPTER NINE

DIRECTIONS FOR A THEORY OF COLLECTIVE BEHAVIOR

The two most obvious sources for a theory of collective behavior are general sociology and the catalogue of descriptions of collective behavior that provided the empirical base for the theories of Smelser (1963) and Turner (1964). However, neither of these sources turns out to be very helpful. Students of collective behavior have derived some interesting working hypotheses from general social theories, but the study of collective behavior has not yet been placed within a well-developed theoretic framework, nor has it been located within a suggestive paradigm. The problems to which general social theories have been explicitly addressed and the intellectual traditions to which social theorists have responded are different from the problems and traditions of the study of collective behavior. As a result, when the sociology of collective behavior has referred to general theories, its phenomena have been described as exceptional, and its propositions have been relatively simple applications or extensions of such theories.

THE SEARCH FOR A DEFINITION OF COLLECTIVE BEHAVIOR

Smelser's use of Parsons' theory of action (see chap. 8) is largely an argument by a frail and often forced analogy. When pressed for specific hypotheses, key concepts become difficult to interpret. For example, does the concept of strain refer to specific frustrations individually felt by a certain large proportion of the membership of a social system? Or does the concept of strain refer to incompatibilities among the conditions of social action, whether or not these incompatibilities are felt by members? The standard indices of strain (Graham and Gurr, 1969) assume the former interpretation, despite the fact that Smelser's theory seems to imply the latter interpretation. Moreover, Smelser listed a number of determinants of collective behavior, but their place in the causal picture is unclear. Smelser's ambiguities seem unfruitful and irremediable, perhaps because the Parsonian model is too generalized. In addition, there are no hints for moving from theory to observation, which accounts for the continual and uncritical reliance, by Parsons and Smelser, on their own common sense understanding of American society—and the ideas of social action commonly held in that society—in order to specify traits of culture or the content of association. Because the meanings of activities and events to participants are essential to Smelser's definition and theory of collective behavior, the failure to find a way of observing those meanings independently of his sense of what they must be, is fatal to his scientific program. This is the criticism that Douglas (1967) made of Durkheim when he said that:

> in the place . . . "objective" measures and the meanings to the individuals involved, he substituted the meanings of the associations to himself as a member of the society and as a social observer . . . . Durkheim was, then, using his common-sense understanding of his everyday social experience to provide the most important part of the data to be used to test his theory. (p. 68).

Smelser's theory lacks power; Turner's lacks scope. The idea of an emergent norm is more a working hypothesis than a theory, although it does take advantage of conventional treatments of interaction and social organization. Its strongest implication is one that Turner left undeveloped—namely, that an emergent norm must arise within a close collectivity rather than within the massive aggregate of a crowd. Although the implications of this proposition are profound for the study of collective behavior, it is not clear how they might be explored within the limits of the emergent norm hypothesis. Apart from Parsons, no other major theorist has provided entry to the study of the crowd or related phenomena. (See chap. 8 for a complete discussion of the theories of Parsons, Turner, and Smelser.)

QUESTIONING THE TRADITIONAL EMPIRICAL BASE

Even if a general social theory had the scope and power to explain collective behavior, the traditional empirical basis for a theory of collective behavior has been put in question by at least three developments. First Bramson (1961) implies that empirical images of the crowd are, themselves, in part, socio-cultural artifacts. Thus, the early empirical illustrations of collective behavior must be questioned. The controversial nature of the crowd has encouraged uncritically partisan descriptions that limit theoretic options. Second, Turner's (1964) insistence on the total inaccuracy of the nineteenth-century image of the crowd—an image that is, as Couch (1968) pointed out, almost as common today as it was then—deprives contemporary students of the catalogue of anecdotes and examples of collective behavior that have illustrated that image. Third, the symbolic interactionists and the ethnomethodologists have called attention to the significance of locale, detail, occasion, and the constructive nature of reality in determining what actions are and are not understood as "normal" or "natural." Their observations dramatize the unsuitability of conventional research tools and static models for the investigation of episodes of collective behavior.

Specifically, survey research deals primarily with phenomena post hoc and at too high a level of abstraction to reveal the moment to moment contingencies in the development of episodes of collective behavior. To study the relationship between individual grievances and participation in collective behavior is to rely too much on memory and to ignore the ways in which individuals enter special circumstances and find themselves subjected to the viscissitudes of events; it is to avoid the sequence of events in favor of the total episode. Moreover, it avoids the issue of the relationship between post hoc statements and situated behavior and the issue of how situated and concerted action can take place. Small group research has dealt primarily with the interaction among transituational variables rather than with the ways in which situated social realities are established and maintained. Interaction process analysis, like many other field research techniques, has been constructed along the lines of survey research. It codes data too early in the process of observation, and at too great a distance from the actors, to permit an adequate description of the emergence of action.

Recent research has destroyed some stereotypes. Turner's (1964) emergent norm hypothesis (see chap. 8), which depended upon an examination of the effects of sudden deorganization on interaction, required a new image of the social structure of the crowd. It is no longer adequate to describe collective behavior in terms of the categories of social pathology—impulsiveness, unresponsiveness, and lack of differentiation. Moreover, it has become clear that classically crowdlike behavior may occur on occasions that are not intensely stressful. Swanson (1953) has replicated in the laboratory some of the peculiar organizational features that classical theorists attributed to crowds. In particular, the apparent susceptibility of crowds to influence was experimentally simulated in face-to-face groups in ordinary problem-solving situations in which some degree of uncertainty had been introduced. Because uncertainty and ambiguity are ubiquitous in social settings, Swanson's research suggested that such behavior may appear on any occasion in which extended interaction takes place.

Turner has provided a way out of the problem that has plagued the study of collective behavior throughout its history: the fallacy of uncritically aggregating data, such that items (e.g., acts and individuals) that appear together are taken to constitute a system (such as a collectivity). The existence of a crowd as a type of collectivity can no longer be inferred from the observation that large numbers of people have gathered at a street corner or are running in the same direction. The premature aggregation of data obscures the local processes by means of which episodes of collective behavior emerge out of interaction. As a result, it becomes necessary to postulate both the unobserved intervening collective states, in order to explain the emergence of the crowd, and the hypothetical psychological states, to account for the participation of otherwise ordinary people in extraordinary events.

Smelser's (1963) theory encounters this same difficulty. He copes with the questions of how people enter collective behavior and how they are bound into active collectivities by assuming that copresence on an observer-defined scene presupposes social forces sufficient to explain individual participation. But the idea of copresence is an inadequate account of the forces that bear on individuals. Smelser, therefore, leaves unanswered the question of the nature of participation and is left with the conventional stereotype of the frustrated and impatient participant in episodes of collective behavior.

SOME PRELIMINARY CONSIDERATIONS

The discussion of disaster will have alerted the reader to the methodolog-ical problems inherent in the subject of collective behavior—chiefly, the interdependence of theory and data (see chap. 2). With reference to people, the problem can be stated in terms of the observer-participant: the positions are distinguishable, but both participation in the events and observation of the episodes are forceful and form-determining. Consequently, the following discussion attempts to warn the reader of several crucial pretheoretic assump-tions that will guide the search for a definition of collective behavior.

Interpretations of episodes of collective behavior are implicated in the settings of such behavior, however the events are described. The nature and the consequences of this implication depend upon the structural origins of the interpretations and their possible uses under the circumstances in which they are presented—that is, on the practice of which the interpretations are an aspect. Throughout the remainder of this book, concern will be focused on the role of interpretation and the uses of theory in settings of collective behavior.

Analyzing the Sequence of Events. Collective behavior is part of a sequence of events that begins and ends outside the boundaries of the episode itself and that can be analyzed as social action. Smelser (1962), for example, failed to distinguish clearly between two empirical problems: that of accounting for societal fluctuations in rates of occurrences, and that of accounting for specific episodes or types of episodes. He moved from studies of incidence to studies of incidents, employing the same model to account for both phenomena. His "value-added" approach (see chap. 8) orders the determinants of an occurrence of collective behavior along a continuum ranging from the general to the specific. The implication is that all determinants operate in the same way. But some of the factors that Smelser listed as determinants (e.g., strain) do not covary, or do not appear to covary, with the phenomena in question, whether they are particular episodes or types of episodes. Therefore, such factors are not determinants in the same sense as those factors that do covary with the phenomena.

Because strain is a characteristic of social systems, it varies with other characteristics of those systems and not with characteristics of their elements. For example, the life of a small business in America depends upon the fact that it takes place in the last third of the twentieth century. But the course of that life can only be understood in terms of factors with which it interacts or to which it responds. Variations in societal strain usually take place over a long period of time relative to the life of the business. For that business, strain in the society is what Parsons (1958) referred to as a parameter rather than a determinant in the strict sense implied by Smelser's value-added scheme. Strain is a relatively stable condition within which the covariations among relevant forces take place.

It is important to remember that, for Smelser, the deprivation of a particular group in a society is not, in itself, evidence of societal strain. Deprivation is not a characteristic of the social system, but rather, of some of its members. Generalized beliefs are tied to specific deprivations; they arise within particular settings and change as collective behavior develops. Thus, system strain is not a part of the causal picture of collective behavior, but generalized belief is a part of that picture. Societal strain is directly relevant only to predicting differential rates of collective behavior among societies or within a given society over time, because strain and incidence of strain are traits of the same social system. Unless determinants are treated as variables with specified ranges and functions, the responsiveness of components of the whole are identified with the responsiveness of the whole, so that each is directly dependent upon the other. Society, collectivities, and individual people are all treated as equal interactants, so that the characteristics of one are used to account for the characteristics of the others. This analytic error tempts Smelser to employ psychological assumptions to explain how strain in a society relates to the collective behavior of its parts and quasi-sociological concepts such as "*shared* generalized beliefs" to account for the way in which a general state of affairs provides the premises for specific actions by collectivities.

The Reordering of Social Elements. The sequence of events that constitutes an episode of collective behavior involves a reordering of social elements that individuates structure and functioning at each stage. The organization of collective behavior changes during its course, depending upon the earlier organization and the new factors that enter the situation. Organization at any stage in the development of an episode of collective behavior is the product of the accumulation of detail and its integration into collective definitions of the situation. Such accumulation and integration are reflexive processes that take time to occur. Moreover, each stage is an organization with a characteristic ordering of its components (Kerckhoff, et al., 1965). The sequence of stages is therefore discontinuous, and the theorist's problem is to account for the transformation from one stage to another. This aspect, therefore, focuses on the movement from stage to stage as a precipitation.

An unwary observer might suppose that the movement initiated by an incident is predominantly caused by that incident, thus overobjectifying its import in the situation. The import of an incident is primarily dependent upon the prior state of the organization in which it occurs and in which it is understood. Precipitation cannot be explained as a property or power of setting-free incidents. What has thus far been called definitions of the situation will be further developed as a type of *collective construction* and the role of collective constructions in precipitation will be discussed. The socially binding properties of constructions in characterizing participation in a collectivity will also be examined. The realization of constructions as practice within socially organized settings will be seen to provide necessary conditions for precipitation.

The Characteristic of Irreversibility. The fact that episodes of collective behavior develop as a series of transformations establishes a further characteristic of such episodes, namely, that their direction is irreversible. Irreversibility is established by the following formal analysis of precipitation: If the transformation from one stage of an episode to the next is designated as a *precipitation*, it occurs as a replacement of one order by another. The agent of that change qualifies as an agent in relation to the order in which it operates. With the replacement of that order, the qualifications for agency change.

If this analysis is accurate, then it follows that behavior that has arisen out of situations of deprivation cannot be eliminated by eliminating the deprivation. Deprivation has been paired with the weakening of authority as a cause of collective behavior; it follows equally that the reassertion of authority will not eliminate that behavior (for an opposing view, see Gurr, 1969; Janowitz, 1968). More often than not, arguments that assert the necessity for a reaffirmation of authority end by affirming the use of coercion by the state (Gurr, 1969; Janowitz, 1968; Nisbet, 1969), a use which is usually understood by sociologists as incompatable with the maintenance of order or the reestablishment of authority (Parsons, 1949, p. 236).

THEORETICAL ORIGINS OF THE DEFINITION

A definition of collective behavior determines the boundaries of a domain of illustration; it also guides theoretical work by introducing key concepts as parts of a basic proposition. Smelser's (1963) definition orders the major determinants of collective behavior as follows: The mobilization of a collectivity depends upon the presence of generalized beliefs that have arisen in response to a crisis in the normal conditions of social action. His definition also designated an empirical domain that is traditionally part of the sociological study of collective behavior. However, this empirical domain—a range of phenomena that includes, among other things, the social movement, the craze, the hostile outburst, panic, and fashion—has been limited to what has been considered abnormal in social life. It will be argued that the distinction between the abnormal and the normal is not an adequate basis for a definition of collective behavior.

PATHOLOGY AS A BASIS FOR DEFINITION

Turner (1964) said that "the assumption that there is a special field of study which can be called 'collective behavior' rests primarily upon the apparent contrasts with normal social and institutional behavior" (p. 382). Moreover, it was formerly assumed that anything considered abnormal must be treated within the logic or common sense framework of the study of pathology. The relevant assumption from pathology was that exceptional behavior and exceptional behavioral products required exceptional circumstances—intense stress or frustration, a failure of socialization, contagion, or the sudden release of deep dispositional aggression among anonymous individuals whose presence in a large standing aggregation has rendered them morally and socially unaccountable for their acts. The contrast with normal behavior implied that collective behavior is sociologically singular and subject to unique principles of explanation. The crowd was thought to be a viral entity that had escaped from either the supersocietal or the subsocietal level of being and had intruded on the otherwise natural and easy life of the social system. For Smelser, impatience as a pathology of instrumentality is the essence of collective behavior.

INDIVIDUAL DISPOSITIONS AS A BASIS FOR DEFINITION

The argument has been advanced that only special types of individuals are present on the occasion of collective behavior. A definition of collective behavior must, therefore, include a description of participants, and this description must be in terms of personality or individual dispositions. Definitions that point to individual frustrations or to individually held beliefs are of this sort, as are the more popular theories and definitions that define collective behavior as the motions of an agitated mass.

This argument has generally been rejected on empirical grounds: participants in collective behavior have not been found to be dispositionally suited to such behavior. It cannot be denied that some episodes of collective behavior attract special participants, but collective behavior cannot be defined as the behavior of special people. The Sans Culottes of the French Revolution were, for the most part, gainfully employed (Rude, 1959); the participants in the 1967 urban disorders in America were often neither migrants to the affected areas nor the poor and the uneducated (National Advisory Commission on Civil Disorders, 1968); the students who occupied buildings, demonstrated against the military and its allied industries, and violated academic protocol during the organized student protest of the 1960s were not underachievers, alienated, authoritarian, or otherwise mentally unhealthy (Sampson, 1967a).

Apart from the failure of empirical research to support a definition of collective behavior in terms of the dispositional deviance of its participants, in any case, such a definition proposes a relationship between individual disposition and action that cannot be maintained. In addition, the typical convergency theory of collective behavior has assumed a direct relationship between the dispositions of participants and their collective behavior, as if the collectivity were simply the individual on a larger scale. Defenders of this theory proceed as if collective behavior involved many individuals doing precisely the same thing for precisely the same reason and as if individual action could only be a result of intraindividual causes.

It is no longer acceptable within psychological theory to link actions directly to dispositions. Cohen (1964), for example, has discussed this linking in regard to the relationship between attitudes and behavior, and Block (1968) has concluded that psychologists have not yet found the consistency of behavior that dispositional analysis and personality theory require. Regardless of whether these reports discredit dispositional analysis itself or the methods by which dispositions have been assessed, and regardless of whether they suggest that behavior must be understood in different terms entirely, it must be stated that, at present, neither the entrance of individuals into collective behavior nor their behavior during participation in collectivities can be explained by their underlying beliefs, attitudes, intentions, or states of motivation. An explanation in such terms either accounts for too little of the variance in the phenomena or obscures the operation of more important factors. These considerations raise questions about the theories that focus on alienation, frustration, special types of belief, and/or special motives and motivational states as major determinants of collective behavior. In its summary report, the National Commission on the Causes and Prevention of Violence (1969) persisted in this theoretical point of view, despite the fact that both the Kerner Commission (1968) and the Skolnick Report (1969) presented facts that discredit it. The summary report referred to a minority of students who "resort to violent disruption as the means best suited to achieve their ends"—their ends being "nihilist" (pp. 213-14). The summary report does recognize the fact that civil disobedience and the collective behavior that often accompanies it can also stem from participants who are not nihilist. However, even in reference to such participants, the report focused on individual belief as the key variable in explaining the collective behavior of the nonnihilist (Allen, 1965; Hoffman, 1965). It is by now a cliche, if not an axiom, of social psychology that individuals do not behave in groups as they do when they are alone—public behavior has public determinants.

OUTCOME AS A BASIS FOR DEFINITION

A definition of collective behavior cannot be based on the outcomes of collective behavior. Violence, property damage, injury, and discontent accompany institutional as well as collective behavior, official actions as well as the actions of persons who have no official standing. For example, urban renewal programs may damage the property interests and lives of people who have lived in areas scheduled for demolition; official economic policies often produce widespread misery and discontent; and military and police actions are often accompanied by considerable violence and injury. Yet, outcome has been used as a basis for defining collective behavior and related phenomena (Levy, 1969) and for classifying such phenomena as pathological. The National Commission on the Causes and Prevention of Violence (1969) relied on outcome to measure violence and strife because it failed to enter the realities of which those outcomes are partly consequence and partly actions rendered accountable. The element of intent in definitions of violence is presumably designed to capture that reality. However, in sociological practice, intent is assumed by virtue of outcome. Thus, the territorial claims of city gangs are often ignored by investigators who exclude them from studies of "civil strife" and "political" behavior (Levy, 1969), presumably because their history of law-breaking is taken to define their intent.

COLLECTIVE VERSUS INSTITUTIONAL BEHAVIOR AS A BASIS FOR DEFINITION

Turner (1964) accepted the contrast between collective behavior and institutional behavior but noted that there is a difference in the occasion on which each behavior takes place. The distinction does not depend upon the nature of the behavior itself, and, in both cases, behavior is normative, regulated and responsive to environmental conditions. Thus, in Turner's view, it is not necessary to explain a singular phenomenon (the crowd) by exceptional causes, nor is it necessary to define it in terms of pathology. His view seems to exclude reference to the essential differences between acting and expressive crowds, mobs and audiences, and hostile outbursts and panic. Instead, it aims to specify the conditions under which various instances of collective behavior occur, in particular, their occasions. Because pure cases are either rare or nonexistent, it is more profitable to focus on occasions of interaction and to derive forms of interaction from those occasions than it is to assume, without question, that an adequate typology of interactions exist and to try to derive the conditions that give rise to one or another of the types. It is possible, then, to accept the contrast between institutional and collective behavior without forging a definition along the lines of those put forth by social pathologists and without using the distinction itself as the basis for definition.

Turner has provided the first element of a definition of collective behavior: that it is *behavior that occurs on a special occasion.* Turner's emphasis on the occasion is obscured by the terms of his definition of collective behavior as social action under the impact of an emergent norm (Turner and Killian, 1957, p. 12). It is, however, clarified by his statements that:

> Because the behavior in the crowd is different either in degree or kind from that in non-crowd situations, the norm must be specific to the situation to some degree—hence *emergent* norms (1964, p. 390).

And:

> Collective behavior occurs only (but not always) when the established organization ceases to afford direction and supply channels for action (1964, p. 392).

These two statements suggest that collective behavior may be defined as situationally contingent interaction rather than as a definite social form. Thus, Turner's definition of collective behavior might well have read: collective behavior is whatever interaction occurs on the occasion of a meaningful disruption of an "established organization" of interaction. In these terms, "collective behavior" refers to interaction at a particular time, namely, following the disruption of a "normal" or nonproblematic social process. *The contrast between collective behavior and institutional behavior is, then, a contrast in situation rather than in form, and collective behavior may be described as isolated from other action by its occasion.* The *occasioned isolation* of collective behavior from institutional behavior provides a sufficient basis for the contrast between the two, and for a definition of collective behavior.

The Types of Isolation of Collective Behavior. Occasioned isolation differs sharply from three other types of isolation that have been attributed to collective behavior and that have been discussed previously in various contexts:

1. Collective behavior is often thought of as expressive and autistic rather than as goal directed and rationally responsive to external conditions. From this point of view, the crowd is *instrumentally isolated,*
2. It is more common to find descriptions of collective behavior as *normatively isolated;* that is, freed from the controls of the conventional norms and values and institutions of the surrounding society,
3. Some accounts of collective behavior still stress the *organizational isolation* of the crowd; that is, its lack of differentiation and internal control. From this point of view, the crowd is a whirlpool of intemperance in a regular and placid social sea.

Contemporary research does not support these descriptions of collective behavior as isolated from institutional behavior. For example, Oberschall (1968) reported that the 1965 riots in the Watts area of Los Angeles were selective responses to needs for which conventional means of satisfaction were apparently unavailable, and selective responses to beliefs about the white power structure that referred to prior discriminatory actions of police and civil government officials. Waskow's (1966) review of the protest activities of the civil rights movement from 1919 to the 1960s stressed the fact that nonauthorized forms of protest by black Americans (sit-ins and demonstrations) have often been the only available political means for countering the effects of racism, just as strikes and industrial sabotage were necessary components in the negotiations that led to the development of collective bargaining in America. Coser (1956), Drake (1969), and Moore (1969) have illustrated the functions of protest, militancy, and violence in socio-political struggle, both for society and for the struggle groups themselves. Coser (1967), for example, wrote that:

> Internal violence within a social system may be seen as a response to the failure of established authority to accommodate demands of new groups for a hearing. It is a danger signal as well as a means by which such groups make their demands heard (p. 96).

Dynes and Quarantelli (1968) found evidence that looting during urban disorders often followed patterns consistent with conventional norms and regulations, and the looting often served community needs when looted goods were shared. Reviews of organized student protests during the 1960s do not support the position that these episodes were internally disorganized, irrational, unresponsive to environmental conditions, or uninfluenced by conventional norms (Sampson, 1967a; Avorn, 1968; Connery, 1969; Skolnick, 1969).

The Occasion of Collective Behavior. Reinforcing the conclusion that the crowd is distinguished by its occasioned isolation rather than by its instrumental, normative, or organizational isolation from conventional social behavior, Turner (1964), following LaPiere (1938) and consistent with the findings of Swanson (1953), has stressed the fact that collective behavior is ubiquitous even within institutional life:

> It is necessary to recognize a collective behavior component in such otherwise institutional phenomena as fashion, financial cycles, organizational morale, and intraorganizational power plays. That the course of group life in any particular situation may have to be explained as a product of the simultaneous operation of an institutional causal system and a collective behavior causal system has been explicitly acknowledged (p. 383).

Thus, the occasion for collective behavior may appear in any social situation. Collective behavior is an aspect of social life in general, not a special social form in itself.

What is the occasion that gives rise to collective behavior? Can the conditions for such an occasion be specified within a definition of collective behavior? For Turner, the generating circumstance of collective behavior is an occasion only in the common-sense use of the term; it is the uncharacterized disruption of established organization—the disruption of the operation of conventional norms within a definition of the situation. Similarly, for Smelser the generating circumstance is the concretization or verification of a shared generalized belief. For Goffman, it can be inferred that the generating circumstance of collective behavior would be something more complex, such as an invasion of the organization of a bounded collectivity. Goffman analyzed action as an emergent of a complex social situation (see chap. 8). Thus, collective behavior would be occasioned by a sudden shift in the contingencies of action in a specific or known situation. Plausible radical alternatives are suddenly exposed. From this point of view, a specific articulate belief, in Smelser's sense of the term, is more often a post hoc rationalization for collective behavior than a determinant of it.

Goffman recognized the fact that collective behavior is, above all, situated; it is not transsituational as is a group, an organization, or a movement. Thus, Goffman is not committed to a view of collective behavior that stresses a questionable similarity among individuals (shared belief) or an equally questionable similarity among acts (conformity to a norm). Instead, he focused on a collective construction of reality within which individuals participate in various ways. The disruption of that collective construction confronts participants with a choice, not simply with normative uncertainty.

A DEFINITION OF COLLECTIVE BEHAVIOR

In part, the direction of theory is set by the categories of phenomena with which the theorist begins. Smelser's theory of the crowd was shaped by his initial concern with large social movements, for which a decision model seemed appropriate (see Turner and Killian, 1957, p. 307). Having begun with social movements, and having defined both the movement and the crowd as collective behavior, Smelser was obliged to employ the same set of concepts and propositions that he had found useful for the understanding of the social movement to the study of the crowd. Social and political movements have been described as rational or quasi-rational organizations that are functionally differentiated and purposive. Consequently, Smelser emphasized conditions of the long run such as strain, consensually valid beliefs, and instrumentality. After choosing to compare his phenomena with an ideal problem solver, he discovered that it is a poor version of its alleged ideal type. Because the goals of social movements seem vaguely millenial and unproductive of programs, he concluded that collective behavior is the action of people who are impatient and who have lost sight of rational means to collective goals. In light of this Smelser's presentation of collective behavior as fundamentally threatening to society can be understood.

Turner's pretheoretic priorities took him along a different path. He began with short-term phenomena—the crowd and its setting. His examination of the crowd used contemporary social psychological concepts and methods and led to a new empirical picture of the crowd and to a more positive view of the role of collective behavior in society. Following Turner's lead in focusing on local interaction, *collective behavior can be defined as interaction on an occasion in which a collective construction of a situation is threatened.* Collective behavior, then, is whatever interaction takes place on a particular type of occasion.

THE TERMS OF THE DEFINITION

The use of the term *interaction* emphasizes the practice to which collective constructions refer. The term *social action* is used to refer both to situated action and to transsituational systems of action such as groups and organizations. Collective action and collective behavior are situated; situated action is bounded; and the participants in the action are distinguished by their simultaneous (in a socially reflexive and not simply physical sense) presence as competent parties to a definitive setting.[1] A meeting of a local labor union about the terms of a new contract is a collective action in which collective constructions of the situation develop and are elaborated. In itself, the local union is a system of social action that is unsituated; it continues beyond any particular meeting. Formally, it is an abstraction of the meetings that anchor it for purposes of reference.

Collective action refers to interaction prior to a precipitating incident. *Collective behavior* refers to interaction subsequent to such an incident. To refer to "meetings of a group" is to confer a particular status on a present—the meeting. That present is thus assigned the status of transition and, therefore, is open to the treatments generally accorded transitional phenomena, including such tension-reducing techniques as adjournment and the tabling of business. To assign transitional status to an episode of collective action is to expand the boundaries of the roles and activities of the participants. Collective action that has assumed transitional status can be contrasted with collective action that is entirely present, such as theatrical performances, ballgames, rituals, and magic. Religious rituals and magic are also distinguished by the extent to which collective action is coordinated over the gestures and appearances by which the occasion is defined. The elevation of the body of Christ during the Catholic Mass is solemn not because of the symbolic import of the gestures but because all behavior is integrated into a form that is self-sufficient. The behaviors of all participants in the mass are mobilized for the consecration of the bread and wine as the body and blood of Christ. The casting of spells can be understood in similar terms. What is accomplished is order, not product. Regardless of whether or not collective action is taken as transitional by its participants and their observers, it has a standing for both groups. It is eventive and regular within boundaries. For participants, situated social action is regularly significant and automatically involving. When collective constructions are complete and utterly plausible, participation may include managing a narrow or wide range of the behaviors produced in the situation.

---

1. Children, patients, and domestic workers are often physically but not socially present at settings in which they live, suffer or work.

COLLECTIVE CONSTRUCTIONS AND ALTERNATIVES

It has been said that collective behavior depends upon the prior state of acting collectivities, in particular, the degree to which collective constructions of reality are well formed or plausible. The definition also asserts that collective behavior depends upon the immediate situation of behaving collectivities, in particular, the presence of intruding items that can discredit existing collective constructions in the life of collectivities. The degree to which individuals are spontaneously involved in collective action depends upon the plausibility of collective constructions of the situation and the implausibility of alternatives.

The Plausibility of Collective Constructions. Constructions are plausible to the degree to which they are clearly and economically organized, detailed, consistent, and complete. The movement of personnel to one collectivity or another depends upon the relative plausibility of the collectivity's construction of the situation. The movement of personnel away from a collectivity, or into the mode of half-hearted or self-conscious participation that Goffman (1961) called *role distance*, is the result of a failure of that particular collective construction of the situation to be plausible and the exposure of plausible (superordinate or coordinate) alternatives.

Collective constructions of the situation seal the reality of the short run for members of a situated collectivity, eliminating participative alternatives. Collective constructions define the site within which action takes place, fill that site with objects of orientation, and yield a range of tolerable activities with regard to the included objects. Dynamically, they are narrative and structural. On the one hand, they place activities within a temporal span. On the other hand, they provide scenarios within which specific activities either fit or do not fit, depending upon the operation of rules of irrelevance and rules of transformation (see chap. 8). In this way, situated social action and the basis for individual participation are defined within collective constructions of the situation.

The Vulnerability of Collective Constructions. It is precisely at the moment when a collective construction is complete and utterly plausible that interaction is most vulnerable to disruption and the presentation of alternatives. Any highly articulated sequence of gestures is vulnerable to being discredited or threatened by accidents or otherwise trivial happenings (Goffman, 1961, 1963b; Koestler, 1964).

When a well-formed collective construction is threatened, what was unimpeachable appears questionable; conduct is no longer felt to be spontaneous or natural; and schedules and routines begin to fail as extraneous gestures and unaccountable appearances accumulate. Under new conditions, elements of the setting (what was environment) can be reevaluated and treated as new definitions require. As individuals' decisions concerning entrance into the group are reviewed and justificatory ideologies of entrance are constructed, the ease of participation that characterizes collective action can dissolve in a new role distance. In a sense, the previous course of events no longer exists, even though it may seem to. For participants, the intelligibility and correctness of behavior may suddenly be open to question. The meanings by which acts had been brought to account, judged, and so forth—meanings that were internal to collective action—are challenged by meanings external to the original setting of collective action. Acts, formerly familiar, now seem to be rooted in other structures or to be parts of other projects. Considerations of means are superceded by considerations of ends. Weighing a particular course of action, people ask the divisive question of "why" rather than "how." When the situation no longer supports common patterns of behavior, participants are thrown back on more local resources. They are forced to reevaluate the basis of continued participation in terms of standards that are not part of their original socially organized practice.

INTERACTION WITHIN THE COLLECTIVITY

After individuals have entered a setting, acts of participation are predicated on collective imperatives rather than on individual imperatives such as attitudes, intentions, or states of motivation. The convergence theories of collective behavior are unacceptable within this framework, regardless of whether they explain participation in collective behavior in terms of personality variables or in terms of specific individual beliefs or attitudes. Individual activities within an episode of situated social action are components of a collective construction of the situation and must be accounted for in terms of that structure.

Social psychologists who have studied attitude formation and change have argued that attitudes are states of readiness (Allport, 1954; Newcomb, et al, 1965), and therefore function as independent determinants of action. This argument has depended in part on an assumption that attitudes are revealed by attitude statements, and an assumption that attitude statements, whose verbal form appears to express tendencies to approach or avoid specific objects, are in fact expressions of such covert tendencies. However, studies of attitude change may be interpreted as studies of replicability of attitude statements rather than as demonstrations of the conditions under which covert tendencies change. The meaning of an attitude statement and therefore its relationship to any other activity, such as approach to or avoidance of the objects listed in the attitude statement, depends on the social structure or action of which it is a component. For example, the statement "I like Ike" has a different role in each of a number of structures in which it might appear: in a situation in which the maker of the statement is a "tourist" in his relationship to others to whom the statement is addressed (he is not affectively involved with the internally organized life of those he observes but with their system and its relationship with other systems), "I like Ike" may simply establish the political location of the speaker. However, where the speaker is a member of the group to whom the statement is addressed, it may simply reaffirm the existence of the group and its ideology. The "I" signifies, in fact, "we." Since people learn to make attitude statements early in life as an essential technique for remaining appropriate in groups and on occasions, they are among the most commonly observed social activities. It is entirely understandable that they would have been taken as clear indices of covert motivational states having a simple and direct relationship to action. From the point of view presented here, constructions do not function according to the logic of motivation. Therefore, the rhetoric of collective behavior is not necessarily representative of the collective constructions within which the behavior takes place, whether that rhetoric is presented through some public operation or by individual responses to questions (Brown, 1967).

Although interaction always depends upon its occasion, it is not a simple phenomenon varying along several continuous dimensions. Nor can it be described in terms of a few specific criteria or attributes which, if changed, would signify a change in an overall pattern of interaction. Interaction is socially open at the same time that it is socially bounded. Incidents can happen and the possible events are uncountable, yet what constitutes a "significant" incident or event is known to the actors. Thus, interaction must be studied directly rather than by means of its verbal traces. An adequate analysis of collective behavior is often largely ethnographic, relying on locally contingent patterns and moment-to-moment descriptions of the details of the action as it transpires, as exemplified by Cohen and Murphy (1966).

The Limits of Interaction. What are the limits of interaction on social occasions? Or, alternatively, what are the limits of situated social action? The answer to this question depends upon the point of view from which the answer is given. From the point of view of members or prospective members of collectivities, the limits of situated social action involve relocation—that is, entrance and exit. From the point of view of the situated collectivity, the limits involve reintegration—that is, dissolution and formation or replacement. For the individual, entrance involves a transition from a position of retrospectively constructed isolation—a situation in which behavior is demonstrably and accountably private in relation to membership in the situated collectivity—to a situation in which behavior is accountable to and in the situated collectivity. The freedom suggested by "privacy" and "liberation" then, is an acknowledged freedom from the constraints and regard of a particular social arrangement rather than a condition of no social constraints whatever.

Entrance into Social Interaction. Milgram and his colleagues (1969a) have reported data that can be interpreted as supporting the hypothesis that the transition from "private" to "social" accounts depends upon the relative plausibility of the settings of the accounts, if it can be assumed that a large aggregate can provide a plausible center for otherwise detached individuals. Milgram's study reported the effects of the initial size of a gathering on the accumulation of additional personnel. Gatherings of from one to fifteen confederates were arranged to occur on a busy sidewalk in New York City. All of the confederates stopped and looked up at the sixth-floor window of a nearby building. Motion pictures were taken in order to analyze the behavior of unknowing passersby. The results of the analysis indicated that "the size of the stimulus crowd significantly affects the proportion of passersby who stand alongside it" (Milgram, et al., 1969a, p. 81). Moreover, the stimulus crowd influenced the behavior of an even greater proportion of people who passed by but did not stop. "A larger number . . . partially adopt the behavior of the crowd by looking up in the direction of the crowd's gaze, while not, however, breaking stride and standing alongside it" (p. 81). (Milgram's use of the term crowd refers only to a gathering of bodies.) The results of the study are summarized in Table 9.1.

Table 9.1 THE BEHAVIOR OF PASSERSBY

Size of Stimulus Gathering	Approximate Percentage of Passersby* Who Looked Up	Who Stopped
1 person	40 percent	4 percent
2	58	10
3	62	8
5	80	16
10	76	20
15	85	40

*Means calculated for five trials for each size of stimulus gathering.

Adapted from Milgram, et al., 1969a, p. 80.

THE INTERTIA OF COLLECTIVE SYSTEMS

In order to explain interaction following a threat to or the disruption of collective action, Parsons (1958) mentioned the "inertial" quality of collective life and tried to explain the persistence of collectivities in terms of the inertia of systems. Inertia depends upon the coherence of the moving body, which is called its mass in physics and its *integration* in sociology. Situated social action is integrated as practice by the collective construction that typifies it. The degree of integration varies directly with the quality of the collective construction. Thus, the persistence of situated social action is a property of the collective construction of the situation and depends upon several variable features of the construction: (1) the degree to which the idea of continuance is either articulated or enacted within a collectivity; (2) the degree to which the subordination of individuals to the collectivity is easy and spontaneous rather than deliberate and stressful; and (3) the degree to which the enactment of a collective construction is complete, consistent, and formulated so that each participant is wrapped in a network of contingencies and opportunities.

Inertia thus depends upon the degree to which collective constructions of the situation are well formed and, therefore, capable of overruling all other constructions, specifically, other frames of reference and standards of action rooted in other perspectives. Because a well-formed construction of the situation is exclusive as well as exhaustible, it is in a competitive position with regard to alternatives. Moreover, because many constructions are possible for any collection of items, collective action is likely to encounter considerable interference from its surroundings. A well-formed collective construction of a situation provides a complete coverage of that situation. It is systematic in the sense that the meanings of the items that the construction includes depend upon the constructed interrelationships among those items and upon the establishment of rules of irrelevance and transformation (see chap. 8) which protect particular constructions. Any unanticipated item that evokes constructive alternatives threatens the whole system of meanings by which the smaller moments in the life of the collectivity are managed. Thus, a well-formed construction of a situation is extremely vulnerable to the disruptive effects of events with which it is bound to interfere. A precipitating incident will produce a relatively complete transformation of a well-formed collective construction of a situation (Goffman, 1961, 1963a). Moreover, items that are extrinsic to a well-formed construction and that would otherwise be trivially annoying can become precipitating incidents.

The transition from collective action to collective behavior is not an objective distinction. For a collectivity, this transition has been identified as occurring under the impact of a definitively disruptive incident on a well-formed collective construction of the situation (a juxtaposition of forms). It should be noted, however, that the transition necessarily need not be perceived by, nor be perceptible to, individuals.

SOME THEORETICAL IMPLICATIONS OF THE DEFINITIONS

The immediate effect of a disruptive event that effectively intrudes on a collective construction of a situation is to demobilize a collectivity. Demobilization shifts the locus of control from the inclusive or superordinate concerns established by the collectivity as a unit to the concerns of individuals or particular local interacting subunits. Thus, collective behavior usually begins with the copresence of suddenly distinct and relatively unassociated acting units. The tension between the sudden demobilization and the integrating force of the prior state of collective action is part of the peculiar urgency of episodes of collective behavior.

THE TENSIONS OF POLAR IDEALS

The tradition of action theory in sociology asserts that collective life includes the tensions of polar ideals. There is a special tension between localization and superordination, one version of which is the tension between the individual and the group. That tension is exaggerated in the crowd because of the fact that it is precisely the question of superordination that is raised by a precipitating incident. The location of individuals, whether they are in a large collectivity or in a more local face-to-face encounter, becomes an issue when collective action is disrupted. The issue is raised locally in terms of the resources—defined in terms of superordinate reference—available to the individual participant or to small gatherings, which is one reason why conventional social distinctions may be sharpened during collective behavior. When thrown back on local resources, people usually begin with what is most ordinary and routine as they reconstruct a disrupted reality. The localization of involvement and the atomization of a gathering during collective behavior also accounts for the wide swings—from loose confederations of small groupings to relatively inclusive collectivities—in crowd organization. Such alternations describe the rhythm of many episodes of collective behavior.

COLLECTIVITIES UNDER PRESSURE

Research on the behavior and organization of collectivities under conditions of urgency, when choices are forced (Swanson, 1953; Festinger, et al., 1950), indicates that small collectivities with limited resources are extremely responsive to the contingencies of their situation. Moreover, such responsiveness may exaggerate organizational trends that had been active prior to the onset of pressure, focusing internal tensions and reinforcing cultural traditions shared by the participants by virtue of their membership in more inclusive and enduring organizations. Solidarity will be enjoined on the basis of traditions unquestionably shared by participants. For example, in struggle groups, such as those that participated in the New Left politics of the 1960s, the pressures of activism led groups to accept, often without criticism, ordinary distinctions of conventional life that they were otherwise bound to criticize. This acceptance allowed the specialized innovation that is essential to political struggle to proceed without the distraction of questions about the grounds and ground rules of social intercourse. In the case of the New Left, for example, roles ordinarily associated with sex differences were taken for granted. Perhaps as a result, the movement contributed to the rise of a radical feminism that produced a pervasive internal criticism of New Left political organization and practice.

Leadership. The localization of precipitated collective action and the responsiveness of local groupings under pressure suggest that what is taken as an act of leadership changes during the various episodes of collective behavior. Particularly, at the point of precipitation, acts that are likely to be acknowledged as leadership will probably identify the problem as an external threat to group identity and demonstrate that identity and its threatened circumstance in relatively orthodox fashion. As the problem of location gives way to the problem of action, leadership will be selected according to whether or not behavior enacts the coordination of collective practice, regardless of extra-collectivity traditions and purely situational considerations. This shift accounts for the way early acts of leadership seem to justify unconventional behavior in highly conventional terms and later acts tend to use novel, and often radical, justifications for limiting collective behavior (see Cohen and Murphy [1966] for a description of these shifts in leadership during the riots in Watts, Los Angeles). It also accounts for the fact that crowds seem to be leaderless at first, because initial acts of leadership are confined to local groupings. When individuals call for coordination among locales that are not themselves well formed, their attempts to lead are usually rejected as irrelevant. Research by Kerckhoff and his associates (1965) indicates that in the early stages of collective behavior, gatherings are not sufficiently solidaristic overall (sociometrically integrated) for acts that point to a gathering-wide solidarity to be defined as leadership behavior. At that stage, the constructions of the situation are poorly formed, which is to say that ideas and behavior have not yet been brought into line. Insofar as the crowd passes through phases of location, crowd formation, definition, and crowd locomotion, what is and is not considered to be leadership shifts in a corresponding fashion.

As the crowd mobilizes for direct action, leadership is limited by the exigencies of proselytization, coordination, goal definition, and the movement of the crowd in relation to various objects and pressures. During late periods of collective behavior, leadership tends to refer to the mobilized collectivity as a persistent unit; it is transsituated and concerned with strategies of the long run. This routinization and relative stabilization of leadership can provide a new basis for patterns of interference within engaged collectivities.

THE PREDICAMENT OF THE OBSERVER

The fact that situated social action is a focused and highly contingent phenomenon limits the analytic options of the observer. If he enters a distant analytic position, the questions he can answer about a particular episode may be trivial or obvious. If he is close at hand or engaged in the action, he may be unable to comment on the collectively produced aspects of his observations and predictions. Moreover, even if he is engaged, the observation of details is lost in the speed of the action.

The rhythm of an episode of collective behavior, its character as a locus of signification, and the changes that occur in its immediate environment require continual assessment. Because the meanings of situations for their participants depend upon how those situations are collectively construed, the investigator himself, at one time or another, must view the situation as a participant. Smelser's (1963) characterization of generalized beliefs assumes at least an intuition about the phenomenology of collective behavior, although he has denied such an approach in principle (1970). The investigator of collective behavior is like the linguist whose capacity to describe the language depends, in part, upon his capacity to understand it. Because the meaning of an incident is never fully encoded in particular analytic units, an examination of the internal life of an episode of collective behavior, to some extent, must replicate it.

An analogy to ethnographic research is appropriate at this point. The ethnomethodologists (Garfinkel, 1967) have demonstrated the theoretical value of the construction of detailed "mechanical models" of situated social reality (Levi-Strauss, 1967). They have also illustrated the power of observer engagement for the detection of social structure in process. Both of these methodological tools are important, though problematic, for the study of collective behavior. The necessity for continual assessment and the fact that predictive power lies primarily in the short run requires the investigator to develop a sensitivity to the small motions of collective life. The study of the relationship between entrance and stimulus collectivity size by Milgram and his associates (1969a) illustrates this problem. As passersby join a gathering, its size increases. It therefore ceases to be the same stimulus gathering for later passersby as it was for earlier passersby. The potential participant's willingness to actually join the gathering, or even to acknowledge it, depends upon when he arrives on the scene.

Situation and Actor. The problems of observation are compounded by the fact that what a situation is to its participants does not depend only upon the items present in the environment; the collective construction of those items must also be known. This knowledge is gained by observing and participating in collective practice. Thus, situations are not knowable independently of the actors, and actors are not knowable independently of the situation.

The importance of this constructive interpenetration of situation and actor is seen when an attempt is made to assess the potential of any item as a precipitating incident for collective behavior. Without knowing how new items are incorporated within a collective construction of a situation, it is impossible to evaluate the potential of any item as a precipitating incident. For example, why does an arrest by a policeman on a street corner result in collective behavior on the part of bystanders on one occasion and not on another, "similar," occasion? Why does the official enforcement of dress regulations at one college meet with no protest but a "similar" enforcement at another college precipitate a demonstration?

Behavior and Action. Because collective constructions of situations are embodied in interaction, when studying collective behavior, the student is ultimately interested in the relationship between two collective constructions, one that has been termed collective action and one that has been termed collective behavior. The definition of collective behavior focuses on a set of factors for the study of situated social action different from those factors usually discussed within the study of group dynamics. The attempt to eliminate "nonbehavioral" aspects—construction—of interaction, which are features that do not fit into an exclusively external and disengaged construction of the event under investigation (as viewed by the social scientist), has not been particularly successful. The attempt has made it difficult to specify the relationship between actor and situation. As a result, predictions are often either trivial, obvious, or unrealized. The behavioral approach to the study of collective action has not eliminated the very elements—elements of construction and, therefore, subjective elements—that it hoped to exclude. For example, when researchers study small groups and criticize a study in terms of whether or not a particular experimental manipulation "took"—that is, whether or not the subjects believed in it—they assume, however unsystematically, the constructions of the situation for the subjects and the groups.

Just as early research on the crowd often failed to recognize and incorporate the role of definitions of the situation in collective behavior, the behavioral study of situated social action has often failed to make explicit, or even theoretically problematic, the constructival basis of collective dynamics. In both cases, nevertheless, conclusions were drawn about how participants in collective behavior or subjects in small groups defined their situations. In neither case were these conclusions based on a systematic examination of definitions of the situation. Moreover, in the field of group dynamics, there have been no methodological tools developed to deal adequately with this aspect of situated social action. Part of this problem may be caused by an overemphasis on induction in the field of group dynamics. To assume the replicability of variables and relationships in all areas may be extending the principle of induction too far. The number of contradictory findings in the literature of group dynamics suggests that apparently similar conditions do not necessarily produce the same results. For the study of collective behavior, structural analysis seems more promising. From this point of view, behaviors are emergents of inclusive and changing structures. For example, a leadership act or an attitude statement are not caused by sets of determinants so much as they are emergents of moments of interaction to be understood by the structures and practices into which they fit.

CHAPTER TEN

A THEORETIC PROSPECTUS

The distinction between collective behavior and collective action depends upon the way an observer orders two episodes of situated social action in relation to a precipitating incident. Whenever situated social action is described without reference to an immediately prior episode with which it is discontinuous, it is called collective action. After such prior episode is invoked, the subsequent situated social action is called collective behavior. Table 10.1 summarizes the conventional distinctions between types of social action depending upon whether the principal actor is described as situated or transsituational and depending upon whether the social action is taken as continuous or discontinuous with another episode with which it comprises a sequence.

Table 10.1 TYPES OF SOCIAL ACTION

		Location	
		Situated	Transituational
Relation to an Earlier Episode	Not Specified or Continuous	collective action	social organization
	Discontinuous	collective behavior	social movement

SOCIAL ACTION: COLLECTIVE ACTION AND COLLECTIVE BEHAVIOR

The term "social action" refers to the collection of organized activities that define a practice for a principal doing that practice and/or its agents. "Situated social action" refers to a practice defined by the relationship of a principal actor to others taken as mutually competent or coordinate parties to a setting. "Unsituated" or "transsituational social action" refers to a superordinate or inclusive practice in which actors are taken as subsidiary elements of competent parties to a setting. For such subsidiary actors, the setting of their principal is a context.

The distinction between the individual and the collectivity is usually an accountable property of transsituational social action. That is to say, when something is taken as a part of a structure, it is ordinarily not defined independently of that structure.

It is possible to say that collective action and collective behavior take place among nonhuman actors and their collectivities as well as among human individuals. For example, some features of bureaucratic life lend themselves to analysis as collective behavior. As bureaus become relatively autonomous within a complex organization, they may compete for scarce resources, such as time, office space, or personnel. This competition may interfere with official practice and sanctioned operations of what is taken to be the organization as a whole (Brown, 1969). For example, in order to accommodate such critical interactions, bureaucracies often develop extra supplies of resources that can serve as the medium of exchange among the competing bureaus without depleting resources necessary to overall operations. Because the regularity of the relationship between the inclusive structure and its local bureaus now depends upon a continuous supply of extra material, any unaccommodated depletion of it can precipitate interactions among the various bureaus that can be described as collective behavior. It is interesting to note that although a majority of individuals in an organization may refer to such exchanges as utterly unserious, corrupt, or funny, these references do not in any way impair them, nor do they mitigate the consequences of official interference with them.

SITUATION AND ACTOR

The concept of situated social action requires some discussion of the term situation. What is situation and what is actor are complex problems rarely addressed, and certainly unsolved in contemporary social science. On the one hand, the dichotomy is philosophically questionable. Yet the ordinary language of social science invokes a logic of transaction in which exchanges take place between actor and other, each assumed to be independently discoverable. On the other hand, given that a distinction between inner and outer cannot easily be avoided within the linguistic strictures of social science, and given the pervasive functional paradigm by which the distinction is brought into theory, how is it possible to deal with the actor-situation complex without laboring over the paradoxes posed by the dichotomy?

To begin with, the terms actor and situation specify different points of entry for an observer. An observer enters a site at some point taken as origin and examines the site as a projection of that origin. The selection of a point of origin has to do with the particular questions that the observer asks, the observer's categories for identifying actors as competent, responsible, and the like, and the particular interests he assumes will be served by observation. From this point of view, actor and situation are artifacts of observation. After an origin is selected, description proceeds in terms of an analysis of the relationship between what is taken as the actor of origin and what is taken as the situation. The situation becomes, then, a projection of a point of origin, which is, in turn, identified and characterized by the observer as part of his own construction of reality.

It should be noted that Parsons' theory of action, although formally capable of accommodating situated social action, has been developed primarily in reference to actors of origin with a continuing identity for the observers who choose them as points of entry. However, Parsons reified the actors that were his points of entry and treated his identification of them as discoveries or acknowledgements of reality. In a sense, Parsons' idealism, especially his failure to explicate the practical frame of reference for his identifications and descriptions of social systems, makes it difficult to interpret his theory. Some of his own attempts to use his theory to understand concrete events often appear to accuse the world of failing to live up to its ideal types (Parsons, 1965a, 1968).

CONTEXT AND SETTING

To specify an actor of origin is to specify a context and a setting. The description of collective behavior determines what is relevant to its explanation. However, the explanation itself follows an order of dependence or contingency rather than the order of projection. Thus, the components of settings are explained in terms of the wider context they project in any given case. Situated social action is ordinarily described within a stable context and a relatively active setting of mutually oriented units. The actor of origin is situated in the sense that it consists of orientations that, in turn, constitute its setting. Context and setting are maps of the social terrain in which action occurs; they are constructions of the situation. The process by which these constructions are attained involves acts of selection and exclusion as well as acts of arrangement. The situation is a projection in the sense that it is one of the possible arrangements of items taken as salient, or not taken as irrelevant, to the actor of origin.

Ordinarily, the items that are arranged as constructions of situations can be described, even though the arrangements themselves cannot be described without becoming engaged in the actor of origin. This possibility depends on the disengaged observer and the observed originating from the same society in that they share objects. As observer and observed, however, they are accountable to different settings and so order those objects differently. When settings are referred to "objectively," the reference is often to the fact that the describer is doing observation, which is to say that he is a party to a different setting from the one about which he testifies. Doing observation, in the sense of adopting special ways of accounting for the observer's own activities, (as scientific, for example,) often involves describing as a setting a collection of objects listed by participants for observers. These objects are then ordered—coded—by the observers for "observers." The observer-based order depends upon the stability of the observer, and therefore the continued plausibility of his setting, relative to the phenomenon to which he testifies. That phenomenon exists for him as summary and, therefore, as static and episodic rather than as eventive and as an "ongoing accomplishment" (Garfinkel, 1967). This fact suggests limits to a sociology of collective behavior that plans to operate outside the setting of the things that it describes, in particular, cross-cultural research (Gurr, 1969).

The arrangement of items in constructions of the situation involves both an order—defined by specific relationships and distributions—and a boundary—defined by what items are excluded from those relationships and distributions. Although the order may be limited to a relatively small set of items at any particular time, the boundary may include other potentially effective items. Goffman (1961) noted that the latter are subjected to rules of transformation as they enter the order of the situation. Thus, to some extent, constructions are open-ended; and the situation and its actors are in flux. Moreover, because any arrangement is only one of many possible arrangements for any given set of items, when an arrangement is brought to notice as an arrangement, it is noticed as an alternative, and is, therefore, noticed as capable of being replaced.

Situated social action takes place within an immediate setting—a present. The initial components of the setting are given by virtue of a wider context taken as a stable set of conditions (parameters) within which activity occurs (Mead, 1932; Parsons, 1958). The Watts riots of 1965 (Oberschall, 1968), for example, took place in a context of racial discrimination, the peculiar ecology of the Watts area of Los Angeles, and the pervasive social structures of American life. The setting for the riots included gatherings of Watts residents and their constructions of the situation, police, and locations vulnerable to force, such as city streets and businesses owned by whites. Contexts change much more slowly than do settings and only in relation to other variables of the large scale and long run. Any inclusive social system changes slower than the items it includes. The behaviors of those items are conceived as behavior relative to constants given by the inclusive system. As a result, for practical purposes the context is static for any particular instance of collective behavior. For example, the views of Watts' residents regarding the oppressed condition of black Americans probably did not change just prior to and/or during the riots of 1965 insofar as oppression was taken as a relatively stable attribute of their lives as black Americans.

It is true, however, that the ecology of an area may change as a result of collective behavior. Public places may be redistributed or redefined by those who retain power over the territory, or the physical makeup of the neighborhood may change as a result of the impacts of particular striking forces (fire). However, before and during collective behavior the ecology of the area, its economy, and the identity and distribution of public places are environmental features—that is, they are contextual rather than implicated in the setting of action. These features are not taken as vulnerable qualities or interactants for the active collectivities. In other words, collective behavior rarely has as its objects or co-interactants the nature of an area. As a result, when the impact of a riot is disclosed as distributional or structural, participants usually register surprise. The surprise lies in the fact that something previously taken for granted (contextual) is *now* seen as *having been* part of the setting of the riot. Damage to a commercial area, for example, may ultimately amount to an impact on the economy of that area so far as post hoc accounts of the riot are concerned. This view of riot impact may amount to a conversion of contextual matters to matters of setting. In this case, the riot appears in retrospect (and prospect) as a confict between two structures, one structure holding power over the economy of the area and the other representing the community. Both structures are taken as original interactants despite the fact that, at early stages of the riot, the economy of the area was not included in definitions of the setting. Looting of the sort described (after the fact—as what might have been) by Dynes and Quarantelli (1968) as the conversion of private property to community resource through an act of appropriation is, at the time it occurs, a highly particularistic, local act; sabotage is not. The former aims at a local reform—putting a commodity to use. The latter treats the larger system as a part of the setting of action and, therefore, tries to affect that system as an actor; sabotage is an act of war.

THE SETTING AS WORLD AND AS FIELD

For any particular actor, the setting for action can be described as a *social world* of relationships and as a *social field* of distributions of items of various types. The social world consists of particular units—competent parties—in their mutual orientations and in their relationships to the actor of origin. The social world is the setting as interaction. It contains relationships of affection, hostility, coordination, relevance, dominance, and so on, which are enacted routinely or inventively, but in either case, as matters of practice. The social field is the distributions of items within the setting according to various characteristics, such as the relation to a particular point or the location along a hierarchy of some value. It is the texture of the setting in terms of gradients, "an increase or decrease of something along a given axis or dimension" (Gibson, 1950, p. 73) relative to the actor of origin. Thus, the social field is characterized by distributions in various dimensions and features of distributions such as areas of concentration (central tendency) and areas of diffusion (dispersion).

The distinction between the social field and the social world is directly analogous to Gibson's (1950) distinction between the visual field and the visual world in his study of perception. The visual world "is the familiar, ordinary scene of daily life, in which solid objects look solid, square objects look square, horizontal surfaces look horizontal, and the book across the room looks as big as the book lying in front of you" (p. 26). The visual field, on the other hand, "is less familiar than the visual world and it cannot be observed except with some kind of special effort" (p. 27). It is bounded and graded by a "central-to-peripheral gradient of clarity: the contours and patterns of the array of surfaces in your field can be observed to become gradually less determinate as you attend to those out toward the periphery" (p. 29). Constancies are not preserved within the visual field, thus "distance is a characteristic only of the visual world" (p. 42) in which objects are seen to overlap rather than eclipse others as is characteristic of the visual field. Gibson argued that "the distinction between the visual field and the visual world is a *substitute* for the traditional distinction between visual sensation and visual perception" (p. 43). Thus, judgment in the psychological sense is an activity referring only to the visual world. Judgment, in the sociological sense, involves orientation. It is tempting to speak of social surfaces on which actors are replaced by bodies having relatively few characteristics as the social field. Here, dominance, for example, can be specified by accessibility rather than by the complex of characteristics that define the relationship of an actor to other actors. Charisma derives in part from the social field. It is the instantiation of plausibility and dominance (an aspect of the social world) as that which overwhelms. A study of the accumulation of personnel in gatherings of various sizes (Milgram, et al., 1969a) illustrates the importance of the social field. The tendency to cluster involves movement within the field; attraction to objects involves movement within the world. In arguing for the potential of gatherings to increase in size, Milgram and his associates argued, in effect, for the relevance of the social field in the analysis of collective behavior.

Accessibility. The perception of any item as isolated, not simply as rejected or excluded, is a condition of its accessibility to an actor and depends directly upon the texture of social reality, the social field rather than relationships of affection, participation, and so on. Gibson (1950) pointed out that "the gradient of density is an adequate stimulus for the impression of continuous distance" (p. 67). By analogy, where clustering (high density) takes place within a gathering of people at a point from which density decreases gradually and continuously to the observer, the cluster will seem accessible to the observer. The gathering will not be seen as a collectivity requiring special effort to join but as a gathering that is open to passersby. Street audiences of the sort that gather at political soap boxes or for street theater performances have this quality (Goodman, 1970). As an observer moves outward from the center of attraction, involvement decreases to the point of incidental concern. At that point, pressure on passersby to participate is low, so that an act of attention appears to take little effort and does not offer the prospect of an intense engagement. Sociometrically diffuse areas are lures requiring little by way of decision. Therefore, although they may not engage people in an intense way, a person easily drifts into them.

The Accumulation of Personnel. The distinction between the social world and the social field suggests that, during an episode of collective behavior, personnel will accumulate only where clusters of participants are not seen by passersby (potential participants) as distinct objects of attention within a social world but as regions of graduated density within a texture or field. Such clusters are accessible in the sense that the individual passerby does not see them as discontinuous with his own activity or his own place; in a sense, it is quite natural to join them. In fact, the term join is too strong; to notice a cluster as a relatively dense area with a graded approach is, ipso facto, to be in it. It is because of this phenomenon that, in large demonstrations, neutral or even hostile bystanders will often undertake exceptional behavior in order to dissociate themselves from the demonstrators. The phenomenon also explains why leadership acts may appear premature or inappropriate unless they occur along the gradients of dimensions that include the activities of other participants. A voice from within a gathering may have more force than a voice from outside, when social world variables are taken as constant. It should be noted that most work in group dynamics does not take account of the social field

(Cartwright and Zander, 1968). The discussion here suggests that the results of experiments that deal with relationships among individuals or groups—the classical experiments of group dynamics, for example—would be modified by systematic variations in the characteristics of the social field.

The relationship between accessibility and the accumulation of personnel during collective behavior suggest that the size of a crowd, given an initially plausible size for what Milgram and his colleagues (1969a) called a stimulus gathering, will tend to stabilize rather early. This stabilization will occur despite an effectively limitless pool of potential personnel, if there is a graded approach to centers of activity and if the crowd itself is structurally superordinate to its local and included encounters, that is, if the crowd is more than a gathering.

Because, as Goffman (1961) pointed out, it is ordinarily difficult to leave well-formed and bounded encounters, it might be expected, given a graded approach and the consequent ease of entry, that the increase in size would be limited only by the availability of potential participants. A number of factors make this unlikely. First, although a graded approach makes it easy to enter, it also makes it easy to leave a center of activity, especially when the center of activity is subordinate to an inclusive collectivity. Second, when local encounters are structurally subordinate to more inclusive collectivities, their members are constantly faced with participative options. Third, the internal conflicts between local and superordinate demands and frames of reference tend to create divisions among hard core participants (and their focused interactions) and the more transient marginals and hangers-on. The numbers of hard core participants stabilize as their encounters become bounded and distinct. Among the marginals, turnover tends to be complete; it is equally as easy to join as it is to leave. Fourth, the ease of entry provided by a graded approach undermines the capacity of encounters to become bounded and distinct relative to participative options and, thereby, increases the rate of turnover. On the other hand, something like perpetual growth will occur—or at least growth to the point of exhausting the pool of available participants—if there are graded approaches to centers of activity and if those local centers of activity are not subordinate to a more inclusive collectivity or located in a milieu of alternative interactions.

Kerckhoff and his associates (1965) observed the spread of a hysterical symptom among workers in a factory. The symptom first appeared among relatively isolated individuals and only later spread through more cohesive interpersonal networks. If the symptom had been initially restricted to highly cohesive collectivities, it would have been less accessible to those women who might have defined themselves as outsiders and for whom the symptom might have been a mark of collective identity that dramatized differences between insiders and outsiders. The "hysterical contagion" observed by Kerckhoff and his associates may have been facilitated by a relatively smooth or slightly graduated texture in which possession of the symptom was a floating attribute, contagious not by virtue of its own qualities or the qualities of its possessors so much as by virtue of the medium in which it floated. Similarly, in hierarchical systems the distribution of positions, not just the structure of hierarchical distinction, may be as important a fact in the life of an individual as his relation to any particular position, or its relation to any other position. Where there is a gradient of status, rather than status discontinuity, individuals tend to perceive their present status as precarious. When ethnic or religious membership is a bar to mobility and statuses are consequently discontinuous, mobility and aspirations for status are expressed politically, as a caste problem rather than as an individual problem.

Reconsideration of Some Classical Phenomena. This discussion of the social field allows a reconsideration of some of the classical phenomena of collective behavior. For example, the apparent suggestibility of individuals in some crowds—in particular, those crowds in which there is a shared object of attention and little direct interaction among participants—may depend upon whether or not the participants face a social field that is evenly graded. If this assumption is valid, there is no particular location or center of activity more compelling than any others, except for the shared object of attention. Such a crowd may be pictured as a set of dyads, in which each member refers his behavior to his relationship with the object of attention rather than to those in his immediate vicinity. This type of gathering has generally been called a mass. Under such conditions, without some change in the object of attention, individuals lack sufficient opportunity to change their orientation or their behavior. As a result, any new element may become a focus of attention that creates new socially relevant dimensions, redistributes the components of the social field, and creates new contingencies of action. A social mass may be described as a focused aggregate in which individuals do not discriminate among their fellow participants. From this point of view, the instability of the mass lies in its inconsequential social order, in particular, in an evenly graded social field in which elements are not comparable.

AN EMPHASIS ON APPEARANCE AND OUTCOME

Early treatments of collective behavior as fundamentally different from institutional behavior depended upon a descriptive emphasis on appearance and outcome, without sufficient regard for the immediate setting and its role in collective behavior. This emphasis gave the accounts of collective behavior in standard texts a quality of objectivity ordinarily associated with certain types of art criticism or with psychiatric case histories. The episodes described in those texts seem clearly out of setting, bearing significant form but utterly detached from what is ordinary in life and from anything that might be called surrounding circumstances. The emphasis on appearance may have been part of a more general tendency to reify the crowd and to ignore the significance of the relationship between the observer and the observed. In any case, it justified an almost exclusive concern with objectively "internal" structure in the sense of norms and style, and with a characterization of the crowd as fundamentally unreasonable in its apparent lack of significant orientation. The rediscovery of the setting in modern research has shifted emphasis to the politics of the crowd experience and the development of collective behavior as it relates to an environment of support, opposition, and incident. Consequently, Waskow

(1966) could describe the history of the civil rights movement as a history of tactics and the exhaustion of authorized means of protest rather than as a collection of outbursts related only in terms of similarities among contextual determinants. Consequently, too, the Skolnick Report (1969) to the National Commission on the Causes and Prevention of Violence could begin to formulate a basis for studying social change from a consideration of the history of collective behavior.

COLLECTIVE CONSTRUCTIONS

Collective constructions are collective demonstrations of collective practice. They are public orders of items taken up by public processes; they are aspects of socially organized settings. (Garfinkel, 1967, has discussed how collective constructions are "accomplished" as a matter of socially organized practice and how this accomplishment can be known.) They are not expressions of consensus, and they are not ideas.

The ongoing and collectively enactive aspect of collective constructions implies that they can neither be summarized by a limited set of verbal statements nor simulated, although they can be indicated. Any stated or modeled version of a collective construction is overspecialized. Such versions are, themselves, products of settings, and their claims are accountable to the projects of those settings. To stress the constructed aspect of a collective construction is to draw attention to its dialectical relationship with the practice of which it is an emergent and to its variability as a demonstration of the "nature of things." Collective constructions place a social present within a context that substantiates or justifies particular arrangements of items available to a collectivity.

Some collective constructions are what Lang and Lang (1968) called inferential structures. For example, Lang and Lang described the inferential structures of various telecasts of the 1952 presidential conventions: "when the same elements were combined into different configurations, viewers on the different networks might draw different inferences . . . . We have labeled this kind of configuration the *inferential structure* of the telecast" (p. 134). Through inferential structures, objects and events are given importance within the array of items available to be collectively noticed and are placed on agenda that relate collective activities to occasions.

LOCATION AND ORIENTATION

Collective constructions of the situation assume or establish perspective by demonstrating a site for the accountable location of action and a general orientation to, or mode of accounting for involvement in, that site. Brown (1969b) reported data that indicated that workers at the Tennessee Valley Authority (TVA) generally located themselves in either the large organization or their local work groups, depending upon which was seen as the site of self-defining activities, such as achievement. There were two major orientations to TVA as the accountable location of individual action: in one, the individual was oriented to the organization itself, without reference to the extrinsic personal gratifications, such as salary and status, that membership might yield; in the other, membership in TVA was seen primarily as a means to the attainment of extrinsic goals. In the first orientation, the worker can be said to have been serious ("symbolically motivated"), and in the second, detached ("pragmatically motivated"). The two components of the workers' construction of the situation—site and orientation—were related: the satisfaction with work of those workers who referred themselves to the organization, rather than to their local work groups, tended to depend upon whether or not they testified that the organization was a source of self-defining attributes—was providing opportunities to achieve and to use personal skills—and was, therefore, intrinsically valuable.

Brown's research was focused on individual constructions of the situation. It did not ask how constructions are sustained within the work situation so that they are available to members. It is assumed here that the definition of site and the orientation of individuals to their site depend upon the practices of collectivities within which site and orientation are enacted. A practice is normally a specialty of a social identity (for example, class membership) and a type of geographical area (for example, the plant). Individuals who share a social identity and a particular type of geographical location and who regularly and collectively notice the same environmental items will probably also participate in—be members to—similar constructions of the general aspects of their situation, in particular, a site to which they refer their activities and an orientation to that site. Moreover, as a constructive tradition emerges for particular social identities and geographical locations, newcomers are able to join that tradition directly, without special socialization.

SITE AND BIOGRAPHY

Site is a priori to action. The meaning of a particular place does not change easily. However, the activities that take place at a particular site are taken to be relatively variable and mutually contingent. Collective constructions include the variable, as well as the recurrent, features of moment-to-moment interaction. As such constructions become increasingly elaborate from moment to moment and are referred to the coded residues of prior constructions that are the records of the situation—the biography of the site—they limit the range of items that are taken as facts. As a result, over time, the relationship between what is taken as fact and what is taken as interpretation is progressively more intimate and progressively more one-sided, which is to say that specific items tend to acquire conventional meanings within a situation that, itself, becomes progressively conventional. Nevertheless, given a site and its record, the construction of the situation is responsive to the events of the moment.

For example, the response of line workers to management demands for greater output depends, in part, upon group discussions and the special dynamics of worker organizations with regard to such matters as the intentions of management, the implications of an increased ratio of output to wages, and related developments in other organizations within the industry. The resulting constructions of the situation are to a large extent ad hoc, or situated; they establish a setting and, thus, are susceptible to verification. A priori constructions, on the other hand, are not verifiable by references to the particulars of a situation. The a priori construction of the situation limits ad hoc constructions: the definition of site establishes boundaries and a general frame of reference for an actor within which events are ordered as they occur. The choice of site by TVA workers, for example, places limits on the items to which individuals are responsive. To be at a site is to be able to decide what is inappropriate or irrelevant. But, action at a site depends upon the specific items that appear, the circumstances of their appearance, and their setting—the situated constructions within which items are interrelated. TVA workers who refer themselves to the organization as a whole are available for the discontents and rewards of mobility, security, and accomplishment over the long run more than they are for the discontents and rewards of peer solidarity, the pressures of particular tasks, and specific short-run achievements. For these workers, the latter are transitional moments in the practical construction of useful biography; disturbances of routine, specific task frustrations, and specific interactions rarely become elements of the work situation but are only incidents of it.

INFERENCE FROM INDIVIDUAL CONSTRUCTIONS

It is important to remember that although constructions of situations may characterize individuals or collectivities, collective constructions, like other collective traits, must be assessed directly. They cannot be inferred from a distribution of individual constructions. Various evidences of collective life must be examined in order to be able to indicate the nature of particular collective constructions of the situation. Many of the early attempts to study "national character" by means of attitude scales may be seen as attempts to describe collective constructions of special situations—specifically, those evoked by the questions on the attitude questionnaires—rather than as descriptions of "typical" Americans, Japanese, or Russians. (The questionnaire provided a situation supposedly shared by subjects and investigators who otherwise were foreign to one another.) Because the data involved distributions of individual constructions, however, even for this purpose, these studies of national character are inadequate.

The use of objective measures was designed to overcome the apparent weaknesses of data in clinical psychology, history, and impressionistic sociology. However, the argument here suggests that certain phenomena must be handled as a problem of judgment. The training of professional sociologists in the use of actuarial techniques has tended to reduce the likelihood that they will be trained in the special skills required for the appraisal of social reality; ethnography and the case method offer possible execeptions. It might be suggested that the authors of the research on national character set about to solve the same types of problems as those who currently study definitions of the situation. Inkeles and Levinson (1954) pointed out that some students of national character defined "national character as a particular way of looking at the coherence of culturally defined values or behavior patterns" (pp. 979-80). However, that literature thrived at a time when sociologists were afraid of the idea of collective traits and collective representations, seeing such traits and representations as mental rather than collectively practical accomplishments (Garfinkel, 1967).

Thus, the fallacy of the typical man was often substituted for the group mind fallacy. Nevertheless, that literature may be recast as providing indications of the accounts by which individuals present themselves, as having a social identity, to anonymous inquiry.

A TYPOLOGY OF COLLECTIVE CONSTRUCTIONS

In describing constructions of the situation, a distinction has been made between setting and context and between constructions that are ad hoc and constructions that are a priori. Although there is a loose correspondence between the two distinctions—both contexts and a priori constructions are given for any action—setting and context are categories of situation, and ad hoc and a priori constructions are categories of action. An actor's setting and context are defined within constructions that are ad hoc and subject to verification and within constructions that are given as primitive assumptions about the nature of social reality. In the simplest sense, some constructions are given and others are issues that are resolved by negotiation. The former are a priori to action; the latter are part of action. The elaboration of articulate constructions is an activity in its own right. The development of collective identity is often a byproduct of elaborating constructions. Wallace (1968) has pointed out that warfare often involves the development of an ingroup-outgroup construction in which a thriving opponent becomes converted into a wholly depersonalized "enemy" and the ingroup becomes a "defender." The mechanisms for this particular development are largely traceable to official acts, taken as contextual, aimed at affecting meanings within particular settings for action.

Collective constructions may be distinguished by their value along two dimensions: the first dimension is their status in the logic of action, that is, whether they are a priori or ad hoc; the second dimension is their temporal reference, that is whether they refer the present action to a past or to a future. Table 10.2 presents a typology of constructions defined by these two dimensions. Perspectives and definitions of the situation are especially important for an understanding of situated social action. Biographies and justifications are essential for an understanding of the relationship between situated social action and its environment of organized support and opposition. Perspectives and definitions of the situation are properties of collectivities engaged in an episode of situated social action, and biographies and justifications are properties of actors who define the episode. Perspectives and definitions of the situation specify the situation for acting collectivities. Biographies and justifications specify the episode as situation for other actors.

Table 10.2 A TYPOLOGY OF CONSTRUCTIONS

		Status in the Logic of Action	
		a priori	ad hoc
Temporal Reference	prospective	perspective	definition of the situation
	retrospective	biography	justification

Definitions of the situation and justifications assert bases for choice, the first in terms of the relation of means to ends, the second in terms of rationalized alternatives for action; they are, then, political in their implications. Perspectives define the site of action, the boundaries or limits of the setting in which situations are defined and enacted. Definitions of the situation specify the variable relationships among the actors (for each other) within a setting. Biographies and justifications pose the problem of entrance; they establish lines around the various actors represented in an episode of collective behavior and determine what "sides" are available to be taken by new participants and how these sides will be understood in terms of both the value of the episode and the functions the episode is alleged to have performed.

When official agencies plot their entrance to an episode of collective behavior, biographical and justificatory materials are used to formulate policy and to engage audiences that will tolerate and perhaps support the official policy (Silver, 1969). Biographies of particular episodes may also play a role in the larger biographies of social movements (Waskow, 1966), which establish a repertoire of available occasions and formats for collective behavior. This repertoire is a part of the context of collective behavior.

Perspectives establish the site at which social action occurs, projected from a particular point of origin. They are taken for granted by those who share them. Perspectives establish the range of items that can be included in a setting, just as the context specifies the most general typifications of those items as parameters for social action. The identity of an act, like any item, depends upon its setting. The identify of a setting depends upon its site. During the 1965 episodes of collective behavior in Watts, Los Angeles, for example, specific acts of hostility against police were intelligible to those who did them or supported them as actions within a setting of community revolt. But the revolt itself was part of a site defined as oppressive and brutal to black people—Los Angeles.

Perspectives assert the minimal conditions for participation. On the other hand, definitions of the situation, arrangements of items as they become locally available, emerge as part of collective practices and account for the ease with which participants are involved in situated social action. Unlike perspectives, definitions of the situation do not demonstrate a practice as a whole. Items defined as part of the setting for collective action substantiate the definitions of the situation by which they are so defined. They are points of reference, items to be arranged so that action may proceed; definitions of the situation refer to such items. For this reason, the collection of items capable of entering a particular setting may be called a *substantiating context* for definitions of the situation.

In summary, definitions of the situation are limited by perspectives and substantiated by reference to what is taken as information. Definitions of the situation arise as information is collectively selected, collectively collated and organized, collectively stored, collectively retrieved, and collectively used. By virtue of the order they give to a setting, definitions determine the range of intelligible activities at any particular time.

Thus, the analysis of collective behavior requires an examination of collective constructions and the conditions under which collective constructions are threatened. At this point, the role of collective constructions in situated social action will be examined, in particular, their consequences for individual participation, individual and collective action, and collective behavior.

Collective behavior occurs when a collective construction of a situation is threatened, when collective action is disrupted by the intrusion of alternative constructions of the situation, when two "bodies" attempt to occupy the same "space." Thus, the analysis of collective behavior requires a discussion of *patterns of interference* among competing collective constructions of the situation and the *points of confrontation* at which that competition is made explicit.

PATTERNS OF INTERFERENCE AND POINTS OF CONFRONTATION

A pattern of interference exists when the same situation—the same collection of items—is construed as a matter of practice in mutually exclusive ways. Ordinarily, these patterns are not explicit. Moreover, the realization of patterns of interference as points of confrontation is often avoided by the parties involved. This avoidance may occur as a result of negotiations about design or detail (practice or activity), as a matter of practice, or because schedules of engagement and areas of exclusive jurisdiction are matters of record or tradition. These mechanisms ensure that the abrasive or uneasy relations of detail that exist between parties to patterned interference do not surface as a confrontation between the parties themselves or, at least, serve to make the timing and circumstances of confrontation reasonably predictable. If the binding quality of practice serves to account for what are usually referred to as consciousness and interest, these mechanisms help account for "false consciousness" in terms of the practices of everyday life.

Competing constructions can come into confrontation as a direct consequence of collective practice, as when, for example, administrators discipline students for engaging in political activity on campus, thereby disclosing that the meaning of the university is profoundly different for students and for administrators. Whether or not this difference leads to student cynicism and apathy or a more positive and political stance on the part of students, to a large extent, depends upon whether students feel that they have the power to force a negotiation. The cynicism and apathy that a number of observers noted following the 1968-1969 school year, during which a number of confrontations occurred, were probably largely because of the fact that the coercive actions of college administrators and others in positions of power confirmed the impotence of students.

Confrontation may also take place as a result of acts of articulation that draw the implications of incompatible constructions of the situation to the point of a hypothetical or constructive confrontation. This point is often reached when decisions must be made that require the explication of various positions and their implications. In general, however, points of confrontation are usually reached when collectivities, through their practical activities, encounter items not consistently accounted for by their collective constructions of the situation and are forced to recognize the existence of competing constructions (Kuhn, 1962).

Even when definitions of the situation are compatible, they may fit into competing perspectives. In this case, points of confrontation will not be reached until the perspectives themselves are engaged, that is, usually not until situational changes require a redefinition of the location of collective action. Perspectives may also be engaged when a succession of definitions of the situation are exhausted through excessive rehearsal or, occasionally, as a result of acts of articulation. As acts of articulation take place, interfering definitions of the situation within a perspective shared by the differing parties will often lead to attempts to set up a reconciled version of the past, either by studying the situation by methods and procedures agreeable to the parties (to negotiate biography) or by compromising on matters whose implications for the future are otherwise unacceptable. However, differences in perspective are not negotiable; because perspectives establish the possibility of action, differences permit only acts that delay confrontation or acts of withdrawal. Thus, differences in perspective are resolved through struggle, which includes behaviors ranging from attempts to proselytize among apparently neutral parties to the use of force to prevent collective action founded on one or another of the competing perspectives. Smelser assumed that collective behavior is founded on interference among competing definitions of the situation. Thus, he was able to compare generalized beliefs to allegedly more accurate ones. The idea of perspectival conflict suggests that many of the incidents Smelser described were based on differences in perspective. Rather than stating what is occurring and what is its cause and remedy, perspectival differences pose conflict about the position from which reality may be drawn.

For Goffman's theory of collective behavior, precipitating incidents are critical events that articulate patterns of interference and force incompatible constructions of the situation to points of confrontation. When this confrontation occurs, the nature of the situation itself becomes an issue and a matter of negotiation, if not a matter of choice. As one side of a critical issue, a construction of a situation is necessarily clarified and simplified. Moreover, the competition among constructions generates a competitive stance for partisans. It is the peculiar character of competition during collective behavior that accounts for the hardening of lines, although the fact has variously been explained by the nature of the participants, the content of attitudes or beliefs, or the need to reduce uncertainty or ambiguity per se. Collective behavior is an expression of certainty, not an expression of uncertainty. Thus, the apparent dogmatism of groups (Bittner, 1963) under pressure may be characterized as a mixture of discipline and articulation by means of which constructions become clear and compelling. The development of relatively hardened positions as a consequence of the emergence of points of confrontation may result in acts that demonstrate identity or acts of style on the part of participants. Acts that demonstrate identity are important in collective behavior. They give intelligible form to individual activities, clarify the collectivity and its constructions, and increase the proselytive capacity of active collectivities.

INTERNAL PATTERNS OF INTERFERENCE

Collectivities may be linked through their independent acknowledgements of the presence of a governing occasion. In disaster, for example, as the occasion is established, the coordination of work becomes a problem. An organic solidarity may be negotiated that preserves the independence of collectivities at the same time that it allows their performances to be coordinated. It is at this point in the development of collective behavior that the collectivity of collectivities is strongest, but it is also at this point that internal cohesiveness is most likely to break down.

As collective behavior stabilizes, new issues that are perhaps raised by the intensity of opposition may reveal patterns of interference among different perspectives within an engaged collectivity. These differences are often obscured by initial agreement on a definition of the situation. For example, student demonstrations in the 1960s initially expressed consensus about the unfairness of campus dress regulations and official acts enforcing these regulations. This consensus broke down with increasing frequency as it became obvious that some students placed official unfairness in the general framework of organizational reform or in the framework of the demand for student power and others placed it within the framework of a more radical critique of American institutions.

A protracted struggle often weakens consensus in the weaker of two parties. Official intransigence frequently meant that demonstrators were faced with the problem of how far to go in the pursuit of their goals. If official unfairness became the issue, then an escalation of tactics was not necessarily called for; it was enough to express indignation. However, if the official unfairness was understood within a more radical framework in which the quality of student life was at stake and in which the official acts were seen as illegitimate or as inevitable expressions of official interests, then a mild escalation of tactics (for example, a boycott of classes) would be called for until officials came to terms. The consideration of means raises the question of whether initially stated goals, as parts of initial definitions of the situation, fit the same perspective. Differences among students on initial goals often led to the articulation of patterns of interference among perspectives on student life, the university, and American society.

The precipitants of collective behavior tend to appear as intrusions from outside during the early periods of an episode and as internal disruptions during later periods, when new definitions of the situation are required, particularly if there has been come organized turnover of personnel. In addition to the effects of time and personnel turnover, several other factors affect the likelihood of internal precipitation. These include fatigue; the exhaustion of meaning through overrehearsal of action at the level of the collectivity; the localization of individual commitment through an excess of free time or debate; the lack of opportunity to rehearse collective constructions of the situation, which is often a result of the official tactic of "waiting out" an episode of collective behavior; and acts of articulation, by means of which competing perspectives are revealed.

SCENARIOS FOR COLLECTIVE BEHAVIOR

Given a collection of items common to different practices, a scenario for collective behavior may be established as a sequence of relatively complete episodes: (1) collective action and its implications, which includes collectivities, their constructions of the situation, and the emergence of patterns of interference; (2) confrontation, which involves the emergence of points of confrontation by virtue of acts of articulation or precipitating incidents; and (3) collective behavior, which includes the crystallization of constructions of the situation and the reaffirmation of collectivities and their constructions in terms

Figure 10.1 A SCENARIO FOR COLLECTIVE BEHAVIOR

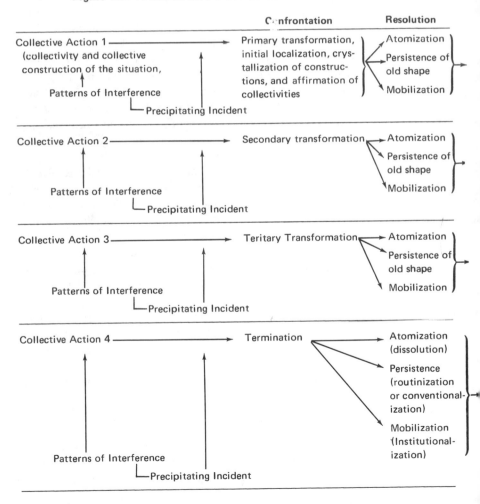

of the exigencies of their situation. It should be noted that reaffirmation is not a return to normal, and collective behavior either dislodges competition or is replaced.

Variations at each point in this scenario account for differences among episodes of collective behavior. Such a scenario and its variations are an alternative to the construction of types of collective behavior based on a prior typology of occasions (Sjoberg, 1962), to a post hoc summary of the content of collective constructions of the situation in terms of beliefs or norms (Smelser, 1963; Turner, 1964), or to a post hoc analysis of outcome (Graham and Gurr, 1969). Within this framework, differences in episodes of collective behavior may be described in terms of different possibilities for social action at different points. Moreover, because few recorded episodes of collective behavior have run only a single cycle, collective behavior is more accurately portrayed as a sequence of related episodes, each of which depends upon the outcome of the preceding one. These outcomes, in turn, establish new bases for confrontation. Three outcomes of collective action are possible: the collectivity of origin atomizes; the collectivity of origin maintains its original action; or the collectivity of origin is precipitated as collective behavior. Figure 10.1 presents an extended scenario for the analysis of collective behavior.

An episode of collective behavior involves interaction among competing parties, each of whom manifests the cycle described in Figure 10.1. Cycles overlap at the point of confrontation and during the process of resolution. It is at these points that elements of one construction of the situation are included in the other. It should be noted that each subepisode represents different conditions for the entrance of new personnel.

AN ILLUSTRATION OF THE SCENARIO

The Watts riots of 1965 illustrate the general development of collective behavior in terms of the scenario described above.

On the evening of August 11, as Los Angeles sweltered in a heat wave, a highway patrolman halted a young Negro driver for speeding. The young man appeared intoxicated, and the patrolman arrested him. As a crowd gathered, law enforcement officials were called to the scene. A highway patrolman mistakenly struck a bystander with his billy club. A young Negro woman, who was erroneously accused of spitting on the police, was dragged into the middle of the street.

When the police departed, members of the crowd began hurling rocks at passing cars, beating white motorists, and overturning cars and setting them on fire. The police reacted hesitantly. Actions they did take further inflamed the people in the streets.

The following day the area was calm. Community leaders attempted to mediate between Negro residents and the police received little cooperation from municipal authorities. That evening, the previous night's pattern of violence was repeated.

Not until almost 30 hours after the initial flareup did window-smashing, looting, and arson begin. Yet the police utilized only a small part of their forces.

Few police were on hand the next morning when huge crowds gathered in the business district of Watts, two miles from the location of the original disturbance, and began looting. In the absence of police response, the looting became bolder and spread into other areas. Hundreds of women and children from five housing projects clustered in or near Watts took part. Around noon, extensive fire-bombing began. Few white persons were attacked; the principal intent of the rioters now seemed to be to destroy property owned by whites, in order to drive white "exploiters" out of the ghetto. . . .

When [National] Guardsmen arrived, they, together with police, made heavy use of firearms. Reports of "sniper fire" increased. Several persons were killed by mistake. Many more were injured.

Thirty-six hours after the first Guard units arrived, the main force of the riot had been blunted. Almost 4,000 persons were arrested. Thirty-four were killed and hundreds injured. Approximately $35 million in damage had been inflicted (National Advisory Commission on Civil Disorders, 1968, p. 37-38).

The Watts riot was a series of related episodes of collective behavior, each having its own development involving the conversion of collective action to collective behavior under the impact of precipitating incidents. It should be noted that the confusion of target—the object of orientation—with goal or aim or intent is common in descriptions of collective behavior. Underlying it is an assumption of the uniformity of crowds and a failure to distinguish appearance from dynamics.

The Kerner Commission (National Advisory Commission on Civil Disorders) summary did not describe the engaged collectivities, their constructions of the situation, and the incidents that brought patterns of interference to points of confrontation. Other accounts (for example, Cohen and Murphy, 1966; Conot, 1967) provide material that is more suitable for analysis. Conot's (1967) account, for example, of the initial periods of the riot suggests that from the point of view of those who later participated in the riot, a juxtaposition of the delayed arrest and the gathering of bystanders allowed the emergence of a pattern of interference between competing definitions of the situation. "Another assault on a vulnerable and helpless community by a powerful representative of white colonial interests" was given time to be challenged by "we can and must protect our own against the intruder." One definition asserted weakness; the other asserted strength. The delay supported the plausibility of strength, at least temporary strength, through numbers. This construction was further bolstered by the fact that the arresting officers argued with bystanders while lingering at the scene, undoubtedly confident of their own strength. Yet the willingness to engage in argument, and the extended time during which that interaction took place, deinstutionalized the arresting officers' presentations of authority. In the ordinary course of events arresting officers perform their task with dispatch and leave themselves little time in which to demonstrate their characteristics as individuals which would reveal their moral and physical vulnerability. In this case, the delay transformed the policeman from an agent of a large and dangerous principal, into an individual whose connection with a main body of force was merely contingent. The altercations between officers and bystanders at the scene of the arrest crystallized the definitions of strength and weakness and, ultimately, yielded a point of confrontation. According to Conot (1967), the result was the mobilization of crowds and the demonstration of collective strength by physical activity and verbal invective—techniques which, if they did not completely validate "strength," at least left it a moot point. When the officers left, their departure did not dissolve the occasion but was treated as an opportunity for a further validation of the threatened definition of collective strength. Members of the crowd hurled stones, bottles, and other missiles at the departing cars and ultimately, attacked all vehicles that unwittingly entered the area. The other episodes (looting and attacks on the business district) occurred later and were apparently actions of relatively small and cohesive units (see also Cohen and Murphy, 1966). These small units may have reflected an atomization of the original collectivities or a natural division of labor corresponding to varied conditions. Available accounts do not indicate which alternative was true, nor is there much information available on the precipitants of these episodes, that is, whether they might have arisen from natural extensions of collective actions already underway.

OFFICIAL ACTION AS COLLECTIVE BEHAVIOR

Although the focus thus far has been on unofficial collectivities engaged in unauthorized behavior, it is clear that much of what transpires during an episode of collective behavior depends upon the actions of officials and their representatives. An analysis of official activities as collective behavior is essential to an adequate understanding of the phenomena usually described in the literature on collective behavior. A recent article by Brown (1969b), for example, suggested that under certain circumstances, coalitions among previously mutually hostile agencies of social control (e.g., police and psychiatrists) can be viewed as collective behavior. These coalitions can form under the impact of special incidents that raise the possibility of an increase in power through coalition or through the establishment of a unity of interest. Coalitions may also emerge as an inevitable consequence of the realization of collective constructions of the situation. For example, when both police and psychiatrists are oriented in practice to the same "problem" (e.g., drugs) in the same way—as a problem of social control—an ideology of coalition may emerge.

Official activity may also assume a more conventional form as collection behavior. The Walker Report (1968) to the President's Commission on the Causes and Prevention of Violence (1968) identified the actions of police during the 1968 Democratic National Convention as a "police riot," thus suggesting the appropriateness of an analysis of some official action as collective behavior in more conventional terms. Along similar lines, Rude (1964) has remarked that, at least for the preindustrial crowd, "it was authority rather than the crowd that was conspicuous for its violence to life and limb" (p. 256). The Skolnick Report (1969) makes a similar case for official responses to the political protests of the 1960s.

COMMUNICATION

A number of topics traditionally related to collective behavior can be discussed in terms of the scenario summarized in Figure 10.1 and in terms of the principles discussed in the theoretic prospectus presented here. For example, communication is different for collective action, confrontation, and collective behavior. Typically, communication is a process by which collective constructions are rendered articulate during the course of collective action.

Shibutani's (1966) concept of rumor as the process by which news is created in interpersonal interaction during crisis can be seen as a characteristic of an advanced stage of collective action. In contrast, Turner (1964) suggested that rumor characterizes the initial state of collective behavior. The elaboration and explication of collective constructions of the situation under the pressure of patterns of interference always involves a significant measure of improvisation and the use of unauthorized channels of communication. Rumor is that collective action that takes place as patterns of interference begin to merge in points of confrontation. Because rumor is a conservative and conservatizing process, it is expected that the content and the acts of the improvised communication process will initially replicate the conventional aspects of collective action (Shibutani, 1966).

As suggested previously, unauthorized channels are not simply a substitute for the temporary malfunctioning of normal channels of communication; they operate in normal times as well as during crisis. During collective behavior, the threat to prior constructions of the situation gives communication a new status. Under the circumstances, improvised news is virtually all the news that is fit to hear. There is no sense of alternative channels, although there may be public reference to the temporary failure of licensed transmitters or the grapevine. The social distinctions and activities that emerge during collective behavior tend to dominate communication as the creation of news becomes an aspect of collective practice.

THE SPREAD OF COLLECTIVE BEHAVIOR

The spread of collective behavior can be accounted for by a number of processes, for example, the development of a social field within which collectivities become accessible, the elimination of plausible participative alternatives, the emergence of proselytive activities during collective behavior, or the continual absorption of new items in collective constructions of the situation. Particularly important is the use by one party of techniques that enforce a change in scale on the opposing party; escalation or the use of overkill techniques by hostile officials often forces bystanders to define themselves as participants in an episode of collective behavior.

SOCIAL CONTROL: A FUNCTION OF THEORIES OF COLLECTIVE BEHAVIOR

Theories always go beyond their facts. They are "projective systems" of a discipline and its practice. Theories reveal the problems and metasocial assumptions of an age, and in their creative stages, when their relation to fundamental moral, political, and intellectual paradigms is explicit, theories are treated dogmatically. Throughout most of their active existence, theories are subject to explication and elaboration rather than to criticism. As dogma, theory tends to carry extratheoretical functions that cannot be justified within the confines of the logic and methodological canons of its discipline. As theory, a set of ideas is subject to criticism, but as dogma it tends to be prescriptive or proscriptive. In short, new theories are frameworks for policy. And because theoretical work is organized within the socio-political framework of the discipline and its practice, it must always be asked: Whose future is served by the normative and practical implications of theory?

THE POLITICAL STANDING OF KEY CONCEPTS

The relation between theory and policy depends in part upon the political standing of key concepts. For example, the relationship between "material deprivation" and "civil strife" is an empirical correlation. It is usually interpreted causally within theories of frustration-induced aggression (Smelser, 1963). However, the key concept, deprivation, the reduction of which is predicted to reduce the level of civil strife (Gurr, 1969), has both a special socio-political standing and paradoxical implications in the United States. As the National Advisory Commission (1968) implied in its report on the urban disorders of 1967, political barriers to the economic reforms necessary to reduce the privation experienced by black Americans probably transcend the capacity of the American polity and the will of its leaders (B. Moore, 1969b). Nevertheless, "privation" is the key concept among liberal reformists in attempting to formulate policies for postindustrial capitalist society (Silver, 1969), which is indicative of the paradoxical status of the concept. The dilemma for the liberal reformer lies in the fact that the sociological theories he cites in support of his program indicate that the liberal capitalist state can survive only if it meets the demands, needs, and emerging political organizations of under-groups, but he is faced with political facts that seem to doom this program even if it should be accepted within the counsels of power. The two major premises of the Kerner Commission (National Advisory Commission on Civil Disorders) Report pose the dilemma clearly:

1. That this nation cannot abide violence and disorder if it is to ensure the safety of its people and their progress in a free society.
2. That this nation will deserve neither safety nor progress unless it can demonstrate the wisdom and the will to undertake decisive action against the root causes of racial disorder (1968, p. 34).

As Silver (1969) has indicated, the notion that privation causes civil strife allows reformists to sympathize with people who have been unruly without accepting unruliness as a tactic for social change. But because the notion is based on a theory of social causation that excludes consideration of the social implications of and political bases for discontent and opposition, it can equally justify reform or repression. On the one hand, even though reform is undertaken, presumably, some measure of repression is necessary in order to contain persons whose privation leads them to collective acts of disorder. On the other hand, if attempted reforms are not followed by an abatement of civil strife, or if reform is not feasible, presumably, repression is necessary to root out the spoiled products of the old regime (Horowitz and Leibowitz, 1968; Skolnick, 1969).

The Kerner Commission (1968) stated the dilemma. In a later report to the National Commission on the Causes and Prevention of Violence, a hint was given for the probable direction of the resolution of the dilema: "If legitimacy, institutional capabilities, and the consistency of techniques of social control are increased and intense discontents alleviated, turmoil is likely to subside" (Gurr, 1969, p. 624).

OFFICIAL PRACTICE

Although the problem is ultimately one of official practice and policy, it depends to a large extent upon conceptions of collective behavior that account for unauthorized action in terms of impersonal and nonpolitical social causes, such as privation or its generic theoretic root, system strain. This position is distinguished as much by what it omits as by what it includes. The deemphasis on the politics-of-protest approach reflects the intellectual and class origins of the theorists, just as it reflects the official perspectives within which theories have been selected to justify policy (Silver, 1969). As C. Wright Mills (1951) pointed out, the profession of social science has developed around the problems of management in an age of corporate capitalism. Consequently, an emphasis on consensus, integration, and administrative problem solving and deemphasis on interest, contradiction, and struggle should be expected.

The elevation of the principle of order above the principles of justice and freedom is a natural consequence of the professionalization and cosmopolitanization of sociology in mid-twentieth-century America. On the national scale, the failure of liberal governments to provide justice and freedom and to prevent social disorder through reform is an expression of the limits of advanced capitalism.

The persistence of the concept of strain in the language of social theory and social policy carries ominous overtones for the future (Silver, 1969; Skolnick, 1969). In the theory of collective behavior, the concept has remained as dogma beyond the creative stages of the theory from which it is derived. As social scientists move into positions of greater political influence, primarily through the bureaucratic or ideological functions they perform for their patrons and clients, and as the option for reform grows dimmer on the political horizon, professional emphasis on social control and the support of traditional official elites can be expected to increase. This tendency can be seen in the growth of service disciplines such as criminology, which is concerned primarily with law enforcement; in the appointment of presidential commissions on violence, protest, strife, insurrection, and so on; and in the funding, by the government and foundations, of extensive research on political dissent and civil strife.

THE GROWING EMPHASIS ON SOCIAL CONTROL

A recent pamphlet, written by Morris Janowitz (1968) of the University of Chicago and released by the University's Center for Policy Study, further illustrates a growing emphasis on social control within sponsored professional sociology. The pamphlet, *Social Control of Escalated Riots*, was prepared for a conference on "Short Term and Emergency Measures to Avert Urban Violence," sponsored by the Center for Policy Study in 1968. Janowitz began with three assumptions, the first dictated by theory, the second by what is apparently an empirical examination of the political economy of the United States, and the third by a more general belief in the inherently progressive tendencies of the American social system.

Janowitz's first assumption is that collective behavior and political violence are caused by system strain in the form of specific deprivations. With minor qualification, Janowitz approached the corollary assumption that a change in the level of strain over time produces a change in the level of strife, a proposition that ignores the irreversibility of emergent phenomena. The second assumption is that reform within America has taken place in the areas of racial and economic discrimination. And the third assumption is that reform will continue to take place until institutionalized injustice, inequality of opportunity, and imposed privation are things of the past.

Janowitz labeled the 1965 and 1967 episodes of collective behavior "commodity riots" which specified his belief that collective behavior is a result of deprivation. Moreover, he easily fitted commodity riots into the framework of his third assumption that the "socio-economic position of the Negro in American society will continue to improve, especially as federal programs of assistance become more effective" (p. 17). According to Janowitz, commodity riots will thus be eliminated, or their likelihood reduced, by providing commodities. Because commodities will be provided, it is only necessary to maintain the peace until they are received by the deprived community or until the deprived community itself develops local institutions capable of channeling residual tensions.

A Prescription for Policy. From his three basic assumptions, Janowitz derived the following proposition: it is essential to develop effective and efficient techniques of social control in order to prevent and contain "outbreaks of mass rioting" and to keep the system intact as efforts at institutional reform proceed (p. 7). In this context, "social control" refers to official coercion through the use of police forces.

Janowitz's position, which is hinted at by his use of the term "outbreak of mass rioting," is revealed by his prescription for policy:

> My basic point of view is that in addition to institution-building aimed at social and economic reform social control of rioting requires independent efforts in the deescalation of violence; domestic disarmament, if you will (1968, p. 8).

Domestic disarmament is not, however, what Janowitz had in mind. The bulk of his pamphlet is devoted to the problem of increasing the capacity of the police for counterinsurgency action and the arming of the quasi-military forces available to official bodies, constituting what by now appears to be a dedicated holding action within the cities of the United States. If Janowitz's assumptions are incorrect, then his suggestions for policy appear to offer no more than technical advice on how to eliminate serious political opposition. Such advice comprises a prescription for what the Skolnick Report (1969) called a police state or, at the very least, a cruel holding action against people who have acted in the light of a condition that was brought about through forces beyond their control and that is apparently unable to be corrected through the available institutions.

Untenable Assumptions. The most important of Janowitz's assumptions is that collective behavior depends upon system strain and that the relationship is reversible. This assumption is not tenable within available theories of collective behavior. Janowitz himself suggested that the assumption was insufficient to explain civil strife when he spoke of a contemporary shift from expressive outbursts to the "instrumental use of violence"—to "political violence or political terror" or what he variably referred to as "mass destruction" and "defiance politics" (p. 18-19). Nowhere did he consider the politics of protest from the point of view of grossly deprived and exploited undergroups or as if those engaged in militant political action were rational in their appraisal of the social system and/or had given that system every chance. Nowhere did he consider the possibility that there may not be a basic consensus in American society and, therefore, no real pluralism. Nor did he consider that official power may be legitimately subjected to radical criticism and, hence, to radical action. Janowitz's only qualification of the notion that riots are caused by strain lies in the suggestion of organization and the growth of determination among the deprived and excluded undergroups. He appears to believe, however, that the only social action that is political is that which takes place within the institutional framework of American politics. Social action that is unofficial and unauthorized is called defiance politics.

UNIT III: SUMMARY

Sociologists have often used the term collective behavior as a label for items that are not easily subsumed by the categories of general sociology. Events as diverse as social movements, public opinion, the crowd, revolution, fashion, and mass communication, at one time or another, have been included in texts on collective behavior. Whether any particular event has been labeled "collective behavior" seems to have depended in part upon four preliminary assertions: that the event is unofficial in its source; that it is unauthorized by official authority; that it is irrational, that is unexpected or unexplained within the prevailing models of social action[1]; and that it involves many people. Thus, until further investigation revealed that many lynchings were actually authorized and legitimate within the community in which they took place, all lynchings were considered collective behavior—that is, unauthorized acts of large unofficial assemblies that were unexpected within what is sociologically taken to be the rational institutional framework for the resolution of social conflicts.

A TYPOLOGY OF SOCIOLOGICAL LABELS BASED ON TWO TYPES OF PRETHEORETIC OBSERVER JUDGMENTS

DEFINITION OF THE INSTITUTIONAL QUALITY OF THE BEHAVIOR OBSERVED

		Source Defined As			
		Official		Unofficial	
		Behavior Defined As		Behavior Defined As	
		Authorized	Unauthorized	Authorized	Unauthorized
Definition of the rationality of the behavior	Rational	Manifest function[1]	Latent function[2]	Agency[5]	Conflict
	Nonrational	Unanticipated consequence[3]	Dysfunction[4]	Spontaneous contribution	Collective behavior

1. Merton, 1957, p. 51: *"Manifest functions* are those objective consequences contributing to the adjustment or adaptation of the system which are intended and recognized by participants in the system." At the sociological level of analysis the self-consciousness implied by Merton's definition clearly suggests legitimacy and the institutionalization of action. Adaptation and the fulfillment of functional prerequisites are definitive of rationality within Merton's framework.

2. Merton, 1957, p. 51: *"Latent functions,* correlatively, being those which are neither intended nor recognized."

3. Ibid.

4. Ibid.

5. Agency involves an act by an authorized but nonofficial actor. The actor is an agent for a principal—often official. While this is a legal concept, it is also pertinent to discussions of political crime, organized crime, scientific productivity, etc.

---

1. In this context, "rationality" refers to whether or not the phenomenon is accounted for by a system of explanation, whether the observer considers it to be in the ordinary course of events. Since the term "collective behavior" appears most often within the framework of structural-functionalism, rationality refers to the relation of means to ends within specific institutions. Insofar as collective behavior has been thought to be the behavior of those who are impatient and as disoriented from the institutional means to various ends, it is nonrational from the point of view of American structural-functionalism. The point is not that the behavior is somehow crazy, but that the observer or theorist does not anticipate the episode. Insofar as his failure to anticipate it is caused by a committment to a paradigm in which predictability is one criterion of rationality, collective behavior is not rational. For Turner, the nonrationality of collective behavior lies in the unpredictability of its occasion and therefore in its lack of continuity with prior activity—and therefore with its resistance to institutional analysis.

The previous typology shows relationships among some of the concepts that have been used to describe the relative institutional quality of social activities. The typology is based on the types of pretheoretic observer judgments corresponding to the assertions, listed above, that determine the application of the label "collective behavior."

One additional judgment is ordinarily prior to the application of the various labels in the typology, namely, that the observer has seen action rather than, simply, motion or something transitional and incidental. This is an instance of a problem discussed throughout this book: To what extent and under what conditions is the attribution of organization to phenomena valid? The labels apply to things taken as complete, known, and episodic.

The study of collective behavior has always been controversial. Theoretical interest in crowds follows in the wake of social change, and the explanations offered to account for crowd behavior usually reflect various political ideologies and perspectives. From its origins, the study of collective behavior has exposed the relationships between analysis and engagement, theory and practice, and political ideas and political problems.

Until very recently, collective behavior was treated as an integral part of the more general concerns of social order and social control. As a result, theories of collective behavior have reflected a special perspective on society—a managerial perspective in which good and bad, health and disease, and function and dysfunction were linked to administrative versions of order and disorder. However, Smelser (1963) has pointed out that collective behavior frequently arises when people are troubled about the conditions of their lives. This particular manifestation of troubled conditions may pose problems for those in power, but it can be both realistic and rational for those for whom unauthorized action may provide the only means for ameliorating their condition, for reorienting official priorities, or for gaining power (Waskow, 1966). As such, collective behavior is part of political conflict. In this sense, the distinction between order and disorder conceals a conflict between those who dominate and those who are dominated, between the official order and the unofficial order. Once this is asserted, collective behavior appears as unauthorized socio-political action. It is only when the crowd, for example, is described apart from its socio-political context that norms, generalized beliefs, and style become focal to an explanation. Then, the crowd appears to be a unit in itself, unresponsive to its environment and, consequently, nonrational and autistic.

Robert Ezra Park argued that the course of history has depended upon episodes of collective behavior that provided entry into intergroup confrontations and led to the formation of new institutions and new bases for power. Yet, Park's view attributes the role of collective behavior in social change primarily to its capacity to provide clues or warnings (see also Turner, 1964; Moore, 1969b) to those in power that there are serious social problems for which policy must be devised. Park's perspective, though its emphasis on the use of the executive function to control societal change and direct it along progressive lines represents a liberal version, is still the perspective of administration.

Since 1966, some of the literature on collective behavior has been written from a different perspective—from the viewpoint of undergroups, for whom authority and power are distinct in terms of the practice of everyday life, and for whom patterns of interest and domination, rather than system, comprise the fundamental operations of society. The shift in perspective poses different problems for sociologists: What are the practical bases for and obstacles to individual participation in unauthorized political action? How does unauthorized political action influence the development of popular-based, progressive movements? What are the official and institutional obstacles to unauthorized political action, and revolutionary change? What are the practical functions of theoretical interpretations of collective behavior?

Many sociologists have accepted the dictum of the late C. Wright Mills that the managerial perspective ultimately reflects the class interests of the powerful. Mills (1961, 1963) argued that sociology written from this perspective tends to justify those interests by ideology in the guise of theory—for example, the notion that unauthorized social action is a form of pathology or disorder—which denies both the legitimacy and the possibility of radical structural change and radical criticism of society. Marcuse (1968) added that this rejection of possibility is a denial of the very rationality of opposition. From this point of view, the "social problem" is not collective behavior but, rather, the growth of new and dangerous forms of social and political control and official opposition to popularly induced change, in short, entrenched and institutionally fortified power (B. Moore, 1969a, 1969b).

Each of the three theories of collective behavior presented in chapter 8 is incomplete but each has a critical core and each is suggestive. The extent to which the theories are opposed or complementary, and whether or not the differences among them are illusory, is a topic for further discussion. It is clear that Smelser, Turner, and Goffman share some concepts. All three deal with strain in one form or another. Smelser conceives of strain in relatively abstract terms—as an incompatibility among the components of a system. For Turner, strain is situated normative ambiguity. For Goffman, it is the potentially intrusive quality of the world external to the encounter and the unease provided by the possibility of role distance. In all three cases, something akin to strain is the most general condition that determines episodes of collective behavior. All three theorists also considered the importance of processes of communication under conditions of strain. They agreed that collective behavior is the behavior of collectivities and not simply of aggregates of unrelated individuals. Each theorist described the environment as organized rather than as a diffuse context of discrete events with isolated effects. Each theorist discussed change in terms of the higher order interaction between crowds, as a type of social entity, and the organized segments of their environments. Each theorist pointed to essential paradoxes of control.

Smelser's distinctive contribution lies in his discussion of the stages of collective behavior. This discussion emphasized the multiple determination of episodes of collective behavior, the shifts in the organization of the crowd over time, and the different conditions of official control at each stage. Turner's contribution lies primarily in his discussion of the normative implications of interaction and their consequences for conformity. He provided a way of questioning the classical picture of crowds, of explaining the illusion of uniformity, and of examining crowds as social structures. Instead of viewing crowds as organized around shared beliefs, he considered them to be organized in terms of norms and, thereby, shifted the theoretical emphasis from culture to social structure. Goffman's distinctive contribution lies in his discussion of the compelling quality of local, ad hoc, face-to-face interaction, which has important implications for understanding precipitation and the organization of collective behavior.

Each theorist orders the major determinants of collective behavior differently. Smelser emphasized generalized beliefs, Turner emphasized emergent norms, and Goffman emphasized the plausibility and engaging quality of local social reality. Each theorist, however, left several important questions unanswered. Smelser did not deal with the rational and organized bases of collective behavior and did not explain how crowds can emerge in which beliefs and moods are not shared. Turner did not deal adequately with the transformation of a collection of interacting normative units into a large-scale, relatively unified crowd. Goffman, like Turner, did not explain the conditions under which nonlocal forms of collective behavior occur. However, the discussion of Goffman's work suggested that the appearance of large-scale crowds, the classically described form of collective behavior, may be either too rare to be of significant concern for a theory of collective behavior or too weak as social forces to account for the phenomena recorded in the literature.

The limits to the application of each of the three theories depend upon the initial data on which the theory was based. Smelser began with the long-range social movement; Turner began with the short-term crowd; Goffman began with face-to-face interaction. Consistent with the choice of entry data, each theory operates from a different paradigm for understanding social action. For Smelser, it is the model of rational organization developed by Talcott Parsons; for Turner, it is the model of normative interaction developed in social psychology; for Goffman, it is the communication model of the symbolic interactionists, the emphasis of which is on praxis, seen in terms of the locally contingent and binding quality of action and the importance of situational definition in collective life.

Important problems remain. For example, all three theorists set out to predict episodes of collective behavior, but they do not account for the frequency of such episodes within a given society. The problems are related, but the solution to one does not necessarily provide a solution to the other. Here, the only clue is in Smelser's development of the concept of structural strain, a concept far weaker and more ambiguous than the Marxist notion of "contradiction," which it is intended to replace in general sociological theory. A society in a condition of strain is more likely to experience episodes of collective behavior than a society that is highly integrated. However, in this proposition, Smelser has merely pointed out that strain, like society itself, is a necessary condition for the occurrence of episodes of collective behavior. It may be that strain in the society at large becomes known only through the appearance of such episodes. In that case, to say that episodes of collective behavior are more likely to appear in societies under strain than in integrated societies adds little to analysis, all the more so if strain is, as Smelser and Parsons seem to imply, a relatively stable attribute of societies.

The question of terminology is particularly important to discussions of collective behavior. The fact that sociological theory necessarily imports the meanings and therefore the practical concerns of daily life is because of the fact that it uses the nontechnical language of its society. The term "riot" evokes a set of meanings that no theory can thoroughly dismiss. Riot connotes the very picture of the crowd that Turner rejected, yet it is a term that appears in the literature time and again. For that matter, the term crowd also carries vivid suggestions of something uncoordinated and unsocial; it evokes the ordinary logic of collective behavior in which milling mobs engage in violent and destructive behavior as excitement mounts. To describe an episode of collective behavior as a riot, a crowd, a mob, an insurrection, a protest, a disturbance, an outburst, or as play or unrest, is to predetermine attitudes toward it. How people think of the episode is related to the possibility of their joining or opposing it. The public opinion that a description fits may sanction or repudiate particular techniques of official control and accommodation (Westley, 1966). Even the more classically technical language of the field carries attitudes and expectations developed within the political and intellectual climate of nineteenth-century Europe, and an implicit logic that, while convenient, has been shown by modern research to be highly questionable.

Is there such a thing as collective behavior? Is there such a thing as the crowd? It has been shown that appearances can be confusing, and the temptation to infer causes from results, known as such within a particular practice, and structure from appearances must be criticized. For now, Goffman and Turner have given good reason to question the appropriateness of the conventional use of the term "crowd" in reference to situated social action. They both suggested that what has been called a crowd has ordinarily been a collection of relatively independent units that are on the scene for an observer at the same time and that may perform in the same ways but that often do not. The image of a riot or a panic may obscure the facts of local interaction and large-scale differentiation. The need for further work in the theory of collective behavior is obvious, especially from perspectives other than those of managerial groups and official policy makers. This need is part of a larger need within sociology itself for greater elaboration and criticism of the perspectives from which theory is generated.

It is possible that collective behavior can be subsumed by the study of social conflict and political action and those studies enlarged by a consideration of the local, the unauthorized, and the short term of social reality. As the contexts of and occasions for collective behavior are made clear, the crowd may be returned to its place in history and to the situations that substantiate it. The most successful analysis of collective behavior from this point of view is Max

Heirich's study of the 1965 Free Speech Movement at the Berkeley campus of the University of California (1971), unfortunately unavailable at the time this book was written.

The theoretical prospectus for the analysis of collective behavior offered in chapter 10 focused on collective practice and the role of collective constructions of the situation. The authors assert that collective behavior is not rare, but is a pervasive aspect of social life insofar as that life is problematic about its grounds. Collective behavior is situated social action occasioned by an incident that threatens the practice of a collectivity by demonstrating the availability of competing constructions of the situation. Collective behavior occurs within a setting that includes support and opposition, and transactions within this setting determine the observable phenomena of collective behavior. But without direct and intensive analysis of collective constructions of the situation, as they change for members under the impact of events, the observable phenomena cannot be explained. Thus, the peculiar nature of collective constructions requires that the investigator, in some sense, be engaged in the situated social action that he analyzes. The difficulties posed by the necessity of this engagement are outweighed by the descriptive and analytic options that it opens for the study of collective behavior.

Sociological theories that have standing within the official circles of society and that are used to formulate and justify policy and procedure are part of the practically projective systems of the society. Such theories are indicative of "official America" and the way it sees the society it rules. Theories of collective behavior are especially revealing in this regard because, for the most part, they are not as carefully cultivated either empirically or formally as sociological theories in other areas, and they tend to have official or quasi-official sponsorship. Nevertheless, modern theories of collective behavior have become significant because of the government's need to account for official policy dealing with what appears to be an increase in unauthorized social action and political struggle in the United States during the last two decades. The theories of collective behavior prevalent in recent government and officially sponsored publications often reveal a distrust of the unofficial and unauthorized; a priority of values in which order replaces justice; a belief that there are no interests in America unrepresented in the houses of power; a faith in the efficacy of the managerial revolution for the administration of the country in the postindustrial technocratic age; and a correlative belief that the "end of ideology" has given way to an end to politics and the possibility of popular government.

In developing some conceptual tools to deal with collective behavior, reference has been made to research on episodes of collective behavior that occur on occasions other than disaster. Most collective behavior, in fact, arises outside of disaster situations and is deeply embedded in the social structures in which it appears. Moreover, episodes of collective behavior often occur "simultaneously" in a number of different but similar sites, as in American universities in the 1960s, in mill towns in early nineteenth-century England, and in urban black ghettoes in the United States in 1967. With accountable repetition—that is, when episodes are known as repeated and repeatable—collective behavior becomes an identifiable form of social action and often a political issue. Repetition encourages a search for determinants and remedies. This search defines an occasion posed by collective behavior itself and is ordinarily accounted for by reference to the correctability of the situation by officially initiated reforms of the conditions that gave rise to the collective behavior or by the discovery of the agents "responsible" for having brought about the break in social order.

From this point of view, the germ theory of social pathology (e.g., riots are "caused by" conspirators or by racist attitudes on the part of Americans) is an account of particular official actions rather than an "objective" statement about the nature of a phenomenon. These accounts tend to become elaborate as the official practice to which they refer becomes elaborate. Thus, once responsibility is attributed to particular agents and their putative responsibility is publicized through acts of retribution or control, the responsible agents are often redefined as a social type to which extraordinary forms of social control may be applied (Turner and Surace, 1956; Brown, 1969a). Heider (1958) has published a discussion of some of the processes involved in the attribution of responsibility to persons designated as agents. A related discussion by Garfinkel (1967) throws light on the socially organized work by which attribution is accomplished. Goffman (1963a) has discussed the nature of official accounts of disorderly behavior and the nature of official practice.

Because collective behavior on the occasion of disaster is accountably—known as—nonrecurrent, and thus largely escapes political appraisal, it is not typical of collective behavior as situated social action. The internal order of collective behavior varies to some extent with the occasion on which the episode takes place, the wider affair that establishes the general meaning of the events and activities that comprise the episode. The question of agency (avoidability) is the definitive element of politically defined occasions and distinguishes collective behavior on those occasions from episodes that occur on other occasions.

Occasions of disaster, as discussed in Unit I, are attributed to a confrontation between the "natural" and the "social" orders of reality. That is, they depend upon the identification of an occurrence as impinging on a social universe in such a way as to threaten the overthrow of that universe by imposing a different and humanly unmanageable order. Politically defined occasions, on the other hand, are predicated on a confrontation between different social orders that refer to the same territory. That is, collective behavior on a politically defined occasion depends upon the identification of an event, incident, or state of affairs as socially universal in its effects; as impinging on a system that participants claim as their own; as sudden in its apparent capacity to undo and replace the project by which that system is defined; and as avoidable, in that it appears to originate from within the affected system itself. The development of an episode of collective behavior depends largely upon the dialectics of the relationship between active collectivities and the socially organized elements of their milieu. Unlike disaster situations, the apparently normal setting of collective behavior on politically defined occasions for social action provides a crucial difference in the meaning of an episode to nonparticipants and, consequently, in the nature of their response.

UNIT IV

SOURCES OF
COLLECTIVE
BEHAVIOR
IN THE UNIVERSITY

CHAPTER ELEVEN

THE STUDENT PROTEST ACTIVITIES OF THE 1960S

The study of organized student protest has been at the margin of both political sociology and collective behavior. Despite the frequent use of the terms "student movement" and "student political activism" to describe the contemporary involvement of American college students in politics, student political activities during the 1960s have been analyzed primarily as crowd behavior. The explanations have relied heavily on the concepts of convergence and contagion and have drawn their predictions from the most general expressions of the frustration-aggression hypothesis.

PUBLIC ACCOUNTS OF STUDENT PROTEST

Most writers have agreed that the protests took place against a background of sharp and protracted conflict in society, punctuated by the issues of war, racism, poverty, the expansion of corporate power, and the consolidation of the state. Setting aside the organization of conflict around these issues, a tradition of sociological analysis has emerged, the roots of which lie in the theoretic legacy of nineteenth-century crowd psychology and in the administrative perspective on society that is typical of modern American sociology. This tradition has dominated both the popular and the professional interpretations of the student political activities of the 1960s. It provides the intellectual basis for recent official policies toward protest and opposition and informs the various mediating publics that have grown in support of those policies. Consequently, an examination of this tradition can reveal some of the crosscurrents of definition that characterize the patterns of interference (see chap. 10) within the university.

There have been other approaches to student activism, as there are other dissenting publics and oppositional movements regarding official acts and policies. But, for the most part, these have focused on personnel, social movements, or societal change. Of the approaches that treated student political activities as situated social action, few presented before 1970 offered theory.

The interest here is in the interpretations, accounts, and traditions that have played significant roles in the development of encounters between students and officials, particularly those that have played roles in the official responses to student political activities.

TRADITIONAL SOCIOLOGICAL ANALYSIS

Many of the writers in the traditional sociological analysis of crowds began with a set of implicit assumptions or recommendations that initially limited their theoretic options. The governing assumption is that the behavior of those persons who protest is theoretically problematic. Supplementary assumptions are that students are adolescents and therefore incapable of engaging in responsible political action centered around issues of genuine concern (Lipset, 1968a, 1968c); current protest is an expression of youth (Moynihan, 1967); the university is one of the institutional elements of society, and its organization as a politically neutral community of scholars is functional to the maintenance and operation of the social system (Parsons, 1968); the polity, as an institutional branch of society, is adequately defined by reference to official structures and officially authorized or recognized activities (Gurr, 1969); and unauthorized political action is, generally, both immoral and irrational and, in any case, dysfunctional for the university and society (Feuer, 1969).

Similar to all intellectual traditions, this view of student political activity has its paradoxes and its moral vision. Thus, reports of officially sponsored investigations and articles in professional journals regularly acknowledged the absence of legitimate channels and opportunities for dissent and at the same time, often expressed agreement with many of the demands listed by students during unauthorized political actions. Yet, paradoxically, the authors of these reports and articles would inevitably conclude that the students were not entitled to engage in unauthorized political activity or that reform could only proceed on the basis of a reaffirmation of official authority, including the administration of sanctions against participation in such activity. For example, the Cox Commission (Cox, 1968), in its report on the protests at Columbia University during the spring of 1968, acknowledged the legitimacy of some of the student demands, agreed that the administration had been unresponsive to those demands, and then denounced the students for conducting themselves in the tradition of labor union job actions.

The Terms of Analysis. The terms (violence, outburst, revolt, disorder) with which commentators regularly described student protest activities illustrate an outrage that reflects their overriding moral and political concern as well as the perspective from which they viewed those activities. The use of the term "protest" itself tends to deny the possibility that the activities of the students were part of a wider conflict between relatively organized segments of American society and, therefore, denies that there was a context within which those activities could be substantiated as more than simply expressions of grievance or discontent. Similar to the term "dissent," "protest" implies a disagreement with specific official acts or policies. It does not imply an objection either to the social order within which those acts and policies are defined or to the definition of reality (setting and context) by reference to which they are accounted for as practical solutions to social problems. Moreover, "protest" suggests that activities can be understood as manifestations of attitude formation and processes associated with public opinion rather than with organized political opposition. Nevertheless, we occasionally use the more conventional terms in speaking of the situated political action of students during this period. This use is not intended to invoke the logic of deviance analysis nor to suggest that student political activities are to be understood by reference to models of public opinion and attitude formation. The use of conventional terminology is intended to avoid more cumbersome phrases in the discussion to follow.

Perhaps the most interesting characteristic of the student protests was the general absence of violence. Students who occupied buildings usually conducted themselves with decorum. Accounts of these student activities charged the participants with littering, graffiti-writing, and the disruption of routine, rather than with the destruction of income-bearing property or injury to people. Despite the use of terms loaded with the imagery of violence, the indignation generated by student protest activities was seldom explicitly justified by reference to physical damage. It was the students' behavior itself and its impact on the social properties of public places that inflamed the administrators and the general public (Cox, 1968).

Tension, Unrest, and Destruction. The view that student protests and academic confrontations involve relatively diffuse, tension-induced, basically destructive episodes of collective behavior appears in many contexts. Richard Hofstadter, in his Columbia University commencement address of 1968, stated this view in very general but apocalyptic terms:

> We are at a crisis point in the history of American education and probably in that of the Western world. Not only in New York and Berkeley, but in Madrid and Paris, in Belgrade and Oxford, in Rome, Berlin and London, and on many college and university campuses throughout this country, students are disaffected, restive, and rebellious. . . . In the short run the escalation of this cruel and misconceived venture in Vietnam has done more than any other thing to inflame our students, to undermine their belief in the legitimacy of our normal political processes, and to convince them that violence is the order of the day (1968, p. 587).

This statement depicts the diffuse unrest described by early theorists of collective behavior. Hofstadter's anguish is evident in his address, as is his sensitivity to the crisis of faith in America. Nevertheless, the terms with which he discusses the results of this crisis make no reference to the structural cources of crisis. It is clear that, more than anything else, Hofstader fears the disruption of social systems, in particular the disruption of the university as it is presently conceived. His statement evokes the image of milling crowds, of social facilitation, of frustration-induced violence, of mass organization, of anxiety, and of alienation. Such descriptions parallel the traditional conception of the mob: a volatile mass of people suddenly melting into a single angry attitude toward official institutions and acting irrationally and violently on the basis of generalized beliefs about those institutions and their role in the contemporary malaise. (See R. Williams, 1960, 1961, for a discussion of the origins of the imagery of the mass and the mob; see also Bramson, 1961.)

This imagery has been further developed by Arthur Schlesinger, Jr., Daniel Moynihan, and a host of other commentators whose articles appeared in large circulation and quasi-scholarly magazines at the end of the 1960s. For example, Arthur Schlesinger, Jr. (1968), writing in the *Saturday Evening Post*, spoke of the detonation of local revolts that "are only the pretexts for the rebellion" (p. 26; see also *Newsweek*, May 6, 1968, p. 40). C. Michael Curtis (1969) described these revolts as the work of "a howling mob" (p. 102) unleashed, as Max Ways (1969) suggested, by the temporary weakness of officials: "these outbreaks . . . could be handled with relative ease if other elements of the university structure. . . were all sound, confident, and united" (p. 94). These descriptions assume a dynamic that Daniel Moynihan asserted in 1967: "that the phenomenon of protest we observe today is more psychological than doctrinal in origin . . ." (p. 539), a manifestation of movements of youth driven by an admirable, but nevertheless irrational, idealism. Moynihan ascribed student protests neither to the social structures in which they emerge nor to ideas. His depiction of protest as idealistic and irrational—and therefore, implicitly impatient and cruel—asserted a virtue but proved a vice. Protest, he declared, often comes from "bloated expectation" that leads to a suspicion of those in authority, a generalized belief that easily erupts in explosive outbursts of collective behavior. He suggested that this short-circuiting of rationality is typically youthful and neither responsive to conditions nor genuinely political.

Similarly, the Harvard Board of Overseers described the unauthorized political actions of students in terms of the imagery of mobbism:

> All of us must protect those who choose reason from those who seek violence . . . . The Board of Overseers is aware of the strains upon the youths of this day: the frustration of a long-continuing war, the climate of violence, the need to reshape American civilization, the urgency of civil rights (*Life*, 25 April 1969, p. 35).

It is the opposition of reason and violence that places the Board of Overseers in the camp of the mass psychologists. It is the use of the concept strain that ties the notion of mass to the phenomenon of collective behavior. Like Moynihan, the board assumed that what is reasonable is a matter of official definition; what is unauthorized is unreasonable and, therefore, violent.

Agitators and Contagion. From the description of mob behavior and the ascription of such behavior to psychological causes, it was a short step to hypotheses that accounted for the episodes in terms of agitators and the contagion of unbridled emotion. Popular literature is replete with references to small exploitative minorities, the "strains upon the youths of this day," and "campus riots" (*Life*, 16 May 1969, p. 23). The titles of the articles are suggestive: George B. Leonard's "A Bold Plan for Peace" is subtitled "Beyond Campus Chaos" (*Look*, 10 June 1969, p. 73); Sidney Hook wrote about "Barbarism, Virtue, and the University" (*The Public Interest*, Spring 1969, p.

23). Such titles frequently struck the keynote for discussions of cause, organization, process, effect, and policy.

In an article typical of the genre, Robert Nisbet (1969) adopted the theoretical program of the convergence theorists by attributing "destructive" and "nihilistic" student dissent to "boredom." The "New Left," he claimed, "has nothing to say. Its program is the act of destruction, its philosophy is the obscene word or gesture, its objective the academic rubble" (p. 7). According to Nisbet, this mindless, yet calculating plan is not grounded in moral concern, substantial motivation, or political sensivitity:

> There is no real alienation in the New Left, only the boredom that is itself the result of erosion of cultural authority, of failure of nerve in the middle-class society, and of adult fear of youth (Nisbet, 1967, p. 8).

Suggestions for Official Policy. Nisbet urged the reaffirmation of conventional authority, but he did not address himself to the New Left's substantive criticisms of that authority. By his assumption that militant action and radical ideology are simply denigrations of "cultural authority," he left the impression that such a reaffirmation could occur only through the heavy application of the coercive power available to the putative representatives of cultural authority in middle-class society. However, such action would entail many of the unintended and paradoxical outcomes—including institutional outcomes that Nisbet would doubtless find repugnant—that accompany the application of coercive control. In part, Nisbet's resistance to these conclusions appears to be a result of an unwillingness to admit that coercive power is often the only means by which discredited authority can be reaffirmed. To make such an admission is to engage in the very debate over the fundamental values of the political order that student political activities have forced into the mainstream of American thought. From this point of view, the question is not the presence or absence of strong and creditable authority but, rather, what system of authority, what values, and what definitions of legitimacy should prevail. Nisbet's position derives from his unwillingness to consider the unofficial and unauthorized actions of American students as political. He takes the view that marginal and oppositional politics are irrational and socially destructive in ways that official institutions rarely are.

Despite their simplicity, such comments on student protest were consistent with more technical accounts in their imagery, hypotheses, and suggestions for official policy. They were "magnifying judgments" that carried the advocacy hidden in professionals' accounts into the arenas where publics are formed and official policies selected. Both popular and technical accounts are illustrated in the influential analyses of student protest activities as collective behavior by Ted R. Gurr, Seymour M. Lipset, and Lewis Feuer.

AN ANALYSIS OF CIVIL STRIFE AS COLLECTIVE BEHAVIOR

In *Violence in America: A Report to the National Commission on the Causes and Prevention of Violence, June, 1969* (Graham and Gurr, 1969), Ted Robert Gurr (Gurr, 1969) listed "major types of civil strife in the United States, June 1963-May 1968" (p. 547). Included in the list were civil rights demonstrations, antiwar demonstrations, student protests on campus issues, antischool integration demonstrations, segregationist clashes and counter-demonstrations, Negro riots and disturbances, and white terrorism against Negroes and civil rights workers.

Gurr's list, presented with modifications in Table 11.1, combines hostile outbursts; small scale, clandestine acts of terror and violence, including bombings, arson, shootings, beatings, and major cross-burning incidents; and peaceful but unauthorized protests and demonstrations under a single heading.

In Table 11.1, the "number of events identified" were gathered from an extensive review of general news sources. Figures in parenthesis are tentative estimates, and Gurr noted (p. 547) that the other figures, despite their apparent precision, are only estimates. In a number of cases (e.g., antiwar demonstrations and student protest) Gurr's estimates do not agree with other sources of data.

Table 11.1 Characteristics of Civil Strife, June 1963 through May 1968

Type of Event	Number of Events Identified	Estimated Number of Participants	Reported Number of Casualties	Reported Arrests
Civil rights demonstrations	369	1,117,600	389	15,379
Antiwar demonstrations	104	680,000	400	3,258
Student protest on campus issues	91	102,035	122	1,914
Anti-school-integration demonstrations	24	34,720	0	164
Segregationist clashes and counterdemonstrations	54	31,200	163	643
Negro riots and disturbances	239	(200,000)	8,133	49,607
White terrorism against Negroes and rights workers	213	(2,000)	112	97
Total for all events	1,094	2,167,555	9,319	71,062

Adapted from Gurr, 1969, p. 547.

"Civil strife" is then defined by Gurr as:

> All collective nongovernmental attacks on persons or property that occur within a political system, but not individual crimes. We included symbolic attacks on political persons or policies such as political demonstrations and political strikes. Their inclusion does not reflect a normative judgment about their desirability or their legality; demonstrative protests are legal under some conditions in some countries, illegal in many others. Whatever their legal status, they are essentially similar to violent forms of protest: they are collective manifestations of substantial discontent that typically occur outside institutional frameworks for action. The violence used by regimes to maintain social control is not included as an aspect of civil strife because we are concerned with the extent to which ordinary citizens, not officials, may resort to force (p. 545).

Despite its title, Gurr's essay is about political opposition in the United States, whether violent or not. For Gurr, civil strife corresponds roughly to

Smelser's (1963) concept of hostile outburst. In order to understand how Gurr treated student protest activities, it is necessary to examine his general theory of civil strife. By classifying student protests about racism and war with riots and terrorism, Gurr is able to apply simple theoretical concepts to what now appears to be a single phenomenon—that is, civil strife. In turn, civil strife is subsumed by the still more general category of turmoil, other phenomena included under the heading of turmoil being conspiracy and internal war.

Gurr treats all opposition as opposition to official authority, including officially permitted oppositional activities. Opposition is defined by the organization chart of a society and not by any selected criterion, such as "prevailing sentiments of legitimacy"—that is, the assumption that what is must have been sanctioned. This initial categorization of data involved precisely the type of error that Horowitz and Leibowitz (1968) warned against: the confusion of marginal politics and criminal deviance, and the development of policy and theory for marginal politics based on a mood evoked by "criminal deviance." Although Gurr admitted that most of the recent turmoil in America had been peaceful and legal (p. 552), he considered even peaceful and legal protest actions to be "symbolic attacks on political persons or policies" (p. 545) and, therefore, covertly violent. That which is unauthorized—in this case, oppositional politics and, by demonstration, the advocacy of opposition—is treated in terms of the imagery and logic of frustration-induced aggression and is systematically deprived of substantial claim, organization, and strategy. In effect, it is treated as expressive action.

Comparative Analysis. Gurr's classification allowed him to compare statistics on civil strife among nations, and thereby to test hypotheses that might serve as bases for official policies of control. Gurr's data indicate that fewer lives have been lost in civil strife in America than in most nations (1969, p. 552) and that the social organization of civil strife is as variable as its outcomes.

> Strife in the more developed and democratic nations is more often organized by legal political groups than in other nations and is less often carried out by clandestine groups. The implications are that strife is a recurrent facet of the political process and that the effect of economic development is to channel it into the political process rather than to insulate politics from violence. At the same time, the intensity and seriousness of violence in politics tends to decline (p. 558).

This statement is problematic. For one thing, Gurr appears to consider the political process to encompass institutional operations alone. In the United States, this delineation excludes oppositional politics by definition. The apparent channeling of strife may simply reflect the lack of serious opposition at the national level until rather late in the 1960s. However, it is still open as to whether the explanation of differences among nations lies in the cooptive properties of "democracies," in the fact that the development of a truly national politics in the United States is a relatively recent phenomenon, or in something else. Until these considerations are grounded in a structural analysis of American society and its polity, the meaning of Gurr's data is difficult to assess. In any case, the data may have to be recombined before they can be used in relation to such an analysis.

Gurr's comparative analysis is noteworthy for its conceptual innocence. Despite a certain intuitive appeal, the meaning of the terms "developed" and "democratic" are not obvious in this context, nor is it clear what he meant by his use of the terms "legal" and "political process" and the phrase concerning a decline in the "intensity and seriousness of violence in politics." The difficulty lies in part with Gurr's apparent assumption that certain political activities—specifically those without official authorization—are not "politics" within the framework of society. Moreover, Gurr left the question of the origin of the judgments of "intensity" and "seriousness" unanswered.

Some structural analysis is essential in any comparative approach that considers differences in outputs of systems. For example, it is not possible to identify a system output without some idea of what the system is. Further, a lack of structural considerations at this point, as usual, leads to an overreliance on official sources for the definition of a social system and the choice of statistical indices. It should also be noted that the subjective meaning of acts must be determined in some fashion before they can be classified. Gurr attributes such meanings to the acts he collates but does not account for that attribution and therefore does not explain his classification itself. As a result, it is difficult to interpret correlations involving his index of civil strife.

Resistance to Civil Strife. The mechanisms by which Gurr explained the apparent resistance of the United States to civil strife are derived from an analysis of several general features of society. One is the relatively high regard for the legitimacy of their political system that Gurr alleges characterizes most Americans (p. 593). Other features of American society are the "coercive potential" of the agencies of social control (p. 592) and the absence of large oppositional movements. The absence or minimization of consensus about the legitimacy of the political system, the reliance of authorities on their coercive potential, and the presence of a vital opposition would indicate what Smelser (1963) called structural strain.

Gurr did not fail to accord conventional importance to deprivation in determining the intensity and frequency of discontent, although, at times, he tended to treat deprivation as an absolute, rather than as a relative condition that predisposes a society to strife:

> The fundamental cause of civil strife is deprivation-induced discontent . . . . The more intense and widespread discontents are in a society, the more intense and widespread strife is likely to be . . . (1969, p. 590).

Gurr's failure to treat deprivation as a significantly relative condition limits his ability to probe the structural determinants of social change. It treats all deprivation as a condition that can be healed socio-medically, without vital changes in a society. In addition, it forces him to accept a simpler notion of deprivation than political conflict theory—as opposed to theories that focus on strain—would require.

Elsewhere, Gurr (1970) does treat deprivation as relative, although he continues to beg serious structural questions regarding both the sources of deprivation and the relationship between deprivation and potential for unauthorized political action (1969, p. 569ff).

Recommendations for Official Policy. Gurr's recommendations for official policy focused on the maintenance of the state. He warned of the danger of revolution and emphasized the need to prevent the "undermining" of "governmental legitimacy and military loyalties" (1969, p. 593).

How did Gurr develop his data to yield these conclusions? First, he lumped together all manifestations of opposition to official authority and its agents, without justifying their unification under a single explanation. Thus, the correctness of his explanation for any single manifestation of civil strife, as well as for the whole set of phenomena, escapes empirical scrutiny.

Second, Gurr relied heavily on psychological concepts as explanations for social phenomena. He assumed, for example, that discontent, or even "deep discontent" and "anger" are necessarily and directly related to the degree of deprivation. He assumed that the two are related—as motivation is to deficit. Thus, he said that a reduction in deprivation produces a reduction in discontent and, in turn, a reduction in strife. He remarked: "If angry men . . . think that protest or violence will help alleviate their discontent, the impetus to civil strife is strengthened" (p. 568). But this assumption was discarded at least once:

> political demonstration, riot, and strike are established tactics of both leftwing and rightwing groups [in Italy, France, and Greece] . . . a manifestation of tactical political moves more than of intense discontent . . . (1969, p. 574). (1969, p. 574).

This conclusion is based on research on strife that did not include the United States. Unfortunately, Gurr lacked the data to examine his proposition for the American situation.

Third, Gurr treated his highly abstract and undeveloped conception of social strain as a cause and related it directly to specific phenomena that were characterized as effects. Variation in the intensity of "substantial discontent" is correlated with variations in the frequency of civil strife and with specific behaviors characterized as "relatively spontaneous," "unorganized," and "violent." Aside from the logical difficulties of this procedure, the extreme generality of Gurr's theoretical concepts premits him to apply generalizations to situations for which they are structurally inapplicable. For example, in reference to developing Latin and Islamic nations, Gurr said that "only high degrees of loyalty to leaders and institutions are likely to inhibit strife under conditions of intense deprivation; . . ." (p. 578). Furthermore, Gurr asserted that:

> Facilitating social conditions, like the existence of extremist political organizations and the provision of external support for rebels, are important conditions of high magnitudes of violence in most types of nations but not in the Anglo-Nordic nations (1969, p. 591).

Gurr's theoretical apparatus is vague and archaic. In order to establish his position, he leans on crude causal assumptions that lack empirical support, indices so general that they obscure sources of variation in strife, and common sense propositions about motivation that are not consistent with psychological theory. Modern psychological treatments of motivation focus as much or more on cognitive states of expectancy and the availability of particular responses as they do on deficit. Moreover, the relationship between motivation and action is certainly not a direct one, nor is it a simple relationship unencumbered with the impact of many other dispositions. Moreover, the frustration-aggression hypothesis has been qualified well beyond the form in which it is used by Gurr. Ultimately, it is the very conventionality of Gurr's theory that gives it its plausibility.

Gurr's disinterest in the complexities of structure yields a concept of strain that is more like general distress than a state of a social system, and the meanings of his outcomes are at best unclear. The attribution of causal efficacy to deprivation-induced discontent for the origin and maintenance of strife allows Gurr to proceed as if social effects were reversible, that is, as if the reduction of strife depended upon only the piecemeal reform of the conditions from which strife presumably originated. In fact, according to Gurr's theory, the reversal of social effects could take place only if collectivities did *not* form under conditions of strain, and if official actions—reform and control—did not generate new responses or lead to changes in official institutions.

Gurr's analysis leads him to suggest economically progressive policies that are unrealizable and officially reactionary policies that are capable of realization. The assumption that enforced order buys time for reform, hinted at by Gurr as a way out of the dilemma, is inconsistent with his finding that the utilization of coercive potential by a government is positively related to the magnitude of strife (p. 591). For Gurr, if the presence of strife is due to incurable ills (or ills that cannot be cured in the short run required, for example, by the Kerner Commission, as the only preventative for internal war), it also justifies coercive control. But if civil strife and official coercion are positively related, then Gurr projects a dismal future for postindustrial capitalist society.

AN ANALYSIS OF UNAUTHORIZED POLITICAL ACTION AS COLLECTIVE BEHAVIOR

Seymour Lipset (1967, 1968a, 1968b) has provided a more specific analysis of student protest. He represented student protest activities as examples of mass phenomena, and he made assumptions about collective behavior that several recent theorists, notably Turner (1964), have rejected. For example, Lipset described the extremism of student movements; the dislocation of students from conventional sources of social restraint; the "tensions which foster the availability of young people for organized 'deviance'"; and situations that "facilitate quick communication, foster solidarity, and help to arouse melodramatic action." Like the convergence theorists, he considered motivation and psychological defense mechanisms, such as displacement, to be more important than cognitive and interactional processes. Lipset and Wolin

(1965) asserted that "participation in politics may be viewed as an alternative to other forms of student extra-curricular activities" (p. 7).

Characterization of Youth. In order to explain the availability of students for "melodramatic action," Lipset characterized youth as idealistic, naive, impatient, vulnerable, and dispositionally prone to protest. By focusing on the extreme idealism of the young—a point not well documented in the empirical literature on adolescence, although consistently maintained by commentators— Lipset joined Lewis Feuer and Daniel Moynihan in suggesting that, at best, the actions of the young are naive and, at worst, irresponsible and dangerous. An implication of student irrationality runs throughout his discussion. At one point, for example, Lipset (1968b) characterized the student conception of sociology in a way that suggests naivete and impatience as unrealistic and entirely at odds with available traditions in the discipline:

> students view some of the social sciences as fields concerned with remedying "social problems." As scholarly disciplines, however, they are essentially concerned with the elaboration of knowledge within scientific- ally rigorous conceptual frameworks and methodology. Since social scientists see crucial political questions as having complex causes and different solutions, they tend to refrain from endorsing simple solutions (p. 19).

Thus, politically active students are implicated as "endorsing simple solutions" and, hence, not rational with regard to "crucial political questions"; they are seen as demanding an orientation that is essentially foreign to sociology; and they are characterized as interested in action as opposed to knowledge. None of these characterizations is valid, yet each endows students with attributes that disqualify them from serious consideration and point to the essentially youthful and irrational nature of their involvements with the social sciences and politics.

The work of Heist (1965), Somers (1965), Watts and Whittaker (1966), and Trent and Craise (1967), among others, does not support Lipset's assumptions about student activists. For example, Trent and Craise (1967) reported that "student activists were found to possess a high degree of autonomy and intellectual disposition and to come from the fields of the humanities and especially the social sciences in disproportionately high numbers" (p. 42). Those findings were representative of the research on student protest available at the time of Lipset's analyses. Moreover, his characterization of sociology represents one point of view among many and, in fact, is not consistent with the standard undergraduate sociology curriculum or with the delineation of issues within the field. For example, if a concern with what Lipset calls "social problems" is foreign to sociology, he has discredited his own work as well as the bulk of what is taught in colleges and universities. Gates (1969) reported that in 1942 and 1957, courses in social problems, marriage and family, social work, and criminology were among the top ten college sociology courses offered in a nationwide sample of more than 600 colleges and universities. In 1966, she reported that a sample of 170 small liberal arts colleges offered these same courses among the top ten offered. Finally, Lipset's characterization of rigor in the discipline has a long tradition of criticism represented by, among others, social phenomenology and Marxism.

Along similar lines, Lipset implied that students are particularly susceptible to influence by more sophisticated agitators and referred to "concentrated efforts to reach students with political messages" (Lipset and Wolin, 1965, p. 6). But he was not sure whether this weakness represented a failure of character or a failure of authority. In one passage, Lipset argued that the success of agitation among protest-prone youngsters is partially caused by a failure of social control within the academic community, with a consequent weakness of traditional academic values:

> A high incidence of intense student political activity is in some sense an indication of the failure of a university as an academic community, particularly since in most cases such activity involves a rejection of the intellectual leadership of the faculty, a denigration of scholarship to a more lowly status than that of politics within the university itself (Lipset and Wolin, 1965, p. 9).

Threat to Scholarship. Lipset's assertion that student political activity threatens scholarship seems to depend upon the following argument:

1. Student political activities involve a rejection of institutional authority in the university,
2. Institutional authority on campus is nonpolitical and depends upon faculty leadership,
3. Faculty leadership affirms the values and norms of scholarship rather than the politics of university management or the politics of professional association,
4. Therefore, student political activities threaten the values and norms of scholarship.

It appears that each of the premises is inaccurate and that the argument is self-serving.

Although ideas related to academic freedom will be discussed in chapter 12, an analysis of Lipset's position requires some attention to his idea of the academic community. Lipset is apparently referring to the classical autonomous community of unpolitical, nonbureaucratic scholars who are guided by the scholarly and disinterested search for truth and defined by a culture of mutual tolerance and respect for hard work and expertise (see Veysey, 1970, p. 243). He implied that the university could be such a community, which would deter the development of politics on campus. However, these propositions are not consistent with what has been written about the American university nor with what is known about the development of political conflict within normative organizations (Hofstadter, 1955; Metzger, 1955; Jencks and Reisman, 1968; Veysey, 1970).

A Repudiation of Student Politics. Lipset's repudiation of politics in favor of scholarship is not a denigration of politics in general as much as a repudiation of student politics on campus and, by implication, the role of students in the organizational life of the university. Lipset appears to view the political activities of students not as politics in the ordinary sense but as what he had previously referred to as "political reactions" (1965, p. 9). He insisted that student protest activities are political only in the most rudimentary sense of the term, much as Smelser considered collective behavior to be only formally instrumental. Although Lipset (1968a) occasionally referred to student protest as a part of wider conflicts in society (1971), he consistently referred to a model of mass behavior in discussing student protest. Such a model is less rational, more antisocial, and perhaps less controllable because it is outside of the legitimate or institutional channels for political action, by which Lipset apparently meant authorized channels. This model is often tied to the more basic assumptions that such channels are sufficient for the resolution for all "realistic" social conflict; that successful socialization produces a hierarchy of commitments, with the primary commitment being to the official order; and that those persons who act outside of authorized channels are either poorly socialized or simply irrational (see also Lipset, 1960).

Thus, in addition to the protest-prone disposition of youth, the impact of agitators, and the failures of institutional authority, Lipset implied that unauthorized student protest is due to the inadequate socialization of the activist minority and of those persons led by them. Adequately socialized individuals, according to Lipset, would understand that official institutions are sufficient for the satisfaction of their needs and that these institutions are parts of a society whose overall direction is good. Lipset appears to believe that part of the problem lies in the fact that young people (students) are utter beginners in the adult world and have not had time to learn about the systems within which they must live. The explosive mixture of idealism, dependency, impotence, and mystification that is typical of young people may be ignited by an unequivocal demonstration of political inefficacy on the part of authorities—weakness, unavailability, and so forth. Lipset (1968b) noted that:

> Confrontation politics is characteristic of politics in which students, and other groups as well, lack legitimate channels of communication to authority. Clark Kerr has observed that political groups turn to activist demonstrations when they find themselves ignored by the adult power structure (p. 15-16).

This statement suggests a benign intent, a good will, on the part of officials that transcends the obligations, capacities, and attitudes of their managerial and political roles and, occasionally, the personal characteristics that led to their selection for those roles. It assumes that, by itself, communication can satisfy the claims of youth and hints that explicit demands are merely the projective overlay of childish needs for attention, acknowledgment, or security. Without the damning label of "youth," Lipset might have been willing to recognize that communication may be adequate but that parties may disagree or that officials may reject, without reason or for bad reason, the demands of those persons who protest (1971, p. 3).

The excerpt quoted above reasserts Lipset's belief that confrontation politics is due to a temporary failure of process in an otherwise sound system and that the character of such politics is reactive and, therefore, amoral (1971, chap. 1). On the other hand, the statement suggests that unauthorized, and therefore nonlegitimate or perhaps illegitimate, political actions ("collective deviance") are often caused by a lack of authorized or "legitimate" alternatives. This reasoning assumes that people will normally pursue their desires and interests following a hierarchy of alternative means from the authorized to the unauthorized.

Although Lipset recognized the consequences of a failure of representation—interpreted in this case as a failure of communication—he ultimately denied the relevance of students' demands for representation and authority. Because he did not believe that their political claims were valid in the context of American society, he found the issues for which representation and change were sought to be essentially trivial or mistaken. Moreover, because of his stated belief that the university is a community in which scholarship precludes political engagement—or, at least political engagement on the part of students—Lipset (1968a) denied the very possibility of responsible student involvement in the organizational life of the university.

Lipset (1968a) considered the politics of student dissent in the United States to be part of "the changing worldwide climate of political opinion" (p. 39). Yet, he argued that students are alienated from their society by the special condition of being a student. It is a condition that is relatively independent of historical considerations, that offers little responsibility, that includes considerable freedom from external constraint, that places them in organizations that are only transitional for them, and that is, therefore, perhaps somewhat unreal. Unappreciative of this respite from reality and impatient for changes in the social order, students and their allies persist in what Lipset called:

> a backlash opposition to systematic and quantitative social science, and the concomitant belief in gradualism, expertise, and planning, with a populist stress on the virtues of direct action against evil institutions and practices (1968a, p. 42).

Lipset alleged that this backlash was supported by a minority of teachers within the social sciences and humanities who resented the development of a technology and technocracy that made them obsolete. In this way, Lipset extended his dispositional analysis of student protest to all unauthorized politics on campus, regardless of the status of participants. (See Rogin, 1967 for a critique of this view and its intellectual origins.)

Lipset's Stereotypes. Lipset's use of nineteenth-century stereotypes of collective behavior cannot be accounted for as a consequence of intellectual naivete or as a result of one-shot analysis. It seems rather to depend upon a general hostility to whatever is unofficial and unauthorized in contemporary American political life. Otherwise, it is hard to explain his failure to select models of collective behavior and political movements that are consistent with theoretical developments in other areas of sociology as well as his willingness to accept cultural stereotypes of youth as the basis for formulating theory.

Similar to the earlier convergence theorists, Lipset persistently focused on motivation conceived of as an irrational force in students'—but not officials'—

political actions. He viewed the emotional and moral elements of student protest as symptoms rather than as aspects of creditable evaluations of a situation. Deprived of its setting by definition, direct action becomes an emotional reaction instead of an organic component of a highly contingent, transactional cycle characterized by patterns of interference among competing constructions of the situation or instead of even a sensible move in a problematic and conflictful situation (Coser, 1956). The particular direct actions taken by students are accounted for by the availability and sudden accumulation under conditions of weakened authority of people who are prone to protest.

Objections to Recent Research. One of the more important weaknesses of Lipset's analysis lies in his failure to assimilate findings of recent research with respect to propositions for which they are apparently relevant. Although he tends to reject most of the available studies of student protesters, particularly leftists, the bulk of Lipset's analysis explicitly pertains to those participants in student political activities (1968a, p. 50). Lipset has voiced general criticisms of the empirical literature on two major grounds. First, he argued that survey procedures fail to distinguish between covert attitudes and the responses to questionnaires. Much of the recent literature on student leftist activists, however, uses more sophisticated techniques than simple questionnaires, including clinical devices, intensive interviews, and complex measures of capacity and disposition that are classical to social psychology (Sampson, 1967) and that Lipset himself has found useful in the past. His studies (1959) of working class "authoritarianism" falls within this methodological tradition.

Lipset's second major objection to this research is that the apparent superiority of leftist activists on a number of measures of intellectualism, tolerance, humanitarianism, intelligence, and so forth is an artifact of a comparison between leftists and the "passive majority," a group Lipset (1968a) nevertheless invoked as politically relevant when he declared that leftist activities represented a tiny minority on American campuses. He concluded that a comparison of leftist and conservative activists indicated that both "are drawn from the ranks of the academically talented in the United States" (1968a, p. 51). Bay (1967) has offered another point of view that depends upon a differentiation of traits within the general category of talented: "Statistically speaking, . . more *conservative views . . . are likely to be less rationally, less independently motivated, compared to more radical-liberal views*" (p. 88). Unfortunately, the evidence is not yet sufficient to choose between these two positions (Lipset, 1971). There are general indications that although intelligence differences may be negligible between right and left activists, there are sharp differences in complexity, intellectualism, tolerance, dogmatism, authoritarianism, and the like (Sampson, 1967). In any case, Lipset's admission that leftists are drawn from the ranks of the talented, on the surface, is not consistent with his analysis of their political activities.

Issues and Implications. Lipset has raised some of the issues with which an examination of student protest activities must deal. His use—whether intended or not—of a collective behavior analysis is important in calling attention to the relationship of context to situated social action, to the rudimentary character of American student politics of the 1960s, and to the even more rudimentary character of the sociology of such events. He also listed some of the factors that have been traditionally associated with student political movements and tied them to the protest activities of the 1960s: the peculiarities of the transitional status of the student, changes in wider socio-political contexts, and institutional failures. He is on weaker ground with his emphasis on small agitational minorities and the inevitable propensities of youth. His belief in the basic irrationality of youth is understandable in the context of his political conservatism, but less so in the light of its lack of basic empirical substantiation.

Lipset's approach has implications both for the prediction of future events and for policy. For example, his analysis implied that student protest activities normally escalate unless checked by direct action, regardless of official efforts at social reform, because: (1) unlike "realistic" struggles over issues of genuine concern, student protests are not responsive to negotiation; and (2) they are based on individual states of motivation that cannot be satisfied and that, therefore, increase in scope and intensity. Lipset's analysis suggests that, as the universities modernize and as society develops technocratically, policies of the short run must reaffirm official authority and restrain unauthorized social and political action. Following the 1964 Berkeley student revolt, in which students of various persuasions united in opposition to a decree by Berkeley officials restricting student political activities on campus, Lipset and Seabury (1965) summarized their perspective in the following terms:

> To restore the Berkeley campus to the normal life of a first-rate American university is still an immensely difficult task. It requires a high and rare level of administrative leadership and intelligence, qualities which fortunately Martin Meyerson seems to have . . . . It requires a faculty which is as sophisticated politically as it is intelligent academically, and which understands how a few extremists can exploit genuine grievances to make the large majority of moderates do their bidding . . . . The indifference to legality shown by serious students can threaten the foundations of democratic order if it becomes a model for student political action (p. 348-49).

Here, as in Hofstadter's (1968) commencement address, the principle of administrative order transcends the principles raised by the issues themselves and their student spokesmen. The spectre of "extremism" and easily led student masses—as the explanation of why there was such campus wide support for the 1964 Berkeley Free Speech Movement—overshadows the question of how disenfranchised people may act politically in the face of official actions that deny them both political rights and the opportunity to question the procedures by which the rights were denied.

Despite its flaws, Lipset's examination of student political activities is among the most comprehensive of those undertaken during the 1960s. It expresses a qualified conservatism in its tacit positive evaluation of elite definitions of "crucial political questions"; its uncritical assumption of the adequacy of authorized channels for the solution of those questions; its consistent denigration of unauthorized political action; and its dictum that the proper political stance for those in managed positions is a mixture of trust, forebearance, and sacrifice. Underlying all, is an intense and personalized anti-communism (1960, 1961, 1971, p. xvii), a calm acceptance of the neutrality and efficacy of central planning under capitalism, and a faith in technical expertise for the realization of progress in American society.

AN ANALYSIS OF GENERATIONAL REVOLT AS COLLECTIVE BEHAVIOR

Lipset's work took for granted the assumptions of early theories of collective behavior. The work of Lewis Feuer (1969) gave those assumptions explicit theoretical status. Feuer's analysis of generational revolt falls between nineteenth-century theories of collective behavior, with their emphasis on convergence and contagion, and twentieth-century theories of social disorganization, with their managerial perspective on social disorder. His analysis is a contemporary version of mass psychology.

The major premise of Feuer's (1969) analysis is the proposition that unofficial and unauthorized political action in the United States constitutes both an irrational challenge to social order and a threat to fundamental human values. Feuer asked: How can the contemporary unauthorized political actions of American students be accounted for? His answer depended upon propositions about the nature of collective behavior and the dispositions of youth. He assumed that student activism arises from within youth movements; he considered the movements themselves to be the collective expression by the society's youth of a deep malaise in the social system. Feuer asserted that these movements were:

> a sign of a sickness, a malady in society. They arise from conditions which have made for a breakdown in the "generational equilibrium" of the society and are reinforced by a mass apathy in which the initiative for political action devolves upon the intellectual elite (1969, p. 11).

He further asserted that the dominant characteristics of student movements are "elitism, suicidalism, populism, filiarchy, and juvenocracy," which he described as traits that typically emerge in response to the "de-authorization of the elder generation" (p. viii).

It should be noted that the definition of "youth" in such analyses is always problematical. Feuer included the graduate students involved in the Berkeley protests as youth and subjected them to the same analysis that had been developed within psychoanalysis to explain the behavior of early adolescence. His enlargement of the category "youth" illustrates the tendency—common in the 1960s—to identify protest and radical politics with "youth" for the purpose of discrediting the former (Brown, 1969a).

De-authorization of the Elder Generation. For Feuer, the public actions of student movements constitute a special type of collective behavior because of the peculiar psychological characteristics of their participants. He derived those characteristics from the concept of youth as typified in orthodox psychoanalytic theory. Feuer's thesis is that student movements manifest the inevitable conflict between generations intensified at various times by the weakness, or "de-authorization," of the elder generation and the peculiar pathologies of adolescence. However, although youth movements, and particularly student movements, are generalized attacks on the authority of the elder generation occasioned by breaks in the cultural order, they are otherwise aimless and expressive. Feuer viewed them as "fitful and transient" and "born of vague, undefined emotions." He asserted that:

> We may define a student movement as a combination of students inspired by aims which they try to explicate in a political ideology, and moved by an emotional rebellion in which there is always present a disillusionment with and rejection of the values of the older generation . . . (1969, p. 11).

According to Feuer, it is the peculiar character of youth and the intensification of its pathologies during the deauthorization of the elder generation that gives violent and irrational form to the collective actions that arise from student movements. Feuer claimed that:

> Student movements are a manifestation . . . of the trauma of adolescence, which is, in large measure, a trauma of renunciation; the young man must renounce his bookish dreams and ideals and come to terms with reality (1969, p. 33).

"Reality," for Feuer, is defined in conservative terms; opposition in any form to any institution becomes "unrealistic" and, hence, in his theoretical scheme, pathological. "Bookish dreams" is what Feuer meant when he allowed student movements their major virtue: "the component of intellectualism." Student intellectualism, said Feuer, "has all the poetry, involvement, and purity of a first love. The students are pure ideologists whose consciousness determines their existence more wholly than that of any other group" (1969, p. 14). But, he asserted that the idealism and purity of adolescence is only superficial. Coupled with the threat to fledgling selves posed by authority and disillusionment with the de-authorized generation that holds the reins of authority, idealism leads to a rage against all authority, attacks on the social order, and "impulses toward self-annihilation" (p. 6). Feuer stated that:

> Nihilism has tended to become the philosophy of student movements not only because it constitutes a negative critique of society; it is also a self-critique that is moved by an impulse toward self-annihilation (1969, p. 6).

Substantiation for the Concept of Generational Conflict. Feuer attempted to substantiate his thesis by citing a large amount of statistical data gathered from historical sources and a considerable body of interested commentary—mostly nineteenth—and early twentieth-century accounts of student movements. His concept of generational conflict is a quasi-psychological, quasi-sociological, quasi-intuitive idea so vague that it can be illustrated in an infinite number of ways without encountering any resistance from common sense. Because of this vagueness, and despite his efforts at substantiation—including statistics, commentary, and anecdotes—the concepts of generational conflict and generational revolt evade empirical scrutiny.

Therefore, although Feuer discussed student protest activities of the 1960s, he did not feel a need to review the research on American student activists, organized protest, and confrontation. By the time he considered the contemporary events, he assumed that his general scheme had been thoroughly justified and was in no need of further substantiation. In fact, in the seventy-five pages Feuer devoted to recent events, he neglected to mention any of the major research on contemporary student protest activities. Instead, Feuer liberally cited anecdotes and writings of activists as illustrations for his view of recent events, although even his sampling of that body of material is not representative.

Methodological Difficulties. In developing his model, Feuer relied heavily on selected documents as the "best evidence"—a strategy that drew on literature in which the quoted documents are, in fact, the best evidence—despite the fact that recent literature is replete with evidence that is methodologically superior within Feuer's own frame of reference.

The recent data that Feuer did mention illustrate only his most general propositions. For example, in reference to the southern student sit-ins of 1960, he remarked that "the chronological list for the month of February 1960 alone indicates the readiness to spontaneous action among the Negro studentry" (1969, p. 392). This comment also points out another, related methodological difficulty in Feuer's approach to his topic: his overreliance on historical material to establish analogues for contemporary events. Such reliance allowed him to use accounts of earlier events without adequately justifying their relevance to the contemporary situation, and without having to develop an intellectual basis for his analogies.

Theory as Politics. What is, perhaps, most interesting about Feuer's discussion is the explicitness and vehemence of the value judgments and political opinions that dominate it. In reference to the Berkeley Free Speech Movement of 1964, he said that it "lowered the whole level of the country's political ethics" (1969, p. 481). Furthermore, like other student movements, it lacked "the substantial dignity which a subject for political sociology should have." Thus, Feuer described the typical participant as follows:

> The young activist, filled with aggressive emotion, found no objective, economic institution against which to direct his feeling. "Free-floating" aggression is much more likely to take a moralistic form; the very values of the System as a whole are rejected, precisely because the System is so economically stable that it provides jobs and opportunities for the willing and capable. The values of Vocation, Work and Success are made the targets of generational revolt; hence the New Left has a propensity toward the beatnik and the hippie (1969, p. 387).

Despite its bizarre logic and use of cultural stereotypes, this statement is similar to Janowitz's (1968) relatively tempered justification for having written *The Social Control of Escalated Riots*, as discussed earlier in this chapter. Feuer also reproduced some of the assumptions of Lipset's analysis of unauthorized social action, although both Janowitz and Lipset occasionally recognized a basis for complaint. All three of these authors assumed the progressive character of the American state and denied the rationality, as well as the legitimacy, of radical criticism and militant action. Janowitz's denial is on the grounds that the social system is inherently progressive despite temporary failures and incidental defects. Lipset's denial is based on the assumption that institutional channels are available and adequate for the resolution of conflict. Feuer made his denial on the grounds that there are no issues in American life that could justify protest or opposition and that students, in any case, are not capable of responsible political action. For Lipset, the study of youth protest is limited by the assumptions of early theories. For Feuer, student protest is essentially illustrative of early theories.

THE INFLUENCE OF EARLY THEORIES OF COLLECTIVE BEHAVIOR ON THE STUDY OF STUDENT PROTEST

The criticism of the classical theories of collective behavior that is presented here is based on the following charges:

1. The classical theories focused on episodes as dependent upon, rather than as integral parts of, larger socio-political processes and structures,
2. The classical theories oversimplified the dynamics of interaction and the emergence of collective constructions of the situation,
3. The classical theories misunderstood the role of circumstance and incident in situated social action,
4. The classical theories emphasized the personal dispositions of participants and characterized those dispositions as causes of collective behavior,
5. These theories left unanswered the question of rationality by regarding the issues raised during episodes of collective behavior as inappropriate or unimportant except as articulate symptoms of discontent, expressions of shared generalized beliefs, or products of rumor,
6. The theories defined social control as exclusively extrinsic to the crowd and characterized all episodes of collective behavior as mass behavior or moblike states of nature,
7. The classical theories described episodes of collective behavior in terms of a model that suggested destructiveness, uniformity, and a lack of competence.
8. These theories assumed without question that the perspective from which they were drawn represented the nature of society.

To the extent that accounts of contemporary episodes of collective behavior depend upon the classical theories, they suffer their defects.

AN EMPHASIS ON PERSONNEL

For example, in summarizing recent research on collective behavior on college and university campuses, Astin (1968) noted that "typically, activists and non-activists are compared in terms of various biographical characteristics and psychological test scores" (p. 2). This emphasis on personnel reflects the influence of convergence theory to a greater extent than is warranted by the weaknesses of that theory. But even those investigations that focus on the context of collective behavior on campuses and the issues of protest (Astin,

1968; Peterson, 1968a, 1968b) rarely approach collective behavior from the perspective of the participants. Perhaps, for this reason, they often fail to provide a detailed examination of the setting or tend to oversimplify the context itself (Avorn, 1968; Heirich, 1971). Peterson (1968b) listed the issues that administrators attributed to the protests of 1967 and 1968 and related the incidence of protest to only the most general characteristics of the university, for example, size as defined by the number of students enrolled. But size, as a determinant, is hardly sufficient to permit the type of analysis ordinarily thought necessary for the study of organizational products. For that kind of study, measures of control and structure, direction and sufficiency of communication, and complexity are usually placed in a network of parameters of social action, only one of which is the number of formally defined members.

Astin's (1968) attempt to examine the interrelationships of personal and institutional variables in predicting the occurrence of episodes of collective behavior on campus is noteworthy as an exploratory look at variables that are expected to be a part of the general picture. Any further extension of his model would, however, be limited by the procedure of mixing a questionable theory of psychological disposition with an overly simplified model of social organization. Such an extension would attempt to establish relationships among variables for a problem that has not been adequately defined. That Astin realized this limitation to the usefulness of his research model is indicated by his summary of his research, in which he suggested that a more sophisticated approach than the correlation of activism with institutional and personal traits is necessary in order to explain student political activities:

> Whether or not an individual student will engage in protest activity during his freshman year in college cannot be predicted very accurately from information provided at the time he matriculates (1968, p. 13).

Apparently, the emphasis on the dispositions and social characteristics of participants is not suitable for an analysis of collective behavior at the university. Commitment and participation are more complex social psychological phenomena that require more data than such analytic schemes can provide. Situated social action cannot be adequately understood without more attention to the imperatives of interaction, the development of differentiated settings, and the role of socio-political and organizational contexts. (Skolnick, 1969).

PROTEST AS UNAUTHORIZED POLITICAL ACTION

Along these lines, Weinberg and Walker (1968) have pointed out that most investigations "do not even hint that the nature of student activism is connected with the political system" (p. 5). Weinberg and Walker continued:

> [Our] perspective on student "activism" moves us to the position where we regard this as another variant of political behavior, constrained by the different limits which societies place on this category of behavior (p. 5).

Furthermore, the emphasis of Weinberg and Walker's investigation is on "student *politics* rather than 'activism'" (p. 6) and, therefore, the emphasis is not simply on political reaction, civil strife, nihilism, energetic idealism, or generational revolt. The program of Weinberg and Walker alters the status and the definition of such major variables as personality, situation, collectivity, and action. Rather than considering the situation as a variable that simply intervenes in the relationship between personality and activity, they considered the primary relationship to be that of situation and action. In this way, Weinberg and Walker emphasized the rational, situated, and social qualities of student political activities (Sampson, 1967; Becker, 1970; Flacks, 1970), which is consistent with what appears to be known about student protest and protesters.

In order to realize this program, it was necessary to treat protest as situated social action and to subject it to the detailed analysis required for such subject matter. Only in this way is it possible to describe the patterns of interference that characterize the settings within which collective behavior transpires among mutually effective participants. This kind of analysis goes beyond the ethnographies that represent the most important methodological tradition in modern research on collective behavior. Many ethnographic investigations captured the gross transactional features of the development of episodes of collective behavior, but they rarely provided sufficient coverage of the particulars of interaction and the settings within which collective behavior transpires among mutually effective participants. This kind of analysis goes beyond the ethnographies that represent the most important methodological tradition in modern research on collective behavior. Many ethnographic investigations captured the gross transactional features of the development of episodes of collective behavior, but they rarely provided sufficient coverage of the particulars of interaction and the settings within which points of confrontation emerge. To say that "the crowd outside had grown to over 800" (Eichel, et al., 1970, p. 89) provides information about a setting, but it avoids the dynamics of the growth of the crowd. To report that groups were engaged in combat is to miss the details that would help to account for the moment in which combat began and the mechanisms by means of which large numbers of people were drawn into the fray. A review of the biographies of participants in collective behavior (e.g., Conot, 1967) may establish the personal origins of individual participation in collective constructions of the situation, but it is not a substitute for a description of the ways in which specific activities fit into the encounters that are, in turn, shaped by the details and incidents of a setting.

Weinberg and Walker's (1968) approach to student political activities is superficially consistent with Lipset's proposition that student activism is common in societies in which the basis for citizen participation—the legitimacy of social and economic arrangements and institutions"—has become problematic for those in transitional positions, that is, for people for whom the future has become a critical aspect of the present. It might be added that as social and economic arrangements and institutions have become more visible to citizens as realizations of specific values and interests rather than as realizations of society per se, socio-political conflict and struggle is inevitable. Lipset missed the point that, in most societies, citizen participation has been so low that citizens can scarcely be referred to as members of the organization of society. It is, precisely, effective membership that was demanded by

American student activists in the 1960s. The role of disappointment, indignation, and outrage in unauthorized political action cannot be denied. However, it must be asserted that these factors are incidental concomitants of collective behavior, and, are themselves emergents of confrontation among mutually exclusive practices determined by power, position, and organization, and reflected in wider contexts.

THE EXTENSION OF THEORY INTO POLICY

The professional as well as the popular and official literature of the 1960s treated student protest activities and academic confrontation as collective behavior from the perspective of theories of mass behavior, a perspective often dominated by an essentially elitist and conservative political ideology. In this literature, that which is official and/or authorized is assumed to be institutional and thus binding on rational, well-socialized participants in socio-political conflict. That which is neither official nor authorized is defined as collective behavior that threatens social, political, and cultural order—ultimately, the very possibility of society.

The resurgence of these old assumptions about collective behavior is not limited to the professional and popular literature on student protest. By the end of the decade of the 1960s, the extension of the a priori into description and theory and the use of theory to justify official policy (Silver, 1967; Skolnick, 1969) became increasingly prevalent. In 1969, attempts to suppress organized protest on campuses increased in Congress and in state legislatures, and the federal government entered a period of intense investigation and repression of oppositional politics in the United States. By the beginning of 1970, Senator James Eastland's subcommittee on internal security had subpoenaed files and bank records for a number of politically oppositional groups, for example, the Institute for Policy Studies in Washington, D.C., Liberation News Service in New York, and, it was threatened, the Vietnam Moratorium.

Against a background of official ambivalence, legislation was introduced to stop financial aid to colleges that did not control protest (New York Times, 6 August 1969), to curtail aid to students who participated in unauthorized demonstrations, to permit judicial injunctions against protest activities before they occurred, and to extend the conventional relationships between law enforcement agencies and educational institutions (Donner, 1969; Wentworth, 1969; New York Times, 17 June 1969, 23 September 1970). At the same time, the pressured university administrations at San Francisco State College, the University of California at Berkeley, the University of Wisconsin, Columbia University, the City University of New York, and elsewhere, began to rely on the police and the courts to control political activity on campus. In some cases, the administrators made small concessions to the demand for student participation in campus governance. This carrot-and-stick strategy had some effect. On the one hand, the strategy occasionally succeeded in isolating the radicals from the larger body of students who interpreted these concessions as indications that the academic system was institutionally progressive and that unauthorized action was not necessary for social change. The strategy also placed the issue of campus governance back within the local framework, relatively dissociated from the other, cosmopolitan, issues—such as war, racism, and political repression—that often had accompanied it.

On the other hand, university officials often found themselves in the embarrassing position of bargaining away their capacity to negotiate with students and, therefore, their opportunity to engage in other than suppressive tactics of accommodation (*New York Times*, 6 October 1970). For example, police in New York City were promised by President Joseph McMurray of Queens College that he would not drop charges or in any way interfere with official procedures in the event of arrests during a campus sit-in in the spring of 1969. The sit-in was held in protest of the selective suspension of three student leaders following a demonstration against recruiting on campus by a military-related corporation (see chap. 12). In many cases, police were called and college presidents were forced to defend police actions that were often excessive and brutal, as in the cases of the Columbia University sit-in of 1968 and the Berkeley "People's Park" protest of 1969 (Avorn, 1968, Barton, 1968; Copeland, 1969; *New York Times*, 28 March 1970).

In such ways, the principle of order became linked to the tactics of suppression and superceded any of the principles raised by student protests. A decision was made to affirm official authority by any means suitable to the containment of youthful mass behavior, either by waiting the students out, as at the University of Chicago, or by relinquishing the problem to the hands of the police. As one student said to a troubled gathering of Harvard students following police action against a group who had occupied campus buildings:

> It doesn't make any sense to have everybody fighting each other [in reference to angry disagreement over whether or not the students should strike the university] because what we just saw was this university showing its true face. What we just saw was this university showing that it couldn't respond to the demands of the people there except by bringing in cops (Eichel, et al., 1970, p. 135).

The use of the courts and the police was a small, dramatic element in the overall texture of official repression (see, for example, *New York Times*, 23 September 1970). The texture consisted of strategies and spontaneous reactions rationalized by the belief that the students were defiant, nihilistic, or simply misguided, and that their actions were explosive and pointless expressions of discontent by adolescents for whom demands were simply excuses. Official responses included the selective suspension of students and student leaders; the withdrawal of funds from campus newspapers and organizations that were seen as antiadministration; the dismissal or threatened dismissal of faculty members who were considered to be too involved with student activists or politics; the refusal to allow some student political organizations on campus; the development of intercampus organizations of college presidents, administrators, and faculty to coordinate the suppression of student groups and activities considered illegitimate; and the development of research on students and student life designed to discover the types of students who engage in political activity on campus.

One of the authors (Brown) was told by an official of the National

Institute of Mental Health in 1969 that several projects were funded that were directed toward the detection and control of student political activities in colleges, universities, and high schools, including the discovery of bases for a quota system that might detect and eliminate potentially "disruptive" elements prior to their entrance to college.

The degree to which these responses comprised a politics of penetration is illustrated by the development of leadership programs on a number of campuses that attempted to select officially acceptable—and to eliminate officially unacceptable—potential student leaders at early stages of their academic careers. In addition, a number of universities, including UCLA, Harvard, and Columbia, made plans to publish official newspapers for students in competition with the regular and allegedly antiadministration campus newspapers (*Newsweek*, 18 September 1969).

The official responses to student protest in the 1960s stemmed from a mixture of archaic theories of collective behavior, external pressures for control on campus, and the particular political sensibilities of college officials (Skolnick, 1969). Archaic theories dominated public expressions of official policies and, thus, served to cultivate publics in support of those policies and in support of the specific official actions that they justified. The channels through which official justifications gathered publics were neither wholly popular nor wholly professional. A large body of semitechnical, social scientific commentary grew up in defense of the establishment of which its authors were often part. The public interpreters of the student political activities of the 1960s, committed as they were to the logic of the analysis of mass behavior, provided sturdy justification for policies of coercive control.

It is surely no accident that both official policies and their intellectual justifications reflect the assumptions of the early theories of collective behavior. Those theories were written from the perspective of official elites to whom unauthorized political action, by definition, was disorderly and nihilistic, particularly when such action originated among undergroups, the "masses," or youth (Bramson, 1961; Rude, 1964; Couch, 1968). The elitist assumptions of those early theories were given root in a modern managerial perspective. According to Horowitz and Leibowitz (1968), a managerial perspective on the internal politics of social systems constitutes:

> a framework limited to the political strategies available to majorities or to powerful minorities having access to elite groups. The strategies available to disenfranchised minorities are largely ignored and thus the politics of deviance also go unexamined. The behavior of rule-makers and law enforcers is treated as a policy decision, rather than as a political phenomenon . . . (p. 283).

From this perspective, confrontation is seen not as part of a political struggle but, rather, as a failure of management or as a failure of the managed to acknowledge the legitimacy of official institutions—that is, a failure of authority or a failure of socialization. From this point of view, the complaints of protesters can arouse sympathy for their condition but can never arouse empathy, identification with their perspective on reality, or an acknowledgment of the plausibility of that perspective.

CHAPTER TWELVE

THE AMERICAN
UNiVERSITY

There are few sociological descriptions of the American university that bear on the organizational and institutional sources of patterns of interference (see chap. 11). Other complex organizations and establishments have been systematically analyzed. The university has not. The sociological analysis of colleges and universities that is available treats them as sites of advanced socialization and as repositories of traditional culture. Jacobs (1957), Lazarsfeld and Thielens (1958), Sanford (1962), Jencks and Riesman (1968), and Feldman and Newcomb (1969) have summarized literature on the organizational features of the university, its relationship to society, and its impact on students. These sources provide descriptions, reviews of individual studies, and, frequently, suggestive discussion about issues in the sociology of higher education; but their scope is limited by the lack of research during the 1960s on the university as a complex organization.

The difficulty of providing a sociological analysis of the university is compounded by the fact that documentation for the links between the university and its environment, the larger society, does not appear in the social scientific literature. With few exceptions, such links must be gathered from popular and nontechnical sources, such as undercover journalism, and from isolated research projects. (See for example, *Saturday Review*, 10 January 1970; *Daedalus*, Winter 1970; *The Public Interest*, Fall 1968; *Viet Report*, January 1968.) Whenever the social structure of the university has become an issue, most sociologists of higher education have drawn their research models from the common sense of institutions and some traditional conceptions of the university. (See for example, Mills, 1951, 1956; Hofstadter, 1955; Metzger, 1955; Caplow and McGee, 1958; Lazarsfeld and Thielens, 1958; Minter, 1966; Morison, 1967; Cox, 1968; Jencks and Riesman, 1968; Ridgeway, 1968.)

THE UNIVERSITY AS AN ENTITY

By and large, the university has been described as a relatively independent community of intellectuals who work in support of universalistic values. The pursuit of material gain or special interest is considered supplementary to their professional commitments (Parsons, 1968). Consequently, the university has been analyzed as a "normative organization" in which all members are presumably controlled through the mechanisms of "normative compliance" rather than through coercion (Etzioni, 1961, p. 48).

NORMATIVE CONTROL

Etzioni's (1961) description of the university as an organization in which "normative compliance prevails and coercion plays a secondary role" (p. 48) is difficult to reconcile with concrete descriptions of the university by students, administrators, and professors. Indeed, for some constituencies of the university, the description seems to be extremely tenuous in its relation to the facts of academic life. It underestimates the importance of coercive control, structural constraint, and nonacademic values to the majority of students and a large number of faculty (e.g., Eckerman, 1963), and it underestimates the importance of normative factors in other types of organizations in order to justify the contrast it poses between universities and those organizations. However, there is little empirical basis for claiming that universities can be distinguished from other organizations by their principle mechanism of control. Without evidence, Etzioni's proposition is most easily understood in reference to its consistency with official statements about the university. His analysis is best seen, regardless of its intent, as an elaboration of an ideological position rather than as a description of social structure.

The extent to which any organization can be characterized as normative depends upon the perspective from which it is presented. Thus, for tenured faculty and advanced students in career disciplines, the organization of the university may be, or may appear to be, controlled by norms. Barton's (1968) report on faculty attitudes toward student political activities at Columbia University in 1968 is consistent with this general hypothesis. Also consistent with the hypothesis is Feldman and Newcomb's (1969) conclusion, based on a review of a number of studies, that values tend to be consensual among older students within individual disciplines. However, there does not appear to be evidence that bears directly on this question.

In any case, a typology of organizations based on presumptive differences in the nature of social control is difficult to use for at least two reasons: (1) there is tremendous variation in members' accounts of control in their organizations; and (2) specific acts of control in any organization, no matter how they are implemented, are usually justified by reference to "normative constraints" and "legitimacy" (Marcuse, 1968). Nevertheless, Etzioni's (1961) typology offers some insight into the differences between the university and other organizations. Universities appear to be distinguished from other organizations in the *accounts* of acts of control offered by agents and groups that have official standing in the organization. Specifically, Etzioni may have been correct in observing that official acts of control in universities and certain other establishments are accounted for by reference to putatively shared ideals, social contract, legitimacy, reasonableness, and so forth, and that such formulations tend to place acts of control beyond dispute. His error lies in his transforming of this observation of official accounting activity into evidence of social structure and process.

On the face of it, asking whether the contemporary American university can accurately be called a normative organization is a conventionally academic question. Yet, it is clearly a political question. If universities do not function like normative organizations, members cannot be expected to act as if they were members of such organizations. The community of scholars, which is held to describe the ideal conditions under which academic freedom can be exercised and the university can perform its societal functions, clearly presupposes the availability of a normatively controlled, politically neutral, and independent organization. The assumption that the university is such an organization may be taken as an axiom of the official ideology of the university.

This ideology was challenged during the 1960s as the campus became, more and more frequently, a setting for unauthorized political action and official repression. The initial concern in the present discussion will be to draw attention to the scope of that challenge. Investigating collective behavior and repression on campus requires attention to the relationship between the university and society. Figure 12.1 charts some of the contextual factors involved in collective behavior on campus and offers some suggestions as to their interrelationships.

THE AMERICAN ACADEMIC SYSTEM

In 1960, there were 3,610,000 students in establishments of higher education. By 1967, the number had increased to almost 7,000,000 in more than 2,300 schools employing 500,000 teachers and administrators; and by 1975, American colleges and universities are expected to have approximately 9,000,000 students (United States Bureau of the Census, 1968). According to Parsons (1968), the exceedingly rapid growth of the "American academic system" is "a critical feature" signaling the university's entry into a phase of "large organization" (p. 175).

Growth of the System. The growth of establishments does not simply extend their characteristics. If other things remain equal, size transforms organizations and introduces new facts of social life. Beyond a certain point, size yields new functions, structural arrangements, operations, and perspectives. For example, according to Rostow (1968), Columbia University's student body, including graduate and undergraduate students, doubled in size between 1947 and 1967, from 8,000 to 17,500 students. The faculty grew from more than 2,300 to almost 3,500, an increase of approximately 50 percent. However, the size of the administration of the university increased nine times, from 78 to 723 people. Changes in the relative size and differentiation of a managerial staff are good indicators of what is happening to an organization. An increase of managerial personnel from 3 percent of the permanent staff to over 17 percent indicates either an enlargment of conventional functions, a shift in some of the major functions of the organization, or both. For Columbia University, the disproportionate increase in the size of the administration was correlative with the development of a competitive research industry, graduate education, and

Figure 12.1 SOME CONTEXTUAL FACTORS IN COLLECTIVE BEHAVIOR ON CAMPUS

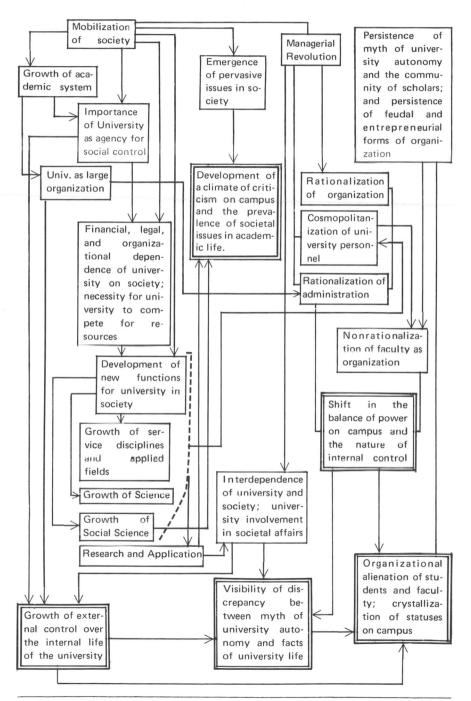

strong institutional ties with other sectors of society. Columbia was transformed from a school into something like an "action bureaucracy" (Krausse, 1968) that provides higher education in addition to its other functions.

Statistics indicate that contemporary American higher education is dominated by service fields such as teaching, fields of applied knowledge such as business and engineering, critical disciplines such as social science, and research (United States Bureau of the Census, 1968, p. 129; Benson, 1966). Of the half-million bachelor's degrees conferred in 1966, degrees in education were most numerous (most of the recipients were women), followed by the social sciences, business and commerce, English, and engineering in that order (United States Bureau of the Census, 1968). More than 18,000 doctorates were granted in 1966. Among the twenty-five major fields listed by the Department of Health, Education and Welfare, Office of Education, the three fields offering the largest number of degrees were the physical sciences, education, and engineering. The social sciences, were fourth (United States Bureau of the Census, 1968). These specialties are directly related to services and professions that are intrinsically cosmopolitan in their orientation. Their extraacademic ties and their positions in the hierarchy of academic disciplines indicate the increasingly intimate relationship between the university and society (Skolnick, 1969, p. 113), a relationship all the more capable of regulation by virtue of the intense concentration of resources at relatively few campuses (Benson, 1966).

Interorganizational Relationships. College and university campuses differ in type, size, quality, location, and prestige. They also hold different kinds of relationships to other organizations: for example, federal, state, and city governments, private foundations, neighborhoods, civic and professional groups, police agencies, religious organizations, and other schools. Parsons (1968) noted that, despite the extent of these relationships, "the system as a whole, though of the greatest importance to society, does not wield much power over that society" (p. 176). In fact, he claimed that:

> the essential point about the academic world is that it is not even self-supporting. It must be heavily subsidized, increasingly from government sources, but very importantly by the private contributions of individuals and foundations. The magnitude of our educational expenditures is not a measure of the academic system's autonomous control of its economic resources (p. 176).

Federal, state, and local governments account for most of the income of higher education and, consequently, the distribution of power over standards and content among campuses and discipline (United States Bureau of the Census, 1968); but the dependence of universities on various sectors of society forces them to compete widely for money, status, and skilled personnel. However, universities offer little that is tangible in exchange for support, which places them in a peculiar competitive position relative to other organizations. Like movie stars, the success of universities in maintaining themselves depends, in large part, upon the public image they present. More than most organizations, universities must justify themselves in conventional cultural terms; in fact, for many people, they represent and symbolize the cultural standards themselves. As a result, supporting universities is often a source of prestige for donors, dignity for officials, and the basis of a reputation for idealism on the part of communities. Universities, however, have often modified their aims and operations to satisfy these interests. For example, during the 1960s, it was not uncommon for those faculty members in the social sciences who did not participate in funded research, and thus draw funds, as well as prestige, to the university and the department, regularly to be referred to as "dead wood." Similarly, the economic views of professors were undoubtedly muted when American business leaders began to support universities on a significant scale at the end of the nineteenth century and in the first two decades of the twentieth.

> Inevitably, the increase in the size of gifts changed the relations of donor to recipient. Borrowing a term from economic history, one may say that givers became entrepreneurs in the field of higher education. They took the initiative in providing funds and in deciding their general purposes . . . . Besides, the patrons of the university received from the academic world the ornate courtesies of gratitude. They did not enter academe as intruders; they were welcomed into the realm and escorted to its high places by its very grateful inhabitants. Within the academic fraternity, to cultivate the good will of donors was a highly approved activity, betokening fine public spirit. To offend the bearer of gifts was an action sometimes defined as the deepest disloyalty and treachery. Cordiality was thus demanded of professors by the most compelling of motives—self-interest and the desire for social approval (Metzger, 1955, p. 140,145).

Despite their impact on the activities of professors, differences in values between academicians and their patrons have had only a minor effect on university life. It is the political economy of the whole system of higher education that accounts for the shape and content of that system and the organization of its local member campuses. As part of the academic system, a given campus, as a matter of practice if not theory, acknowledges economic, political, social, and cultural standards that are incompatible with both the idea of the university as an enclave of detached scholars, and the idea of the university as a normative organization (Minter, 1966).

THE UNIVERSITY, SOCIETY, AND POLITICS

The link between university and society is complicated in the case of public universities that depend heavily upon governmental budgets and that are ultimately accountable to the political organization of the state. The degree of dependence, the intensity of scrutiny, and the special regulations that qualify the life of a public university influence campus goverance, curriculum, academic standards, and the order of academic priorities. For example, public and private colleges differ, to some extent, in the criteria by which they evaluate student applicants and select faculty and in the capacity to negotiate their own positions during internal disputes. Samuel B. Gould, the president of the State University of New York, has described the ways in which the state legislature of New York can affect the state university:

They can give expanded authority; they can take it away. They can cut budgets; they can increase them. They can investigate and chart new paths of constructive legislative enactment; they can also investigate and destroy. They can reach into public higher education and force additions to the master plan; they can curtail enrollments; they can even create new professiorial chairs on their own recognizance (1966, p. 7).

Gould illustrated his point with several hypothetical situations, each of which "represents the start of a tendency toward outside dictation which, if unchecked, could have anything but trivial consequences":

A legislative committee eliminates certain academic positions relating to a previously approved academic program on the grounds that their own judgment on the way the program is to be developed is the ruling one.

* * *

A legislator expounds in the public press his doubts about the wisdom of a university decision regarding the site of a new campus, giving unmistakable signs that he expects such a decision to take into account political considerations for the region rather than educational ones.

* * *

A committee is recommended to the legislature for the purpose of maintaining surveillance over students and faculty as to actions that might be interpreted as subversive because they reflect unpopular or unorthodox attitudes and opinions (p. 10-11).

Gould's description of the state university supports McConnell's (1966) judgment that, at least for public institutions, "academic self-government is not the American way" (p. 92). In California, the relationship of the university system to the state government is a particularly strong example. The University of California is composed of branches that are relatively autonomous but, nevertheless, subordinate to a central board and accountable to the state government. Each chancellor is responsible to his local campus and to the state university as an administrative entity. Daniel C. Aldrich (1966), chancellor of the University of California at Irvine, commented that, "As an institution in a publicly supported system of higher education, the campus is viewed as a public trust requiring accountability to all whom it serves or is served by" (p. 21). The interaction of each campus of the University of California with the central administration and "other segments of higher education in California" is mediated by a Coordinating Council for Higher Education. The Council:

(1) reviews the annual budgets and capital outlay requests . . . and presents to the governor comments on the general level of support sought; (2) interprets functional differentiation among the junior college, state college, and university system; and (3) develops plans for orderly growth and the need for, and location of, new facilities (Aldrich, 1966, p. 19).

The Coordinating Council is, in turn, part of the Master Plan for Higher Education in California, which is implemented by the state legislature. In addition to the Coordinating Council and the legislature, accrediting organizations, professional associations, and other governmental agencies exercise constraints on the university and its campuses.

Under these circumstances, it is easy to understand the cosmopolitan overtones of local decisions, and the fact that such decisions take place under a variety of extracampus influences—including the overall structure of the academic system—that feed directly into campus policy. It can be seen why many administrators would agree with Aldrich's evaluation of the belief that "the university is a sanctum for a collection of unencumbered free intellectuals" as a myth (p. 24). This belief is also implicitly rejected by Jencks and Riesman (1968) in broad political and generational terms. They asserted that "colleges have always been institutions through which the old attempt to impose their values and attitudes on the young" (p. 35).

Nevertheless, the belief that the university is an autonomous enclave of intellectuals (a belief that will be discussed in greater detail later) is supported by a strong rhetorical tradition that justifies a protected status for the university and its intellectuals in terms of its potential for social reform. Wiebe (1969) argued that this tradition:

> has continually raised expectations that the schools, more or less as autonomous agents, could promote a basic national reconstruction if only narrow and timid officials would grow wise and courageous . . . . Public education has never even approximated the resources for such independent action, [but] it has always derived its strength and purpose from institutions around it . . . . Only a revolution in social relationships would enable the school to fulfill the strange role the rhetoric of reform has set for it (p. 164).

ADMINISTRATION: STRUCTURE AND PRACTICE

Two of the most important developments shaping administrative practice have been the rationalization of administration along particular lines and the professionalization of administrators. The shift from a conventionally supportive and relatively minor role for administrative personnel to the enlargement of managerial and institutional operations and the reorganization of administrations has moved along classical bureaucratic lines. It includes the development of a professional field of higher education and the socialization of administrators directly into management.

THE RESTRUCTURING OF THE ACADEMIC SYSTEM

The rationalization of administration within the university heralds an important restructuring of the academic enterprise and accounts for many of the tensions that accompany profound organizational change. Specifically, the shift in operation from the traditional practice of caretaker to the more differentiated and instrumental practices of management entails the assumption of new powers by administration on campus, a realignment of administrators' organizational commitments, and the redefinition of university operations in terms of modern managerial practice. To a larger extent than ever before, administration has assumed the responsibilities and prerogatives of a polity within what it projects as the academic "system." That is, it performs executive as well as coordinating operations for a charted entity. As will be seen, these operations are directly functional to the system that includes the university. Administration, primarily is the agent of what can be thought of as an absentee landlord.

The rationalization of administration is not simply the consequence of organizational growth. For example, the managerial authority of administration at public colleges and universities is confirmed by developments within the administrative field and controlled by the fact that the activities of administration are under "close supervision by various state officials—budget officers, comptrollers, purchasing agents, and legislative auditors" (McConnell, 1966, p. 94). More and more of the ordinary operations of the university are becoming subsidiary to transactions at and beyond its boundary, that is, to relationships with the official agencies to which it is legally and practically subordinate (Jencks and Reisman, 1968, chap. 1). This state of affairs encourages a relatively formal and one-sided relationship between administration and the particular campus it manages. It also entails an enlargement of the setting of administrative practice from the strictly local to the more cosmopolitan regions—what Jencks and Reisman refer to as "established rational institutions" (1968, p. 18)—of society. In turn, the enlargement of the site of administrative practice has defined a new frame of reference for administrators that evokes new values, norms, structures, and loyalties.

Professionalism. *College and University,* the journal of the American Association of Collegiate Registrars and Admissions Officers, now in its forty-fourth volume, is a starkly professionalist publication. It is spotted with articles dealing with managerial operations in terms of systems analysis and draws a careful line between the older caretaker operation of administration and the newer operations of management. Harold Temmer, president of the association, referring to association members as "middle management," (Jencks and Riesman have used the term middle management to refer to faculty [1968, p. 17]) discussed the impact of management and data systems. He pointed out that systems analysis and computer techniques require particular types of input and particular codes, which, by inference, place important limits on such academic decisions as evaluations of academic performance by professors and the construction of curricula (Temmer, 1969). In discussing the output of these "information systems," Temmer (1969) tells middle management:

> You decide what comes out of the system, when it comes out and how, i.e. in what form. Here is where you will have an excellent opportunity to sharpen your educational statesmanship. As a professional you will put the top on the management system by involving top management in creating management tools in terms of output. You will even be involved in training department chairmen how to use all the data you can now give them—data they have not had before (p. 218).

As need for special training in the evaluation of this data increases, and as this data replaces other data in the construction of educationally relevant facts, many academic judgments will depend upon nonacademic specialists increasingly removed from traditional academic settings, criteria, and procedures. Actuarial techniques (and the judgments they select), already in remarkable evidence at larger universities, become institutionalized under the broadening managerial jurisdictions within the university.

Craftsmanship. Despite the inevitable and irreversible incorporation of local administration into the more cosmopolitan systems of society, local administrators still demand the prerogatives of craftsmanship within their local jurisdictions. Insofar as the claim to university autonomy supports the traditional organizational chart, it provides a basis for retaining local jurisdiction over and above the managerial argument for efficiency. Both arguments are contained within the following excerpt from a report by the Committee on Government and Higher Education (1959) entitled *The Efficiency of Freedom*. In a personal preamble, McConnell (1966) particularly approved the report's criticism of the fact that:

> state finance officers frequently made decisions, not alone on the general level of support which should be afforded higher education in competition with other governmental services, but also on specific items of proposed expenditure involving such fundamental matters as educational program, faculty salaries, and admission policies. The committee passed forthright judgment on this practice when it said:

> "Viewed from a management perspective alone, it violates the canons of sound administration for a college governing board to be vested with legal and public responsibility for the conduct of educational affairs, while the real decision making power resides at some remote spot in the state bureaucracy. The maxim that authority should be commensurate with responsibility is grossly violated on a campus where routine decisions on financial matters are in fact made by a state official. Carried to an extreme, as it has been in some places, such a system of remote control denies to governing boards and college presidents the power they are intended and entitled to have. In such a situation, public officials who may be ill-equipped to make educational decisions are moved into a position where they govern higher education without bearing any visible responsibility for its success or failure" (p. 94-95; quoting the Committee on Government and Higher Education, 1959, p. 9).

THE DISTRIBUTION OF POWER

Rationalization of administration and its concomitant developments have profound implications for the distribution of power on campus. Commenting on the components of this distribution, Frederic Heimberger, dean of faculties emeritus at Ohio State University, has stated that:

> Within the university itself, major responsibility for charting a course into the future will reside in three groups or centers of power. These are the governing board, the president and his principle administrative associates, and the university faculty (1967, p. 72).

Although functional specialization within the academic system ideally accounts for the jurisdictions of these three centers of power, their control over the university as a whole depends upon the types of decisions they can make, the organization of their activities, and their extracampus alignments. Thus, there are stringent structural limits to the distribution of power on campus by systemically functional considerations alone. For example, faculty, as a collection of individuals who perform similar operations, has not been organized in the same way as administration. Resistance to unionization and the ambiguous role of faculty governing bodies illustrates the lack of unity within faculties that leaves administrators with "broad powers to make policy" (Jencks and Reisman, 1968, p. 18).

It is, therefore, difficult to credit Heimberger's (1967) statement that the faculty is still capable of exercising significant control over the university. Universities may be judged by the quality of their faculty, but that is quite different from their being controlled by faculty. Jencks and Riesman (1968) have discussed the "managerial revolution," which has led to a transfer of power from boards of directors to professional administrators (p. 18), thereby reinforcing a distribution of power on campuses in favor of administration. Heimberger's discussion of the structural determinants of the distribution of power campus is weakened by his suggestion, *sui generis*, that the erosion of faculty power is voluntary, that faculty has somehow permitted administration to assume more and more control over a wider and wider range of problems. Rather, it appears that the redistribution of power within the universities in favor of administrations and their extracampus constituencies is institutional, an irreversible consequence of recent developments within the academic enterprise and society.

Ramifications. This consequence can clearly be seen in the case of public universities and colleges. In many public schools, decisions that affect curriculum, personnel, priorities for the distribution of resources, and the development of new academic programs may rest primarily with the president, his administrative associates, and the governing board. Such decisions are often subject to further review by other governmental agencies. Control is often exercised indirectly on the range of possible decisions as well as directly on specific matters. As specific decisions move form academic to managerial jurisdiction, they take their places within a hierarchy of priorities governed by the long-range plans and the systemic and contextual considerations of administrative officials. These plans and considerations reflect the values, ideologies, locations, and practice of administration. Thus, administrative decisions affect more of the college for a longer time than do other decisions, and they are intelligible primarily in the context of administrative practice. Although faculty control of some aspects of curriculum planning and personnel selection still exists, it is largely restricted to individual departments and, thus, is of little importance to the university as a whole compared to the larger policy decisions upon which curriculum planning, personnel selection, and the use of facilities ultimately depend. For example, one chairman at Queens College of the City University of New York remarked, during the fall 1969 meetings of the college personnel and budget committee (the body responsible for recommending personnel to the president of the college), that department recommendations for tenure and promotion were being questioned more intently by representatives of administration than ever before. And, according to T.R. McConnell (1966), professor of higher education at the University of California at Berkeley, "the instances in which faculty members sit on governing bodies of their own institutions are extremely rare" (p. 93).

Paradoxically, departmental autonomy, a value that has been at the core of many faculty demands, reduces the faculty's power to affect the total organization. The capacity of individual departments to initiate the reforms essential to the maintenance of their autonomy is thereby reduced. Department chairmen, ordinarily marginal to both administration and faculty, often deal more with each other and the administration than their own departments. Departmental negotiation for scarce resources, such as space, personnel lines, clerical assistance, and materials, ultimately depend upon the relationship of a chairman to the administration. Whatever bargaining takes place generally occurs between administrators and department representatives rather than between chairmen.

Administration is neither handmaiden nor mediator. The gradual decline in faculty power over university policies and the diminution of the faculty's local jurisdiction has left most of the crucial tasks of university policy, governance, and organization in the hands of specially trained nonacademic or quasi-academic personnel whose organizational site includes, but is not identical to, the university. Moreover, the rationalization of campus governance and the redistribution of power from the faculty to the administrative bureaucracy has shifted the locus of accountability for decision makers. They are now less responsive to those whom they manage than to those to whom they must report. Decisions that are vital to the academic life of the university are processed through administrative structures, and the conclusive criteria are more often rooted in extraacademic political and economic affairs than in academic practice. Administration no longer operates simply to facilitate the educational operations of faculty; it shapes the environment within which teachers must work. This can be seen as an example of a general process of social change. Functional units developed for one organization often become functional units for another, at the same time preserving their power over their former co-interactants. Their tasks are transformed, but the material on which they work is the same. However, their relationship to that material is no longer one of interdependence but of power, in the sense of domination.

Heimberger (1967) has summarized some of the changes and developments on campus and has offered a projection of the future of the university in terms of present trends.

> Within the next decade the nature of many a state university will be greatly affected by the choice of one man, and through him, a relatively small group of persons in important administrative positions . . . . Given a little time, their day-to-day decisions have a cumulative effect that weighs heavily upon any campus . . . . Thus it is not fanciful to suggest

that in the selection of a president and, subject to his strong influence, a few other important administrative officers lies the greatest power of any board to govern a state university (p. 74).

This comment is sensitive to the ways in which rational and centralized organization reduces the control held by lower and middle strata, reaffirming hierarchy and concealing the domination involved. Nevertheless, Heimberger's emphasis on specific personnel is short-sighted. For the implications of rationalization and the structural penetration of the university by society are wider than he recognized.

THE ADMINISTRATION AND CRISIS

Although the rationalization of administration, the cosmopolitanization of administrators, and the redistribution of power have important consequences for the development of settings for collective behavior on campus, the same factors also shape official responses to collective behavior after it is underway. During the Columbia University crisis of 1968, students occupied buildings in an effort to force the administration to yield on three issues having to do with due process for students, the role of the university in the life of the surrounding community, and the involvement of the university in secret military research. Grayson Kirk, then president of Columbia, remarked that his response to the protest depended upon extracampus considerations rather than on his judgment regarding the local issues raised by the protestors. This approach reflected the relatively recent development of cosmopolitan commitments on the part of top level university officials, an outcome of many of the changes in university life mentioned above. Kirk, following the arrest of students who had occupied campus buildings, stated that:

> If Columbia had been prepared to accede to the students' demand for amnesty from all disciplinary action resulting from their illegal conduct, we would have dealt a near-fatal blow not only to this institution but to the whole of American higher education. Columbia's action tonight thus is not merely in the interest of its own future but that of its sister institutions . . . (quoted in Avorn, 1968, pp. 198-99).

Strategies for Crisis. As has been indicated, the cosmopolitan commitments of administrators have been translated into organization as well as into strategy during crisis. For example, Handler reported that:

> Nine university and college presidents urged yesterday that their colleagues across the country refuse to negotiate with student protesters under duress and reject requests for amnesty in civil and criminal cases (*New York Times*, 1 July 1969).

That conference of university and college presidents adopted eleven other guidelines, apparently intended to operate as a regional or national strategy for maintaining the present organization of control at local colleges and universities and for the academic system as a whole. Several guidelines clarified local obligations to the larger strategy. Thus, according to Handler, one guideline read:

When student governments are representative and legitimate, college administrations should support them against the challenges of "coalitions" and "ad hoc committees," generally a tiny minority purporting to speak for the students (*New York Times*, 1 July 1969).

In deciding what governments are or are not representative and legitimate, administrators engage in protracted political struggle from a prepared cosmopolitan position, with the various competing political groups on campus. Though the language of the quoted guideline obscures its political intent, the position represented is clearly political in interest as well as in strategy. This position results from the enlargement of the administrative frame of reference, the fact that—as a consequence of the systemic relocation of administration—administrative control is reinforced by appeals to cosmopolitan publics and cosmopolitan sources of support, the redistribution of power on campuses in favor of administration, and the consequent determination of top level administrators to consolidate their power. This last result, a kind of "captain of the ship" dictum, was forcefully stated by Grayson Kirk, "There is no part of this university that is immune from the central authority" (quoted in Avorn, 1968, p. 25).

Centralization of Control. Insofar as Kirk's "central authority" was conceived of as managerial and took its cues from extralocal sources, his pronouncement dramatizes the conflict within the university between the laissez faire ideal of an autonomous community of scholars and the rational organizational practice of modern management, applied to the university as an included and subordinate entity. The importance of normative control is minimized and the coercive potential of university management as the primary mechanism of internal order is reemphasized (Wallis, 1967). Vaccaro (1969) has described this conflict as the "confrontation of professional and administrative authority in the modern university" (p. 232), a confrontation that can occur only as an incident of the crystallization of statuses within the university. As has been discussed, the confrontation has been resolved in favor of the administration and, thus, in favor of the rationalized centralization of control within the university along very specific lines and the incorporation of local campuses into larger establishments. Nevertheless, the conflict remains as tangible evidence of the lack of a higher order educational practice capable of integrating currently and vividly incompatible approaches to the organization of higher education.

These trends doubtless reflect the general growth of bureaucracy, the concentration of power, and the increase in prestige of managerial personnel that characterize the consolidation of the ruling class in America. But within the university, the change has generated patterns of interference among the competing perspectives of faculty and administration. It is the traditional ambiguity of faculty roles that has prevented these patterns of interference from yielding points of confrontation. Many universities retain the formal elements of faculty governance, including the belief that administration performs essential services for faculty in the pursuit of their primary functions of education and research. The persistence of such beliefs simply limits the likelihood that patterns of interference will yield points of confrontation between faculty and administration.

ADMINISTRATIVE PRACTICE AS CONTROL

External involvement in university affairs has always reflected the relationship of the university to society. Lazarsfeld and Thielens (1958) have pointed out that "institutions of higher education are not immune from scrutiny and challenge. Criticism of their objectives and of the means used to attain them is to be expected in the normal course of events" (p. 71). Lipset (1968a), who may have been looking at a special sample, has called the American university "an institution where 'liberalism' in politics and 'modernism' in culture has become an established if unofficial Weltanschauung" (p. 41). Whether or not Lipset's characterization is accurate, it has become part of the public image of the university and has provided a basis for twentieth century versions of the historic conflict between town and gown. The university's political reputation has, more often than not, played a part in an increase in external surveillance and control over campus life. When criticism takes the form of surveillance and control as a part of the regular operation of established agencies, the impact of criticism may be institutional for both the university and its relation to society.

Administrative Conservatism. The Skolnick Report to the National Commission on the Causes and Prevention of Violence (1969) places the institutionalization of surveillance and control at the center of attention in response to the problems raised by academic confrontations during the 1960s. According to the report, "the development of workable internal mechanisms of order and justice is critical, since the alternative is recurrent outside intervention" (p. 123). Skolnick and other authors have implicitly claimed that a conservative emphasis on the maintenance of order has been forced on administrations by outside interference. Indeed, it is true that academic conservatism is partly based on the assumption that external surveillance and control threaten the freedoms that traditionally have been claimed for the university. However, this assumption alone is not enough to account for administrative conservatism as a general practice. Administrators who are not politically dependent upon faculty support—for example, at large public university systems—often act regardless of, and occasionally in defiance of, the wishes of faculty organizations.

Two additional factors must be taken into account in explaining the conservatism of administrative practice. First, administrators are likely to be selected by the degree to which they are committed to the principles of social order and superordination. Such a commitment enables them to deal with external organizations such as governmental agencies. Moreover, the commitment to order increases both their willingness to stifle dissent when it threatens the official order of the university and the likelihood that they will see any organizational conflict as a sign of disorder. Second, and more important, is the nature of the administrative enterprise. Such an enterprise, although it may be benevolent, is always conservative relative to its administered population. Administrative practice is, by its nature, exclusive—devoted, in principle, to maintaining an internal order within an official perspective.

In the contemporary university, the relative power and frame of reference of administrators places the very practice of administration at odds with students and, often, with faculty as well. Thus, as a practical matter, it becomes difficult for administrators to maintain the "community of scholars" position that ordinarily engages faculty support for the official order. Nevertheless, insofar as administrative conservatism remains consistent with the socially organized practice of faculty, it gains considerable support or acquiescence from faculty members who see conflict as a threat to the stability required for their work and mobility within the academic system, and student dissent as subversive to the principle of rational discourse that justifies the characterization of the university as a liberal establishment.

The Position of the Student. Although faculty-administration relationships are relatively clearcut, the way in which student practice is subject to administrative practice has been less frequently noted. For example, the student's ability to determine the course of his education depends upon his freedom to choose courses and select major fields. However, these choices are controlled by administrative allocations of facilities to departments, by registration practices, and by other limitations on options that are enforced by the contingencies of management, the cosmopolitanization of staff, and the requirements of heavy research. These factors, in turn, reflect the properties of the society in which the university is embedded. Teachers and counseling staffs can only translate the structural arrangements of the university into criteria and options for students. Therefore, the particular arrangements that prevail, and the values and perspectives that they entail, are critical parameters of student life. Although courses that are in great demand by students—such as courses in social movements, women's studies, and deviance—are available on many campuses, their educational status and, thus, their usefulness to the extra—and post-academic aspirations of students is seriously impaired by the fact that they are rarely treated as courses in a major program.

Whether or not the apprentice-master relationship identifies the student as powerless and immature, it defines the student's position as one in which he and his "master" must be mutually accessible to each other in the sense of sharing a practice. When organization of higher education makes apprenticeship obsolete as practice—that is, when the student-teacher relationship is formal rather than practical—the student's ability to initiate demands on his master is substantially decreased. The emergence of a service ethic in the university—the attempt to cultivate in students a sense of service to society rather than to a particular skill or area of knowledge—doubtless reflects the development of a difference in class between students and teachers relative to the organization of the university. In addition to its compatibility with the requirements of a managed society, this ethic denies the possibility of conceiving of education as relevant to class struggle and other forms of intrasocietal conflict.

Although administrative control over students has been most visible in relation to political issues, it is simply an extension of normal practice into other areas. Attempts on the part of university officials to suppress leftist student political activities should be understood in the context of the general mobilization of society around the consolidation of rule. Such actions on the part of university officials are attempts to keep internal control a university matter, but paradoxically, they often increase the very pressures they are presumably designed to reduce. Controversy in politically or culturally sensitive areas has often been reduced by trading in some measure of autonomy. What is ultimately sacrificed is the principle of free discussion of controversial issues that is traditionally claimed to be essential to the liberal university. This sacrifice was the case during the 1960s, when many university officials acquiesced to the deployment of undercover agents on campuses, participated in governmental investigations of the political activities of students and teachers, and enforced regulations that limited the political activities of students and the tenure of radical professors.

Parsons (1968) has described student political activities as attempts to implicate the university in politics and to reduce its alleged complicity in the actions of "the power structure" or "the establishment." But if the university is implicated in societal politics, it can be argued that the campus conflicts of the 1960s involved a struggle between officials and a wide range of opponents over the question of whether students and faculty can legitimately take a left-oriented political initiative. Because university officials are usually in a position to legalize or outlaw any campus group, the possibility of total political repression of the left is virtually unlimited. The fact that this possibility has not gone unnoticed may be illustrated by the actions cited above, of a number of university and college presidents during the summer of 1969. They joined in a statement urging their colleagues to oppose student political organizations that are not formally recognized by the college administration as legitimate or representative (*New York Times*, 1 July 1969).

THE COSMOPOLITANIZATION OF THE ACADEMY

Various features of contemporary life have exposed the university to public scrutiny to an extent unique in the history of American higher education. To some extent, this exposure is an aspect of factors that have been mentioned—the growth of the academic enterprise, the development of service and applied disciplines, the emergence of a heavy research industry, the expansion of the university's operation as an agency of socialization, and the shift in patronage from the private to the public sector. The articulation of an official ideology of academic autonomy reflects the new vulnerabiltiy of the university in its publicly controversial position. But the idea of the university as a sovereign entity runs counter to some major trends in recent American history. The force of the coordination of societal operations, the development of superordinate systems of control, and the rationalization of social life under the impact of the "managerial revolution" and the consolidation of rule must be acknowledged.

Since World War II, a national mobilization has been taking place in which local units and operations of American society are increasingly subordinated to the political and economic imperatives of state and national government. New superordinate establishments are coordinating the activities of what had been comparatively simple and sovereign social entities. At the same time, these changes have been the focus of national movements concerned with the distribution and use of economic and political power. From the perspective of ruling elites, this mobilization is described as the inevitable consequence of technological developments that require coordination and planning as efficiency measures. But the very mobilization that provides the opportunity for a fully managed society places the institutions of society under official and public scrutiny. In the United States, scrutiny from the perspective of rule conventionally focuses on two features of its object: the extent to which a given institutional component ensures the performance of tasks deemed essential for the society, and the extent to which the component does not violate the putative values and ideals by which it is institutionally defined. Both features are thought to contribute to the stability of the social order. Consequently, public and official scrutiny of institutions is often accompanied by the development of special processes and structures of control in particular institutional sectors. Such structures and processes work to check the growth of organizational tendencies that are inconsistent with the national mobilization (Brown, 1969b).

As an "agency of socialization" (Jencks and Riesman, 1968, pp. 28, 35), higher education has become prominent under the impact of the national mobilization. Its operations have become a national topic and, since the dramatic news coverage of student political activities during the 1960s, a political issue. The academic enterprise has become a more intimate part of the political, economic, social, and moral conflicts of American society, susceptible to the new forms of centralized and highly coordinated processes of social control that have developed since World War II.

THE COSMOPOLITANIZATION OF FACULTY

During the same period, research and consultation have become the dominant cosmopolitan options for faculty members. Moreover, as research and consultation improved the competitive position of universities relative to other organizations and as the prestige of a university came to depend upon the publication and consultative record of its academic staff, the utilization of cosmopolitan options became increasingly important. It became a prerequisite for the promotion of individual faculty members and a criterion for establishing the academic and intellectual (as well as political) orientation of a faculty or a department. By defining productivity, this criterion selects faculty members who work to perpetuate a cosmopolitan orientation based on officially sponsored research and consultation and eliminates those who do not.

As academic operations came to rely on a heavily elaborated research industry, this source of the relationship between the university and society was institutionalized within the university. Consequently, two polar practices have crystallized for faculty with regard to the relationship of the professor to his local campus: a *cosmopolitan* practice in which the local situation is subordinate to a wider national, historical, and professional scene governed by the contemporary organization of American society; and a *local* practice in which external and inclusive collectivities are subordinate to the specific site of employment. Although both practices tend to include, as justification, the conventional notion of academic autonomy, this justification has a special meaning for parties to cosmopolitan practice. For such parties, it asserts the freedom of the professional from the details of running the organizations in which he works and from the political and economic pressures that influence those organizations.

Recent developments within higher education have produced a sharp division between disciplines where the cosmopolitan option is available and those disciplines where it is not. This division can also be found, to some extent, within disciplines. For those whose practice is local, autonomy is essentially based on the local educational enterprise (Blau and Scott, 1962). The occupational focus of the cosmopolitan practice is research; the focus of the local practice is teaching (Ridgeway, 1968; Wallis, 1967; Morison, 1967; Rossi, 1967). Nevertheless, individual productivity is measured by cosmopolitan standards, regardless of the orientation and practice of faculty members.

INCREASED IMPACT OF THE RESEARCH INDUSTRY

C. Wright Mills (1963) discussed the "ascendency of the technician over the intellectual in America" (p. 157). In *White Collar* (1951) and in *The Sociological Imagination* (1961), Mills elaborated the thesis that the academic disciplines have become oriented to techniques and products that serve specific and often unexamined or unexaminable interests, values, practices, and ideologies. Although both the technician and the intellectual tend to be cosmopolitan in their practice, the former is professional and the latter is critical with regard to the problems they attempt to solve. For the technician, the problems are given; for the intellectual, the selection of problems is, itself, a subject of concern. The site of activity for the technician, or in less pejorative terms, the professional, is national and organizational; the site of activity of the intellectual is international and historical.

Mills viewed the professional social scientist as performing two functions within an ethos of service: bureaucratic and justificatory. The bureaucratic function of social science serves a given official order; the justificatory function provides argument in support of that order. "The ascendency of the technician," an inevitable consequence of the consolidation of the ruling class within the framework of contemporary capitalism, has been assured by the development of heavy research within the academic system and its impact on the institutional life of that system. The attractiveness of research to the individual professor lies in its putative capacity to provide him with an entrepreneurial and meritocratic setting. But it also lies in the opportunity that research provides for drama and a sense of scale in his life, which includes a tradition and a mission, a national audience, increased prestige and income, professional advancement within the academic hierarchy, sponsorship, and the facilities with which to practice his craft and to realize what is often, in retrospect, his calling. Sponsored research is attractive to universities because it places them in more favorable positions with regard to each other and with regard to competing types of organizations.

However, interest alone does not explain the institutionalization of heavy research within the university. As patronage came to depend upon research imbedded in the business economy and the government, the university changed. Research began to dominate more and more aspects of university life, including the distribution of facilities, the relative strength of disciplines, curricula, and standards of performance. As this criterion of productivity becomes recognized and because the prestige of a university depends upon the publication record of its faculty, the selection of personnel itself affirms the system of heavy research. In fact, the balance between teaching duties and research time is often a matter for negotiation between faculty members and their departments as a condition of employment. Rossi (1967) has described the impact of heavy research, in particular, campus research centers, on university organization:

> The essential nature of the American university is being affected by these organizational developments . . . certainly the extraordinary diversity of activities which are now put within one large organizational framework must necessarily affect the nature of teaching, research and the administration of our foremost institutions (p. 112).

The Cox Commission (1968), appointed by the administration of Columbia University to investigate the student protests of 1968, viewed the impact of heavy research in terms of its relationship with the official order of society and described the impact in terms of the ideology of the official order. The Commission asserted:

> The increasing complexity and sophistication of all aspects of the industrial and social order have enormously increased the demands upon universities to join in applying to practical uses the knowledge, skills, and equipment they assemble. State and federal governments, industry, foundations, and community organizations are constantly calling upon individual professors for active participation in action programs as well as for expert opinion; and both the professors and their institutions value the opportunity. Universities, as others have said, have become knowledge factories with much wider and possibly more powerful constituencies than the students whom they educate. At least some branches of the university, moreover, are attracting to their faculties a new type of academician—the man of action as well as intellect whose interest is not the pursuit of truth for its own sake but to shape society from a vantage point combining academic security, intellectual weapons, and political action.
>
> The trend raises questions of extraordinary difficulty, of which we mention only two.
>
> 1. What is the proper role of the university in the immediate practical application of knowledge to military, industrial, social, and economic problems? . . .
> 2. If universities are to be actively engaged in social endeavor, how and by whom are decisions to be made concerning when, how, where, and to what uses their knowledge shall be applied . . .
>
> Making decisions on the application of its knowledge to society must, to some degree, politicize the university . . . . And this leads back to the initial question concerning the university's role in the application of knowledge" (pp. 19-21).

The Economics of Research. By 1968, research accounted for one fifth of all university expenditures (United States Bureau of Census, 1968, p. 129). Moreover, resources were highly concentrated. Benson (1966) noted that, at the beginning of the 1960s, 66 percent of the total federal disbursement to colleges and universities went to seven states, California, Illinois, Maryland, Massachusetts, Michigan, New York, and Pennsylvania (p. 63) and to relatively few campuses. Moreover, in 1964, organized research commanded 85 percent of federal funds for higher education (p. 63). Thus, by the end of the 1960s the structure and content of higher education were controlled by the political and economic sectors of society to a greater degree and more intricately than ever before. The facts cited by Ridgeway (1968) in *The Closed Corporation: American Universities in Crisis* were part of the stock of analysis that radicalized campus protest. For example, Ridgeway noted that "more than two thirds of the university research funds come from the Department of Defense, the Atomic Energy Commission or the National Aeronautics and Space Administration . . ." (1968, p. 5). He cited the total federal obligation to the University of Michigan by August 1966 as $66,265,000, of which $21,579,000 was from the Department of Defense. According to Ridgeway, Michigan was the fifty-eighth largest nonprofit defense contractor in the United States in 1967:

> The University of Michigan's Willow Run Laboratory . . . works on (among other projects) photo-reconnaissance measures for the military, and . . . is involved in counter-insurgency in Thailand. Willow Run has an annual budget of about $11 million, most of it from the Defense Department, and for some time has been recognized as an expert in infrared imagery. About 160 undergraduate and graduate students have secret clearances for their work at the labs. Willow Run . . . maintains its own fleet of airplanes.

> Because of its intimate ties with the military over the years, it seemed natural enough for Willow Run to accept the Pentagon's invitation to send out some men to Thailand and set up a laboratory to train the Thais in photo-reconnaissance methods. This was part of an extensive U.S. effort to spot communist movements in the northeast of Thailand. The University of Michigan's part in the Thailand project remained secret until the fall of 1967, when the *Michigan Daily* made it known. The university then declared the project was nearly finished; however, Willow Run had consultants in Thailand in the winter of that year (1968, p. 118).

Most colleges and universities are affected by such developments only indirectly, by virtue of their participation in the official systems of higher education (Rossi, 1967). Many of the colleges and universities most directly affected, those "at the head of the academic procession," were sites of protest and confrontation during the late 1960s (Ridgeway, 1968, p. 5).

Effects on the Definition of Status. So far as "the basic structure of American universities" is concerned, Rossi (1967) noted that:

> There can be little doubt that the teaching function of universities, especially of undergraduates, is carried out differently today than when research was carried out by professors primarily as an extra-curricular activity (p. 127).

This redistribution and reorganization of faculty energies has left the organization and direction of university life largely in the hands of management and subject to both the imperatives of a managerial perspective and the cosmopolitan commitments of university administrators. Because this perspective is more compatible with the perspective of professional researchers than with either intellectuals or locals, the question "knowledge for what" has been answered within the university along organizationally and societally conservative lines. One president of a large midwestern university has remarked that his university is a "knowledge factory," with undergraduate education simply one of its "byproducts." Although not all university presidents would agree with that statement, it illustrates the extent to which sponsored heavy research has penetrated the culture of the academy and the imagery of higher education (Cox, 1968, pp. 19-21).

The impact of research on the distribution of power on campus may be seen in the way in which heavy research has affected the quality and tenure of department chairmanships, the administrative linking pin between academic authority and managerial authority. Rossi (1967) asserted that:

> Perhaps the most serious inroad upon the university arises out of the rise of research as an alternative to entering upon a career of academic statesmanship. Departmental chairmanships appear to be going begging and on occasion few candidates have appeared as contenders for deanships (pp. 127-28).

Although many chairmen and deans still come from the academic ranks, there is a trend toward the socialization of individuals directly toward those positions, and departmental chairmanships are already occasionally seen as way stations to higher organizational ranks. This trend contributes to the crystallization of statuses within the university; to an increase in the distances among administration, faculty, and students; and to an increase in the number of dimensions by which interstatus distance is defined.

The crystallization of statuses and the increased dependence of faculty members upon organizations that they cannot control have opened the way for a reinterpretation of the faculty role of teacher as employee. Because organizational control is in other hands and because many teachers have increasingly important off-campus economic interests, it is not surprising that faculty occupational identifications are moving slowly toward an acceptance of Mills' (1951) judgment that: "The professor is, after all, an employee, subject to what this fact involves, and institutional factors select men and have some influences upon how, when, and upon what they will work" (p. 151).

As employees, faculty members find themselves occasionally subject to procedures more often experienced by students. For example, following a demonstration at Queens College of the City University of New York during the spring of 1969, at which a young professor and thirty-seven students were arrested, the dean of faculties summarily suspended the arrested professor without a hearing. The suspension was lifted following expressions of concern by some faculty members and students. The professor was then invited to attend a hearing by a committee appointed by the president of the college. When he requested a delay in the hearing so that he might prepare a case and solicit testimony from witnesses in his behalf, the chairman of the committee is reported to have told the professor that the committee would appreciate his appearance at the hearing as scheduled because the president wished to "expedite the case." Similarly, at Queensboro Community College during the same school year, the president refused to rehire a professor who had been active in leftist politics, despite the recommendations of his department and of the faculty at large. Demonstrations and strikes followed the president's refusal to reconsider his decision, which the local chapter of the United Federation of College Teachers referred to as a violation of academic freedom. Nevertheless, the president called the police on campus and suspended some of the faculty, as well as students, involved in the protest.

Neither local nor cosmopolitan practices support faculty involvement in campus government or in the determination of university policy. Cosmopolitan orientations are constrained by professional and extracampus commitments. Local orientations tend to emphasize either local work conditions or the problems of teaching in a particular discipline. Thus, the cosmopolitanization of administration and the cosmopolitanization of faculty have opposite consequences.

The subject matter of administration (its material) has always been the local campus, whether or not the local campus is treated as subordinate to larger administrative entities. As university management has become craft, it has brought administrators closer to the campus and, at the same time, has rechanneled loyalty and accountability from local organization to external agencies and inclusive structures. On the other hand, the traditional subject matter for faculty members has been that of a discipline, whether enacted through teaching, participation in professional associations, or research. The cosmopolitanization of faculty has intensified involvement with a field of study or with the problems of sponsors of research. Neither development encourages participation in campus government, in the formulation of university policy, in local faculty organizations (by means of which faculty power could be retained and enlarged). For the administration, local power is essential to the managerial enterprise, although the development of polar frames of reference for faculty members reinforces indifference to local power, an indifference that is also incorporated into the weakness of faculty organization relative to the organization of administration. Thus, the community of scholars has given way to an administrative structure that temporarily accommodates a new class of academic entrepreneurs. As geographical mobility decreases for professors or market conditions increase the instability of their employment, it is likely that the dominance of management within the university will yield to the conventional labor-management relations of collective bargaining and a corresponding redefinition of higher education and the academic enterprise.

ACADEMIC AUTONOMY: IDEOLOGY AND PRACTICE

Conceptions of academic autonomy and academic freedom play an imporant part in articulating the patterns of interference (see chap. 10) that characterize the university as an establishment and as a setting for collective behavior. Academic freedom may be taken as a political ideal, the practical interpretation of which is a political issue. Academic autonomy is the interpretation of academic freedom that has become prominent among those persons concerned with the social and political problems of academic life. Their concern has established "academic autonomy" as the critical component of an official ideology of the university. This ideology relates the ideal of freedom to the organization, the situation, and the institutional values of the university and assigns the university to a place among the higher ideals and institutions of society. The ideology is presented as a justification for specific actions and policies that are alleged to support the practical application of the ideal.

In discussing the contribution of these conceptions to the patterns of interference that characterize the university, the concern is with the assumptions made by those persons who have defined "freedom" as autonomy. Concern also centers on practical uses and political consequences of the claim that the university is and must remain independent of external political forces. These uses and consequences define the role of academic autonomy in the emergence of points of confrontation from the patterned interference of student, faculty, and administrative practice.

THE IDEAL OF ACADEMIC FREEDOM

What is sociologically most significant about statements of political ideals is the setting in which the ideals are made explicit as premises for or justifications of action, that is, their operational location. The ideal of freedom may be made operational as autonomy of the putative members or components (the groups, operations, people) of an assembly. However, making freedom operational as autonomy is practical only for social establishments in which independence is an accountable property of members or components. It is not possible to incorporate that operationalization into a practice for which components are vaguely defined, accountably interdependent, or accountably interpenetrant. Any practical interpretation of "freedom" assumes the parameters of action for a particular socially organized setting. When it does not assume those parameters, it is usually taken as a comment on that setting as a whole or as a principle of control—that is, as an unimpeachable rule, the enforcement of which protects the components from any infringement on their prior state, in particular, on the way in which they are usually addressed. For example, to express the classically liberal ideal of freedom within a bureaucratic system is to criticize bureaucracy because the degree of autonomy ordinarily taken as sufficient to constitute freedom cannot be incorporated into bureaucratic practice. Etzioni's (1961) characterization of students as lower participants, and the standard definition, in human relations research, of formal or credentialed members as members in practice, do not acknowledge the critical implication of the application of the liberal ideal of freedom to bureaucracy (see also Parsons, 1949, pp. 767-68). Consequently, both assume that the segregation of people by class and power within an establishment does not significantly alter both their relation to that establishment as "free participants" and the conception of that establishment as "organization" or "system."

Sometimes the operational definition assumes a principle of organization that is incompatible with the setting in which the ideal is claimed as an aspect of practice. This has been the case with academic freedom. The operational interpretation of "academic freedom" as autonomy for individuals and groups does not reflect the parameters of collective action provided by the structure of the university and its links to society. (The belief in university autonomy is still passionately affirmed by academicians as diverse as Malia, 1965; Taylor, 1965; Bell, 1968; Hofstadter, 1968, and Parsons, 1968.) However, this interpretation of freedom has not been taken as a criticism of the contemporary organization of the university or its involvement in societal affairs. It has, rather, been taken as a principle of control.

Academic Freedom as Control. Two factors contribute to the use of the ideal of academic freedom as a principle of control: (1) the practical problem posed by an attempt to adjust the idea of autonomy to the structural and definitional constraints of the modern university, and (2) the distribution of power within the academic system. With regard to the first factor, the helplessness and vulnerability of academic personnel during the era of McCarthyism demonstrated how unlikely it was that the principle of individual autonomy could be applied to the university without changing its social structure and without seriously revising academic practice itself. In fact, the "social system" in which the ideal was to be applied shifted from the university to the societal setting of the university, and the unit for which autonomy was claimed was no longer the individual or the academic department but the university itself (Hofstadter, 1968). To claim autonomy for the university, however, was to assert that there is a stable unit for which autonomy could be claimed. The claim that the university should be autonomous thus implied that its constituents—students, faculty, and administrators—should be subjected to a degree of constraint sufficient to insure the stability of the university as an identifiable social order. In other words, autonomy for the university implied little autonomy for its members, unless the social structure, norms, and processes of social control within the university assured order by virtue of a general consensus. The argument assumes that no such consensus exists, that the university is not, in Etzioni's terms, an organization in which authority is fully legitimized by shared values and "coercion plays a secondary role" (1961, p. 48). The accuracy of this assumption depends upon the accuracy of the description of the university throughout this chapter.

Much like the moral paradox implicit in the application of a universalistic ideal—freedom to a limited class of members (e.g., teachers)—the intellectual paradox implicit in the operational interpretation of academic freedom as university autonomy expresses a state of affairs that has been taken for granted since the end of World War II. Caplow and McGee (1958) have described the way in which techniques endemic to the academic system limit the autonomy of individual students and professors in the interest of the official internal order; the regular use of such techniques tends to enforce limits on the range of tolerable opinion and conduct. Control over the individual teacher is built into the processes of hiring, personnel review, promotion, and the allocation of department duties, all of which are processes that tend to be controlled by specific groups within the university and routinized in administrative practice. Similarly, the distribution of intellectual and political points of view at a given campus are profoundly influenced by curriculum, policies of hiring and firing, and other devices essential to the ordinary operation of the university. Because these processes are part of that ordinary operation, there are built in justifications for any particular outcome, and it is difficult to detect pressure and discrimination. It is still more difficult to discover the sources of a given intellectual climate on campus. The traditional insulation of the university agencies that determine policy on budget, curriculum, and personnel, the secrecy of the operations of those agencies, and the informal and covert political processes that affect specific decisions compound the difficulty.

The distribution of political opinions and organizations on a campus also depends upon the traditional relationship of students to the university. The degree of control exercised over students has varied, but the potential for administration control over students has always been greater than for faculty. The suspension of politically active students, selective financing of student organizations, and official restrictions on the capacity of groups to function on campus have always limited student activities. The absence of due process procedures for students is often justified in terms of either a client or parental model of the student-university relationship. Rules affecting behavior in the political, social, cultural, and personal spheres, and post hoc interpretations of vague but inclusive definitions of misconduct have been traditional burdens of the student's position.

The Relation of the University to Society. The transformation of the setting in which freedom is to be practiced assumes that the relation of the university to society is cultural rather than structural (see Parsons, 1968). If the relation of the university to society is primarily cultural, that is, controlled by the values realized for society through the action of the university's polity, then there are no critical structural limitations to the attainment and maintenance of autonomy for the university, and the degree of autonomy presently held by the university is directly responsive to moral and political persuasion.

Academicians, like other employees, are largely ignorant of the intricacy, strength, and scope of the university's links to the political and economic sectors of society and the extent to which those links affect the university. Academic life is a career for professors. It is not one of many equally potent and interrelated practices shaping their lives. They have had little involvement in the operations by which the links between the university and society were manifested. They are not in a position to evaluate, as a matter of the overall practice of their lives, the links between the university and society. Consequently, academicians regularly overestimate the extent to which universities can operate internally as autonomous systems of control. Moreover, what they do not see is the enormous range of implications following from the university's dependence upon the powerful sectors of society.

The Position of Students. Students are in a different position than faculty. The growth of academic operations within an expanding economy and concentrated polity make the university more than a place for students to become cultivated or to learn the practice of "rationality" (see Parsons, 1968). Career, political involvements, family pressure, and the military draft are prominent considerations in the lives of students. A competitive grading system, cooperation by university officials with the military, and curriculum channeling are among the additional factors that demonstrate for students, the university's imbeddedness in society. As it touches their lives, the university is not an autonomous establishment or a "citadel of intellectualism." Consequently, as a matter of socially organized practice, students, like administrators, often act inconsistently with the conception of the university as an autonomous and normatively organized enclave of scholars devoted to the value of rational discourse, the production of knowledge, and the preservation of culture.

Some activities of students are relatively innocuous as far as faculty and university officials are concerned. For example, selecting a schedule of courses designed to provide an academic degree with a maximum of efficiency; selecting a field of concentration that provides entry to an economically advantageous position; participating in the type of social life that increases prospects for a favorable marriage; complaining that courses are not relevant; and cheating on examinations to avoid being drafted into the military forces or to achieve a valuable academic credential.

Some student activities are not innocuous. Some students, and some professors as well, translate their sense of the relationship of the university to society into demonstrable socio-political and moral propositions. Their organized activities, often prompted by a confrontation of official and student practice, directly challenge the assumptions by which academic freedom has been defined as autonomy for the university. (By 1968, such activities had challenged the cosmopolitan practice of faculty that provided the assumptions necessary for the ideology of academic autonomy.) Because the balance of power so overwhelmingly favors university administrators and because it is difficult for students to develop the type of organization that could establish a base of student power, university officials and faculty do not have to meet the challenge. The practical interpretation of freedom has not become a matter of conflict and negotiation so far as university officials are concerned. Instead, academic freedom, regularly interpreted as university autonomy, became a principle of control applied against those persons defined as threatening the legitimacy of academic authority, and, thus, the freedom of the academy itself.

Political Alliances. Faculty members are often drawn by their endorsement of academic autonomy into political alliances with administrators and external agencies that threaten their own practice and the validity of their perspective on the modern university. Those alliances reinforce the power of administrators and support the very status quo within which patterned interference between faculty and administrative practice has become increasingly prominent in the university (Eichel, et al, 1970). Those who claim autonomy for the university often support or directly initiate acts of control that are easily seen as scape-goating, repression, and a reenactment of McCarthyism. These acts of control, like all such actions, involve the establishment of new standards, tactics, and agencies, and the prospect of the extension of official control into other areas of university life (see Brown [1969b] for a discussion of this process).

The foregoing discussion is one possible interpretation of a recent survey by Martin Trow, reported in the *New York Times* (23 April 1970), in which 80 percent of 60,447 university and college faculty members agreed that "campus demonstrations by militant students are a threat to academic freedom," despite the fact that most professed "liberal views on national and international affairs," and despite the fact that many stated that they agreed with the aims of the demonstrators. The respondents also rejected student participation in policy making with regard to faculty appointments and promotions, undergraduate admissions, curriculum course content, and degree requirements. One of Trow's associates, Everett C. Ladd, was quoted as saying, "there is a strikingly clear shift toward a more conservative attitude where the faculty's self-interest is involved." In its content, this shift toward conservatism was consistent with the dictates of managerial order, as is illustrated by the resolution of the Harvard Faculty of Arts and Sciences following the occupation of campus facilities during a student protest in 1969 (*New York Times*, 10 June 1969, p. 31; see also Eichel, et al, 1970). The preamble to that resolution suggested that members of the "university community," while not obliged to be "silent and passive," are required "to see how easily an academic community can be violated." Although affirming the right to dissent and to act on the basis of dissenting opinion, the faculty listed several activities as "unacceptable," presumably regardless of the issues at stake, one of which was "obstruction of the normal processes and activities essential to the functions of the university community." Trow's survey suggests that the notion of academic autonomy is more qualified than has been indicated in the present discussion, that it serves to reject particular instances of governmental involvement in faculty affairs in the university rather than to define academic freedom as a value. Although this suggestion is probably accurate regarding the practical application of "academic autonomy" to particular cases (when a faculty intiates or addresses specific acts), it is nevertheless not consistent with the way in which the concept has been developed in relation to the idea of freedom (when a faculty addresses the problem of allocating loyalty to specific agencies). Published documents of the sort reviewed here suggest that many prominent academicians endorse the general claims (regardless of their endorsement or nonendorsement of any particular application) that academic autonomy is an adequate interpretation of academic freedom; that university autonomy serves all real or legitimate interests; and that autonomy refers to independence from any but minor controls over the political, social, and cultural functions of the university.

OFFICIAL IDEOLOGY

Krausse (1968) has discussed the role of official ideology in gaining and maintaining support for an official order and official policies. Krausse mentioned several major types of definition of the term "ideology" (p. 130); but in the broadest sense, an official ideology is a consensus-inducing statement, issued or endorsed by officials, that justifies a policy for a particular establishment in terms of certain ideals, and that is used to mobilize support for official actions from a target assembly. (This use supposes an organized and plural setting in which the policy is already a political issue.) Krausse does not consider a set of propositions an official ideology if it urges the initiation of action by the target assembly; if it justifies a particularistic action by officials; if it refers to specific interests or aims; if it is offered as a comment or memorandum by officials; or if the target assembly is not a party to an already politicized setting.

Academic Autonomy as an Ideology. As has been discussed, the ideal of academic freedom plays an important role in the political life of the university. Expressed as university autonomy, it is part of the official ideology of the university. This ideology is widely endorsed by professors and administrators who write about the university and its place in society during periods of crisis. The ideology is regularly presented as a justification for official policies that are adopted during episodes of collective behavior. An account of how this ideology came to be endorsed has been offered here. In addition, the effect of this endorsement on the willingness of faculty members to support official policies that ultimately threaten their conception of the university has been discussed. Two additional questions have a bearing on the relationship of official ideology to official practice and, thus, to the patterns of interference in the university: How has this ideology become an official ideology within the academic system? What has been its role in the development and implementation of official policy during confrontations between students and university officials?

Justificatory Ideologies. Krausse (1968) suggested that justificatory ideologies develop when officials of an organization need public support or protection. He argued that officials of organizations, such as universities, that are the most vulnerable to external interference, the most dependent upon outside sources of support, and the internal order of which is accounted for by reference to shared ideals, are in the greatest need of ideological justification. Because of the university's alleged importance as a site of advanced socialization (the last directive link between the individual and agencies of general socialization), the involvement of universities in heavy research, and perhaps the cost of education relative to other governmental priorities, universities have increasingly come to be seen as "action bureaucracies." As reputed agents of change, universities are controversial organizations. Krausse noted that "it is these socio-political factors which lead the 'action bureaucracy' to develop ideologies to increase the acceptability of their actions to the influenced public" (1968, p. 136). Presumably, these factors increase the likelihood that action bureaucracy officials will define the boundary of the organization in such a way that many structurally interpenetrating organizations will be taken as sources of external interference or intrusion. Krausse implies that officials issue ideological statements in order to gain support for policies. The policies for which support is sought, however, are usually already established and, often, practically irrevocable (Brown, 1969b).

In addition, the same socio-political factors are likely to require an expansion of official control within the action bureaucracy (or to reflect the expansion of official control) in order to bring operations into line with new policy. In any case, it is clear that officials of action bureaucracies must continually expand their control within the organization in order to be able to devise new policies and make reliable presentations to the publics and organizations upon which the action bureaucracy depends. Because the university's environment—in particular its relationship with the state—is presently undergoing tremendous change, officials need a degree of operational flexibility that requires more control—in the sense of constraint rather than enforced accountability—over the internal life of the organization than is required in most action bureaucracies.

History, social structure, and culture limit the range of publicly acceptable justifications. Official ideology, like rumor, conventionalizes what is potentially most controversial about an establishment. It is incumbent upon officials to assemble ideology that fits prevailing views of the publics and organizations they wish to influence. This usually requires that the elements of ideology—statements of ideal, situation, and appropriate modes of support—have already been well-established and are relatively uncontroversial for those publics and organizations either because the ideological elements are settled or because relations of power have trivialized dissent. The content of the mainstream official ideology of the university incorporates elements that are estabished within the public traditions of higher education—and is presented by academicians who are the putative representatives of those traditions—because the university is normally presented as an institution of society rather than a specific organization or type of organization. The ideology of academic autonomy is, like most official ideologies, generated in response to crisis. During the 1960s, this particular ideology was addressed to organized forces inside and outside of the university (Hofstadter, 1968; Parsons, 1968), and it was usually presented by faculty members in justification of particular official decisions about unauthorized political activities on campus. The presentation of this ideology transformed specific responses by officials into putative matters of policy.

Wherever an official ideology justifies a policy in regard to what is taken as the environment of the organization, officials appeal to the more or less organized and powerful sectors of the society on which the organization depends for resources and legitimation or those sectors into which the official bureaucracy is integrated. In the case of the university, during the 1960s, officials regularly appealed to agencies of government and public loyalties to the state, and referred to those academic values or products that could be claimed to be functional for the society as a whole. In this commencement address at Columbia University in 1968, Richard Hofstadter (1968) described the university as an institution "firmly committed to certain basic values of freedom, rationality, inquiry, discussion, and to its own internal order; but it does not have corporate views of public questions" (pp. 583-84). But the values and products provided by the university are not tangible and, therefore, do not lend themselves to appeals, by officials or specific interest groups, for support.

Consequently, the values and products mentioned in ideological presentations, and described as essential to society and threatened unless official actions are supported, were nonpragmatic or symbolic (Brown, 1969b). Thus, official ideology referred to the most inclusive identity and most general values of its targets.

Official Ideology and Official Practice. Various discussions of the academic system (for example, Parsons, 1968; Jencks and Riesman, 1968) support the proposition that the conventional view of the university has less to do with its products and services than with the value—that is, rationality—that is alleged to be its societally institutional specialty and with which it is identified. This view of the university is ordinarily presented as part of published and politically significant accounts (qualified accounts that refer to topical focuses of organized settings.) of the university in crisis. It is the intellectual foundation of official ideological work. The university becomes a public issue in terms of its public identity as a social institution, regardless of the underlying economic and socio-political forces that control its shape and direction, and regardless of the source of its troubles. The use of official ideology in such accounts attempts to guarantee that no matter how complex and controversial university problems appear, the institution is presented as a familiar phenomenon and as an element in the proper comprehension of society itself.

Administrative practice can proceed only if its setting is maintained as limited to parties that are taken as competent to that setting. Those social actors—such as specific legislative committees, foundations, and supraadministrative bodies—with which an administration is mutually reflexive, or taken as mutually effective, are ordinarily taken as the competent parties to the setting of administrative practice. This setting is vulnerable to the intrusion of "noncompetent" parties whenever the university becomes a public issue, that is, whenever public discussion of the university includes those persons or groups who are not ordinarily taken by administration as parties to the setting of administrative practice. As Krausse (1968) suggested, official ideology is indeed useful under these circumstances, but official ideology is used to *decrease* public involvement in the setting of official practice rather than, as Krausse assumed, to *increase* support for officials and, therefore, to increase the involvement of "external" assemblies in that setting.

Thus, the presentation of official ideology is not only designed to influence public opinion, but to ensure that, whatever conflict the university is embroiled in, there is relatively little interference with administrative practice and its structures. In this respect, official ideology is an element of the struggle of administration to assume the institutional prerogatives of management, thereby establishing hegemony over the internal order of the unversity. Official ideology is, then, a matter of practice insofar as it is used to manage particular controversies; and it is a matter of metapractice insofar as its use is intended to influence arrangements of power and economy that are the parameters of administrative practice.

Ideological work—that is, assembling and presenting official accounts of the university in a crisis—cannot, by itself, keep noncompetent parties at a distance from the setting of administrative practice. As in disaster, the capacity of officials to pursue a course of action depends upon the degree to which they can control the information that is used to evaluate their activities. Officials must prevent facts that could discredit the institutional identity of the university from coming to public notice. In addition, officials must act to ensure their credibility with the assemblies they address or, at least, must refrain from acting in a way that raises the issue of their credibility. This attempt to ensure credibility may include publicized support of official university policies by acceptable public figures, such as a state governor, or the demonstration of a consensus among university officials at a number of campuses about the issues. Finally, in addition to maintaining ideological claims, officials may have to demonstrate the validity of the claims of their crisis accounts to powerful, formerly noncompetent, formally neutral parties. For this operation officials must demonstrate that the university (and, therefore, society) is under attack and that they can control the attack without additional help or interference from noncompetent parties. These danger and capability claims are often demonstrated by the establishment of procedures—boards or committees—whereby interested but noncompetent (to the setting of administrative practice) parties, such as faculty, judicial officials, and community groups, temporarily participate in administrative affairs.

Most importantly, a demonstration of the validity of these claims may involve engaging in specific acts of control. With regard to such acts, on the one hand, accounts of the university in crisis that incorporate official ideology justify particular acts of control. On the other hand, insofar as such acts dramatize the danger and the official capability to handle the danger, they demonstrate the validity of the accounts themselves.

Official acts of control often exacerbate a conflict or are presented as a step along an escalatory scale of official response. As a result, they may create new conditions for collective behavior on the part of the student or faculty at whom they are directed, which can result in "evidence" of the validity of the official account of the crisis but can also increase the likelihood of interference by outside parties. The risks of too subtle an approach to control during campus confrontation have prompted officials at many universities either to vacillate in an attempt to avoid a noticeable escalation or to hit hard in order to terminate the episode before it attracts the attention of other parties. Vacillation may, however, prevent officials from demonstrating the validity of the claims of their crisis accounts, and a hard-line approach, as in the case of Columbia University in 1968 (Barton, 1968), may discredit those claims with those persons to whom official accounts are directed. The advantage of choosing a hard line—and perhaps one reason why officials at so many universities adopted such an approach—is that it permits officials to publicize established but covert arrangements with the nonuniversity parties to the setting of administrative practice without endangering those arrangements (see "Growing Number of Colleges Taking Tougher Stand in Guidelines on Protests," *New York Times*, 6 October 1970).

The success of official presentations depends upon a number of factors, including a low degree of organization based on position on the part of faculty; an available audience for public displays of social control (Westley, 1966); a bias against initiative by managed groups, the persistence of faculty belief in both the viability of the community concept of the university and faculty control of the university; and the presence of structurally secure—and therefore potentially intrusive—links between local administration and cosmopolitan agencies. As has already been noted, the domination of the university by management is an accomplished fact. The neutralization of faculty is an aspect of this domination. Faculty members who endorse the ideology of academic autonomy and for whom it does not violate professional practice are more likely to support the administration than the protesting students, regardless of the issues raised by students or their tactics (Barton, 1968). By and large, these faculty tend to remain disengaged from official practice except to the extent of debating votes of confidence. Rarely are faculty members or their organizations more than simply bystanders. Occasionally, and usually unsuccessfully, they attempt to mediate between students and administrators (Avorn, 1968). Faculty inactivity or support for official policy is likely to be strengthened when official accounts of campus confrontation refer to an exclusively professional practice of professors (Cole and Adamsons, 1969) because such a practice tends to engage a relatively orthodox and locally detached orientation to the administration.

Thus, the translation of cosmopolitan and structurally determined pressures on local campuses into campus polices depends upon the articulation of an official ideology of academic autonomy, which must engage internal support for the official order and external support for policies directed at maintaining that order as the visible evidence of the institutional identity of the university. The translation also depends upon the presentation of crisis accounts that offer to demonstrate the dangers inherent in attacks on managerial authority within the university.

"Attacks" on Managerial Authority. The "activist" label, with its associated imagery, belongs to the practical logic of official response—order, as a whole, is at stake rather than a specific order, specific operations, or particular products (see, for example, Howe, 1968; Riesman, 1968; Kristol, 1968). Having recast student protest activities as a nihilistic, or at best a naively idealistic, and, therefore, ruthless attempt to destroy the university, and having developed politics of control that were consistent with that proposition, university officials contributed heavily to the radicalization of student political activities during the late 1960s. As the system became the topic of official presentations and the referent of particular acts of control (Skolnick, 1969), students also began to address this definition of their protest. Peterson's (1966, 1968b) research indicates that the emphasis of organized protest shifted during the 1960s from the specific conditions of student life to the more structural issues of campus governance and the relationship of the university to society.

This escalation was an inevitable consequence of the use of the official ideology of academic autonomy as a justification for official policies that, in any case, were committed to the task of maintaining managerial authority at the university. There were other incidental consequences of even greater importance. Policies designed to maintain the official order and the institutional identity of the university occasionally engaged forces with results that were sharply at odds with academic autonomy itself. The introduction of police on the campuses of Columbia University, Queens College of the City University of New York, and the surrounding community of the University of California at Berkeley, for example, tended to both raise the level of internal support for protestors (Barton, 1968) and increase the likelihood of surveillance and control by outside agencies of social control—the police, the courts, and the legislatures (Brown, 1969a; Donner, 1969; *New York Times*, 4 June 1969, 13 June 1969).

At Queens College, during the spring of 1969 (as previously mentioned in chap. 11), rallies and the occupation of part of a campus building (an administrative facility) followed the refusal of administrative officials to address over 400 students who had petitioned for a meeting with the president and the dean of students. The meeting had been petitioned after the suspension of three student leaders of a demonstration against recruitment on campus by the General Electric Corporation, a military-related corporation. The suspensions were issued without a hearing for the accused students. The refusal of the president and the dean to meet with the students led to the occupation of the building and to the development of a set of student demands that went beyond the initial issue of due process. After several weeks, and following what appeared to be a promise not to call the police, the president of the college asked the city police to clear the campus. In exchange for police cooperation, the president agreed not to drop charges if students were arrested. (This agreement was later admitted by the president during a convocation of students following the police action.) Immediately afterward, a statement was released by the district attorney's office in Queens to the effect that there would be a far-reaching investigation of the episode that would examine the roles of faculty and students, including those persons who were present during the building occupation and those whose actions might have been part of the background of the episode. Although this investigation never materialized and, ultimately, was repudiated by the district attorney, the threat of surveillance and a "witch hunt" hung heavily over the college during the last part of the semester and the following year (during which many politically radical instructors were not rehired), dampening enthusiasm for the expression of unpopular views and arousing fears that the students had somehow brought on the forces of repression. Ultimately, the role of the police became rationalized in policy, and local campus control became more completely dominated by the inclusive administration of the City University of New York.

A similar situation arose when the president of the University of California and the chancellor of the Berkeley campus urged that a section of university property be reserved for the city of Berkeley as a recreational park. Earlier, police had violently suppressed a large demonstration in support of students and Berkeley residents who had converted the unused land into a "people's park." The president and the chancellor reversed their initial opposition to the project after the violent police assault—which included the killing of a bystander, the wounding of many others, and vicious treatment of prisoners—because the incident aroused widespread public sentiment against both the police and the administrators who had called them. However, according to an article in the *New York Times*, 21 June 1969:

> Over the objections of Charles J. Hitch, president of the University, and Roger W. Heyns, chancellor of the Berkeley campus, the Regents committee on grounds and buildings had recommended for board approval that student housing be expeditiously developed on the site, "subject to a determination of the economic feasibility thereof."

The introduction of police set into motion forces that denied university officials autonomy in adjusting their relationship with students and the surrounding community, and engaged a larger system of control than had been publicly prefigured or admitted in the initial official call for police (see also Goodman, 1970).

AN HISTORICAL INTERLUDE

The absorbing vividness of the here-and-now, which is such an important consideration in the present topic and the present theoretical conceptions, is elusive and fragile only when gauged from a distance. For those who live in an epoch, for whom the "epoch" is present and eventive, the constructive force of the epoch is not fragile at all. It selects and enshrines constructions of the past and affects definitions and institutions that continue to shape the present.

As the nature of the university of the 1960s and 1970s is comprehended as part of contemporary events that comprehension projects a search for illustrations of that nature in the past. From the perspective of the present, the anticommunism of the 1950s exposes the forces that underlay campus confrontation in the 1960s. In unmistakable terms, it dramatizes the links between the university and society, the irrevelance of conventional notions of academic autonomy in a contemporary capitalist society, and the central ambiguities and mystifications of liberalism in the university.

ANTICOMMUNISM AND THE UNIVERSITY

The simple anticommunism of the post-World War II period is no longer the major justification proposed by those persons who press for wider applications of state control over socio-political affairs and the elimination of the left. Instead, many liberal academicians, by the end of the 1960s, claimed that the repression of the left was not politically motivated, but was directed at violent, authoritarian, or antisemitic tendencies of leftists. Nor is the ideal of academic freedom, which was occasionally and ineffectually used in an attempt to mobilize opposition to governmental investigations, interpreted in the same way today as it was then. The right of communists and socialists to teach was rarely raised as a point in opposition to political repression. It was generally assumed that practicing communists and Marxists were beyond the scope of application of the value of academic freedom. The issue for most liberals who argued against governmental intervention in the affairs of the university was the "right" of professors not to be occupationally disabled or otherwise punished for past (and present) disavowed ideas and activities. The viscissitudes of academic freedom as a stated ideal, specifically its interpretation as an operational construct, cannot be understood without seeing its paradoxical role during the official persecution of the political left in the 1950s.

Moreover, although some of the consequences of anticommunism were pervasive (e.g., the elimination of Marxism as a paradigm for social science) other effects were felt and responded to differentially within the academic system. In general, it may be said that external pressures on the university brought about a remarkable degree of participation in political repression on the part of faculty and university officials. The extent of this participation suggests that those pressures reinforced tendencies that were dormant within the university itself and that were responsive to the relationship between the university and the postwar society. Political repression by the state was the cutting edge of a wider official policy tied to "the Cold War," and to participate in university life was to participate in the society of the Cold War. Beyond that, political repression had specific effects on the socio-political tone of academic life. Most significantly, for the present consideration of the unauthorized political activities of students in the 1960s, repression affected the structure of the university. McCarthyism reinforced the power of university officials and strengthened alliances between those officials and politically and economically powerful groups outside the university. Repression was only one of several consequences of the new relationship between the university and society affecting the social structure of the university. Other consequences were the emergence of research as an economic and political base for the expansion of the university and the growth of the public university.

Repression and Control Within the University. New and subtle means for organizational control, originally part of the extension of management within the university were applied to political matters, often with the complicity of liberal faculty members who saw anticommunism as a legitimate exception to academic freedom or as accidentally repressive but essentially legitimate tools for upgrading the professional tone and quality of academic disciplines (Caplow and McGee, 1958). Whether or not they supported these repressive measures, faculty members clearly saw the need for caution and self-protection. However, there were few cases of organized resistance. University teachers continued to resist the proletarianization of their occupational identity and often chose membership in paper associations over unionization or collective protest. Many liberal professors withdrew from or overtly opposed public controversy or governmentally proscribed organizations and activities, which is not to imply that without governmental repression they would have engaged in such controversy. In fact, there had been little left-oriented criticism of American society during the period preceding the McCarthy charges and investigations. In the social sciences, a strong anti-Marxist tradition was reinforced, and leftist professors came under attack by liberal as well as conservative colleagues. In most college and universities, socialists, communists, Marxists, and criticism in general became targets of repression as university officials made their peace with the official polity of the country or, in any case, vigorously participated in its affairs. Anticommunism became academically and intellectually respectable and administratively secure (see, e.g., Lipset and Smelser, 1961, especially p. 50).

Private Schools and Public Colleges. That the institutionalization of surveillance and control depends upon the relationship between the university and society is supported by the fact that McCarthyism had less impact at prestigious private schools than it did at public colleges and universities. Harvard, for example, was relatively more insulated from external influence than Brooklyn College of the City University of New York. Although the character of top level administrators and trustees may account for some of the difference, Lazarsfeld and Thielens (1958) presented data that indicate that private schools were more insulated from external influence than public schools because of the relative independence of their officials from sources of influence. It must be remembered that the officials of public universities are officials of the state, in which case the vulnerability of public universities to political attack is only an expression of the nature of their organization (Lazarsfeld and Thielens, 1958). For example, Lazarsfeld and Thielens noted that public schools that experienced a high degree of political pressure were seen by their faculty members as highly unlikely to offer administrative support for a threatened teacher. Private schools under greater pressure were seen by their faculty members as highly likely to provide such support. Lazarsfeld and Thielens stated that:

> Political pressures . . . are lighter on the private schools. The Trustees are then less inclined to pass them on. And the administration is often prepared to follow a policy of interposition (p. 183).

"Externally" Imposed Pressures. Lazardsfeld and Thielens evaluated the impact of McCarthyism on academic life in the decade following World War II. They solicited faculty for incidents of pressure on colleagues in apparent violation of academic freedom, which they defined as the capacity of the individual teacher to speak without political, social, or cultural restrictions imposed coercively by government officials. Of those faculty members sampled, 54 percent mentioned charges involving political point of view (p. 50). However, there were charges involving nonpolitical issues as well: religion, personal unconventionality, intramutal conflict over teaching techniques, and so forth. According to Lazarsfeld and Thielens, 39 percent of the charges were made by "visiting committees of the state legislature, right-of-center individuals and groups in the community, and other sources outside the school" (1958, p. 68). What was startlingly demonstrative of the receptiveness of university administrations to these off-campus pressures were the facts that a large number of such charges originated inside the university and that the actions against the individuals charged were ordinarily taken by university personnel. Lazarsfeld and Thielens reported that 36 percent of the charges were made by persons "formally connected with the university—trustees, administrators, alumni, colleagues, students, and relatives of students . . . (1958, p. 68). In 44 percent of the 990 reported incidents, unfavorable action was taken; in 18 percent the individual charged was fired (p. 70). Lazarsfeld and Thielens remarked that "whatever else may be said about them, the pressures against teachers in the post-war decade often got results" (p. 70).

McCarthyism illustrates the propositon that the vulnerability of the university to externally imposed controls, in part, depends upon conflicts among groups that have varying degrees of official standing and recognition in society (Hofstadter, 1955; Metzger, 1955; Lazarsfeld and Thielens, 1958; Minter, 1966; Jencks and Riesman, 1968). Moreover, the multiplication and increased pervasiveness of the links between the university and the ruling sectors of society suggest that it is no longer possible to delineate strictly "external" influences on the university. It is only recently that unrepresented groups within the university have been able to apply internal pressures on university officials even remotely comparable to the pressures alleged to be applied by external agents in the past. This turn of events has occurred precisely at the time when the nature of the university, the costs of academic operations, the problems of rechanneling youth into vocational and service positions, and the need for protected research establishments have become issues within official circles. The emergence of a student movement may be seen as parallel and coordinate to the developments in university teaching and administration that have been discussed. Rather than generating a "backlash" of administrative harshness and outside interference, the student movement must be seen as a relatively late manifestation of the managerialization and cosmopolitanization of the official structures and operations of the university.

THE UNIVERSITY AS A TOPIC OF CONFLICT

The 1960s saw two shifts in the recent history of the university as a topic of socio-political conflict. On the one hand, from authorized political interaction among officially recognized groups, the source of conflict shifted to unauthorized action of officially unrecognized and unrepresented groups which, traditionally, have been subject to official regulation within the university. On the other hand, the focus of conflict (the specific issues) shifted from the apparently incidental products of the system (particular attacks on faculty members; particular decisions by administrators; particular conditions of student life, including dress, food, curriculum, and housing) to the system of government within the university and the proper relationship between the university and society. The issue of military recruitment on campus, so prominent in the organized student protests of 1967 and 1968 (Peterson, 1968a), not only raised the question of what the proper function of the university is, but also raised far more basic questions: How shall the uses of the university be determined? And, in whose interests shall it function? After those questions were raised, analytic responses to them were formed; further issues began to arise:

How does power develop?
How are academic operations organized?
In what respect can academic operations be said to be systematic?
What is the university's relationship to the basic problems of America, including the physical environment, racism, sexism, exploitation, poverty, the lack of civilian control over the police and the military, the expansion of empire, and the concentration of power?

How does the university participate in society?
Who should control the university?

This sequence of events indicates that Parsons (1968) is mistaken in equating, as historical conflicts over academic freedom, "the effort of boards of trustees to impose their views on economic policy on the faculty members," McCarthyism's identification of orthodoxy and loyalty, and "left attacks" on "the alleged 'complicity' of the universities with the establishment, or power structure" (pp. 177-78). These various events did not constitute the same sort of threat to the academic "system." The "attack" by the "left" that Parsons saw as the modern version of the university's historic struggle to maintain the values of rational and disinterested inquiry is distinguished by the *source* of the protest—not "the left" so much as the unrepresented—and the *issues* around which protest had been mobilized—not incident and product but structure and purpose (Skolnick, 1969). It is in these terms that the contemporary left criticism of the university resembles and is part of a more general movement in society. Parsons himself has forcefully illustrated the interpenetration of the "academic system" and society, substantiating the substance of the claim that the university is thoroughly implicated in the life of its society. The issue for the 1960s was not whether or not the university should be involved in society but, rather who should determine how it should be involved and for what ends.

CHAPTER THIRTEEN

STUDENTS AND
THE UNIVERSITY

Sometime in the future, when historians write about the domestic scene of the Sixties one of the major themes that will emerge undoubtedly will focus on the related issues of general unrest, dissent, organized activism and mass protest. Somewhat surprisingly, a select group of students from a few universities will emerge as having been of major importance. (Sampson, 1967a, p. 1).

SETTINGS FOR CONFRONTATION

The Berkeley student rebellion of 1964 surprised everyone (Parsons, 1965, pp. 113, 139; Sampson, 1967a, p. 2; Skolnick, 1969, p. 79). Parsons, writing at the beginning of the 1960s, recognized that college is a site peculiarly sensitive to societal strains. Nevertheless he argued that:

> The main orientation of youth seems to be in tune with the society in which they are learning to take their places.

* * *

> Given the American value system we have outlined, it seems fair to conclude that youth cannot help giving a *relative* sanction to the general outline of society as it has come to be institutionalized.

* * *

> Clearly, American youth is in ferment . . . . Yet the general orientation appears to be, not a basic alienation, but an eagerness to learn, to accept higher orders of responsibility, and to "fit," not in the sense of passive conformity, but in the sense of their readiness to work within the system, rather than in basic opposition to it (1965, pp. 134-40).

In retrospect, it is tempting to try to find reasons for the failure to anticipate the unauthorized political actions that rocked the academic world during the last half of the 1960s. The present analysis suggests that available models of the university failed to consider the settings within which collective behavior can occur. The failure to move from an institutional to organizational and situational analyses obscured the relative instability of the American university at the end of the 1950s. Part of the problem undoubtedly lies in the acceptance of some dubious assumptions about the university, the society, and students, just as part of the problem lies in the conventions of theoretic discourse regarding social change. With regard to the latter problem, the tendency to adopt a macrosociological approach of excessive inclusiveness with a correlative focus on official elites as exclusive sources of stability and change is significant.

SOME THEORETICAL ASSUMPTIONS

Prior to 1964, sociological writing fundamentally overemphasized the stability and integrity of American institutions (Parsons, 1965; Rogin, 1967). Thus, Parsons referred to American society "running a scheduled course" in which "we find no cogent evidence of a major change in the essential pattern of its governing values" (p. 139). The success of the university as an insulated, normative organization that was institutionally committed to the preservation of elite culture, the development of knowledge, and the socialization of upwardly mobile pre-adults was more or less taken for granted. The assumption that the university was autonomous, and divorced from social movements, the national polity, and societal problems precluded a consideration of the university as a site for unauthorized political action.

Even if no assumptions were parametric to analyses of society and the university, prevailing views of youth and students drew attention away from them as potential political actors. On the one hand, students as adolescents were considered motivationally disabled so far as politics was concerned. Their energies were thought to be directed toward reducing identity diffusion, a problem that appears to privatize young people and limit their capacity to engage in collectively instrumental activities that do not bear directly on self-definition. On the other hand, students as role-players were largely described as pure cases of the man-in-society paradigm, objects of the "overly socialized view of man." Too young to work, too old to play, the student's relation to society, though not unaffected by traditional occupational, economic, and social groupings, was seen as unmediated by them. The emphasis on the socializing function of the university assumes this paradigm by placing the student in direct contact with agents of society and characterizing this contact as affected by such factors as peer solidarity.

These assumptions were consistent with prevailing views of the American society and its institutions. In academic sociology, the exclusive emphasis of theories of social change on planning, and consequently on the role of the official polity and authorized political action, undoubtedly drew attention away from the perspectives of those not in official or authorized representative positions. The national mobilization following World War II led to a focus on the problems of technique and administration that seemed endemic to postindustrial society. Although these problems contributed most to theory, there were occasional attempts to anticipate and deal with a growing reaction to expressions of discontent, largely by exploring inconsistencies within the institutions of American society. Thus, research on authoritarianism during the 1950s and the impacts of prejudice and officially sponsored or officially sanctioned discrimination during the 1960s were designed to humanize the society but not to affect the social theories by means of which it is understood.

In the light of such assumptions about American society, the university, and students, it was entirely appropriate for the poet Steven Spender (1969) to describe the unauthorized political activities of students and what was called the American student movement as the "politics of the non-political." And it was at least understandable, if not appropriate, for sociologists to grasp uncritically at available theoretic straws in their efforts to understand in retrospect that which apparently had had no prospect. Aside from the empirical and conceptual difficulties this uncritical theorizing often entailed, the most serious flaw lies in the failure to examine, in any other than a perfunctory fashion, the episodes in their settings. Descriptions of concrete episodes of collective behavior were often uncertain as to the relevance of specific details and, in any case, were rarely used as data for the construction of theory. In fact, theoretic accounts moved from the particular to the general with a speed that reflected the unease with which investigators approached a problem that was both intellectually stimulating and occupationally threatening.

COLLECTIVE BEHAVIOR: PATTERNS OF INTERFERENCE

Thus far, it has been suggested that collective behavior is interaction following a confrontation among competing collective constructions of a situation that appears to be claimed by a number of active parties. The confrontation occurs under the impact of a precipitating incident. Such an incident transcends the capacity of transformation rules (see chap. 8) to assimilate potentially intrusive items in collective action by positing exclusive and fully plausible practical options. The crucial components of confrontation, then, are collective constructions of the situation, the enactment of which demonstrates the incompatibility of collective constructions. This formulation does not require large aggregates to be precipitated as a whole.

For any situated social action, there are two sorts of collective construction of the situation that are relevant to the analysis of collective behavior: perspective and the definition of the situation. The first is parametric to the second. Moreover, relative to its active origin, a definition of the situation is a variable product and aspect of collective practice. It is intertwined with available coded constructions and is subject to continual demonstration through the enactments and codes that comprise collective action. The concept of collective action ties situation to collectivitity analytically, so that situation, collectivity, and action cannot be defined independently of each other. Thus, the structure of collective action is extended in time as well as in space and in meaning. In this sense, the term "pattern of interference" signifies only that more than one episode of collective action is observed in reference to some set of items. Any plural setting is characterized by patterns of interference.

In chapter 12, it was argued that the university is a plural setting by discussing the crystallization of position-based, collectively accomplished practices on campus. The alternative description of the university as a normative organization, consensual about its institutional value for society and controlled largely by an internal normative order to which members are socialized was rejected. As a plural setting in which practices have crystallized, the university is characterized by the copresence of different collective constructions of the situation. That these constructions are also mutually exclusive is indicated by the discussion of the links between the university and society, particularly the links that engage administrators and faculty in cosmopolitan enterprises; the power structure of the university; the shifts in occupational identifications of administrators and teachers; and the practical differences in the conditions of students, faculty, and administrators.

The patterns of interference that characterize the campus as a plural and highly differentiated setting can be illustrated by reference to one of the consequences of the organization of power within the university. The distribution and character of power on campus influences the normal evaluation of student activities by nonstudents. Such evaluation is ordinarily taken to be an administrative task. Therefore, some activities outside the classroom are processed through administrative perspectives and definitions of the situation. Within these constructions students, by their position, are excluded from participation in structures having to do with managerial and institutional decisions affecting the organization of the university, its relationship with other establishments, and its overall direction. Students are enjoined to be local in the site to which they refer their activities and nonserious with regard to that site, in the sense that they are obligated to recognize their studenthood as a transitional condition—important only for its bearing on their future. This construction of the student position is not compatible with the cosmopolitan and serious perspective of those students whose practice defines the university as structurally related to society and subject to the political operations inherent in that relationship.

The various collective constructions establish social worlds of competent actors with social identities, relationships, boundaries, and plans, as well as the other features of the environment. These features of the social world are variable in reference to an actor of origin and constitute the setting of situated social action. The discussion here will focus on the perspectives within which situated social action transpires and the patterns of interference that are requisite to confrontation.

CONFRONTATION: INCIDENCE, ISSUES, AND PARTICIPATION

By the end of the decade that Boskin and Rosenstone (1969) described as a decade of protest unique in American history, the American college campus was firmly established as an arena for situated unauthorized political activity. John Naisbitt, president of the Urban Research Corporation of Chicago, reported that "major incidents of student protest occurred on 92 campuses from mid-January through March 23 of this year [1970]. Eighty-eight were reported during the same period last year" (*New York Times*, 29 March 1970), and "at least 215,000 students participated in campus protests during the first half of 1969" (Levine and Naisbitt, 1970, p. 24). Levine and Naisbitt defined protest "as an organized attempt by a student group to (1) stage a disruption of college activities or (2) make a formal set of demands of a college or university" (1970, p. 24).

Naisbitt was quoted by the *New York Times* (29 March 1970) as indicating that protest is spreading: "Of the protests this year, more than half occurred at campuses that had had no previous protests." Despite this apparent spread, unauthorized political activities were still concentrated at large, heterogeneous, elite, urban universities in the Far West, the Mideast, and the Great Lakes area, particularly in New York, Iowa, Michigan, Massachusetts, California, and Illinois. Harold Hodgkinson, project director for the research on which Naisbitt's conclusion was based, argued that data support the hypothesis that there is a relationship between campus protest and the political economy of university life:

> In support of our assessment that the high protest institution tends to be research-oriented and "on the make," in which the student is frequently lost in the struggle to acquire as much research support as possible, we cite the figure of 68 percent of the high protest institutions reporting an increased proportion of the budget based on federal support compared to 56 percent reporting such an increase in the national sample (*New York Times*, 30 May, 1970).

The findings reported by Naisbitt and Hodgkinson are consistent with those reported by Peterson (1966, 1968b) for the periods 1964 to 1965 and 1967 to 1968. Thus, from the 1964 Berkeley student revolt through 1969, unauthorized political action tended to occur at campuses that were plural settings, that is, where the differences among student, faculty, and administrative practice had become highly crystallized and intricately linked to other, parallel and inclusive establishments.

THE RELATIONSHIP BETWEEN INCIDENCE AND ISSUES

Peterson's early research on "organized student protest" showed not only that there was a relationship between the incidence of unauthorized politics and the characteristics of colleges and universities but also that this relationship varied with the primary political issue and, in addition, that at least one important characteristic of colleges and universities—size—was significantly, but not linearly, related to unauthorized student political action. With regard to issues, Peterson (1968b) listed twenty-seven separate issues of unauthorized student political action during the academic year of 1967 to 1968, which ranged from strictly local conflicts over regulations governing student conduct to the cosmopolitan issues of civil rights and the Vietnam War. He listed (1968b, p. 11) the ten most frequent issues and the percentage of deans of students who reported protests in relation to each issue (see Table 13.1). Peterson's research was based on a sample of approximately 850 accredited, four-year colleges.

Table 13.1. STUDENT PROTEST ISSUES, 1967 to 1968.

	Issue	Percentage of Deans Reporting Protest
1.	U.S. policies regarding Vietnam	38
2.	Dormitory and other living-group relations	34
3.	Civil rights	29
4.	Insufficient student participation in establishing campus policies	27
5.	On-campus recruiting by the armed services	25
6.	The draft	25
7.	Food service	25
8.	On-campus recruiting by firms or agencies such as Dow, the CIA, etc.	20
9.	Dress regulations	20
10.	Controversy surrounding a particular faculty member	20

Adapted from Peterson, 1968, p. 11.

Peterson found that, although unauthorized political action about the traditional role of students in campus governance and curriculum development grew more frequent between 1965 and 1968 (1968b, p. 39), the number of incidents of unauthorized student political action regarding the Vietnam War doubled. The overall increase was greatest in the fifty largest public universities; outside of those fifty universities, the increase was relatively independent of size. These data indicate that, at least for the years included in Peterson's study, the size of the establishment is an important factor only when a distinction is made between the very large and the not so very large colleges and universities. Size is not an important variable for predicting unauthorized political action within the population of universities and colleges as a whole (see also, Peterson, 1968a, p. 311).

Apart from size, the incidence of unauthorized politics was found to vary with the quality of the college or university as crudely measured by the proportion of faculty doctorates (see *New York Times*, 30 May 1970). Here again, the relationship between an organizational variable and unauthorized politics depended upon the particular issue. For the academic year of 1964 to 1965, for example, Peterson (1968a) found that:

> Correlations involving the faculty-doctorates dimension and the six off-campus issues ranged from .18 on the Dominican Republic situation to .43 for the Vietnam issue (p. 311).

Peterson also found that the incidence of unauthorized politics varied with the different types of campus just as it varied with specific characteristics of colleges and universities regardless of type. Again, the relationship depended upon the particular issue. For example:

Civil rights involvement was most frequently reported by the independent universities . . . . At the other extreme, about one in eight teachers' colleges reported student involvement in civil rights. A crude ranking of the eight types of student bodies in terms of civil rights activism would be: independent universities, independent liberal-arts colleges, public universities, and Catholic institutions—all standing above the "national norm"; ranged below the norm would be the public liberal-arts colleges, Protestant institutions, technical institutions, and teachers' colleges (1968a, p. 309, in reference to the period from 1964 to 1965).

But the greatest variation by institutional type, according to Peterson, was for the foreign-policy issues:

On the Vietnam issue, the incidence of organized student protest ranged from a high of 61 percent in the independent universities to 8 percent in both the Protestant and Catholic institutions and 6 percent at the teachers' colleges (1968a, p. 309).

Thus, although episodes of unauthorized student political action occurred at a large number of campuses during the 1960s, they were concentrated at certain types of colleges and universities. Moreover, the degree of this concentration depended upon whether or not the issue was local or cosmopolitan in scope. These findings, and additional findings on the social and personal characteristics of participants in unauthorized student politics, suggest that variations in the prevalence of various student perspectives may help to account for variations in the incidence of unauthorized politics. This statement is not to argue that unauthorized politics is dispositional to perspectives but, rather, that the enactment of prevailing constructions of the situation in a setting characterized by patterns of interference tends to yield points of confrontation that, in turn, may yield situated social action organized and interpreted as unauthorized politics or protest (Turner, 1970).

PARTICIPATION IN CONFRONTATION

The American Institute of Public Opinion's survey of fifty-five college campuses in 1969, found that 28 percent of the 1,030 students polled reported that they had "participated in a demonstration of some kind" (*New York Times*, 25 May 1969). The relatively large percentage of participants may reflect the generality of the question because "participation" was left undefined. But even when unspecified as to quality, degree, and timing, participation depended to some extent upon the background and orientation of the students. Thirty-one percent of the men and 24 percent of the women reported that they had demonstrated.

Characteristics of Participants. There was a tendency for demonstrators to have been over twenty years of age and to have come from the East; to have described themselves as politically independent (34 percent of the independents demonstrated) or Democrats rather than Republicans (31 percent of Democrats demonstrated compared with only 13 percent of Republicans); and to have described their ideological position as "extremely liberal" (61 percent). They often came from families with an annual income of $15,000 or more, although differences across the economic spectrum were quite small, and most were either young—freshmen and sophomore—or graduate students (41 percent of graduate students reported participating in a demonstration).

In addition to these differences, it is generally agreed that participants in unauthorized politics differed from their fellow students in terms of their major fields of academic concentration, their religious orientation, their political experience, and their family background. Those students initially involved in demonstrations tended to be more antiauthoritarian, more socially conscious, more unconventional, more intellectual, more open-minded, more egalitarian, more academically oriented, better socialized to democratic values, and academically more talented than nonparticipants (See Bay, 1967; Flacks, 1967, 1970; Keniston, 1967; Sampson, 1967; Trent and Craise, 1967; Block, et al. 1968; Skolnick, 1969; Levine and Naisbitt, 1970).

Characteristics of Episodes. Several investigations have provided information on the characteristics of the episodes of situated social action on campuses. The Skolnick report, completed by the beginning of 1969, described "confrontations arranged by students" as:

> usually more "symbolic" than "disruptive" or "destructive." Much rhetoric flows in university circles, and elsewhere, about "interference with institutional functioning." Whatever the intent of radicals, however, they have usually not been successful in disrupting the routines of most university members—until massive police formations were called to campus (p. 106).

More specific details have been offered by a report of the Urban Research Corporation on the "292 major student protests on 232 college and university campuses in the first six months of 1969" (Levine and Naisbitt, 1970, p. 24). The report listed several general findings:

> Black students were involved in more than half of all the protests
>
> Black recognition was the issue raised more than any other
>
> Issues related to the Vietnam war and the military were raised in only 22% of the protests
>
> Racially integrated protests were uncommon
>
> Violence of any kind occurred in less than one-fourth of the protests
>
> Twenty-two schools were closed temporarily as a result of protests
>
> The longer the protests, the more likely the protesters were to get demands granted (p. 24).

Changes in Student Protest. Although the overall findings regarding student protest are fairly consistent from year to year, there have been interesting changes. As Naisbitt reported, more and, presumably, different types of colleges and universities experienced protest in 1969 than in any of the preceding years. There were also differences in personnel; in the relative numbers of black students involved in incidents of organized student protest; in the number of participants; and, to some extent, in the issues of protest. Black recognition and curricula became important issues only after the Columbia revolt of 1968 and concomitant with related political developments in the black communities outside of the university. The issues of black recognition and curricula, similar to the foreign policy and domestic issues of campus protest, are evidence of the responsiveness of politically engaged students to cosmopolitan movements and the politically engaging affairs of society, such as war and racism, that the Skolnick Report (1969) called "events."

After issues were joined, the decade of the sixties saw changes in the scope of collective behavior on campus, as well as changes in the incidence of protest, the issues of protest, and the participants in protest. These changes may be described as a shift in political practice an escalation in which both students and university officials became increasingly militant, although not necessarily increasingly violent. The conclusion of the Urban Research Corporation (Levine and Naisbitt, 1970) that the militancy of the students was rarely violent during 1969 but, rather, appeared to involve a wider range of tactics than in earlier year is consistent with the analysis of student protest as political action. The Urban Research Corporation reported that of the 292 actions that occurred during the first six months of 1969, 26 percent involved strikes or seizures, 24 percent were classified as disruptive, 25 percent included sit-ins, 18 percent included boycotts; 50 percent involved rallies or demonstrations, and 13 percent involved petitions (Levine and Naisbitt, 1970, p. 147).

THE NATURE OF SUPPORT

The episodes of collective behavior did not take place in a vacuum. Nor were they always local quarrels, the interactions of combatants. They usually took place in a setting in which a variety of points of view had considerable support and opposition. The nature of support is problematic: Is support a pool of potential participants? Or is it simply a background of sympathy? Does it refer to audiences and publics who are collectively involved in the episode? Support varied with issues, tactics, constituencies, and time. Research by Olson (1968) and by Barton (1968) indicated that support is often imbedded in the local community within which collective behavior occurs; that it is quite concrete in its reference to issues, tactics, and groups; that it varies with the particular constituency tested; and that it is highly responsive to the events as they transpire.

Olson (1968) reported the results of an analysis of interviews with 154 Ann Arbor, Michigan, residents taken during 1965. The population sample as a whole was above the national average income and 50 percent were college graduates; 28 percent were over the age of 60; almost all persons interviewed were white; 46 percent considered themselves Republicans, 25 percent were Democrats, and 29 percent were independents. The sample is clearly not representative of a national population, but it may represent Ann Arbor, and it may indicate the presence of a considerable body of support for unauthorized political action near the University of Michigan. Olson measured "the perceived legitimacy of various types of social protest actions" (p. 298) by the following question:

> If a group of people in this country strongly feels that the government is treating them unfairly, what kinds of actions do you think they have a right to take in order to try to change the situation? . . . Which of these actions do you think groups have a right to take in our country? (1968, p. 298).

Table 13.2 presents the actions listed by Olson and the percentages of favorable responses.

Table 13.2. ATTITUDES TOWARD VARIOUS TYPES OF UNAUTHORIZED POLITICAL ACTION.

Type of Action	Percentage of Favorable Responses
1. Hold public meetings and rallies	92
2. March quietly and peacefully through town	70
3. Take indirect actions such as economic boycotts or picketing	60
4. Take direct actions such as strikes or sit-ins	46
5. Stage mass protest demonstrations	41
6. All five of the above are legitimate	31

Adapted from Olson, 1968, p. 299.

These findings may indicate nothing more than the types of statements individuals were apt to make during 1965, when confronted by an abstract question such as Olson's. But if these responses indicate a background of support for or tolerance of unauthorized political action, or if they represent the presence of a pool of potential participants, they raise the problem of the role of support and its relationship to the extent of participation in unauthorized political activities. Regardless of the intentions of those persons interviewed, and regardless of the personal meanings and determinants of their answers, the public expression of such attitudes may be part of the patterns of interference that are essential to the emergence of collective behavior.

Barton's (1968) research dealt with support as it developed during the course of the Columbia University crisis of 1968. During that period, five campus buildings were occupied by over 1,000 students who were subsequently dispersed by approximately 1,000 policemen. Almost 600 students were arrested, and the spring semester ended in a mixture of confusion, dismay, and enthusiasm. Barton found that 58 percent of the students and 51 percent of the faculty supported the goals of the student protestors during the 1968 crisis, although only 19 percent of the students and 10 percent of the faculty supported their tactics (p. 336). Although it is not clear how this support related to the action, the extent of the support suggests that the unauthorized political action tapped tensions that reflected underlying patterns of interference. At the same time, the findings suggest either that the political climate was not clearly in favor of the administration or that there was disapproval of certain features of Columbia's tradition of community and government relations.

Following a violent, and often brutal, police intervention (Cox, 1968, p. 142), Barton found that campus support for the tactics of the occupiers of university buildings increased siginificantly among those persons who had previously been undecided and who were present at the police action: 17 percent of faculty and 19 percent of students. The percentage increases do not exhaust the political significance of the change, however, the political significance of support for the Columbia protesters is problematic. Descriptions of the climate at the campus following the police action indicate that there may have been an increase in the intensity of the support among those who witnessed the "bust" and who were already in support of the students as well as an increase in the relationship between support and participation (see Cole and Adamsons, 1969), including, for example, cancelling of classes, attending meetings, and expressing opinions.

THE EXTENT OF PARTICIPATION

The problem of the extent of participation arises when the frequency of unauthorized political action is juxtaposed to the relatively small proportion of students reportedly engaging in such activities. Is it sufficient to describe organized student protest as the work of a small and unrepresentative minority (Lipset, 1968a, p. 45)? Is the political significance of this minority limited to their capacity to agitate among uncommitted masses of students? Peterson (1968a) stated that:

> The student movement is still a minority phenomenon. Members of the student left amount to something on the order of two percent of the national student population. An additional eight to ten percent are strongly sympathetic with the "movement for social change" and are capable of temporary activation depending on the issues. And the numbers of activist students, while not increasing spectacularly, are nevertheless rising steadily (p. 39).

Yet there is something impressive about the 28 percent reported to have participated in unauthorized political actions on campus during 1969 (American Institute of Public Opinion, New York Times, 25 May 1969). The Urban Research Corporation reported that 215,000 students participated in student protests (participation was defined more stringently in this report than in the survey of the American Institute of Public Opinion) during the first six months of 1969 (Levine and Naisbitt, 1970), although that figure constitutes only 3 percent of the national student population. If 215,000 is divided by 2,300, the number of establishments of higher education in this country, only about ninety-three students per establishment participated in student protests during that period. But if, instead, the divisor is 232, the number of campuses that experienced major protests during the first half of 1969 (Levine and Naisbitt, 1970), the number of participants in authorized political action per campus increases tenfold, to about 930 (See Cox, 1968, p. 142). Moreover, if the student population is considered to include only those who attend college during the day as regular fulltime students in nonprofessional programs, a definition that conforms to normal usage, the proportion of students who engaged in unauthorized political action on each of the 232 campuses would be still higher (see Lipset, 1968a, p. 45).

In addition to justifying the population—of which students who engaged in unauthorized political activities are a sample—and weighting sites within the academic system, there are two other problems that make it difficult to estimate the extent of participation in unauthorized student politics. The first problem has to do with the source of information and the second has to do with the definition of participation. With regard to the first, conservative estimates of participation were more likely when university administrators were the source of information than when students themselves were interviewed. Each source can be questioned. Students may translate casual interest or sympathy into participation. University officials, who are partisan and often lack independent sources of information, may speculate in the light of bias and desire. This problem is illustrated by the report of the San Francisco State College Study Team (Orrick, 1969) to the National Commission on the Causes and Prevention of Violence:

> The student newspaper, the *Daily Gater*, a strong supporter of the strike, said that class attendance was substantially reduced in the departments of economics, English, art, philosophy, and psychology, and down slightly in humanities, chemistry, music, and the school of education. The *Gater* said the strike was 40 to 50 percent successful. The administration has insisted that the *Gater* coverage of the strike has often been unreliable.
>
> Newsmen regularly assigned to the strike estimated that it was 20 to 50 percent successful at times late in the fall semester. However, this did not mean that half the students at the campus supported the strike goals and agreed with the tactics. Many were frightened, or they had no class to attend because their teachers were on strike—or afraid to teach. The most successful rallies of the students drew more than 5,000 persons, but it was difficult to separate the curious from the committed. San Francisco State College had an enrollment of about 900 Negroes in the fall semester. The administration claimed that only 100 to 200 of them supported the BSU and its demands. To many observers it appeared that the percentage of support was much higher . . . .
>
> Strike leaders were claiming in mid-November that their effort was 40 to 50 percent successful. President Smith said a majority of the classes were meeting (pp. 40-41).

The Definition of Participation. The problem of defining "participation" is even more critical than the problem of obtaining reliable information about the extent of participation. Is a participant someone who is present when confrontation erupts? If so, is it possible to specify precisely when presence at a confrontation takes place? Is a participant someone who is present at places taken to be centers of activity, or is he anyone who contributes to the various activities as they are taking place, in prospect, or even in retrospect? Because episodes take place over time and seem to have periods, does even the distinction between the event, before the event, and after the event make sense in defining participation?

Certainly it can be said that someone has participated even when he has been absent from the scene of concentrated activity and even when his complicity is indirect, peripheral, or even marginal. Participation can be enacted in a range of behavior, from moral and financial support to public expressions of approval and physical assistance. Moreover, the range probably widens as an episode develops and the political implications of various activities become increasingly articulated and intertwined. The point is that collective behavior, much less conventional political activities, cannot be understood by simply counting bodies at particularly vivid places.

Lipset and Peterson are undoubtedly correct in saying that student protest is a minority phenomenon. However, it is necessary to consider the size, political significance, and representative quality of student protest in the light of the above discussion. For the analysis of collective behavior, an examination of the social and political base of situated social action is essential. Moreover, a formal problem arises in designating those persons who participate directly in academic confrontations or unauthorized political organizations as a minority. The terms "minority" and "majority" ordinarily designate mobilized or mobilizable collectivities, that is, constituencies and not statistical aggregates. The political scientist's preference for the term "public" as opposed to the simply statistical "mass," makes the same distinction between numbers and collectivity. It is by no means correct to assume that all those who are not politically active in universities constitute a majority in the political and social sense of the term.

To make this point, it is not necessary to agree with Trent and Craise's (1967) assessment of the numerical majority of American students as apathetic and conformist (p. 34). Only reconsideration of what can be meant by the terms "student," "participant," and "majority" is needed.

It is not at all clear that unauthorized political action is unrepresentative and that its political significance is limited to agitation and force. Nor is it appropriate to consider such action representative only if it comes in the wake of a mass movement. Private and vague sentiments of distress or outrage can be mobilized by dramatic actions which come to be representative as a movement grows around them. This idea is far from the notion of easily led masses that are active for any cause that they can share with a leader.

THE PRACTICAL ORIGINS OF PERSPECTIVES

College is a different place to different people. This difference is not simply a result of variations in character or background. For example, the library is a workplace to its librarians and its custodians, but it is not the same workplace. In one case, the library is a site where the significant items include books, systems of order, fellow professionals, a reputation, and clients. In the other case, the library consist of material such as floors, windows, and lighting system components, work conditions, a class-based system of authority. The conditions and practice of work are not alike for workers in the two positions. However, those who hold similar positions within an establishment usually share a "sense" of that establishment that corresponds to a socially organized practice, a perspective that is different from the perspective of those in other positions

(Gibb, 1954, p. 894. See also Stouffer, et al., 1949; Merton and Lazarsfeld, 1950).

In general, when an organization is stratified along a dimension of dominance and when statuses are crystallized, as in the army, or in a large university, perspectives will include those features of organization that bear on the structure of social action (practice) at the various positions. This principle leads to the identification of the links between the university and society, and the organization of power on campus as critical factors in determining the perspectives held by faculty, students, and administrators. The proposition that perspectives can be significantly grounded in positions within an established organization and position-based practice has two important implications: first, a hardening of divisions between positions will usually be accompanied by sharpened differences in perspective; second, when differences bear on the structure of social action at the various positions, perspectives will ordinarily refer to those differences in position (see Speier, 1950; Seashore, 1954; Brown, 1969b).

American college students share a distinctive position. They constitute a lower order of transients in establishments in which positions and practices are highly crystallized within a rigid hierarchy of dominance and control. Students are designated but not functional members of the university and, in this respect, they are outsiders to its operations, capable of influencing the organization only by breaking its rules. They are, relative to administration, functionally strange. This position yields a perspective on the university insofar as that position provides a common organizational experience (and experience of organization) for students and to the extent to which that common experience is collectively practiced. The fact that unauthorized student political actions have been able to find support among unmobilized peers substantiates the hypothesis that those for whom studenthood becomes an issue can enact a general sense of the university that is distinctive, that is shared or accomplished with most other students, and that refers to their relative position at the university. This shared sense may be characterized as a sense of being locked into a position, that is, of being overdetermined by a status that gives its members a highly generalized social identity and at the same time deprives them of the opportunity to exercise control over the conditions of that identity. It may be associated with feelings of being tested for obedience, of being forced into an individualism by official restrictions on positionally interested organization and collective expression, or of being denied significant access to academic authority while at the same time being encouraged to participate in campus governance. To acknowledge one's position or to share a "sense of the organization" is not to acquire a perspective on the organization; it merely states the problems of position. It does not define the organization from that position by identifying ranges of significant items and specifying that they are interrelated. Formally, however, a sense of the organization is a metaperspective in that it establishes the dimensions along which different perspectives may be defined. The extent to which perspectives are defined in practice depends upon the possibility and scope of collective action within a given position.

STUDENT PERSPECTIVES

In order to arrive at a description of student perspectives, some of the literature on differences and similarities among college and university students will be reviewed. It will be argued that this literature can more aptly be used to specify perspectives than to describe "student culture," character, or personality.

A Critique of the Concept of Student Culture. Jencks and Riesman (1968) explain "the war between the generations" on campus by reference to the increased autonomy of the youth culture (p. 30) and its internal functions or content—to "resist adult pressure" (p. 46). They describe the relationship of officials to students by reference to demographic characteristics rather than to organizational characteristics. But they do not justify their assertion that the degree of autonomy of what they take to be the youth culture is greater today than during the nineteenth century (p. 30). Nor do they justify the three main assumptions of their analysis: (1) that the degree of autonomy is sufficient to account for campus conflict; (2) that this autonomous culture refers primarily to the student's relationship to officials at the university as a collectively practical matter and, thus, accounts for the content of unauthorized action; and (3) that the content of student politics is adequate described as resistance to adult pressure.

Jencks and Riesman (1968) stated:

> But there has always been such a thing as student culture; it has always had a significant effect on the individual students who came to a given college; and it has always been to some extent shaped by the mix of student types at college (p. 7).

The use of the term "culture" in this context is structural. It is intended to have theoretic import. Jencks and Riesman are referring not to the totality of student activities but to a "system" that is self-sustaining and, to some extent, reflexive, and within which individuals know themselves as students in relation to the university (p. 46). The use of the term "culture," much like the use of terms such as "style" and "national character" (Brown, 1970), often converts a simple attribution of similarity, for an observer, among individuals or their activities into a "system of action." In this way, it attributes relationships among items that fall within the boundaries of the observer's category and reifies the category by asserting a mechanism of integration. Thus, the effective use of such terms requires a specification of the observer's relation to his data, and attention to facts that substantiate the inference of structure, given the observer's relation to his data.

Student Culture as an Administrative Projection. The facts ordinarily cited to justify the structural implications of the term "culture" point to the values and associations of student life that are "manifest" within an administrative perspective. Thus, by and large, the associations that are taken to represent student culture are, traditionally, those associations sponsored or authorized by university officials or otherwise considered suitable for public display. Such associations certainly include student government, fraternities, sororities, sports, and many campus extracurricular activities. Whether membership in such association is evidence of a generic youth culture is certainly open to question. Moreover, the antiorganizational outlook ascribed to students by Jencks and Riesman (1968, p. 45) may reflect a disaffection from specific organizations and particular types of social control rather than a general value orientation. Certainly there is as much reason to believe one description as there is to believe the other In any case, an anti-organizational bias cannot distinguish students from the rest of white-collar society. If students are antiorganizational, which the authors doubt, they share the malaise attributed to many lower and middle members of large-scale organizations, a malaise apparently enforced by the role distance and coercion characteristic of bureaucracy. Such speculation, however, does not establish an integrated culture supposedly engaged in "the war between the generations." Thus, what is usually taken to be student culture appears instead to be a congerie of officially authorized or permitted organizations, activities, and appearances that are most easily accounted for by reference to official, rather than student, constructions of the situation.

The "collegiate" character of this sponsored culture is apparently at odds with some of the other currents of thought and action that have been described in reports of research on students. Jencks and Riesman (1968) noted that many students now reject the "traditional juvenile counterpart" of the "adult world of big business and bureaucracies," that is, the authorized and "formally organized extracurriculum" (p. 45). But it is not necessarily a rejection *sui generis*, nor is it necessarily an attribute of an autistic student culture. Indeed, the rejection appears to reflect a pattern of interference between the perspective of those who administer college life and who implement its traditions and those who practice college life as students. In addition, it appears to the authors that officials are not less, and are perhaps more, given to stylistic display, reaction, and generational hostility than are students.

The collegiate model of the student fits a university relatively dissociated from its surroundings, in which each person's place is securely grounded within the autonomous academic community, and in which the problems of citizenship are strictly local. If the political and economic interpenetration of the contemporary university and society has been demonstrated, then the collegiate model and its sponsored culture is an anachronism. The sponsored culture of the putative collegian is not simply at odds with stylistic traits of contemporary students, it is inconsistent with what they know about and practice at the university. Similarly, an apparent student reaction to "adult" authority may be a resistance to the continued imposition of outdated restrictions and modes of organization resulting from the university officials' failure to acknowledge changes that have taken place in the university and society. From this point of view, the relationship between students and university officials is no more than that of children to adults than is the relationship between those in controlled and controlling positions in any establishment.

Specific Concepts of Differentiation. Moving from a vaguely global concept of culture, it is necessary to examine more specific and systematic concepts of differentiation among students as well as between students and other members of the university. Some of these concepts have been provided by an investigation of the degree of student satisfaction with the curricular and extracurricular aspects of college life. Paulus (cited by Peterson, 1968b, pp. 304-6) administered the College Student Questionnaire to three types of students at Michigan State University: student government leaders; leaders of leftist political groups, including Students for a Democratic Society, the Student Non-Violent Coordinating Committee, and a local politica.! group called the Committee for Student Rights; and a sample of politically inactive students with backgrounds similar to those of the activists.

Paulus found that the activists differed sharply from the other students on two indices of satisfaction with academic life, an index of "satisfaction with administrative rules and practices" and an index of "extracurricular involve ment." First, the activists rejected the ordinary "'collegiate' brand of extra-curricular activities" and, second, they "were highly provoked by the university's posture regarding student life outside the classroom" (Peterson, 1968a, p. 305) and, second, they "were highly provoked by the university's posture regarding student life outside the classroom." However, the activists scored approximately the same as the other subjects on an index labeled "satisfaction with faculty and student-faculty relations," which Peterson interpreted as a measure of "satisfaction with the non-academic side of college life. Insofar as "satisfaction with administrative rules and practices" and "extracurricular involvement" pertains to student's attitudes toward officially sponsored student culture, the findings illustrate the difficulties entailed by the notion of student culture. They reinforce the conclusion of the authors that unauthorized student political activity does not express a culture of hostility but, rather, results from the emergence of issues and the interference of perspectives. In his review of Christopher Lasch's *The Agony of the American Left* (1969), McDermott (1969) placed this conclusion in a more general, critical context. He spoke of the:

> almost unremitting failure to perceive the current left movement in this country as a political movement per se giving expression to profound social and economic grievances. Instead Lasch . . . insists on portraying today's radicals as animated by moral or cultural (or even) generational protests only marginally related to American politics and social life (p. 797).

STUDENTS: TYPES AND TYPOLOGIES

Clark and Trow (1966) constructed an influential typology of student orientation to college. They identified four student "subcultures": vocational, academic, collegiate, and nonconformist. Peterson (1968a, pp. 293-317) expanded the scheme of Clark and Trow to eight types of students distinguished by their "dominant value commitment" and by their attitudes toward "prevailing American institutions" (p. 299): vocationalists, collegiates, ritualists, academics, intellectuals, professionalists, left-activists, and hippies. Peterson's expansion of the Clark-Trow typology was accompanied by a shift in concept from subculture to character.

According to Peterson, vocationalists are devoted to the acquisition of skills for use in later life. The vocationalist "views his college education chiefly in instrumental terms—as a means of acquiring a skill that will ensure the occupational security and social prestige that his family has lacked" (pp. 299-300). Vocationalists tend to specialize in technical fields, education, or business, and are relatively stable in their commitment to their chosen vocations. They are passive in their attitude toward learning, culturally unsophisticated, and less liberal than other types of student. "The vocationalist, in sum, is preparing himself to 'make it' within the American system, which he accepts uncritically" (pp. 300-301).

Academics are career-oriented and seriously involved in their chosen disciplines. They are relatively satisfied with college, have good study habits, are relatively liberal and sophisticated, are fairly independent of both their family and their peers, and are more likely to come from middle-class backgrounds than are vocationalists.

Collegiates are locally oriented and absorbed in the customary extra-curricular cultural and social activities of the college. They are less satisfied with school than are academics and vocationalists, although they are considerably more satisfied with it than are the nonconformists. Collegiates have fair study habits, are relatively dependent upon their peers and family, conservative, apolitical, extracurricular, unsophisticated, and conformist.

Finally, the nonconformists, a category that Peterson rejected as too general, are highly sophisticated, liberal, and independent. Their study habits are poor, and they are neither involved in local campus life nor satisfied with college. Table 13.3 presents the four student types listed by Clark and Trow and their ranks on eleven scales of the College Student Questionnaire. Each type is ranked 1, 2, 3, or 4, from high to low on each scale. The questionnaire was administered to over 120,000 American college students (Peterson, 1968a, p. 299). Clark and Trow's specification of the types as "subcultures" is problematic in that a scheme for classifying subcultures has been developed from a device for classifying individuals. There is no reason to assume that the characteristics of groups are also the characteristics of their members or that interpersonal interaction has the qualities of its component individuals. Peterson's characterological interpretation is more consistent with the data.

In addition to describing the nonconformist, academic, collegiate, and vo-cational types of Clark and Trow, Peterson included in his typology the pro-fessionalist, the ritualist, the left-activist, the intellectual, and the hippie types as a refinement of the Clark-Trow scheme.

The professionalist is conservative, is accepting of American institutions, is achievement oriented, and is "born of upper-middle-class and professional parents" (p. 301). He "aspires to much the same life pattern as his highly successful father—achievement, expertise, *noblesse oblige*" (p. 301).

Ritualists are distinguished by a "lack of commitment to anything" (p. 302). The ritualist is oriented toward home rather than the campus, tends to be an isolate, is apolitical, and has little interest in the college environment.

The left-activist is committed "to personal involvement in action directed at reforming some facet of American life . . ." (p. 303). Left-activists tend to have "noncareer-oriented academic interests" centered largely in the social sciences and humanities.

Intellectuals are similar in many respects to the left-activists and to the academics. However, their interests are not specific to a discipline. They are individualistic, liberal, aesthetically sensitive, and probably are critical in their attitude toward dominant American institutions.

Table 13.3. CLARK-TROW STUDENT TYPES.

	Scales	Vocationalists	Collegiates	Academics	Nonconformists
1.	Satisfaction with faculty	2	3	1	4
2.	Satisfaction with administration	1	3	2	4
3.	Satisfaction with major field	1	3	2	4
4.	Satisfaction with students	2	3	1	4
5.	Study habits	2	3	1	4
6.	Extracurricular activities	3	1	2	4
7.	Family independence	3	4	2	1
8.	Peer independence	3	4	2	1
9.	Liberalism	4	3	2	1
10.	Social conscience	4	3	1	2
11.	Cultural sophistication	4	3	2	1

Adapted from Peterson, 1968a, p. 300.

In Peterson's view, hippies are estranged "from American values and institutions . . ." (p. 303). They are apolitical and tend to reject the usual student roles and sponsored culture.

Peterson's descriptions of those types not included in the typology of Clark and Trow are, as he admitted, "largely inferential and speculative." Their plausibility lies more in the fact that the labels evoke culturally available responses, or stereotypes, than in the degree to which they fit available information. The major dimension along which Peterson classified his eight types, "stance vis-a-vis American institutions" (p. 299) indicates his purpose: to demonstrate the "diversity in student characteristics" in order to account for the emergence of a student political left in America during the 1960s. The weakness of this program lies in its assumptions that student activism can be explained by describing student activists and that action directly reflects character—activists are active, and activism is the action of activists.

Peterson's classification is an improvement over the Clark-Trow typology insofar as it distinguished career-minded academics from humanistic intellectuals, and identified various kinds of nonconformity. However, aside from the difficulties entailed by the emphasis on character, there are several reasons for the failure of Peterson's classification as a genuine typology in which the types are defined as the intersection of a number of canonical dimensions. First, it is not at all clear that Peterson's types can be distinguished by their position on the dimension of "stance vis-a-vis American institutions," nor is it clear that "dominant value commitment" (p. 299) is a dimension on which observations can be ordered. Both the left-activists and the hippies are said to reject American institutions to the same degree, but the differences between their dominant value commitments do not seem to be of the same sort as the differences in value commitment between the vocationalists and professionalists, both of whom are said to accept American institutions to the same degree. Peterson has presented a list of value commitments without specifying the dimension or dimensions that underly the list and, thus, has not provided a basis for distinguishing and comparing various commitments.

The second difficulty with this typology is that there is some ambiguity in Peterson's descriptions of his two types of nonconformists—left-activists and hippies—that suggests a failure to separate, adequately, observation from expectation. On the one hand, left-activists are described as rejecting the very institutions that they hope to reform. Similarly, the cohesion implied by Peterson's acceptance of Keniston's (1967) description of the hippies as constituting "a kind of hidden underground" is not apparently consistent with the characterization of them as "pessimistically apolitical" (p. 303). (See Brown, 1969a, for a different characterization of hippies.)

The third problem involves Peterson's insistence on the importance of the psychological variable he called value commitment, which suggests that disposition is the real basis for his classification of students. He does not adequately acknowledge the participatory bases of action and the experiential and practical bases of participation. Moreover, this idea of value commitment bypasses the organizational bases of constructions of the situation by its implication that the various student outlooks enter college with the individual, which ignores the possibility that outlooks may originate within the structure of the establishment.

The use of the concept value commitment suggests that only activists can be mobilized for collective behavior. It also implies that protest takes place largely because of the massing of activists. Individual characteristics, including disposition, may help to explain the presence of certain individuals at the various sites and collectivities on a campus, but they do not account for the availability of those sites and collectivities that are organizationally disposed toward unauthorized action. Nor do dispositions account for the activities of an individual who is a participant. The social forces surrounding a participant at a given site and in a given assembly must be examined in order to understand his participation in situated social action. The aggression of armies cannot be explained in terms of the aggression of soldiers. A soldier may do violence, but his violent activities are determined more by the collectively practical facts of membership than by his initial dispositions or intentions to do violence.

The reversion to a psychological explanation of student protest indicates that something was lost in Peterson's translation of the Clark-Trow typology. The Clark-Trow "subcultures" may have been more to the point than Peterson's "dominant value commitment" and more useful for the understanding of collective behavior on campus than Peterson's classification of students based on character. Instead of being refined and extended, the theoretical emphasis on subculture—and thus on the collective base of student orientation—was sacrificed to methodological expediency. Rather than attempting to find a basis for classifying subcultures by reference to the university and the conditions of student life, Peterson classified students or, more precisely, the responses of individuals to questions. Thus, Peterson is forced into the view that the student political activities of the 1960s were expressions of individually prior value commitments and, therefore, were alien to the college as an establishment. Nevertheless, if his scheme is taken as an exploratory outline of differences in prevailing outlooks of students, it may be possible to rearrange his descriptions along the dimensions of a genuine typology of student perspectives.

The earlier suggestion that students are transient lower members—by designation—of the university implies that the various student perspectives on the university can be described by a limited set of dimensions that reflect the practical articulation of position. Each attribute of position is problematic and each is, on occasion, a reflexive aspect of a collective practice. For example, as transients, students may take their temporary status seriously, or they may take it as a momentary interruption—essential but not the main point—of the business of life. As designated lower members of an establishment, students may handle the disabilities of dependency, impotence, and subordination by stressing their membership in inclusive systems—for example, the imperatives of citizenship may dominate the imperatives of studenthood. Thus, students' perspectives are responsive to their condition as students, and are specified both in terms of a site for which they are taken as actors and as a practical relationship to that site.

Before adapting Peterson's classifcation to the analysis of student perspectives, it is worthwhile to inquire whether or not all of his categories refer to students in the organizational sense of the term. At least two of the categories do not seem adequate as labels for student outlook: the estrangement of the hippies and the privatization of ritualists removes these two as participants in social action on campus. Neither qualifies as an actor within the settings of collective action for students. All the other categories listed by Peterson are potential interactants and are situated within the academic establishment as a matter of practice. Thus, the problem of classification can be simplified by eliminating those two categories as not referring to genuine constituencies—that is, students in the organizational sense of the term—although it should not be assumed that the authors accept Peterson's characterization of hippies or ritualists as an accurate portrayal of observable types.

The remaining categories appear to be distinguished by two factors: the site in which student activities are accountable as collective action—*local* or *cosmopolitan*—and the collectively accomplished quality of involvement that reflects a practical relation to that site—*serious* or *nonserious*. The academics, collegiates, and vocationalists appear distinctively local in their site of accountability as compared with the cosmopolitanism of the intellectuals, left-activists, and professionalists. The academics are oriented within their disciplines as those disciplines are enacted departmentally and within the confines of particular campuses. The vocationalists are largely concerned with the local routines and requirements of their apprenticeship rather than with the cultivation of their discipline and a sense of mission. The collegiates, operating within the officially sponsored student culture, enact their localism by participating in whatever extracurricular activities are officially sponsored on the local campus. The cosmopolitanism of the professionalists, intellectuals, and left-activists is reflected in their assimilation of student practice to a career, to an historic discipline, and to contemporary society, respectively.

Equally significant differences appear when the quality of involvement of academics, intellectuals, and left-activists is compared with that of collegiates, vocationalists, and professionalists. The former groups are serious in their practice—Goffman would say that they are, as a rule, spontaneously involved. The latter groups tend to be role-distant or practice-conscious. In this sense, studenthood is not serious for them, although it is consequential: they accept their position as transients and work within that position as its practice is officially implemented.

A distinction need not be made between the collegiate and the vocationalist for the purpose of establishing a typology that specifies active campus constituencies. If the two dimensions discussed are sufficient to describe student perspectives, and if student perspectives are critical elements in an explanation of unauthorized political action, then it is sufficient to note that both vocationalists and collegiates share a perspective entirely consistent with the limits of transient lower membership. Similarly, intellectuals and left-activists share the perspective of serious actors within a cosmopolitan site. Later, it will be apparent that the differences between collegiates and vocationalists and between intellectuals and left-activists are not differences in perspective but differences of a lower logical order, specifically, in their definitions of the situation.

A TYPOLOGY OF STUDENT PERSPECTIVES

A perspective is a point of view. It is often thought of as a personal trait or as an idiosyncratic version of an objective situation. But the distinction between a priori and ad hoc constructions of the situation, and the discussion of the importance of that distinction for the analysis of situated social action, requires a different use of the term. Perspective can be treated as a collective trait that is linked to organizational position. As such, for an observer, it refers to the location of an actor of origin (a collectivity) in relation to a specific range of items, the significances of which are, by virtue of that location, stable throughout the range.

The authors are concerned primarily with the availability of perspectives within organizations rather than with their origins or their special appeal to or construction by special persons. The interest is in their organizational sources and their consequences for the collective actions for which they constitute limits of accountability. The indentification of perspectives as collective constructions of the situation implies that perspectives appear as relatively exclusive constructive options imbedded in collectively accomplished practice. Thus, that students shift from one perspective to another over their academic career does not imply that perspectives change but only that personnel may change for a given practice over a period of time. During episodes of situated social action, individuals tend to be stable in their participation although the bases for participation may shift as precipitating incidents occur. This way of describing constructions of the situation allows consideration of collective behavior in terms of such concepts as mobilization rather than as an expression of individual disposition within a mass.

POLITICAL CONSEQUENCES OF PERSPECTIVES

The political consequences of perspectives arise because perspectives locate conditions of life by pinning them to positions and collectively accomplished practices within an establishment that is taken as either extended or nuclear. Perspectives establish context and settings for situated social action. They make it possible to identify the components of social structure and to select action by limiting what will be taken as settings for action. A perspective binds a social reality within a range of identities, goals, means, places, and potential interactants. Concomitantly, it implies the presence of locale-specific influences and values. Thus, it is the most general map of a social world available to an actor; and it is available by virtue of its collective enactment—an individual normally takes a perspective by virtue of his participation in collective practice. In this sense, perspectives are the most general type of "rules" of irrelevance (see chap. 8); what they exclude is more important than what they include as relevant for social action.

Insofar as perspectives are embodied in collective action, they are inescapable for members of the collectivity. In fact, it is appropriate to say that perspectives define the limits of intelligibility for action within a collectivity, which they do by establishing the member's site and how he is to be there—his mode of involvement in a practice. Perspectives do not establish the specific components of settings, the identity of the site as a social place, nor the precise activities of the actor of origin and its members. The location, or site, and the quality of involvement taken as normal and, therefore, consistent with practice for that location are analytically sufficient dimensions for the specification of perspectives.

Location. Location consists of a boundary that limits what are taken as the social facts of a situation. (Although the terms location, site, and place have been previously used, each refers to a different aspect of the situation. Location is a boundary; site is the collection of items available for public consideration at a location; and place is the social identity of a site as that identity is determined within establishments that include the actor of origin. The distinction is not a satisfying one, nor has it been invariably conformed to. However, it has a heuristic value at this point in the development of theory.) When an individual's position is defined by reference to the nuclear establishment in which he is formally designated a member by reference to a rule of inclusion, the site of membership is considered to be local. When his position is defined by reference to an extended establishment that includes the nuclear, the site of membership is cosmopolitan. For example, employees who act as if their position is part of a wider membership are engaged in a practice at a cosmopolitan, rather than simply a local, site. Their local activities are subjected to standards that are applicable to citizens, workers, professionals, and others, as well as to employees. There is evidence from studies of establishments other than college that these two constructions of site are mutually exclusive for the situations to which they refer (Brown, 1969b).

Quality of Involvement. The quality of involvement taken as normal or natural within a site places actors in a particular relationship to other actors and to events. As a matter of practice, involvement may be serious or it may be nonserious. If it is the former, members are properly *engaged* or, at least, vulnerable to the challenges of their settings. If the quality of involvement is nonserious, members are properly *role-distant* or *practice-conscious* in the ways in which tourists and conformists are distant from their performances. For the nonserious student, college is a place of passage rather than a place in which one takes on meaning for others and accomplishes social identity. For the nonserious, middle-range executive, his position is a temporary disability, a momentary step in the acquisition of ideal status, wealth, or security. It is possible to get the "flavor" of nonseriousness by noticing the terms associated with it: behavior rather than action, ground rather than figure, transition rather than presence, ritualism rather than participation, inauthenticity rather than authenticity, extrinsic motivation rather than intrinsic motivation, manipulation rather than responsiveness. In this connection, Friedenberg (1969) has pointed out that students are often enjoined to be nonserious: "Students are not paid for attending school; they are held to be investing in their future . . ." (p. 36). In this sense, college is at best an investment and at worst a trial. Similarly, during a speech at the Colorado Conference on World Affairs in 1968, Leslie Claude Green, professor of political science at the University of Alberta, speaking to a large audience of students, stated less delicately: "If you think that this [college] is the *real* world, you're in trouble." Parsons (1968) has given the injunction formal status within his model of the university. He asserted that the limited decentralization that allows college to function as an academic community "implies that a particularly important location of the student's autonomy must lie in his relations to his instructors *taken individually*" (p. 186, italics added).

FOUR TYPES OF STUDENT PERSPECTIVE

The two dimensions discussed—site and quality of involvement—yield four types of student perspective, as presented in Table 13.4.

The Customary Perspective. The customary perspective yields a practice and collective action that is strictly local in its objects, interactants, and standards. Its participants take their studenthood as transitory and college as an insulated, nonfateful site. The links between college and society are not acknowledged within customary definitions of the situation. Thus, the experience of college is discontinuous with life experience, as rehearsal is discontinuous with the play or as an introduction is discontinuous with the conversation.

Within the customary perspective, the context of collective action is the formal structure of the nuclear organization. Because this structure affects students largely in terms of control, the parameters of collective action have to do with academic authority, as in the case of Peterson's vocationalists, and managerial authority, as in the case of the collegiates. Violations of routine, jurisdiction, and conventional authority are capable of precipitating collective behavior when those violations are processed through the assemblies that accomplish the customary perspective on the university.

Because college is not serious, and because it is nonfateful, the relationship between the statements made by customary students and their on-site activities is probably weaker than the relationship between the statements and on-site activities of students who share the other perspectives. Because statements are, among other things, situated activities, and because the situated activities of customary students are conventional, their statements about their attitudes toward college are likely to be conventional rather than directly responsive to their condition, their collectivities, or their intentions. This consideration suggests that it is not adequate to compare students sharing different perspectives by reference to survey data alone.

Table 13.4. A TYPOLOGY OF STUDENT PERSPECTIVES.

		Site			
		Local		Cosmopolitan	
	Nonserious	(A.)	Customary	(B.)	Traditional
Quality of Involvement	Serious	(C.)	Responsive	(D.)	Engaged

The Traditional Perspective. The traditional perspective yields collective action that is cosmopolitan in its objects, interactants, and standards. Student-hood is transitory and college is a site of passage. The links between college and society are acknowledged within the limits of the functional relevance of college to students who share the traditional perspective. From this perspective, the function of college is not simply training for a vocation but developing values and attitudes consistent with the values and attitudes associated with a student's chosen career. Thus, college is the initial stage of a career rather than a preliminary to a vocation.

Within the traditional perspective, the context of collective action is the extended organization—those aspects of society, including college, that determine the outlines of a career. The student is a client rather than a child, and he sees the college primarily as a service organization whose obligation is to introduce him to a career by providing preprofessional practice, including facilities for learning, models of professionalism, and temporary relief from the social pressures of childhood, which would divide loyalty, and adulthood, which would bypass adequate preparation for professional practice. This obligation includes both the preservation of the status quo (identified with expertise), and the development of the plant. When a college fails in its traditional obligations, students who share the traditional perspective may change to another school or may exaggerate their specialization within the available curriculum. When, however, such failures are processed through assemblies within which the traditional perspective is a matter of practice, such students may participate in collective behavior directed against college officials and official practices.

The politics of traditional students is not simply reactive; they might be called slow progressives. Neither the customary nor the traditional perspective imposes a generalized practice and a generalized social identity on students. For the traditionalist, studenthood is a stage of a career and social identity is framed by that career rather than by any of its stages.

The Responsive Perspective. The responsive perspective yields collective action that is local in its objects, interactants, and standards. Its participants take their studenthood as serious and as conferring a generalized social identity on them. The links between college and society are not acknowledged within responsive definitions of the situation. The experience of college is discontinuous with other life experiences in the sense that working for the telephone company is exclusive of working for a department store, or playing chess at a particular time is exclusive of building a cabinet at that time.

Within the responsive perspective, the context of collective action is the formal structure of the nuclear organization skewed in the direction of the academic and the inclusively local rather than in the direction of the managerial and particular, included groups. Students who share this perspective often work for the college newspaper, are active in student government, or play prominent roles in student activities in general. The quality of their involvement includes a political practice regarding their campus that claims a limited jurisdiction over the establishment. College is an organization defined less by its structural and institutional characteristics than by the mechanical solidarity that underlies its community.

Collective action takes place within the limits of authorized student jurisdiction, processes that define the proper relationship of students to nonstudents, and the individualized politics that characterizes a liberal community. Students who share the responsive perspective, as a matter of collectively accomplished practice, may engage in collective behavior when the jurisdiction claimed by participants in responsive practice is put into question by administrative favoritism; when that jurisdiction remains stable and fails to enlarge; when due process is violated by faculty or administration; or when events occur that are inconsistent with community, such as the firing of a popular teacher.

The Engaged Perspective. The engaged perspective yields collective action that is cosmopolitan in its objects, interactants, and standards. Its participants take their position as students seriously, as conferring a social identity on them, and as qualifying their participation in the larger society. College is defined largely in terms of its institutional characteristics—its links to the rest of society—and its internal life is subject to cosmopolitan standards. In other words, college is a setting where cosmopolitan movements and issues are of immediate local concern.

The relationship between college and society for the student is analogous, within the engaged perspective, to the relationship between the city and the state in which it is located, for the city resident. Because of this relationship, definitions of the situation will include facts pertinent to the inclusive establishments, and activities on the campus will be responsive to the cultural, social, economic, and political life of the society.

Students who share the engaged perspective within active assemblies can be mobilized by events that deny the links between society and the university, that deny the relevance of societal issues on the campus, or that deny the opportunity for students to be collectively serious within the site of this practce. Thus, some student protest must be seen simply as an active extension of the engaged perspective—not collective behavior but collective action—and other protests must be seen as situated social action produced by official acts that are entirely inconsistent with an engaged perspective of the university. Because, as has been pointed out (Keniston, 1967), students who share the engaged perspective are likely to be academically talented, intellectual, open-minded, and humane and, thus, represent what has been taken by many educators to be an ideal for college students in general (Sampson, 1967), it may be in the confrontation between the engaged student perspective and the modern administrative perspective that the significance of patterns of interference for collective behavior can most clearly be seen.

In Table 13.4 the labels in the four cells describe the limits of participation under the standard conditions of everyday life—in other words, within a collectively accomplished practice (Berger and Luckmann, 1967). Given the previously discussed modifications of Peterson's classification, each of his described types can be placed (reclassified) within one of the cells in Table 13.4. Cell A includes both the collegiates and the vocationalists, cell B includes the professionalists, the academics fall within cell C, and the left-activists and the intellectuals fall within cell D.

RESEARCH ON STUDENT PARTICIPATION

There is still something appealing about including left-activists in a typology that purports to be useful for the analysis of academic confrontation and collective behavior on campus during the 1960s. However, from Peterson's description, it appears that left-activists are more accurately characterized as mobilized intellectuals than as a separate and dispositionally volatile type. Most of the research done during the late 1960s on students who had been arrested following demonstrations on campus or who admitted to regular participation in leftist political organizations supports this characterization of left-activists. Trent and Craise (1967) summarized some of the research that was available by the time Peterson formulated his classification:

> For example, research by Heist (1965), Somers (1965), and Watts and Whittaker (1965) showed that the students in Berkeley's Free Speech Movement at the University of California were exceptionally high in measured intellectual disposition, autonomy, flexibility and liberalism, as well as in level of ability, and that they exhibited marked qualities of individuality, social commitment and intellectuality not observed among

more representative samples of college students. They were, in fact, atypical Berkeley students and represented some of the University's most able and intellectually dedicated students" (p. 39).

The import of this research (see also, Block, Haan, and Smith, 1968) can be seen more clearly by looking at a particular study. Flacks (1967) intensively interviewed a small sample of "activists" and "nonactivists" at the University of Chicago in 1966. He observed how activists differed from nonactivists on four values: romanticism, intellectualism, humanitarianism, and moralism. Romanticism was defined as a concern with aesthetic experience and the "realm of feeling," intellectualism as a "concern with ideas" and an "appreciation of theory and knowledge," humanitarianism as a "concern with plight of others" and "particular sensitivity to the deprived position of the disadvantaged," and moralism as a conventional "opposition to impulsive or spontaneous behavior" and a "reliance on a set of external and inflexible rules to govern moral behavior." Each "value pattern" represented at least ten items coded from the interview protocols. Table 13.5 presents the percentage of each sample scoring high, medium, and low on each value pattern.

Table 13.5. ACTIVISTS AND NONACTIVISTS: DIFFERENCES IN SELECTED VALUES.

	Activists (percentage)	Nonactivists (percentage)
Romanticism		
High	35	11
Medium	47	49
Low	18	40
Intellectualism		
High	32	3
Medium	65	57
Low	3	40
Humanitarianism		
High	35	0
Medium	47	22
Low	18	78
Moralism		
High	6	54
Medium	53	35
Low	41	11
Number of students interviewed	34	37

Adapted from FLACKS, 1967, p. 69.

The problem of the relatively small sample recedes, to some extent, in the face of the sharpness of the differences and the method employed by Flacks. In addition, these results are consistent with those of larger surveys. By 1970, Keniston felt confident enough of the results of research on politically active students (leftists) to say:

One study of several hundred American colleges and universities showed that about 90 percent of all protests involving the war in Southeast Asia could have been predicted simply by knowing the characteristics of the student body. Students who mark "none" for religion, have high IQs, are intellectually oriented and politically liberal, and who come from educated professional families are likely to "cause trouble," especially if you put a lot of them on one campus. In short, Harvard . . . .

Studies of the psychological characteristics of "protest-prone" students merely amplify the Harvard profile. Compared with their inactive classmates, protesters turn out to be more independent, more free thinking, less conventional. The vulgar theories of student neuroticism, Oedipal rebellion, boredom, paranoia, hedonism, or family permissiveness as causes of protest all prove to be wrong. But the cliche about student activists being "idealistic" is empirically correct: differences in "level of moral reasoning" distinguish protesters from nonprotesters more decisively than any other variable, with the protesters being greatly more "principled" and less "conventional" (p. 6-10).

Apart from Keniston's conceptualization of the findings in individually dispositional terms, the research clearly indicates that the left-activists display the traits usually associated with intellectualism, as described by Peterson, except for the fact that they are mobilized for unauthorized political action, and their collective practice is likely to include a political practice. Thus, it does not seem profitable to distinguish left-activists from intellectuals. Instead, activism appears to be what certain students do rather than what they are, and there is no need to restrict the engaged cell (cell D) of Table 13.4 to left-oriented students. Furthermore, it is only in relatively advanced stages of wide-spread political mobilization that activists may emerge as a distinct type.

This discussion suggests that unauthorized political action is neither the activity of a particular type of student nor is it an expression of a hostile youth culture, but it is situated social action—collective behavior—limited by perspectives on the university. As such, it can occur within any of the four perspectives that have been described. Each perspective, as a matter of collectively accomplished practice, posits the conditions of its own disruption; each is limited in its capacity to exclude or transform potentially intrusive items or events and therefore is, limited in its capacity to resist the precipitation of the collective action within which each perspective is shared. This conclusion depends upon the adequacy of a perspectival basis (rather than a culturological or characterological basis) for classifying collective action, the logical statuses of perspective and practice in the analysis of situated social action, and the logic of precipitation characterized as confrontation.

As the issues of the larger society become more visible and contribute to the formation of political movements outside of the campus, and as the university becomes increasingly tied to the official sectors of society, it is to be expected that the engaged perspective will be shared by a greater number of students and the customary will recede in importance. Whether or not these shifts will lead to more collective behavior on campus concerning cosmopolitan issues depends upon, among other things, the degree to which there are changes in official perspectives; the extent to which official coercion and other techniques of control prevent the collective expression of a serious involvement with student life and the organization of engaged students for collective action; the degree to which the university appears to be representative of its inclusive systems or of minor importance in the life of the society; and the extent to which an ethos of service can professionalize the engaged students and thereby neutralize their political potential. What seems more likely is the eventual elaboration and articulation of patterns of interference between faculty and administration, and between administration and other student perspectives, as a consequence of the trends described in chapter 12. The future of the university then, is expected to be a future of conflict in which opposing parties will be more widely representative, and in which conflict will assume the forms that characterize institutional crises in American society.

UNIT IV: SUMMARY AND CONCLUSIONS

Links between the university and external establishments made student life reflexively societal—"society" had become an accountable feature of student practice. As a result, that practice increasingly referred to both authorized and unauthorized cosmopolitan politics. Specifically, the unauthorized political activities of students during the late 1950s and throughout the 1960s were part of larger unauthorized movements in support of civil rights and against militarism, repression, and economic and political exploitation.

The timing and organization of collective behavior on campuses depended upon patterns of interference among distinct and naturally competing parties to the university. A number of factors contributed to the formation and articulation of these patterns of interference. Among these were the gradual crystallization of positions; the separation of managerial and academic authority; a distribution of power on campuses in favor of administration; and the cosmopolitanization of administrative and faculty practice. The decisive facts for students were their own imbeddedness in the cosmopolitan structures that gave moral, political, and economic dimension to their lives and their collective dislocation from the power, interests, initiatives, and moral claims that governed their lives—that is, their quality as "object" for the administrators who managed them and the faculty whose work excluded them.

To examine unauthorized student political activities without reference to the structures in which they occurred encourages an emphasis on spurious determinants, such as youth, leisure, a failure of communication, extended adolescence, character, or a failure of the university to provide the models necessary for fulfilling its putative function as an agency of socialization. Moreover, such an examination encourages distinctions between student political activities and the political activities of other protesting groups. This distinction would require special explanations for "student revolt" that are consistent with neither the recent developments in the study of collective behavior nor the available evidence.

Jencks and Riesman (1968), for example, conceive of the conflicts between students and administration and faculty as hostile projections of impatient young people. They attribute this impatience to an extension of adolescence "both back into what was once childhood and forward into what was once adulthood" (p. 47) and to a critical generational discontinuity between the young and the wise within the contemporary academy. They remarked that:

> the academic profession is at least as elitist and exclusive as the American professional norm. This makes it in some ways very unsuited to the socialization of young people, who are by definition outside the charmed circle. While some students nonetheless identify with their professors, the majority cannot afford to take the professorial model too seriously, for they have no reason to think they could approximate it if they tired (1968, p. 45).

Nor, it might be added, is the intellectual, moral, or cultural superiority of the professorial model any longer obvious (Landers and Cicarelli, 1970).

Views that emphasize psychological processes in order to account for dissent, protest, opposition, hostility, or revolt have been criticized. The present analysis of the university indicates that the structures of the establishment can account for many of the attributes and interactions of its parties. The authors do not agree with the generational accounts of unauthorized student political action which assert that these activities differ in principle from the unauthorized political activities of other dissenting, protesting, and resisting groups throughout history (Rude, 1964). In descriptions of student protest, whether by Feuer, Lipset, or Jencks and Riesman, no evidence whatsoever can be found to support the idea that student political actions are different in principle from the unauthorized actions of other unofficial political assemblies (see, for example, Waskow, 1967, p. 226n). It is not age that makes students revolt, nor is it a failure of their elders to teach them good manners or to provide models for identification. Rather, it is the circumstances that locate and give structure to their lives. The generational explanation must be understood as an expression of both an administrative perspective on the university and a cosmopolitan practice of academic personnel.

The interactions between students and their faculty and administration are by no means usually, or even often, collectively hostile; they are, however, almost always uneasy. The rarity of collective behavior on the part of students does not mean that patterns of interference do not exist, only that confrontation has been temporarily avoided or that there is no collective base from which points of confrontation can be made articulate for collective behavior. The same can be said about faculty in its relationship to administration.

Challenges to the conventional structure and rhetoric of academic practice, and shifts in occupational identity brought about by, among other things, the ascendance of the public university, unionization, and civil service status have created considerable ambivalence and occupational alienation among university teachers. Needless to say, those teachers who display this alienation as a serious (practical) matter tend to be cut from the corps of academic workers or isolated from their assemblies. The conception of the meritocratic scholar who shares ideas in an open forum is not, if it has ever been, consistent with the structure of contemporary academic practice. Job security, heavy research, and the universalism of a union contract are not consistent with meritocratic and laissez faire notions of academic professionalism and scholarship. Moreover, the fact that collective bargaining and the imperatives of civil service place negotiations for faculty positions in the realm of power politics creates a vital relationship between the academy and the rest of society and irrevocably implicates the university in the processes of state and national politics and government.

The professor in the contemporary American university is an employee, above all. Even his professional activities depend upon his continued employment by a university, a fact that Jencks and Riesman (1968) failed to give sufficient importance in their discussion of the "professorial model." The justification for professorial work depends less upon the relation of that work to a discipline than upon its relation to university management, the operations of extra-academic establishments, and the requirements of professional associations (Mills, 1951; Goodman, 1968; Marcuse, 1968; Lazarsfeld, et al, 1967).

The client model of the student, so common a decade ago, was an early expression of trends within the academic enterprise that now include the occupational changes that threaten traditional accounts of faculty practice. The ambivalence and alienation that characteristically accompany such developments have had serious implications for the involvement of faculty in the affairs of the university, for the relative slowness with which faculty organizations have grown, for the weaknesses of such organizations, for shifts in the balance of power on campuses, and for the willingness of faculty to acquiesce to administrative policy during campus confrontations.

For students, the articulation of points of confrontation depended upon a number of things: the presence of small political associations that constituted plausible centers of comprehension and action; the structural revelations that occurred as administrative personnel enacted their own constructions of the differences between students and administration; a cosmopolitanization of the university that bypassed the cosmopolitan aspects of student life; the emergence of issues in the larger society and the consolidation of criticism around an undergroup perspective on society; and the gradual collective dislocation of students from the institutions of the academy—the erosion of student government and the fraternity and sorority systems and the decline of sports.

The most important factor contributing to a leftist student movement was the continual demonstration of administrative power within the university setting. Other issues provoked complaint, but the issue of power addressed the collective capacity of students. Consequently, it was the only issue that could provide even temporary coalition among student assemblies and, at the same time, focus on the structural basis of the student condition.

The issue of power polarizes unequal assemblies along highly general lines. In addition, it asserts a relationship between the products and operations of an establishment and the structure of the establishment. Power is the initiating element of a political consciousness within an undergroup perspective. It is from that topical base that radical analysis proceeds to elaborate an identity of interest among undergroups, the necessity for undergroup initiative in promoting social change, the relevance of the cosmopolitan setting of local affairs to the disposition of those affairs, and the positional basis of the particular interests and practices that are decisive in establishing the overall directions of an establishment.

Single issue protests address their topics as arbitrary products or incidents of society. For example, early protests against the United States invasion of Indo-China treated the war as an administrative error rather than as, with poverty and racism, a projection of the structural imperatives of American capitalism. Because it does not address itself to structure, single issue protest is readily converted to participation in or support of the very structures that gave rise to the events about which people protested in the first place. Radical criticism develops as a collective construction of the situation only when those in power threaten the collective potential of undergroups for whom topics of collective protest already exist. Moreover, the effect of this threat is not to shift the *attitudes* of the assembled members of undergroups but, rather, to articulate gross internal differences that ultimately precipitate radical and conservative realignments.

The impact of the issue of power on the development of student movements as part of larger movements is illustrated by the relationship of early manifestoes and political actions to later political activities. Many of the early manifestoes articulated positions that focused on moral and cultural values and the opportunities for societal reform (Newfield, 1967; Long, 1969; Lothstein, 1971). The 1961 Port Huron Statement of the Students for a Democratic Society (SDS), the most prominent of the "new left" campus organizations of the 1960s begins:

> We are people of this generation, bred in at least modest comfort, housed in universities, looking uncomfortably to the world we inherit . . . . We ourselves are imbued with urgency, yet the message of our society is that there is no viable alternative to the present . . . . The search for truly democratic alternatives to the present, and a commitment to social experimentation with them, is a worthy and fulfilling human enterprise, one which moves us and, we hope, others today . . . . Today, for us, not even the liberal and socialist preachments of the past seem adequate to the forms of the present . . . . Subjective apathy is encouraged by the objective American situation—the actual separation of people from power, from relevant knowledge, from pinnacles of decision-making . . . .
>
> The first effort, then, should be to state a vision; what is the perimeter of human possibility in this epoch? . . . The second effort, if we are to be politically responsible, is to evaluate the prospects for obtaining at least a substantial part of that vision in our epoch. What are the social forces that exist, or that must exist, if we are to be successful? And what role have we ourselves to play as a social force?

The SDS manifesto reflected the spirit of the Freedom Rides of 1961 (Waskow, 1967). It also reflected the outlaw consciousness of the 1950s, the decade that established the existential basis of the "new left," a radical culture, and a principled rejection of corporate capitalism (Newfield, 1967; Oglesby, 1967; Nuttall, 1968). Events gradually forced new leftists to see American society in terms of the growing distance between classes. The ecological isolation and concentration of black people, the erosion of opportunities for individuals to move across class lines, the war against Indo-China, militarism, and the development of a national secret police (Miller, 1971) were factors that challenged both the prevailing notions of solidarity as the basis of social organization in American society and "system" as an adequate model of social control (see also, *New York Times*, 28 June 1970, article entitled "Federal Computers Amass Files on Suspect Citizens"). The recognition that much that had passed for theory and "objective" analysis was, in effect, ideological work in support of ruling interests was seen as an instance of a more general epestemological view of the interpenetration of theory and practice, and of politics, work, education, and life. This epistemology, in turn, gave still greater intellectual impetus to the development of analyses of social change that focused on undergroup struggle rather than on elite initiative. (For an example of the traditional American sociological emphasis on elite initiative as the mechanism of social change, see Moore [1963]).

The experience of protesters in the South against legal segregation, in the North against more subtle forms of repression and exploitation as well as war, and on the campuses often turned single issue protests that envisioned negotiation into hard opposition when the actions of officials demonstrated the emphasis on power characteristic of official definitions of the situation. A political practice developed out of this experience, and with it emerged paradigms by which American society came to be known as well as new ways of describing the products of that society:

> The civil rights movement came to be known as a struggle against racism, which, in turn, was seen as a source of divisiveness among undergroups that operated in the interest of the ruling class.
>
> Government was identified with the military-industrial complex.
>
> United States involvements abroad were viewed as extensions of empire.
>
> Poverty was characterized as an inevitable product of a wider exploitation and oppression.
>
> The American political and economic structure was identified as corporate capitalism.
>
> The use of the coercive power of the state—law enforcement—to contain and suppress unofficial political associations and unauthorized actions, through infiltration, surveillance, intimidation, and arrest, was identified as political repression.

As protest grew during the period between 1958 and 1968, it became increasingly radical in three ways.

1. The war, racism, and poverty were no longer viewed as unfortunate and reversible incidents of an otherwise sound social system but came to be seen as the inevitable products of an official order in need of revolutionary change,
2. The shift from concern with the war, racism, and poverty as incidents to a concern with the social structures that produced them resulted in a shift from an ad hoc, or single issue approach to isolated issues to an analysis of their interrelationships, structural origins, and supports,
3. The failure of the government to find solutions to the problems of undergroups, or to implement the ameliorative devices already avail-

able, led to the development of new forms of protest—unauthorized political actions.

The attempts by university administrators to consolidate their managerial prerogatives on campus threatened the possibility of collective action by students. Administrative actions raised the issue of power and, therefore, of collective capacity. But the radicalization of the white student movement was aided by the growing presence of militant black students. The refusal to trade their political initiative for white student support forced white students to reconsider the relationship between their own condition within the university and society and the conditions of other unrepresented groups. Sympathy for the condition of these other groups gave way to a recognition of a more widely shared undergroup practice and its perspective. At the same time, the women's movement forced leftist political associations, especially those based at the university, to develop more democratic procedures, a greater sense of collectivity, and a more internally critical practice than had existed before. For example, by the beginning of the 1970s, the New University Conference had developed procedures to maximize individual participation in meetings, to shift leadership, and to engage members in consciousness-raising activities, and group exchanges, by means of which they could face the pervasive discriminatory conventions that otherwise often governed their activities within the organization.

Richard Flacks and Douglas Dowd have indicated the importance of events in the growth of a political practice among students that reflected patterns of interference in the university and society. Flacks (1970) wrote:

> more Vietnams, more racial turmoil, more squalor in the cities, more political stagnation, more debasement of popular culture—in short, more of the status quo is likely to increase the availability of this stratum for radical politics (p. 356).

Dowd added, in particular reference to the university as a setting for unauthorized political action:

> The young now know what their teachers are reluctant or unable to see: the schools are an integral and functioning part of an American socio-economic-military system that combines deadlines with boredom, oppression with triviality, deceit with foolishness . . . .

> There is much dispute about whether the university can afford to involve itself in political affairs. It seems irrefutable, instead, that the university was always, is, and must always be, political to its very core in the deepest sense of "political." The problem today is that the *status quo* politics of the university are under attack for the larger *status quo* is under attack . . . . In education, it is the entire system that is now under deserved attack; not because it is entirely valueless, but because what is valued most by its entrenched defenders are the causes not of all, but of only a few Americans—the causes of business, of war, of power, of status.

> Of the many matters faculties find difficult to grasp these days, perhaps the most elusive is that the acceptance of this *status quo* is as political as its rejection; that to try to maintain R.O.T.C. on campus, for example, is as political as trying to get rid of it (*New York Times*, 28 May 1971).

BIBLIOGRAPHY

Abney, G.F., and Hill, L.B. "Natural Disasters as a Political Variable; the Effect of a Hurricane on an Urban Election," *American Political Science Review* 60 (1966): 974-97.

Aldrich, Daniel G., Jr. "Maintaining Institutional Identity and Autonomy in Coordinated Systems." In *Campus and Capitol*, edited by W. J. Minter, pp. 17-27. Boulder, Colo.: Western Interstate Commission for Higher Education, 1966.

Alexander, C. Norman, and Knight, Gordon W. "Situated Identities and Social Psychological Experimentation," *Sociometry* 34 (1971): 65-82.

Allen, Vernon L., "Situational Factors in Conformity," In *Advances in Experimental Social Psychology*, edited by L. Berkowitz, vol. 2, pp. 133-75. New York: Academic Press, 1965.

Allport, F. H. *Social Psychology*. Boston: Houghton Mifflin, 1924.

Allport, G. W. "The Historical Background of Modern Social Psychology." In *Handbook of Social Psychology*, edited by G. Lindzey, pp. 3-56. Reading, Mass.: Addison-Wesley, 1954.

Altbach, Philip G. *Select Bibliography on Students, Politics, and Higher Education*. Cambridge, Mass.: Center for International Affairs, Harvard University, 1967.

Astin, A. W. "Personal and Environmental Determinants of Student Activism," Address delivered to the American Psychological Association meetings, San Francisco, 30 August, 1968.

Avorn, J. L. *Up Against the Ivy Wall: a History of the Columbia Crisis*. New York: Atheneum, 1968.

Baker, G. W., and Chapman, D. W., eds. *Man and Society in Disaster*. New York: Basic Books, 1962.

Baker, G. W., and Rohrer, J. H., eds. *Human Problems in the Utilization of Fallout Shelters*. Washington, D. C.: National Academy of Sciences, National Research Council, 1960.

Barton, Allen H. " The Emergency Social System," In *Man and Society in Disaster*, edited by G. W. Baker and D. W. Chapman, pp. 222-67. New York: Basic Books, 1962.

_____. "The Columbia Crisis: Campus, Vietnam, and the Ghetto," *Public Opinion Quarterly* 32 (Fall 1968): 333-35.

_____. *Communities in Disaster: A Sociological Analysis of Collective Stress Situations.* Garden City, N. Y.: Doubleday, 1969.

Bates, F. L.; Fogleman, C. W.; Parenton, V. J.: Pittman, R. H.; and Tracy, G. S. *The Social and Psychological Consequences of a Natural Disaster: A Longitudinal Study of Hurricane Audrey.* Washington, D.C.: National Academy of Sciences, National Research Council, 1963.

Bay, Christian. "Political and Apolitical Students: Facts in Search of Theory," *Journal of Social Issues* 23 (1967): 76-91.

Beach, H. D., and Lucas, R. A., eds. *Individual and Group Behavior in a Coal Mine Disaster.* Washington, D.C.: National Academy of Sciences, National Research Council, 1960.

Becker, Howard S. *Campus Power Struggle.* New York: Trans-action Books, 1970.

Bell, Daniel. "Columbia and the New Left," *The Public Interest*, Fall 1968, pp. 61-101.

Benson, Charles. "The Effects of Federal Support on Allocation of Campus Resources," In *Campus and Capitol*, edited by W. J. Minter, pp. 63-72. Boulder, Colo.: Western Interstate Commission for Higher Education, 1966.

Berger, Peter L., and Luckmann, Thomas. *The Social Construction of Reality.* Garden City, N. Y.: Anchor Books, 1967.

Berkowitz, L, ed. *Advances in Experimental Social Psychology.* Vol. 2. New York, Academic Press, 1965.

Besag, Frank. *The Anatomy of a Riot: Buffalo, 1967.* Buffalo, N.Y.: University Press, 1967.

Bindler, Paul; Granat, Michael; Weiner, Neil; and Brown, Michael E. "The Effects of Prior Interaction on the Emergence of Norms in Ambiguous Situations," *Nucleus: The Queens College Journal of Science* 8 (Spring 1970): 33-35.

Bittner, Egon. "Radicalism and the Organization of Radical Movements," *American Sociological Review* 28 (1963): 928-40.

Blau, P. W., and Scott, W. R. *Formal Organizations.* San Francisco: Chandler, 1962.

Block, Jack. "Some Reasons for the Apparent Inconsistency of Personality," *Psychological Bulletin* 70 (1968): 210-12.

Block, Jeanne H.; Haan, Norma; and Smith, M. Brewster. "Activism and Apathy in Contemporary Adolescents," In *Understanding Adolescents*, edited by F. Adams, pp. 198-231. Boston: Allyn and Bacon, 1968.

Blumer, Herbert. "Collective Behavior," In *New Outline of the Principles of Sociology*, edited by A. McC. Lee, pp. 167-224. New York: Barnes and Noble, 1951.

_____. "Collective Behavior," in *Review of Sociology*, edited by Joseph B. Gittler. New York: John Wiley and Sons, 1957.

_____. "Collective Behavior," In *Dictionary of the Social Sciences*, edited by J. Gould and W. L. Kolb, pp. 100-101. New York: Free Press, 1964.

Boskin, J., and Rosenstone, R. A. "Protest in the Sixties," *The Annals*, March 1969, whole issue.

Bramson, Leon. *The Political Context of Sociology.* Princeton, N.J.: Princeton University Press, 1961.

Brown, Michael E. "Some Uses of Attitude Statements," Unpublished manuscript, 1967.

_____. "Draft Resistance: Crimes of Agency and Crimes of Conscience," Unpublished manuscript, 1968.

_____. "The Condemnation and Persecution of Hippies," *Trans-action* 6 (September 1969a): 33-46.

_____. "Identification and Some Conditions of Organizational Involvement." *Administrative Science Quarterly* 14 (1969b): 346-55.

_____. "The Impact of Life Styles on the Future of Sociology," Paper read at the American Sociological Association meetings, Washington, D.C., Fall 1970.

Brown, Roger W. "Mass Phenomena," In *Handbook of Social Psychology*, edited by G. Lindzey, pp. 833-76. Reading, Mass.: Addison-Wesley, 1954.

_____. *Social Psychology.* New York: Free Press, 1965.

Bucher, R. "Blame and Hostility in Disaster," *American Journal of Sociology* 62 (1957): 467-75.

Campbell, James S. "The Usefulness of Commission Studies of Collective Violence," *The Annals*, September 1970, pp. 168-76.

Camus, Albert. *The Stranger* (transl. by Stuart Gilbert). New York: Knopf, 1946.

Canetti, Elias, *Crowds and Power.* Translated by C. Stewart. New York: Viking Press, 1963.

Caplow, Theodore, and McGee, Reece J. *The Academic Market-Place.* New York: Basic Books, 1958.

Carmichael, Stokely, and Hamilton, Charles V. *Black Power.* New York: Random House, 1967.

Cartwright, Dorwin, and Zander, Alvin, eds. *Group Dynamics.* 3d ed. New York: Harper & Row, 1968.

Chapman, D. W. "A Brief Introduction to Contemporary Disaster Research," In *Man and Society in Disaster*, edited by G. W. Baker and D. W. Chapman, pp. 3-22. New York: Basic Books, 1962.

Chicago Commission on Race Relations. *The Negro in Chicago.* Chicago: University of Chicago Press, 1922.

Cisin, I. H., and Clark, W. B. "The Methodological Challenge of Disaster Research," In *Man and Society in Disaster*, edited by G. W. Baker and D. W. Chapman pp. 23-49. New York: Basic Books, 1962.

Clark, Burton R., and Trow, Martin. "The Organizational Context." In *College Peer Groups*, edited by T. M. Newcomb and E. Wilson, pp. 17-70. Chicago: Aldine, 1966.

Clifford, R. A. *The Rio Grande Flood: a Comparative Study of Border Communities in Disaster.* Washington, D.C.: National Academy of Sciences, National Research Council, 1956.

Cloward, Richard A., and Pliven, Frances Fox. "The Urban Crisis and the Consolidation of National Power," In *Urban Riots: Violence and Social Change*, edited by R. H. Connery, pp. 164-73. New York: Vintage Books, 1969.

Cohen, Arthur. *Attitude Change and Social Influence.* New York: Basic Books, 1964.

Cohen, Jerry, and Murphy, William S. *Burn, Baby, Burn. The Story of the August Los Angeles Race Riot, 1965.* New York: E. P. Dutton, 1966.

Cole, Stephen, and Adamsons, Hannelore. "Determinants of Faculty Support for Student Demonstrations," *Sociology of Education* 42 (1969): 315-29.

Committee on Government and Higher Education. *The Efficiency of Freedom.* Baltimore, Md.: Johns Hopkins Press, 1959.

Connery, Robert H., ed. *Urban Riots: Violence and Social Change.* New York: Vintage Books, 1969.

Conot, Robert. *Rivers of Blood, Years of Darkness: Rebellion in the Streets.* New York: Bantam Books, 1967.

Cook, Thomas D., et al. "Demand Characteristics of Three Conceptions of the Frequently Deceived Subject," *Journal of Personality and Social Psychology* 14 (1970): 185-94.

Copeland, Alan, ed. *People's Park.* New York: Ballantine Books, 1969.

Coser, Lewis. *The Functions of Social Conflict.* Glencoe, Ill.: Free Press, 1956.

————. *Continuities in the Study of Social Conflict.* New York: Free Press, 1967.

Couch, Carl J. "Collective Behavior: An Examination of Some Stereotypes," *Social Problems* 15 (1968): 310-22.

Cox Commission. *Crisis at Columbia: Report of the Fact-finding Commission Appointed to Investigate the Disturbances at Columbia University in April and May 1968.* New York: Vintage Books, 1968.

Currie, Elliott, and Skolnick, Jerome, H. "A Critical Note on Conceptions of Collective Behavior," *The Annals,* September 1970, pp. 34-45.

Curtis, C. Michael. "Taking Students Seriously," *The Atlantic* (May 1969).

Daedalus, Summer 1967, whole issue. "Toward the Year 2000."

Daedalus, Winter 1970. whole issue. "The Embattled University."

Danzig, E. R.; Thayer, P. W.; and Galanter, L. R. *The Effects of a Threatening Rumor on a Disaster-Stricken Community.* Washington, D. C.: National Academy of Science, National Research Council, 1958.

Disaster Research Group. *Field Studies of Disaster Behavior: An Inventory.* Washington, D.C.: National Academy of Science, National Research Council, 1961.

Donner, Frank. "The Injunction on Campus," *The Nation,* 9 June 1969, pp. 718-720.

Dotson, Floyd. "Patterns of Voluntary Association Among Urban Working Class Families," *American Sociological Review* 16 (1951): 687-93.

Douglas, J. *The Social Meanings of Suicide.* Princeton: Princeton University Press, 1967.

Douglas, Mary. *Purity and Danger: An Analysis of Concepts of Pollution and Taboo.* Middlesex, Eng.: Penguin Books, 1970.

Drabek, Thomas. "Disaster and Family Evacuation," *Social Problems* 16 (1969): 336-49.

Drabek, Thomas, and Boggs, Keith. "Families in Disaster: Reactions and Relatives," *Journal of Marriage and the Family* 30 (1968): 443-51.

Drabek, Thomas, and Hass, J. Eugene. "Laboratory Simulation of Organizational Stress," *American Sociological Review* 34 (1969): 222-36.

Drake, St. Clair. "Urban Violence and American Social Movements," In *Urban Riots: Violence and Social Change*, edited by R. H. Connery, pp. 15-26. New York: Vintage Books, 1969.

Dynes, Russell, and Quarantelli, Enrico L. "What Looting in Civil Disturbances Really Means," *Trans-action* 5 (May 1968): 9-14.

Eckerman, W. A study of attitudes toward college, Cited and summarized in the *Michigan Daily*, 12 November 1963.

Eichel, L. E.; Jost, K. W.; Luskin, R. D.; Neustadt, R. M. *The Harvard Strike.* Boston: Houghton Mifflin, 1970.

Erikson, Erik H., ed. *The Challenge of Youth.* New York: Anchor Books, 1965.

Etzioni, A. *A Comparative Analysis of Complex Organizations.* Glencoe, Ill.: Free Press, 1961.

Evans, Robert R., ed. *Readings in Collective Behavior.* Chicago: Rand McNally, 1969.

Faris, Robert E. L. "The Discipline of Sociology," in *Handbook of Modern Sociology*, edited by Robert E. L. Faris, pp. 1-36. Chicago: Rand McNally, 1964.

Feldman, Kenneth, and Newcomb, Theodore N. *The Impact of College on Students.* San Francisco: Josey-Bass, 1969.

Festinger, L.; Schachter, S.; and Back, K. *Social Pressures in Informal Groups.* New York: Harper & Row, 1950.

Feuer, Lewis S. *The Conflict of Generations.* New York: Basic Books, 1969.

Flacks, Richard. "The Liberated Generation: an Exploration of the Roots of Student Protest," *Journal of Social Issues* 23 (July 1967): 52-75.

———. "Social and Cultural Meanings of Student Revolt: Some Informal Comparative Observations," *Social Problems* 17 (1970): 340-57.

Fodor, Jerry A. *Psychological Explanation: An Introduction to the Philosophy of Psychology.* New York: Random House, 1968.

Form, W. H., and Loomis, C. P. "The Persistence and Emergence of Social and Cultural Systems in Disasters," *American Sociological Review* 21 (1956): 180-85.

Form, W. H., and Nosow, S. *Community in Disaster.* New York: Harper & Row, 1958.

Fortune, "Youth in Turmoil." New York: Time-Life Books, 1969.

Freire, Paulo. *Pedagogy of the Oppressed.* New York: Herder and Herder, 1970.

Freud, Sigmund. *Group Psychology and the Analysis of the Ego.* Translated by J. Strachey. London: Hogarth, 1922.

Friedenberg, Edgar. "The Generation Gap," *The Annals*, March 1969, pp. 32-42.

Friedsam, H. J. "Older Persons in Disaster." In *Man and Society in Disaster*, edited by G. W. Baker and D. W. Chapman, pp. 151-82. New York: Basic Books, 1962.

Fritz, C. E. "Disaster," In *Contemporary Social Problems*, edited by R. K. Merton and R. A. Nisbet. New York: Harcourt Brace Jovanovich, 1961, pp. 682-694.

Fritz, C. E. and Marks, E. S. "The NORC Studies of Human Behavior in Disaster," *Journal of Social Issues* 10 (1954): 26-41.

Fritz, C. E., and Mathewson, J. H. *Convergence Behavior in Disasters: A Problem in Social Control.* Washington, D.C.: National Academy of Sciences, National Research Council, 1957.

Gamson, Zelda. *Social Control and Modification: A Study of Responses to Students in a Small Nonresidential College.* Unpubl. PhD. Diss., Harvard University, 1965.

———. "Utilitarian and Normative Orientations Toward Education," *Sociology of Education* 39 (1966): pp. 46-73.

Garfinkel, Harold. *Studies in Ethnomethodology.* Englewood Cliffs, N. J.: Prentice-Hall, 1967.

Gates, Davida P. "Sociology in Small U.S. Liberal Arts Colleges" *The American Sociologist* 4 (1970): 324-30.

Gerbner, George. *Mass Media.* London: Penguin Books, 1969.

Gibb, C. A. "Leadership," In *Handbook of Social Psychology*, edited by G. Lindzey, pp. 877-920. Reading, Mass.: Addison-Wesley, 1954.

Gibson, J. *The Perception of the Visual World.* Boston: Houghton Mifflin, 1950.

Goffman, Erving. *Encounters.* Indianapolis, Inc.: Bobbs-Merrill, 1961.

———. *Behavior in Public Places.* New York: Free Press, 1963a.

———. *Stigma.* Englewood Cliffs, N. J.: Prentice-Hall, 1963b.

———. *Interaction Ritual.* New York: Anchor Books, 1967.

Goodman, Mitchell, ed. *Movement Toward a New America.* Philadelphia: Pilgrim Press, 1970.

Goodman, Paul. *People or Personnel and Like a Conquered Province.* New York: Vintage Books, 1968.

Gossett, William T. "Mobbism and Due Process," *Case and Comment* 73 (July-August 1968): 3-6.

Gould, S. B., "The University and State Government: Fears and Realities," in *Campus and Capitol.* edited by W. John Minter, pp. 3-16. Boulder, Colorado: Western Interstate Commission for Higher Education, 1966.

Gouldner, A. W. "Cosmopolitans and Locals: Toward an Analysis of Latent Social Roles, Part 1," *Administrative Science Quarterly* 2 (1957): 281-306.

———. "Cosmopolitans and Locals: Toward an Analysis of Latent Social Roles, Part 2," *Administrative Science Quarterly* 2 (1958): 444-80.

———. "Anti-Minotaur: The Myth of a Value-Free Sociology," In *The New Sociology*, edited by I. L. Horowitz, pp. 196-217. New York: Oxford University Press, 1965.

Graham, Hugh Davis, and Gurr, Ted Robert, eds. *Violence in America: A Report to the National Commission on the Causes and Prevention of Violence, June, 1969.* New York: Signet Books, 1969.

Grosser, G. H.; Wechsler, H; and Greenblatt, M. eds. *The Threat of Impending Disaster: Contributions to the Psychology of Stress.* Cambridge, Mass.: M.I.T. Press, 1964.

Gurr, Ted Robert. "A Comparative Study of Civil Strife," In *Violence in America: A Report to the National Commission on the Causes and Prevention of Violence, June, 1969*, edited by H. D. Graham and T. R. Gurr, pp. 544-605. New York: Signet Books, 1969.

———. *Why Men Rebel.* Princeton, N. J.: Princeton University Press, 1970.

Heider, Fritz. *The Psychology of Interpersonal Relations.* New York: John Wiley & Sons, 1958.

Heimberger, F. "The State Universities," In *The Contemporary University: U.S.A.*, edited by S. R. Morison, pp. 51-76. Boston: Beacon Press, 1967.

Heirich, Max. *The Spiral of Conflict: Berkeley, 1964.* New York: Columbia University Press, 1971.

Heist, Paul. "Intellect and Commitment: The Faces of Discontent," In *Order and Freedom on the Campus: The Rights and Responsibilities of Faculty and Students*, edited by O. W. Knorr and W. J. Minter, pp. 61-69. Boulder, Colo.: Western Interstate Commission for Higher Education, 1965.

Hill, Reuben, and Hansen, Donald A. "Families in Disaster," In *Man and Society in Disaster*, edited by G. W. Baker and D. W. Chapman, pp. 185-221. New York: Basic Books, 1962.

Hoffman, L. R. "Group Problem Solving," In *Advances in Experimental Social Psychology*, edited by L. Berkowitz, pp. 99-132. New York: Academic Press, 1965.

Hofstadter, Richard. *Academic Freedom in the Age of the College.* New York: Columbia University Press, 1955.

———. "The 214th Columbia University Commencement Address." *The American Scholar*, Autumn 1968, pp. 583-89.

Hook, Sidney. "Barbarism, Virtue, and the University," *The Public Interest*, Spring 1969, pp. 23-39.

Horowitz, David. *Empire and Revolution.* New York: Vintage Books, 1969.

Horowitz, Irving Louis, ed. *The New Sociology.* New York: Oxford University Press, 1965.

Horowitz, Irving Louis, and Leibowitz, Martin. "Social Deviance and Political Marginality: Toward a Redefinition of the Relation Between Sociology and Politics," *Social Problems* 15 (1968): 280-96.

Hovland, C. I., and Janis, I. L., eds. *Personality and Persuasibility.* Vol. 2. *Yale Studies in Attitudes and Communication.* New Haven, Conn.: Yale University Press, 1959.

Hovland, C. I.; Janis, I. L.; and Kelley, H. H. *Communication and Persuasion.* New Haven, Conn.: Yale University Press, 1953.

Howe, Irving, "The New Confrontation Politics is a Dangerous Game," *New York Times Magazine*, 20 October 1968.

Hudson, B. "Anxiety in Response to the Unfamiliar," *Journal of Social Issues* 10 (1954): 53-60.

Ibrahim, A. "Disorganization in Society, but Not Social Disorganization," *The American Sociologist* 3 (1968): 47-81.

Ikle, Fred Charles. *The Social Impact of Bomb Destruction.* Norman: University of Oklahoma Press, 1958.

Inkeles, Alex, and Levinson, Daniel S. "National Character: The Study of Modal Personality and Sociocultural Systems," In *Handbook of Social Psychology*, edited by G. Lindzey, pp. 977-1020. Cambridge, Mass.: Addison-Wesley, 1954.

Jacob, P. E. *Changing Values in College*. New York: Harper & Row, 1957.

Janis, I. L. *Psychological Stress*. New York: John Wiley & Sons, 1958.

———. "Psychological Effects of Warnings," In *Man and Society in Disaster*, edited by G. W. Baker and D. W. Chapman, pp. 55-92. New York: Basic Books, 1962.

Janis, I. L., and Feshbach, S. "Effect of Fear-Arousing Communications." *Journal of Abnormal and Social Psychology* 48 (1953): 78-92.

Janowitz, Morris. *Social Control of Escalated Riots*. Chicago: University of Chicago Center for Policy Study, 1968.

Jencks, C., and Riesman, D. *The Academic Revolution*. Garden City, N. Y.: Doubleday, 1968.

Katz, Elihu, and Lazarsfeld, Paul. *Personal Influence*. Glencoe, Ill.: Free Press, 1955.

Kelley, H. H.; Coutry, J. C.; Dahlke, A. E.; and Hill, A. H. "Collective Behavior in a Simulated Panic Situation," *Journal of Experimental Social Psychology* 1 (1965): 20-54.

Keniston, Kenneth, "The Sources of Student Dissent," *Journal of Social Issues* 23 (1967): 108-37.

———. "Harvard on My Mind," *The New York Review of Books*, 24 September 1970, pp. 6-10.

Kerckhoff, A. C.; Back, Kurt W.; and Miller, Norman. "Sociometric Patterns in Hysterical Contagion," *Sociometry* 28 (1965): 2-15.

Killian, L. M. "The Significance of Multiple-Group Membership in Disaster," *American Journal of Sociology* 57 (1952) 309-314.

———. *An Introduction to Methodological Problems of Field Studies in Disasters*. Washington, D. C.: National Academy of Sciences, National Research Council, 1956a.

———. *A Study of Response to the Houston, Texas, Fireworks Explosion*. Washington, D. C.: National Academy of Sciences, National Research Council, 1956b.

Kilpatrick, F. "Problems of Perception in Extreme Situations," *Human Organization* 16 (1957): 20-22.

Klapper, J. T. *The Effects of Mass Communication*. Glencoe, Ill.: Free Press, 1960.

Koestler, Arthur, *The Act of Creation*. New York: Macmillan, 1964.

Krausse, Elliott. "Functions of a Bureaucratic Ideology: 'Citizen Participation'." *Social Problems* 16 (1968): 129-42.

Kristol, Irving. "The Old Politics, The New Politics, the New New Politics," *New York Times Magazine*, 24 Nov. 1968.

Kuhn, T. S. *The Structure of Scientific Revolutions*. Chicago: University of Chicago Press, 1962.

Kurtz, Seymour, ed. *The New York Times Encyclopedic Almanac, 1970.* New York: New York Times, 1969.

Landers, Clifford E., and Cicarelli, James S. "Academic Recession," *The New Republic,* 9 May 1970, pp. 14-16.

Lang, Kurt, and Lang, Gladys Engel, "The Unique Perspective of Television and its Effect: a Pilot Study," *American Sociological Review* 18 (1953): 3-12.

_____. *Collective Dynamics.* New York: Thomas Crowell, 1961.

_____. "Collective Responses to the Threat of Disaster." In *The Threat of Impending Disasters: Contributions to the Psychology of Stress,* edited by G. H. Grosser, H. Wechsler, and M. Greenblatt, pp. 58-75. Cambridge, Mass.: M.I.T. Press, 1964.

_____. *Politics and Television.* Chicago: Quandrangle Books, 1968.

Lanternari, V. *The Religions of the Oppressed.* New York: Knopf, 1963.

LaPiere, Richard T. *Collective Behavior.* New York: McGraw-Hill, 1938.

Larsen, Otto N. "Social Effects of Mass Communication," In *Handbook of Modern Sociology,* edited by Robert E. L. Faris, pp. 348-81. Chicago: Rand McNally, 1964.

Lazarsfeld, Paul F. and Thielens, W. *The Academic Mind.* Glencoe, Ill.: Free Press, 1958.

LeBon, G. *The Crowd.* New York: Viking Books, 1960.

Leonard, George. "A Bold Plan for Peace," *Look,* 10 June 1969, p. 73.

Levine, M., and Naisbitt, J. *Right On: A Documentary on Student Protest.* New York: Bantam Books, 1970.

Levi-Strauss, Claude. *Structural Anthropology.* New York: Anchor Books, 1967.

Levy, Sheldon. "A 150-year Study of Political Violence in the United States," In *Violence in America: A Report to the National Commission on the Causes and Prevention of Violence, June, 1969,* edited by H. D. Graham and T. R. Gurr, pp. 84-100. New York: Signet Books, 1969.

Lieberson, Stanley, and Silverman, Arnold R. "The Precipitants and Underlying Conditions of Race Riots," *American Sociological Review* 30 (1965): 887-98.

Lindzey, G. *Handbook of Social Psychology.* Reading, Mass.: Addison-Wesley, 1954.

Lipset, Seymour Martin. "Democracy and Working Class Authoritarianism," *American Sociological Review* 24 (1959): 482-501.

_____. *Political Man.* Garden City, N. Y.: Doubleday, 1960.

_____. "University Student Politics," In *The Berkeley Student Revolt,* edited by S. M. Lipset and S. S. Wolin, pp. 1-10. New York: Anchor Books, 1965.

_____. *Student Politics.* New York: Basic Books, 1967.

_____. "The Activists: a Profile." *The Public Interest,* Fall 1968a, pp. 39-51.

_____. "Students and Politics in Comparative Perspective." *Daedalus,* Winter 1968b, pp. 1-20.

_____. *Rebellion in the University.* Boston: Little, Brown and Co., 1971.

Lipset, Seymour Martin, and Seabury, Paul. "The Lesson of Berkeley." In *The Berkeley Student Revolt,* edited by S. M. Lipset and S. S. Wolin, pp. 340-50. New York: Anchor Books, 1965.

Lipset, Seymour Martin, and Smelser, Neil. "Change and Controversy in Recent American Sociology." Reprinted by Berkeley: Institute of Industrial Relations, 1961, pp. 41-51.

Lipset, Seymour Martin, and Wolin, Sheldon S., eds. *The Berkeley Student Revolt*. New York: Anchor Books, 1965.

Lipsky, Michael, and Olson, David J. "Riot Commission Politics," *Trans-action* 6 (July-August 1969): 8-21.

Livingston, L.; Klass, B.; and Rohrer, J. *Operation Walkout, Rideout, and Scat*. Washington, D. C.: National Academy of Sciences, National Research Council, 1954.

Long, Priscilla, ed. *The New Left*. Boston: Porter Sargent, 1969.

Loomis, C. P., and Loomis, Z. K. *Modern Social Theories*. Princeton: Van Nostrand, 1961.

Lothstein, Arthur, ed. *All We Are Saying: The Philosophy of the New Left*. New York: G. P. Putnam & Sons, 1971.

Lubell, Samuel, "That 'Generation Gap,' " *The Public Interest* (Fall, 1968): 52-60.

Lynd, Robert Staughton. *Knowledge for What? The Place of Social Science in American Culture*. Princeton, N. J.: Princeton University Press, 1939.

Mack, R. W., and Baker, G. W. *The Occasion Instant: The Structure of Social Responses to Unanticipated Air Raid Warnings*. Washington, D.C.: National Academy of Sciences, National Research Council, 1961.

Mackay, Charles. *Extraordinary Popular Delusions and the Madness of Crowds*. Boston: L. C. Page, 1932.

Malia, Martin. "The Nature of a University and Academic Freedom," In *The Berkeley Student Revolt*, edited by S. M. Lipset and S. S. Wolin, pp. 448-50. New York: Anchor Books, 1965.

Mankoff, M., and Flacks, R. "The Changing Social Base of the American Student Movement." *The Annals* (May, 1971): 54-67.

Mannheim, Karl. *Ideology and Utopia*. New York: Harcourt Brace Jovanovich, 1936.

Marcuse, Herbert. *One-Dimensional Man*. Boston: Beacon Press, 1968.

_____. *An Essay on Liberation*. Boston: Beacon Press, 1969.

Marks, E. S., and Fritz, C. E. *Human Reactions in Disaster Situations*. Unpublished Report, National Opinion Research Center, 1954.

Marx, Gary. "Issueless Riots," *The Annals*, September 1970, pp. 21-33.

Masotti, Louis H., and Corsi, Jerome R. *Shootout in Cleveland: a Report to the National Commission on the Causes and Prevention of Violence*. New York: Bantam Books, 1969.

McConnell, T. R. "The University and the State—a Comparative Study," In *Campus and Capitol*, edited by W. J. Minter, pp. 89-118. Boulder, Colo.: Western Interstate Commission for Higher Education, 1966.

McDermott, John. "Politics of the Movement," *The Nation*, 23 June 1969, pp. 797-99.

McHugh, Peter. *Defining the Situation*. New York: Bobbs-Merrill, 1968.

Mead, G. H. *The Philosophy of the Present*. Edited by A. E. Murphy. Chicago: Open Court, 1932.

———. *The Philosophy of the Act.* Edited by C. W. Morris. Chicago: University of Chicago Press, 1938.

Meadows, Paul. "The Metaphors of Order: Toward a Taxonomy of Organization Theory," In *Sociological Theory: Inquiries and Paradigms*, edited by L. Gross, pp. 77-103. New York: Harper & Row, 1967.

Menashe, Louis, and Radoh, Ronald, eds. *Teach-ins: U.S.A.* New York: Praeger, 1967.

Merton, R. K., and Lazarsfeld, P. F., eds. *Studies in the Scope and Method of "the American Soldier."* Glencoe, Ill.: Free Press, 1950.

Metzger, W. P. *Academic Freedom in the Age of the University.* New York: Columbia University Press, 1955.

Milgram, Stanley. "Some Conditions of Obedience and Disobedience to Authority," *Human Relations* 18 (1965): 57-76.

Milgram, Stanley; Bickman, Leonard; and Berkowitz, Lawrence. "Note on the Drawing Power of Crowds of Different Size." *Journal of Personality and Social Psychology* 13 (1969a): 79-82.

Milgram, Stanley, and Toch, Hans. "Collective Behavior: Crowds and Social Movements." In *The Handbook of Psychology*, edited by G. Lindzey and E. Aronson, vol. 4, pp. 507-610. Reading, Mass.: Addison-Wesley, 1969b.

Miller, Arthur, R. *The Assult on Privacy.* Ann Arbor: University of Michigan Press, 1971.

Mills, C. Wright. *White Collar.* New York: Oxford University Press, 1951.

———. *The Power Elite.* New York: Oxford University Press, 1956.

———. *The Sociological Imagination.* New York: Evergreen, 1961.

———. *Power, Politics, and People.* Edited by I. L. Horowitz. New York: Ballantine Books, 1963.

Minter, W. John, ed. *Campus and Capitol.* Boulder, Colo.: Western Interstate Commission for Higher Education, 1966.

Mintz, A. "Non-adaptive Group Behavior," *Journal of Abnormal and Social Psychology* 46 (1951): 150-159.

Moore, Barrington. "Revolution in America?" *New York Review of Books*, 30 January 1969a, pp. 6-12.

———. "Thoughts on Violence and Democracy." In *Urban Riots: Violence and Social Change*, edited by R. H. Connery, pp. 3-14. New York: Vintage Books, 1969b.

Moore, H. E. "Toward a Theory of Disaster," *American Sociological Review* 21 (1956): 733-37.

———. *Tornadoes Over Texas.* Austin: University of Texas Press, 1958.

Moore, H. E. and Friedsam, H. J. "Reported Emotional Stress Following a Disaster," *Social Forces* 38 (1959): 135-39;

Moore, Wilbert E. *Social Change.* Englewood Cliffs, N. J.: Prentice-Hall, 1963.

Morison, Robert S., ed *The Contemporary University: U.S.A.* Boston: Beacon Press, 1967.

———. "Foundations and Universities," In *The Contemporary University: U.S.A.*, edited by R. S. Morison, Boston: Beacon Press, 1967. pp. 77-109.

Moynihan, D. "Nirvana Now," *The American Scholar* 36 (Autumn 1967): 539-48.

Myers, R. C., "Anti-Communist Mob Action," *Public Opinion Quarterly* 12 (1948): 57-67.

National Advisory Commission on Civil Disorders. *Report of the National Commission on Civil Disorders.* New York: Bantam Books, 1968.

National Commission on the Causes and Prevention of Violence. *To Establish Justice, to Insure Domestic Tranquility.* Washington, D. C.: Government Printing Office, 1969.

Newcomb, T. M.; Turner, R. H.; and Converse, P. E. *Social Psychology.* New York: Holt, Rinehart and Winston, 1965.

Newfield, Jack. *A Prophetic Minority.* New York: Signet Books, 1967.

Nisbet, Robert. "The Twilight of Authority," *The Public Interest,* Spring 1969, pp. 3-9.

Nuttall, Jeff. *Bomb Culture.* London: Kee and MacGibbon, 1968.

Oberschall, Anthony. "The Los Angeles Riot," *Social Problems* 15 (1968): 322-42.

Oglesby, Carl, and Shaull, Richard. *Containment and Change.* Toronto: Macmillan, 1967.

Olson, Marvin. "Perceived Legitimacy of Social Protest Actions," *Social Problems* 15 (1968): 297-310.

Orrick, W. H. *Shut It Down, a Report on San Francisco State College, October 1968 to April 1969.* Washington, D. C.: Government Printing Office, 1969.

Park, R. E., and Burgess, E. W. *Introduction to the Science of Sociology.* Chicago: University of Chicago Press, 1921.

Parsons, Talcott. *The Structure of Social Action.* New York: Free Press, 1949.

———. "An Approach to Psychological Theory in Terms of the Theory of Action." In *Psychology: A Study of a Science,* edited by S. Koch, vol. 3 pp. 612-711. New York: McGraw-Hill, 1958.

———. "Social Strains in America," In *Structure and Process in Modern Societies,* edited by T. Parsons, pp. 226-47. Glencoe, Ill.: Free Press, 1960.

———. "Full Citizenship for the Negro American?" *Daedalus,* November 1965a pp. 1009-1054.

———. "Youth in the Context of American Society," In *The Challenge of Youth,* edited by E. H. Erikson, pp. 110-41. New York: Anchor Books, 1965b.

———. "The Academic System: A Sociologist's View," *The Public Interest,* Fall 1968, pp. 173-97.

Paulus, George. *A Multivariate Analysis Study of Student Activist Leaders, Student Government Leaders, and Non-Activists.* PhD. Diss., Michigan State University, 1967.

Permanent Subcommittee on Investigations of the Committee on Governmental Operations of the United States Senate. *Riots, Civil and Criminal Disorders.* Washington, D.C.: Government Printing Office, 1967.

Peterson, Richard E. *The Scope of Organized Student Protest in 1964-1965.* Princeton, N. J.: Educational Testing Service, 1966.

_____. "The Student Left in Higher Education," *Daedalus,* Winter 1968a, pp. 293-317.

_____. *The Scope of Organized Student Protest in 1967-1968.* Princeton, N.J.: Educational Testing Service, 1968b.

Powell, J. W. "A Poison Liquor Episode in Atlanta, Georgia," In *Conference on Field Studies of Reactions to Disasters.* Chicago: National Opinion Research Center, 1953.

Powell, J. W.; Finesinger, J. W.; and Greenhill, M. H. *An Introduction to the Natural History of Disaster,* Vol 2. College Park, Maryland: University of Maryland, 1954.

Powell, J. W. and Rayner, Jeannette. *Progress Notes: Disaster Investigation July 1, 1951-June 30, 1952.* Edgewood: Army Chemical Center, Chemical Corps, Medical Laboratories, 1952.

Quarantelli, E. L. "A Study of Panic: Its Nature, Types and Conditions," *National Opinion Research Center Survey 308* (1953).

_____. "A Note on the Protective Function of the Family in Disaster," *Marriage and Family Living,* 22 (1960): 263-65.

Quarantelli, E. L., and Hundley, J. R. "A Test of Some Propositions About Crowd Formation and Behavior," In *Readings in Collective Behavior,* edited by R. R. Evans, pp. 538-54. Chicago: Rand McNally, 1969.

Raker, J. W.; Wallace, A. F. C.; Rayner, J. F.; and Eckert, A. W. *Emergency Medical Care in Disasters: A Summary of Recorded Experience.* Washington D. C.: National Academy of Sciences, National Research Council, 1956.

Ridgeway, J. *The Closed Corporation: American Universities in Crisis.* New York: Ballantine Books, 1968.

Riseman, David. "America Moves to the Right," *New York Times Magazine,* 27 October 1968.

Rogin, Michael Paul. *The Intellectuals and McCarthy.* Cambridge, Mass.: M.I.T. Press, 1967.

Rosow, I. L. *Conflict of Authority in Natural Disaster.* Ph.D. dissertation, Harvard University, 1955.

Ross, E. A. *Social Psychology.* New York: Macmillan, 1908.

Rossi, Peter H. "Researchers, Scholars and Policy Makers: The Politics of Large Scale Research," In *The Contemporary University: U.S.A.,* edited by R. S. Morison, pp. 110-29. Boston: Beacon Press, 1967.

Rude, George. *The Crowd in the French Revolution.* New York: Oxford University Press, 1959.

_____. *The Crowd in History, 1730-1848.* New York: John Wiley & Sons, 1964.

Rudwick, Elliot M. *Race Riot at East St. Louis, July 2, 1917.* Carbondale, Ill.: Southern Illinois University Press: 1964.

Rustow, D. "Days of Crisis," *New Leader,* 20 May 1968, pp. 5-10.

Ryan B. "Resuscitation of Social Change," *Social Forces* 44 (1965): 1-7.

Sampson, Edward E., issue ed. "Stirrings Out of Apathy: Student Activism and the Decade of Protest," *Journal of Social Issues* 33 (July 1967a): whole issue.

———. "Student Activism and the Decade of Protest." *Journal of Social Issues* 23 (1967b): 1-33.

Sanford, Nevitt, ed. *The American College*, New York: John Wiley & Sons, 1962.

Sartre, Jean-Paul. *Search for a Method.* Translated by H. E. Barnes. New York, Alfred A. Knopf, 1963.

———. *Saint Genet: Actor and Martyr.* Translated by B. Frechtman. New York: Mentor Books, 1964.

———. "Intellectuals and Revolution: Interview with Jean-Paul Sartre," translated by B. Rice. *Ramparts*, December 1970.

Schiller, Herbert I. *Mass Communications and American Empire.* Boston: Beacon Press, 1971.

Schlesinger, Arthur, Jr. "Joe College is Dead," *The Saturday Evening Post*, 21 September 1968, pp. 24-26.

Schneider, D. M. "Typhoons on Yap," *Human Organization* 16 (1957): 10-15.

Schultz, D. P. *Panic Behavior: Discussion and Readings.* New York: Random House, 1964.

Scott, Marvin B., and Lyman S. M. "Accounts," *American Sociological Review* 33 (1968): 46-62.

Scott, W. A. *Public Reaction to a Surprise Civil Defense Alert in Oakland, California.* Ann Arbor: University of Michigan Survey Research Center, 1955.

Seale, Patrick, and McConville, Maureen. *Red Flag, Black Flag: French Revolution 1968.* New York: Ballantine, 1968.

Seashore, Stanley. *Group Cohesiveness in the Industrial Work Group.* Ann Arbor: University of Michigan Press, 1954.

Shibutani, Tamotsu. *Improvised News: a Sociological Study of Rumor.* Indianapolis Ind.: Bobbs-Merrill, 1966.

Short, James F., and Wolfgang, Marvin E. "On Collective Violence: Introduction and Overview," *The Annals*, September 1970, pp. 1-8.

Silver, Allan A. "The Demand for Order in Civil Society: A Review of Some Themes in the History of Urban Crime, Police, and Riot," In *The Police*, edited by D. Bordua, pp. 1-24. New York: John Wiley & Sons, 1967.

———. "Official Interpretations of Racial Riots," In *Urban Riots: Violence and Social Change*, edited by R. H. Connery, pp. 151-63. New York: Vintage Books, 1969.

Sjoberg, Gideon. "Disasters and Social Change," In *Man and Society in Disaster*, edited by G. W. Baker and D. W. Chapman, New York: Basic Books, 1962, pp. 356-84.

Sjoberg, Gideon, ed. *Ethics, Politics, and Social Research.* Cambridge, Mass.: Schenkman, 1967.

Skolnick, Jerome H., ed. *The Politics of Protest: A Report to the National Commission on the Causes and Prevention of Violence.* New York: Ballantine Books, 1969.

Smelser, Neil J. *Theory of Collective Behavior*. New York: Free Press, 1963.

———. "Theoretical Issues of Scope and Problems," *Sociological Quarterly* 5 (April 1964): 116-22.

———. "Two Critics in Search of a Bias: A Response to Currie and Skolnick," *The Annals*, September 1970, pp. 46-55.

Somers, R. H. "The Mainsprings of Rebellion: a Survey of Berkeley Students in November, 1964," In *The Berkeley Student Revolt*, edited by S. M. Lipset and S. S. Wolin, pp. 530-57. New York: Anchor Books, 1965.

Sorokin, P. A. *Man and Society in Calamity*. New York: E. P. Dutton, 1942.

Speier, Hans. "The American Soldier and the Sociology of Military Organization," In *Studies in the Scope and Method of "the American Soldier,"* edited by R. K. Merton and P. F. Lazarsfeld, pp. 106-32. Glencoe, Ill.: Free Press, 1950.

Spender, Stephen. *The Year of the Young Rebels*. New York: Vintage, 1969.

Spiegel, J. P. "The English Flood of 1953," *Human Organization* 16 (1957): 3-5.

Spitzer, Stephen P., and Denzin, Norman. "Levels of Knowledge in an Emergent Crisis," *Social Forces* 44 (1965): 234-37.

Stouffer, S. A., et al., *The American Soldier*, Vol. 1. Princeton, N.J.: Princeton University Press, 1949.

Students for a Democratic Society. *Port Huron Statement, 1962*. Reproduced in part in Massimo Teodori, ed. *The New Left: A Documentary History*, Indianapolis, Ind.: Bobbs-Merrill, 1969, pp. 163-172.

Suttles, Gerald D. *The Social Order of the Slum*. Chicago: University of Chicago Press, 1968.

Swanson, G. E. "A Preliminary Study of the Acting Crowd," *American Sociological Review* 18 (1953): 522-33.

Swanson, Thor, "A State in Emergency," *National Civic Review* 53 (1964): 483-88.

Tarde, G. *L'Opinion et la Foule*. Paris: Librairie Felix Alcan, 1901.

Taylor, Harold. "The Academic Industry: a Discussion of Clark Kerr's 'The Uses of the University'," In *The Berkeley Student Revolt*, edited by S. M. Lipset and S. S. Wolin, pp. 60-63. New York: Anchor Books, 1965.

Temmer, Harold. "Topless Management or the Anatomy of Data Systems," *College and University* 44 (1969): 213-19.

Teodori, Massimo, ed. *The New Left: A Documentary History*. Indianapolis, Ind.: Bobbs-Merrill, 1969.

Thompson, James D., and Hawkes, Robert W. "Disaster, Community Organization, and Administrative Process," In *Man and Society in Disaster*, edited by G. W. Baker and D. W. Chapman, pp. 268-300. New York: Basic Books, 1962.

Trent, J. W., and Craise, Judith L. "Commitment and Conformity in the American College," *Journal of Social Issues* 23 (1967): 34-51.

Turner, Ralph H. "Collective Behavior," In *Handbook of Modern Sociology*, edited by R. E. L. Faris, pp. 382-425. Chicago: Rand McNally, 1964.

———. "The Public Perception of Protest," *American Sociological Review* 34 (1969): 815-31.

Turner, Ralph H., and Killian, Lewis M. *Collective Behavior*. Englewood Cliffs, N. J.: Prentice-Hall, 1957.

Turner, Ralph H., and Surace, S. J. "Zoot-suiters and Mexicans: Symbols in Crowd Behavior," *American Journal of Sociology* 62 (1956): 14-20.

United States Bureau of the Census. *Statistical Abstract of the United States: 1968*. 89th ed. Washington, D. C.: Government Printing Office, 1968.

Vaccaro, Louis C. "The Conflict of Authority in the University," *College and University* 44 (1969): 232-39.

Veblen, T. *The Higher Learning in America*. New York: Sagamore Press, 1957.

Veltfort, Helene Rank, and Lee, George E. "The Cocoanut Grove Fire: A Study in Scapegoating," *Journal of Abnormal and Social Psychology* Clinical Suppl. 38 (1943): 138-154.

Veysey, L. R. *The Emergence of the American University*. Phoenix ed. Chicago: University of Chicago Press, 1970.

Von Wright, George Henrik. *Norm and Action: A Logical Inquiry*. New York: Humanities Press, 1963.

Walker, Daniel. *Rights in Conflict: The Violent Confrontation of Demonstrators and Police in the Parks and Streets of Chicago During the Week of the Democratic National Convention*. (Report to the National Commission on the Causes and Prevention of Violence.) New York: Bantam Books, 1968.

Wallace, A. F. C. *Tornado in Worcester: An Exploratory Study of Individual and Community Behavior in an Extreme Situation*. Washington, D. C.: National Academy of Sciences, National Research Council, 1956.

————. "Psychological Preparations for War," In *War: The Anthropology of Armed Conflict and Aggression*, edited by M. Fried, M. Harris, and R. Murphy, pp. 173-182. Garden City, N. Y.: Doubleday, 1968.

Wallis, W. Allen, "Centripetal and Centrifugal Forces in University Organization," In *The Contemporary University: U.S.A.*, edited by R. S. Morison, pp. 39-50. Boston: Beacon Press, 1967.

Walter, E. V. *Terror and Resistance: A Study of Political Violence*. New York: Oxford University Press, 1969.

Waskow, Arthur T. *From Race Riot to Sit-In: 1919 and the 1960s*. Garden City, N. Y.: Doubleday Anchor, 1967.

Watts, W. A., and Whittaker, D. N. "Some Socio-psychological Differences Between Highly-committed Members of the Free Speech Movement and the Student Population at Berkeley." *Journal of Applied Behavioral Sciences* 2 (1966): 41-62.

Ways, Max. "The Faculty is the Heart of the Trouble," *Fortune*, January 1969, pp. 94-99.

Webster's New Twentieth Century Dictionary of the English Language, Unabr. 2nd ed. New York: World Publishing Co., 1962.

Weinberg, Ian, and Walker, Kenneth N. "Student Politics and Political Systems: Toward a Typology," Revised version of paper read at the American Sociological Association meetings, Boston, 26-29 August 1968.

Wentworth, Eric. "U.S. Colleges," *International Herald Tribune*, 8 September 1969.

Westie, Frank R. "Race and Ethnic Relations," In *Handbook of Modern Sociology*, edited by R. E. L. Faris, pp. 576-618. Chicago: Rand McNally, 1964.

Westley, W. *The Formation, Nature, and Control of Crowds.* Canada: Defence Research Board, Directorate of Atomic Research, 1956.

_____ "The Escalation of Violence Through Legitimation," *The Annals*, March 1966, pp. 120-26.

Wiebe, Robert. "The Social Functions of Public Education," *American Quarterly* 21 (Summer 1969): 147-164.

Williams, H. B. "Some Functions of Communication in Crisis Behavior," *Human Organization* 16 (1957): 15-19.

_____ "Human Factors in Warning-And-Response Systems," In *The Threat of Impending Disaster: Contributions to the Psychology of Stress*, edited by G. H. Grosser, H. Wechsler, and M. Greenblatt, pp. 79-104. Cambridge, Mass.: M.I.T. Press, 1964.

Williams, Raymond. *Culture and Society 1780-1950.* Garden City, N. Y.: Doubleday, 1960.

_____ *The Long Revolution.* London: Chatto and Windus, 1961.

Williams, Robin. "Racial and Cultural Relations," In *Review of Sociology*, edited by J. Gittler, pp. 423-64. New York: John Wiley & Sons, 1957.

Wolfenstein, Martha. *Disaster: A Psychological Essay.* Glencoe, Ill.: Free Press, 1957.

Young, M. "The Role of the Extended Family in a Disaster," *Human Relations* 7 (1954): 383-91.

Zajonc, R. "Social Facilitation," *Science* 149 (1965): 269-74.

Zelditch, Morris. "Can You Really Study an Army in the Laboratory?" In *A Sociological Reader on Complex Organizations*, edited by A. Etzioni, 2nd ed., pp. 528-39. New York: Holt, Rinehart & Winston, 1969.

Ziegler, Jerome M. "Continuing Education in the University," In *The Contemporary University: U.S.A.*, edited by R. S. Morison, pp. 130-151. Boston: Beacon Press, 1967.

Zinn, Howard. *The New Abolitionists.* Boston: Beacon Press, 1965.